The New Illustrated
MEDICAL
ENCYCLOPEDIA
and Guide to
FAMILY
HEALTH

the enlarged
and revised

8th edition

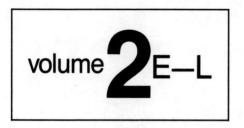

volume **2** E–L

the enlarged and revised 8th edition

The New Illustrated
MEDICAL
ENCYCLOPEDIA
and Guide to
FAMILY HEALTH

Edited by
Robert E. Rothenberg, M.D., F.A.C.S.

LEXICON PUBLICATIONS, INC.
95 Madison Avenue, New York, N.Y. 10016

Note to the reader

No prescription or course of treatment is intended to be recommended in this volume; for such purposes a doctor should be consulted. The *Medical Encyclopedia's* function is informational only.

Library of Congress Cataloging in Publication Data

Main entry under title:

The New illustrated medical encyclopedia for home use.

Includes index
1. Medicine, Popular. I. Rothenberg, Robert E.
II. Medbook Publications, inc.
RC81. A2N44 1982   616.02'4   81-7981
ISBN 0 – 7 1 7 2 – 4 5 6 2 – 4   AACR2

**Enlarged and Revised 8th Edition,
Updated 1988**

Printed and bound in the United States of America

This Table of Contents lists all topics in this particular volume only. For a complete Table of Contents listing all topics in the entire four volumes of this *New Illustrated Medical Encyclopedia,* see Volume One. A special section of Definitions of Common Medical Terms will be found at the end of Volume Four.

CONTENTS | Volume **2**

CHAPTER **22** ENDOSCOPY

What is endoscopy?

Endoscopy is the study of internal organs with the use of optical instruments that permit direct viewing. The purpose of endoscopy is to aid in diagnosis and treatment.

Recent advances in fiber optical instruments have made endoscopy a safe and exceptionally useful procedure.

What is esophagoscopy?

It is the study of the foodpipe (esophagus) with the use of an optical instrument. The lining of the esophagus can be seen and examined by peering through the esophagoscope, which transmits light.

What is gastroscopy?

Gastroscopy is the study of the stomach with the use of an optical instrument. The instrument is passed through the mouth into the esophagus and down into the stomach. The source of light for all endoscopic instruments remains outside the body, and the light travels into the stomach by means of glass fibers.

Are endoscopic instruments rigid or flexible?

The portion of the instrument within the body is flexible, unlike the old-fashioned gastroscope or the present-day proctoscopes and sigmoidoscopes.

What is gastroduodenoscopy?

It is the combined study of both the stomach, and duodenum. (The duodenum is the first portion of the small intestine.)

323

Endoscopy

Is the same instrument used both for gastroscopy and gastroduodenoscopy?

Yes.

What are the indications for doing an esophagoscopy, gastroscopy, or gastroduodenoscopy?

These procedures are helpful in making the following diagnoses:

a. The source of bleeding that may arise from a tumor or varicose vein in the esophagus, from a polyp, cancer, or ulcer of the stomach, or from an ulcer of the duodenum.

b. The presence or absence of an ulcer in the esophagus, stomach, or duodenum.

c. The presence of a tumor in the esophagus, stomach, or duodenum.

d. The presence of stones or a tumor in the common bile duct.

e. The presence of inflammation of the esophagus, stomach, or duodenum.

These procedures are also helpful in that biopsies, the snipping off of small pieces of tissue, can be taken from diseased areas of the esophagus or stomach, especially to determine if cancer is present.

Is gastroduodenoscopy ever helpful in treating disease?

Occasionally, yes. Stones in the common bile duct can sometimes be removed with use of this instrument. The outlet of the common bile duct is stretched, thus permitting stones to pass into the duodenum. However, it must be noted that this procedure is not always successful.

Is endoscopy of the esophagus, stomach, and duodenum painful?

No. Before the examination begins, the patient receives sedative and pain-relieving medications. Moreover, the instrument is made out of flexible, rather than rigid, material, such as metal.

How accurate is endoscopy of the esophagus, stomach, and duodenum?

Approximately 90 percent of cases are diagnosed correctly. In many instances, the accuracy is checked by taking a biopsy.

Does endoscopy of the esophagus, stomach, and duodenum make x-ray examinations unnecessary?

No. The procedures are complementary to x-ray studies and will not supplant them.

What is proctoscopy?

Proctoscopy is the study of the rectum through direct viewing. Either a rigid metal or a flexible nonmetal instrument can be used for this examination. Through proctoscopy, diagnoses can be readily made by use of the proctoscope, biopsies easily taken, and certain lesions, such as polyps, can be burned or snared off. The average proctoscope is between five and six inches long.

What is sigmoidoscopy?

Sigmoidoscopy is the study of the sigmoid colon—the portion of the colon that lies just above the rectum—with the use of optical instruments.

It has the same diagnostic and therapeutic usages as the proctoscope but differs in that the instrument goes up ten to twelve inches, rather than five to six inches, from the anal opening.

What is colonoscopy?

Colonoscopy is the study of the large intestine with the use of a flexible optical instrument. It is passed through the anus and is threaded through the entire extent of the colon, a distance of several feet.

What conditions can be diagnosed through colonoscopy?

a. Inflammations of the colon, including the various types of colitis.
b. Diverticulosis or diverticulitis of the colon.
c. Polyps of the colon.
d. Cancer of the colon.
e. The sources of bleeding within the colon.

Can biopsies be taken through a colonoscope?

Yes. This is one of its great values.

Can polyps frequently be removed through a colonoscope?

Yes. This is a great asset since in many instances it does away with the need for an open surgical procedure.

Is colonoscopy helpful in explaining puzzling findings on x-ray examination of the colon?

Yes. Frequently an x ray may point toward the presence of a tumor in the colon, but colonoscopy may prove no tumor to be present.

Can colonoscopy ever reveal a tumor when x rays fail to show it?

Yes. This occurs on many occasions.

Is colonoscopy painful?

Yes, at times it can be painful. For this reason sedatives and pain-relieving drugs are given prior to colonoscopy.

How accurate are diagnoses made through colonoscopy?

There is a high degree of accuracy provided the examiner is well trained, the colon thoroughly cleansed prior to examination, and providing that bleeding has not obscured the site of disease.

Can polyps and malignant tumors be removed through the colonoscope?

In many cases, polyps can be completely removed. However, if the base of the polyp is broad, it may not be possible to do so.

Malignant tumors of the colon must be removed surgically.

What are examples of the rigid metal endoscopes?

a. The gastroscope. This is used infrequently now as it affords much less opportunity to view the entire lining of the stomach. However, it is a good instrument for removal of foreign bodies that have lodged in the esophagus or stomach.
b. The bronchoscope. This is still used, but to a lesser extent than the flexible instrument. However, the rigid metal bronchoscope affords a better way to remove foreign bodies.

325

Endoscopy

c. The laparoscope. This is an instrument inserted through a small incision in the abdominal wall near the navel. Through it, one can view the abdominal organs. Recently it has been used widely to carry out sterilization in women. The Fallopian tubes are identified and are fulgurated (burned electrically) at their midpoint, thus blocking the passageway and preventing conception.

d. The culdoscope. Culdoscopy is a procedure whereby the instrument is inserted through the vagina into the abdominal cavity. Through its use the gynecologist can diagnose many abnormalities of the ovaries, Fallopian tubes, and the uterus. The doctor can also note the presence of blood in the abdominal cavity, often seen in tubal (ectopic) pregnancy.

e. The cystoscope. The instrument is passed through the urethra into the urinary bladder. (See Chapter 76, on The Urinary Bladder and Urethra.)

Are there specialists in endoscopy?

Yes. Most gastroenterologists are trained in both upper and lower endoscopy. Gynecologists perform laparoscopy and culdoscopy whereas urologists perform cystoscopy. Most otolaryngologists and chest (thoracic) surgeons are trained in bronchoscopy.

Is endoscopy painful?

The various procedures are uncomfortable, but pain is kept to a minimum by medications administered prior to endoscopy.

Is anesthesia required for endoscopic procedures?

Anesthesia is not given for upper or lower endoscopy, but it may be given for laparoscopy, culdoscopy, and cystoscopy.

Is endoscopy carried out in a physician's office or in a hospital?

Both places are utilized. To perform endoscopy in an office requires a special setup with special equipment to prepare the patient properly and highly trained personnel to assist the endoscopist.

Are special courses given to train physicians in endoscopy?

Yes. The various procedures should be carried out only by those gastroenterologists or surgeons who have been specially trained.

CHAPTER 23 THE ESOPHAGUS

(See also Chapter 70 on Stomach and Duodenum)

What is the esophagus?

It is a muscular tube that connects the pharynx, or back of the throat, to the stomach. Through it, swallowed food and fluid are conducted to the stomach. The esophagus has no digestive function, but acts merely as a conduit.

Is the drinking of excessively hot liquids harmful to the esophagus?

Yes, as it may burn the lining membrane. Also, some investigators believe that the taking of extremely hot foods over a period of many years may stimulate cancer formation.

Is the drinking of excessively cold liquids harmful to the esophagus?

No.

Can one choke from swallowing too large a quantity of food at one time?

If food enters the esophagus and not the trachea (windpipe), choking does not take place. However, taking too much food in one swallow may cause it to become stuck somewhere along the course of the esophagus. This may require the passage of an esophagoscope to remove the excess food particles.

327

The Esophagus

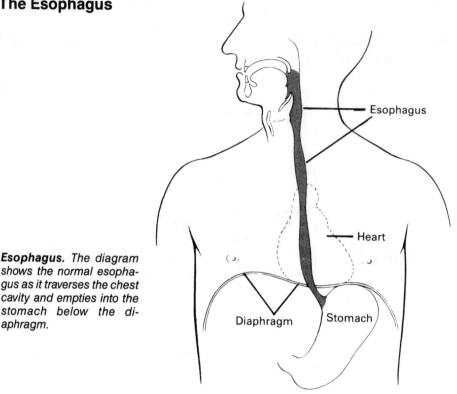

Esophagus

Heart

Diaphragm

Stomach

Esophagus. The diagram shows the normal esophagus as it traverses the chest cavity and empties into the stomach below the diaphragm.

What is the significance of inability to swallow?

It usually signifies an obstruction due either to a mechanical cause or to spasm.

What does it mean if there is regurgitation of undigested food?

It signifies either an obstruction of the esophagus or the presence of an esophageal diverticulum (pouch).

What is the significance of regurgitation of sour-tasting food or stomach contents?

This is caused in most instances by conditions within the stomach, duodenum, or gall bladder, and not by esophageal disease.

What is the significance of tightness in the throat, especially in women in their forties?

This is a tightening of the muscles of the throat encountered in women during their menopausal years. It is not due to organic disease but is thought to be caused by the tenseness that many women exhibit during these years of their life.

What are some of the common conditions affecting the esophagus?

a. Birth deformities.
b. Inflammatory conditions.
c. Injuries, including burns and foreign bodies.
d. Diverticulum of the esophagus.

328

e. Chronic spasm (achalasia).

f. Varicose veins.

g. Tumors.

BIRTH DEFORMITIES

What types of birth deformities of the esophagus are encountered?

The most common type of birth deformity is known as a tracheoesophageal fistula. This is an abnormal communication between the esophagus and the trachea (windpipe). As a result of such an abnormal opening, saliva, milk, or other swallowed materials get into the lungs and cause irritation, often resulting in pneumonia.

Is tracheoesophageal fistula a serious condition?

Yes. If untreated, it always results in death.

What is the proper treatment for these fistulae?

Surgery must be performed promptly. This will involve severing the abnormal communication and stitching

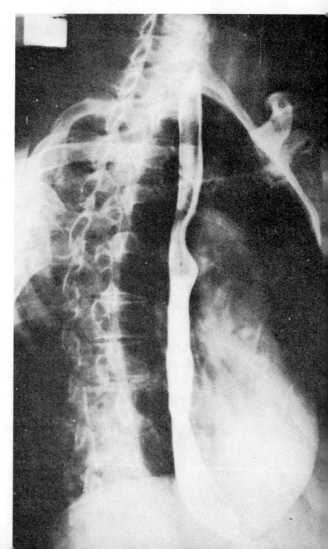

X-ray of Esophagus. *This x-ray shows the normal esophagus within the chest cavity. It should be noted that its contours are smooth and that no constrictions obstruct the passage of the barium.*

The Esophagus

the openings left in the esophagus and trachea.

What are the chances for recovery following this operation?

The mortality rate is approximately 25 percent. However, in the days before operation was feasible in this type of case, the mortality was 100 percent.

Are there other birth deformities of the esophagus?

Yes. There may be an interruption in the continuity of the esophagus, with failure of the structure to reach the stomach. This is known as congenital atresia. Occasionally, a web, or diaphragm, is found coursing across the passageway. Such an abnormality may completely obstruct the channel of the esophagus.

What is the treatment for an incompletely developed esophagus?

By an extremely extensive operation performed through the chest, the two normal ends of the esophagus are sutured together. If the lower half of the esophagus is not developed at all, it may be necessary to bring the stomach up into the chest and sew it to the lowermost portion of the normally developed section of the esophagus.

Is there any urgency in the performance of this operation?

Yes. This operation must be performed as soon as the diagnosis of the congenital abnormality is made. If surgery is not instituted immediately, the condition will result in the death of the child.

What procedure is carried out for a congenital web of the esophagus?

It must be removed surgically or dilated and stretched. This is not as serious an operation as for congenital atresia.

INFLAMMATION OF THE ESOPHAGUS *(Esophagitis)*

What conditions cause inflammation of the esophagus?

Inflammation of the esophagus (esophagitis) is either found in association with a hernia of the diaphragm (hiatus hernia) or with an ulcer in the stomach. In hiatus hernia, a portion of the stomach protrudes into the chest cavity through a widening of the opening in the diaphragm. This permits stomach contents and juices to go up into the esophagus, where they often cause irritation and set up a secondary inflammatory reaction. Patients with ulcers in the duodenum are also prone to regurgitate highly acid contents from the stomach into the lower portion of the esophagus. This may create an esophagitis.

Is esophagitis a serious condition?

Yes. It is serious because it can result in an ulcer of the esophagus, bleeding, or stricture formation, with consequent interference with swallowing.

What is the proper treatment for esophagitis?

The underlying cause must be removed. If a hiatus hernia is present, it should be corrected by surgery. If a duodenal ulcer is present, adequate medical treatment should be instituted. This should include a bland diet, drugs that prevent spasm, and medicines that counteract the excess acid secretions of the stomach.

Is it ever necessary to surgically remove that portion of the esophagus affected by esophagitis?

If the esophagitis fails to respond to the usual medical measures, its removal, followed by reestablishment of the continuity of the esophagus, may be necessary to bring about a cure.

Is removal of a portion of the esophagus a serious operation?

Yes, indeed; but approximately 90 percent of patients recover.

INJURIES OF THE ESOPHAGUS

What are some of the common injuries to the esophagus?

The most frequent injury to the esophagus is caused by the swallowing of corrosives such as lye. All too often this happens to small children because adults have carelessly failed to keep these dangerous substances out of a child's reach.

What changes occur in the esopha- **gus as a result of swallowing corrosive substances?**

Severe esophagitis, complicated by stricture formation, may result.

What is the treatment for this kind of injury?

The esophagitis is treated much the same as esophagitis from any other condition. If a stricture develops, it is treated by forceful, frequent dilatations over a period of several months. If dilatations do not produce a satisfactory increase in the diameter of the passageway, then removal of the constricted portion of esophagus may be required. If the involved area is extensive, it may be necessary to bring the stomach up into the chest and to suture it to that portion of esophagus that is normal and uninvolved in stricture formation.

What other types of injury of the esophagus are encountered?

The esophagus is, on rare occasions, ruptured as a result of severe vomiting. It may also be perforated by the swallowing of a sharp foreign body such as a safety pin, a fishbone, or a denture.

What is the management for a ruptured esophagus?

Rupture of the esophagus demands immediate surgery with closure of the opening and drainage of the chest cavity. On occasion, if the patient's condition is too poor to permit surgery, this condition may be treated conservatively by surgical drainage of the chest. In such cases, a permanent leak from the esopha-

331

gus may develop, which will eventually require surgical correction.

DIVERTICULUM OF THE ESOPHAGUS

What is a diverticulum of the esophagus?

It is an outpouching, or hernia, of the mucous membrane through the muscle wall of the esophagus that produces a saclike protrusion in an otherwise smooth mucous membrane channel.

Where are diverticula usually located?

The most common location is in that portion of the esophagus that traverses the neck. They may also be located within the chest, in the midportion of the esophagus, or in the lowermost portion, near the diaphragm.

Do diverticula ordinarily produce symptoms?

Those in the neck usually cause symptoms because they tend to fill with fluid and grow larger, thus leading to obstruction of the esophagus. In addition, fluid or food that collects within the diverticulum may be ejected into the main passageway of the esophagus, thus causing regurgitation or vomiting. Occasionally, bleeding takes place from a diverticulum, and in rare instances, malignancy may develop within one of these sacs.

Do all diverticula cause symptoms?

No. Only those that occur in the neck or in the lowermost portion of the esophagus are symptomatic. Those that occur within the midportion of the esophagus ordinarily do not cause symptoms.

What treatment is recommended for diverticula of the esophagus?

Surgical removal of those diverticula that cause symptoms. If the diverticulum is located in the neck, the incision is made in the neck. If the diverticulum is located in the lowermost portion of the esophagus, the operation is performed through the chest cavity.

ACHALASIA (Esophageal Spasm)

What is achalasia, or spasm of the esophagus?

This is a condition in which certain nerves of the esophagus are absent, probably since birth. As a result of this deficiency, there is inability of the lower end of the esophagus to dilate and relax. As a consequence of this continued spasm, the esophagus above the area of spasm becomes tremendously widened and dilated.

What causes achalasia?

It is thought to be associated with a birth deformity in which there is absence of certain nerve elements within the wall of the esophagus.

What age groups are usually affected by this disease?

People in their twenties and thirties.

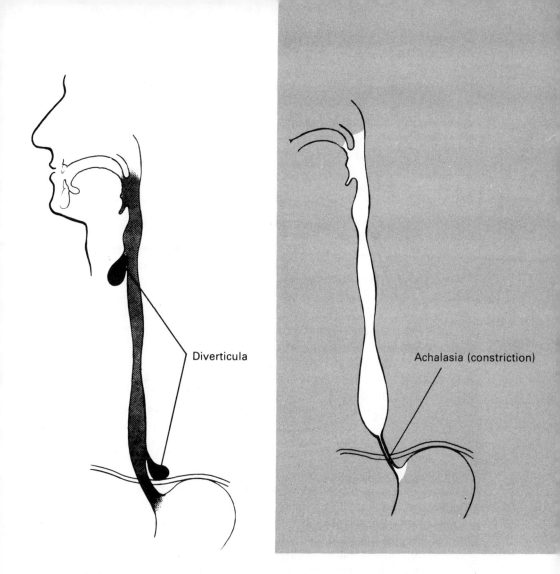

Diverticula

Achalasia (constriction)

Left:

Diverticula of the Esophagus: *The diagram shows diverticula or out-pouchings of the esophagus. Food tends to collect and stagnate within these pouches and to be regurgitated into the mouth from time to time, causing considerable discomfort. This condition can be cured by removing the diverticula surgically.*

Right:

Achalasia. *The diagram shows a condition affecting the esophagus known as achalasia or chronic constriction of the esophagus. Sufferers from achalasia are unable to hold down food thay have swallowed. If this condition continues for too long a time, it may cause fear of eating and even emaciation. Fortunately, this condition can now be relieved by a safe operative procedure.*

333

The Esophagus

What symptoms are associated with achalasia?

The most common complaint is inability to swallow normally. This symptom becomes progressive and severe. In addition, there is often a foul odor to the breath because of retained food particles within the esophagus. Sufferers from this condition are undernourished and show evidences of marked weight loss.

What is the treatment for achalasia?

Seventy-five percent of patients with achalasia respond satisfactorily to repeated dilatations of the esophagus. However, about 25 percent require operation because they fail to obtain relief from repeated dilatations.

What type of operation is performed for achalasia?

The thickened muscle fibers overlying the area of spasm are severed in a longitudinal direction. This permits outpouching of the mucous membrane of the esophagus at that site and creates an inability of the esophageal muscles to contract or become spastic.

Is this a safe operative procedure?

Yes. It is carried out through an incision in the chest but is not associated with great surgical risk.

What are the results of this operation?

The majority of patients are greatly improved, but an occasional patient may develop esophagitis as a complication.

334

VARICOSE VEINS OF THE ESOPHAGUS

What causes varicose veins of the esophagus?

Obstruction of the portal circulation, that is, the circulation of blood through the liver. This is seen in cirrhosis. (See Chapter 40, on The Liver.) Since the blood cannot get from the intestinal tract through the liver, it bypasses that organ and travels along the veins of the esophagus. This vastly increased blood volume causes the esophageal veins to dilate and become varicosed.

What harm can result from esophageal varicosities?

Eventually, when the veins become too distended and dilated, they may rupture and cause a tremendous hemorrhage.

How is the diagnosis of esophageal varicosities made?

a. By noting the evidences of cirrhosis of the liver.
b. By x-ray studies of the esophagus after taking a barium swallow.
c. By noting the bringing up of large quantities of blood through the mouth.

What can be done to relieve esophageal varicosities?

a. Attempts should be made to relieve the portal circulatory obstruction. This is attempted by either suturing the large portal vein (in the abdomen) to the vena cava, by suturing the main vein of the spleen to the main vein of the left

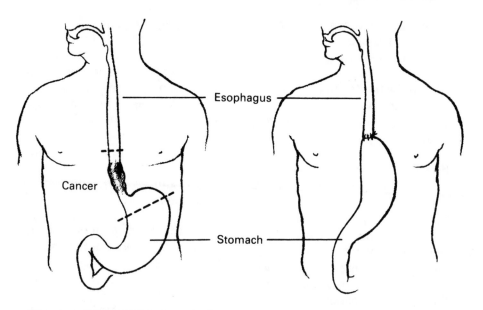

Esophagus

Cancer

Stomach

Surgery in Esophageal Cancer. *In the diagram at the left, the affected part of the esophagus and a portion of the stomach to be removed with it are shown between the dotted lines. At the right, the stump of the stomach has been sutured to the cut end of the esophagus.*

kidney, or by performing a meso-caval shunt. This operation entails placing a graft between the superior mesenteric vein (from the intestines) and the vena cava.

b. When life-threatening hemorrhage from esophageal varicosities is taking place, it may be necessary to open the chest, isolate and open the esophagus, and tie off the bleeding veins.

TUMORS OF THE ESOPHAGUS

What are the different types of tumors of the esophagus?

a. Benign tumors.
b. Malignant tumors.

What is the relative frequency of tumors of the esophagus?

It is said that approximately 1 percent of all deaths from cancer are due to cancer of the esophagus. Benign tumors occur much less frequently.

Is there any variation in the incidence of this disease in either sex?

Yes. Males are much more commonly affected than females.

What symptoms are associated with malignancies of the esophagus?

a. Difficulty in swallowing.
b. Loss of desire to eat.
c. Weakness and weight loss.

335

The Esophagus

What are the usual age ranges for cancer of the esophagus?

Fifty to seventy years.

What is the treatment for cancer of the esophagus?

Either surgery or x-ray therapy, or a combination of both.

How effective are these forms of treatment in the cure of the disease?

Radiation treatment rarely results in a cure for a cancer of the esophagus. Surgery can effect a cure in approximately 20 percent of all patients with cancer involving the lowermost portion of the esophagus.

Are benign tumors of the esophagus curable?

Yes. Practically all patients with this condition can be cured by surgical excision of the tumor.

What type of operation is performed for malignant esophageal tumors?

Those that can be attacked most successfully are usually located in the middle or lower third of the esophagus. In these cases, through a chest incision, it is possible to remove that part of the esophagus involved in tumor formation and a generous portion of normal esophagus surrounding it. Through an opening made in the diaphragm, the stomach is drawn up into the chest and is sutured to the remaining stump of esophagus.

What other forms of operation are available for cancer of the esophagus?

In another, less commonly used operation, the tumor and adjacent esophagus are widely removed and replaced by a plastic tube. This has a disadvantage, however, of being followed in many cases by leakage.

Are operations for removal of esophageal malignancy serious?

Yes. They are among the most formidable of all operations and should be performed only by a specially trained surgeon.

CHAPTER **24** THE EYES

(See also Chapter 7 on Allergy; Chapter 18 on Contagious Diseases; Chapter 26 on First Aid; Chapter 47 on Newborn Child)

Is it necessary for an eye specialist to perform an eye examination, or is an optometrist capable of performing the entire examination?

When an optometrist works in association with an ophthalmologist, it is often sufficient to have him examine the eyes if it is solely for the purpose of obtaining eyeglasses. However, an examination by an ophthalmologist (eye specialist) is always advisable when the patient feels something is wrong with his eyes or when the optometrist notes some abnormality. Also, people over forty years of age should have a yearly examination by an ophthalmologist.

How often should one have a routine checkup of the eyes?

The average person should have his eyes checked at least every one to two years.

The nearsighted person should be checked once every six months to one year.

The farsighted patient under the age of forty should be examined at least every one to two years.

All people over the age of forty should be checked every one to two years.

All people over the age of sixty-five should be checked once a year.

What are the common causes of eyestrain?

a. The need for eyeglasses.

b. Reading under a poor light.

c. Reading in any position other than sitting up.

d. Reading for excessively long

337

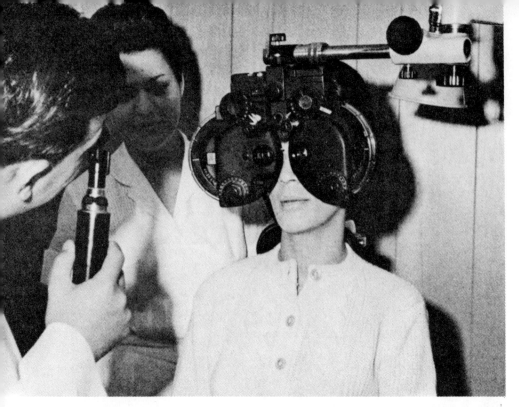

Testing the Eyes for Glasses (Refraction). *People should have their eyes tested about once a year, as changes in vision tend to take place as one ages. Changes in eyeglass prescriptions are sometimes difficult to adjust to, but it is always wise to use the glasses your oculist recommends.*

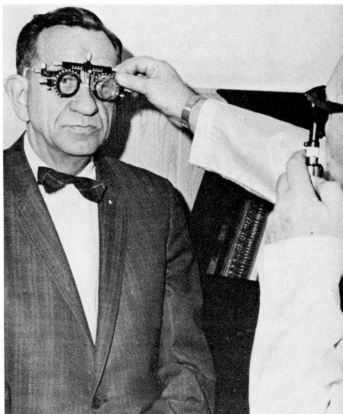

338

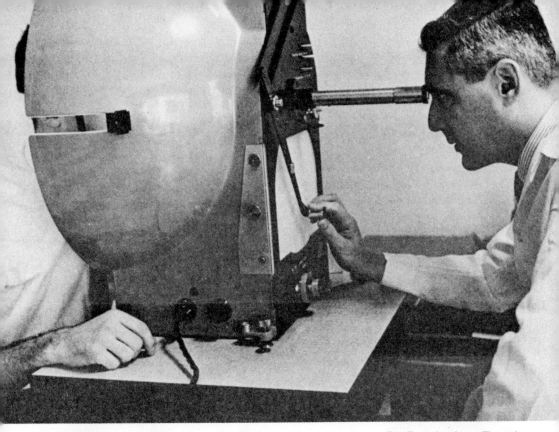

Eye Examinations. *The ophthalmologist measures the patient's visual field with this device and determines his peripheral vision (above).*

It is just as important to test children's eyes regularly as it is to test the eyes of adults (at left).

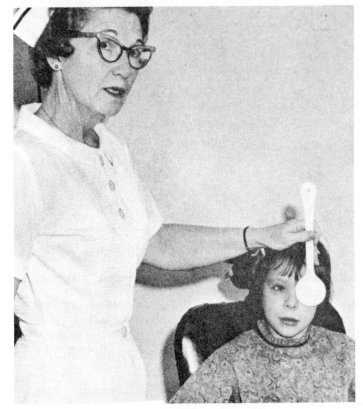

339

The Eyes

periods of time without resting the eyes.

What are the symptoms of eyestrain?

Blurring of vision, smarting and burning of the eyes, slight tearing, and headaches.

Can eyestrain be caused by reading too much?

Yes.

What is the treatment for eyestrain?

a. Wearing corrective glasses.
b. Reading under a good light.
c. Sitting in a good reading position.
d. Proper rest periods.
e. Eyedrops prescribed by a physician to reduce eyestrain.

Can permanent damage to the eye result from overuse?

No. The eyes will recover if properly treated.

Why do people have different colored eyes?

The color of the eyes depends on the amount of pigment in the iris. The less pigment there is, the bluer the eye; the more pigment, the browner the eye. The less pigment, the more sensitive the eye is to bright light.

Is it significant if a person has one eye of a different color from the other?

No. This has no significance other than cosmetic, as long as no inflammation is present.

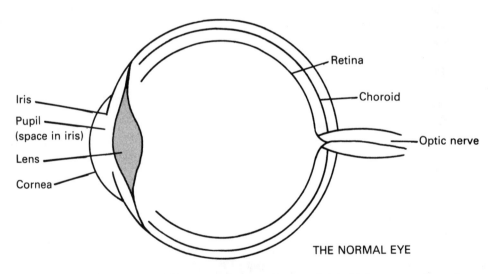

THE NORMAL EYE

The Normal Eye. This diagram illustrates the mechanism of sight. Light rays pass through the pupil and through the lens, where they are bent so that they focus on the retina in the rear of the eye. This apparatus is almost exactly like a camera, with the pupil corresponding to the opening of the camera. The lens of the eye is similar to the lens of the camera, and the retina in the back of the eye is comparable to the photographic film in a camera.

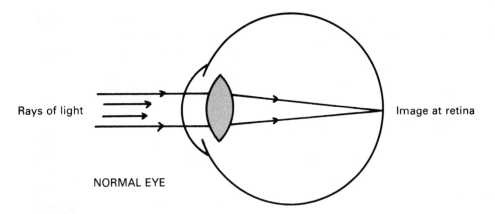

Rays of light

Image at retina

NORMAL EYE

The Normal Eye.
This diagram shows another view of the normal eye, with the light rays focusing exactly upon the retina in the back of the eye. When these rays hit the retina they are transmitted to the brain along nerve pathways and are interpreted by the brain as sight.

Is it natural for the pupils of children's eyes to be exceptionally large?

Yes. As a child grows older, the pupil will appear smaller.

What causes tearing of the eyes?

This may be due to irritation from excessively bright lights, allergies, a sharp wind, smoke, inflammation of the eye, a foreign body in the eye, or a blocked tear duct. It occurs more frequently in older people.

What are the common causes for itching and swelling of the eyes and lids?

Itching may be due to an allergic condition such as hay fever or sensitivity to smoke or face powder or soap.

Swelling of the lids should be a signal to see a physician to make sure that kidney function is normal.

Slight swelling of the lids is sometimes caused by insufficient sleep.

What causes red lid margins?

This condition may be caused by dandruff or seborrhea of the scalp, exposure to irritating smoke, dust, or wind, eyestrain, allergy, or chronic conjunctivitis. Children may develop red lid margins when they rub their eyes with dirty hands.

What causes the spots that are seen floating in front of the eyes?

Spots are caused by opacities of protein matter that float in the internal portion (vitreous) of the eyeball. These opacities become visible as small spots or threads and are usually seen when a person looks at a bright background such as a clear sky or white paper. Usually they are of no significance unless associated with blurring of vision and/or flashes

341

of light. If either should occur, consult an eye doctor for a thorough examination to rule out inflammation or disease of the retina.

What causes bulging of the eyes?

Bulging or prominent eyes may be due to overactivity of the thyroid gland, inflammation, tumor behind the eye, or to excessive nearsightedness. In some people it is a normal anatomical feature and has no significance.

How does one treat the so-called "black eye"?

An eye specialist should be consulted to make sure there has been no damage to the eyeball itself. Then, for the first twenty-four hours, cold wet compresses should be applied to lessen swelling. After twenty-four hours, warm compresses should be used to hasten absorption of the blood clot.

NEARSIGHTEDNESS (Myopia)

What is nearsightedness?

In nearsightedness, the eyeball is longer than it should normally be for that individual. Vision is better for near objects than for distant objects.

How common is nearsightedness?

About one-third of all people who wear glasses are nearsighted.

Are boys more likely to be nearsighted than girls?

No.

Is nearsightedness inherited?

It often runs in families, particularly if both parents are nearsighted.

Can anything be done to prevent nearsightedness?

No.

Does nearsightedness tend to get better by itself?

No, except very occasionally.

Will wearing the proper eyeglasses lead to an improvement in nearsightedness?

No, but it will permit the eyes to function normally.

How early can children be fitted for eyeglasses for nearsightedness?

Usually at three years, but if necessary, at one year of age.

How can the doctor detect nearsightedness in small children?

By shining a light in the eye and performing a test known as retinoscopy. Prior to the test, the pupils are dilated with eyedrops.

Why does nearsightedness get worse as one matures?

As the body grows, the eyeball gets larger while the optical system of the eyes remains unchanged.

Does watching television have any adverse effect on the eyes of nearsighted people?

None at all.

Should nearsighted people spare their eyes from excess reading?

No. This is necessary only if the

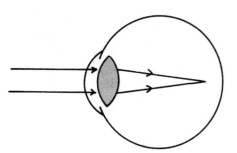

(image focused in front of retina)

NEARSIGHTED EYE

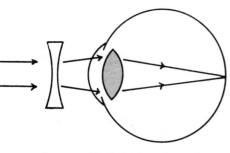

Corrected by lens (eyeglasses)

Nearsighted Eye (Myopia). The diagram of the nearsighted eye shows the image focusing in front of the retina. When this defect is corrected by eyeglasses, the image is made to focus exactly upon the retina.

nearsightedness is very severe and associated with degeneration of the back of the eye.

What are contact lenses?

These are molded plastic lenses that fit directly over the eyeballs and therefore disguise the fact that "glasses" are being worn.

When are contact lenses recommended in nearsightedness?

When the nearsightedness is of moderate severity, and the patient does not want to give the appearance of wearing glasses.

Are contact lenses worn directly against the eyeball harmful?

Not if they are well fitted.

Are soft contact lenses advisable?

Yes, for many people they represent a considerable improvement over the rigid lenses. However, they do not provide clear vision for people with astigmatism. (See the section on Astigmatism in this chapter.)

Is there any medication to help nearsightedness?

No, although certain eyedrops are being tried with some apparent success.

Is there any surgical procedure that can help nearsightedness?

In extreme cases of nearsightedness associated with weakening of the walls of the eyeball, implants of fibrous tissue are sewn to the weakened areas. Recently, a new operation on the cornea known as keratomileusis — an operation involving a change in the curve of the cornea — has been devised. This procedure can benefit both nearsighted and farsighted patients. Although the operation is still in the experimental stage, it has been used successfully on patients who have also had cataract operations, Keratomileusis may do away with the need for heavy spectacles or contact lenses among this group of patients.

How effective are the newer operations for nearsightedness?

Although the number of cases in

343

which they have been performed is relatively small, first reports are that if patients are properly selected for these procedures, results are successful in a fair number of instances.

Is there any surgical procedure that can arrest or decrease nearsightedness?

In a few selected cases, operations to shorten the eyeball can be performed. These operations have just been developed recently and have not yet been perfected. They consist of taking out crescentic portions of the eyeball along the inner and outer aspects. This will shorten the length of the eyeball and thus bring the lens closer to the retina, overcoming some of the nearsightedness. In addition, surgery upon the cornea to change its optical properties has been tried recently. (See above.)

Does nearsightedness ever lead to blindness?

In the very rare case, nearsightedness may lead to degeneration—with or without detachment of the retina—with some loss of vision. (See the section on Detached Retina in this chapter.)

FARSIGHTEDNESS
(Hyperopia)

What is farsightedness?

In farsightedness, the eyeball is shorter than it should normally be for that individual. Vision is better for distant than for near objects. In marked cases, vision is also blurred for distant objects.

How common is farsightedness?

About one-third of all people who wear glasses are farsighted.

Are boys more likely to be farsighted than girls?

No.

Is farsightedness inherited, or does it tend to run in families?

Yes, in some cases.

Can anything be done to prevent farsightedness?

No.

Does farsightedness tend to get better by itself?

No, but in growing children, farsightedness may change into nearsightedness.

Will wearing the proper eyeglasses lead to an improvement in farsightedness?

It will not bring about a cure but will improve the vision.

Is it ever bad to wear eyeglasses for farsightedness?

No.

How early can children be fitted with eyeglasses for farsightedness?

Usually at three years of age.

How can the doctor detect farsightedness in small children?

By a special examination known as retinoscopy.

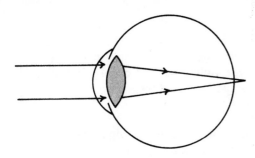

(Image focused beyond retina)

FARSIGHTED EYE

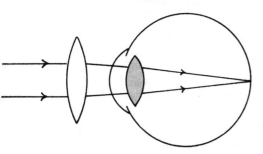

Corrected by lens (eyeglasses)

Farsighted Eye (Hyperopia). This diagram of the farsighted eye shows the image focusing beyond the retina. This too can be readily corrected by appropriate eyeglasses.

Why does farsightedness get worse as one gets older?

As one gets older, the lenses of the eye grow more rigid and the patient is less able to compensate for his defect by muscle contraction.

Should farsighted people spare their eyes from excessive reading?

This is not necessary if the patient wears proper eyeglasses.

Does watching television have any harmful effect on the eyes of far-sighted people?

No.

When are contact lenses recommended for farsightedness?

When the farsightedness reduces vision enough to require constant use of spectacles and when it is desirable to avoid the latter for cosmetic, occupational, or athletic reasons.

Is there any medication that can be given to help farsightedness?

No.

Is there any surgical procedure that can help farsightedness?

Yes, keratomileusis.

Does farsightedness ever cause blindness?

No.

ASTIGMATISM

What is astigmatism?

A defect in the curvature of the cornea and/or lens whereby there is an inequality preventing the light rays from hitting the retina at a point of common focus.

What produces astigmatism?

The manner in which the eyeballs grow. This is inherited.

How does a person know if he has astigmatism?

Astigmatic people are more prone to eyestrain and blurred vision. They soon become aware that something is wrong.

What is the treatment for astigmatism?

The wearing of proper corrective

The Eyes

glasses will relieve the symptoms and improve vision greatly.

Does astigmatism ever get better by itself?
No.

Can astigmatism lead to blindness?
No.

CONJUNCTIVITIS

What is conjunctivitis?
An inflammation of the conjunctiva, the thin membrane that covers the white part of the eyeball and the inner surface of the eyelids.

What can cause conjunctivitis?
An injury, an infection, or an allergy. Injury can be caused by exposure to sunlight, dust, or wind. Infection may be caused by a streptococcus, staphylococcus, gonococcus, or any other bacteria.

What are the symptoms of conjunctivitis?
The symptoms of the traumatic (injury) type are redness, itching, burning, and tearing of the eyes. The symptoms of the infectious type are the same as for traumatic conjunctivitis, plus the fact that there is a pus discharge from the eye. The symptoms of the allergic type are redness, burning, tearing, and itching of the eyes and lids, often accompanied by symptoms in the nose and throat.

What is the treatment for conjunctivitis?
For the traumatic type, mild astrin-

gent eyedrops. For the infectious type, antibiotic eyedrops. For the allergic type, antihistamine or cortisone eyedrops.

Is conjunctivitis contagious?
Only the infectious type is contagious.

How can one prevent the spread of the contagious type of conjunctivitis?
By isolating the patient and having him use his own soap and towel.

How long does it take for conjunctivitis to get well?
Usually two to four days if there are no complications and proper treatment is instituted.

Does permanent damage to eyesight result from conjunctivitis?
No, unless there are complications.

What is the most common complication of conjunctivitis?
An ulceration of the cornea, which may leave a scar obscuring vision to a greater or lesser degree.

If conjunctivitis is due to a gonorrheal infection, can it be cured?
Yes, by proper use of an antibiotic medication, usually penicillin.

What is the treatment for gonorrheal conjunctivitis?
The use of penicillin eyedrops.

What are the preventive measures to avoid gonorrheal conjunctivitis?
If one has gonorrhea, strict personal hygiene is essential! The hands must be kept away from the eyes,

and penicillin eyedrops should be used prophylactically.

What is "pinkeye"?
"Pinkeye" is a very contagious type of infectious conjunctivitis caused by special bacteria.

What are the symptoms of pinkeye?
The same as for any infectious conjunctivitis.

How is pinkeye treated?
By eyedrops that will bring about a cure in two to three days.

Can pinkeye permanently injure the eyes?
No.

LACERATIONS, ABRASIONS, ULCERATIONS, AND FOREIGN BODIES OF THE CORNEA

What is the first-aid treatment for a scratch or foreign body in the eye?
The use of anesthetic eyedrops and a bandage to cover the eye. After anesthetizing the eye, a foreign body can usually be wiped away with sterile, moist cotton on a stick.

What should one do if this occurs late at night when the eye doctor is not available?
The use of the anesthetic drops and a patch will relieve the patient of pain and keep the eye clean until the patient can consult an eye doctor in the morning. However, it is much wiser to go to the emergency room of the nearest hospital than to leave a foreign body in the eye overnight.

Can serious damage to the eye result if one waits several hours before receiving medical treatment?
No, but one should not wait more than twelve hours before seeing a doctor.

What is the treatment for an abrasion (scratch) or ulcer of the cornea?
The use of an antibiotic and cortisone eyedrops or ointment and a bandage to keep the eye covered. See your eye doctor.

Can a laceration of the cornea be successfully sutured?
Yes. This is done when there has been a deep or extensive laceration.

Is there any serious danger to the eye from a foreign body such as a small cinder or piece of steel?
If the foreign body is on the surface of the eye, there is usually very little danger. If the foreign body has penetrated the eyeball, there is serious danger to the eye.

Do abrasions and lacerations tend to heal by themselves?
Small abrasions will heal by themselves. Lacerations usually have to be treated.

How does one prevent scar tissue from forming when abrasions or lacerations heal?
By the use of cortisone eyedrops and the use of warm compresses to the eye.

The Eyes

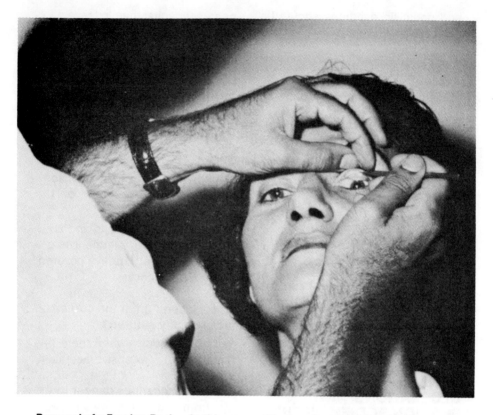

Removal of a Foreign Body—in this case a Cinder—from the Eye. Foreign bodies which cannot be easily and quickly removed should be treated by a physician. The cornea (the membrane over the pupil) may be scratched and infection may take place if untrained people attempt to remove firmly embedded foreign bodies.

Is impairment of vision often found after an injury of this type?

If a corneal abrasion is superficial and does not become infected, there is usually no impairment of vision. Intraocular foreign bodies very often result in impairment of vision.

How long do corneal abrasions take to heal?

With proper treatment, two to four days.

How long do corneal lacerations take to heal?

Usually two to three weeks.

What causes chronic ulceration of the cornea?

Chronic ulceration of the cornea occurs when the patient's resistance is low, as in diabetes or other debilitating illnesses. Infection of an abrasion can produce the same result.

What is the treatment for chronic or recurrent ulcers of the cornea?

The use of antibiotics, cauterization of the ulcer, and a bandage to keep the eye covered and safe from possible external contamination.

Is it possible to replace a cornea that has been damaged irreparably by scars?

Yes. Corneal transplants have recently been used for this purpose with great success. There are now eye banks in which normal corneas are preserved for long periods of time, to be used for purposes of transplanting to other individuals.

Do corneal transplants usually survive?

Yes, in the great majority of cases a cornea transplanted from one human to another will live and will function normally.

Is it possible to restore vision through a corneal transplant?

Most certainly, yes. There are now thousands of people who were formerly blind but can now see because they have received a corneal transplant.

If one operation with corneal transplantation fails, is it possible to reoperate?

Yes. Every once in a while a transplanted cornea will fail to survive. In such cases, success may follow a second operative procedure.

Can all blind people be helped by corneal transplants?

Unfortunately, no. It is estimated that

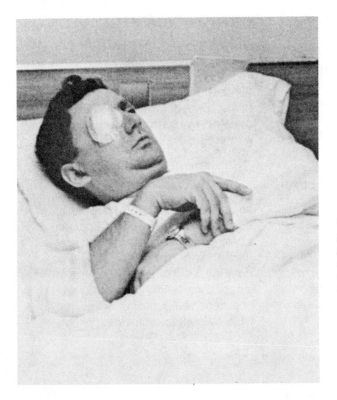

Corneal Transplant. Transplantation of the cornea has proved to be very successful in helping to restore vision to an eye which has been scarred by injury.

349

approximately 5 percent of those who are blind have lost their sight because of scarring of the cornea. It is this small group that can be benefited by a corneal transplant.

Can an entire eye be transplanted?
No.

STYES AND CYSTS OF THE EYELIDS

What causes recurrent styes of the eyelids?
a. Lowered body resistance due to poor health.
b. Conjunctivitis (inflammation of the covering of the eye).
c. Blepharitis (inflammation of the eyelid).
d. Lack of cleanliness.

What is the treatment for styes?
Warm compresses and mild antiseptics will usually cause most of them to heal. Occasionally it is necessary for the eye surgeon to open them. Severe cases are treated with antibiotic drugs.

How long does it take for the usual stye to disappear?
About five to eight days.

What causes cysts of the eyelids (chalazion)?
An inflammation of one of the small glands in the lid with a clogging of its opening to the surface.

What are the symptoms of a stye or cyst of the eyelid?
A markedly painful swelling and redness of the lid.

What is the treatment for chalazions?
Most of them will respond to warm compresses and eyedrops. If they do not subside by themselves, they must be opened and removed under local anesthesia in the ophthalmologist's office.

Do these cysts have a tendency to recur once they are cured?
No, but there is a tendency for people who have developed one cyst (chalazion) to develop others.

ENTROPION AND ECTROPION

What is entropion?
It is a condition in which the margin of the upper or lower eyelid turns in, causing eyelashes to rub against and irritate the eyeball.

What causes entropion?
It usually develops as a result of scarring consequent to an old inflammation of the eyelid. Occasionally it results from an injury with scarring. Another type is caused by overdevelopment of the muscle that closes the eyelids. This is the result of excessive squeezing of lids, particularly in older, high-strung people.

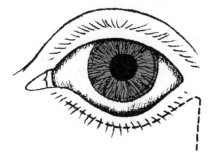

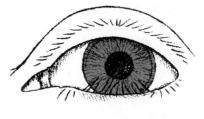

Below:
Operation for Entropion. *The lashes are shown rubbing against the eye in the diagram at the top. Center, a wedge from the upper lid is inserted. The lengthened lid, with the lashes drawn away from the eye, is shown at the bottom.*

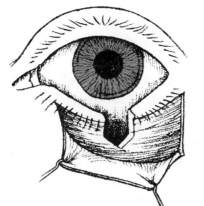

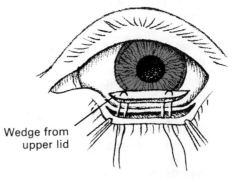

Wedge from
upper lid

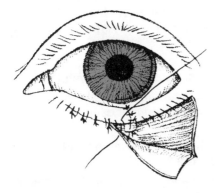

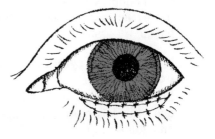

Above:
Operation for Ectropion. *The top diagram shows the line of incision. In the center, a wedge-shaped piece has been cut out of the lid. Below, the shortened eyelid is sutured.*

351

The Eyes

Is it important to operate to repair an eyelid with entropion?
Yes, because the continued rubbing of the eyelashes against the eyeball will lead to permanent scarring and loss of vision.

What operation is performed to correct entropion?
It is a simple plastic procedure, carried out under local anesthesia, in which a portion of the inside of the eyelid is cut away in such a manner as to cause the lid to bend outward.

Are the results of operation for entropion successful?
Yes.

What is ectropion?
It is a condition in which the margin of the upper or lower eyelid turns outward.

What is the most common cause for ectropion?
With advancing age there is a loss of elastic tissue within the eyelid, allowing it to fall away from the eyeball. Other cases are caused by scarring secondary to inflammation or injury.

Who is most likely to develop ectropion?
Older people whose elastic tissue of the eyelid is replaced with fibrous tissue.

What are the symptoms of ectropion?
Since the eyelid—usually the lower one—has fallen away from the eyeball, tears run out onto the cheeks rather than into the tear duct.

Can ectropion be corrected surgically?
Yes, by a simple operative procedure a portion of the inside of the eyelid is excised so as to cause the lid to turn inward.

How successful are operations for ectropion?
They are very successful in most cases.

DACRYOCYSTITIS

What is dacryocystitis?
Dacryocystitis is an inflammation of the tear sac of the eye.

Who is most likely to develop dacryocystitis?
It is a common condition in infants under a year or two of age. It also occurs sometimes in elderly people whose tear ducts tend to become clogged or to be narrowed by fibrous tissue.

What causes dacryocystitis?
Dacryocystitis is usually secondary to a blocked tear canal.

What are the symptoms of dacryocystitis?
Pain and swelling of the inner corner of the eye, sometimes extending down toward the nose.

What is the treatment for dacryocystitis?
The use of antibiotics and an incision for drainage of pus.

Is recurrence frequent after cure of this condition?
Yes, unless the blockage of the tear canal is released by probing or by surgery.

How long does it take for someone with dacryocystitis to get well?
Usually about a week.

IRITIS

What is iritis?
An inflammation of the iris, the colored part of the eyeball.

What causes iritis?
Iritis may be caused by an immunological response to local infection, tuberculosis, syphilis, or other generalized diseases.

What are the symptoms of iritis?
Pain, redness, and tearing of the eye, with inability to tolerate light.

What is the treatment for iritis?
The treatment will depend upon the cause of the disease. It will consist, usually, of eyedrops containing atropine and cortisone.

Is recovery possible after iritis?
Yes.

Is the eyesight frequently damaged after iritis?
In some cases, a severe iritis may leave permanent damage to vision.

How long does it take for iritis to get well?
In some cases, one to two weeks. In others, it may last for months and even years.

Do some cases of iritis affect the deeper structures of the eye?
Yes, and if it involves the choroid, the inflammation may extend all the way back to the retina. In severe cases, vision may become greatly impaired, or even lost.

GLAUCOMA

What is glaucoma?
A condition in which the pressure within the eyeball is elevated above normal.

What causes glaucoma?
The cause is unknown in most cases. Injury, hemorrhage in the eyeball, and/or displacement of the lens cause this condition.

How often does glaucoma occur?
Two percent of all adults over the age of forty will develop glaucoma.

Is it more common in males than in females?
No.

Does it occur in children?
There is a rare form of glaucoma in children that is present from birth. This is called congenital glaucoma.

Does glaucoma tend to run in families or to be inherited?
Yes.

What are the harmful effects of glaucoma?
If untreated, it will cause serious de-

353

The Eyes

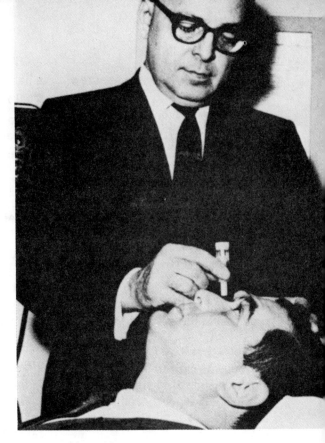

Glaucoma Test. *A simple test for glaucoma is to measure the eyeball pressure with a tonometer.*

crease in vision and may result in blindness.

What are the symptoms of glaucoma?

In the acute type, there is severe pain in the eye, redness of the eye, vomiting, and blurring of vision. In the chronic type, the patient may have no symptoms whatever until late in the course of the disease, when it is either difficult or too late to treat.

How can one tell if he has glaucoma?

In the acute type, he will know very quickly because of the severe pain and blurring of vision. In the chronic type, it may be discovered on routine

eye examination by the ophthalmologist.

Is there any way to prevent getting glaucoma?

If the eye doctor suspects the patient of being a potential glaucoma case, he may prescribe prophylactic eyedrops, which will protect against the disease. Also, such patients require constant supervision.

What tests are performed to make the diagnosis of glaucoma?

a. Taking the pressure of the eyeball with an instrument known as a tonometer.
b. Checking the visual fields.
c. Performing provocative tests.

354

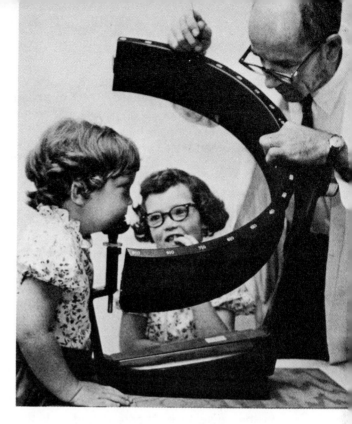

Glaucoma Tests. The visual field of a child born with glaucoma is being checked at the right. Her sister also has congenital glaucoma. A tonometer is being used below to measure a patient's ocular pressure.

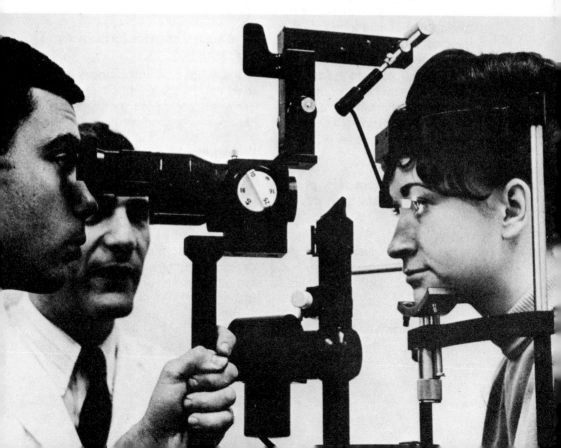

The Eyes

Should people be tested regularly for pressure of the eyeball?

Yes, this is an extremely simple test, and all adults should have it performed as part of their annual eye examination.

Is it painful to have pressure of the eyeball tested?

There is no pain whatever.

Does glaucoma usually affect both eyes at the same time?

Yes, except in an acute case. A patient who has developed the condition in one eye is more prone to develop it in the other eye at some later date.

What is the treatment for glaucoma?

In the acute type, eyedrops and medications given by mouth or intravenously are used to reduce the intraocular pressure. If the pressure cannot be reduced after eight hours, surgery is indicated. In the chronic type, eyedrops may be continued for years as the sole means of treatment provided the pressure remains controlled; otherwise surgery is necessary.

Is hospitalization necessary, or can the patient be satisfactorily treated at home?

Hospital care is necessary if surgery has to be done. Otherwise the patient may stay at home, but only if he maintains contact with his eye specialist.

Is surgery always necessary?

It depends upon the pressure and the visual fields. If these can be controlled by eyedrops, surgery will not be necessary.

What will happen if surgery is not performed when indicated?

Blindness will result.

What will happen if the eyedrops are not used when indicated?

The patient may eventually lose the sight of the involved eye.

Does glaucoma clear up by itself without treatment?

Usually not.

Is the surgery for glaucoma dangerous?

No, but results are not always as good as one might wish. However, it is more dangerous in many cases *not* to operate.

What are the chances for recovery after surgery?

In the acute type, the chances are excellent. In the chronic type, the earlier surgery is done, the better the chances for a good result.

What kind of operation is performed?

An iridectomy, wherein a small piece of the iris is removed to allow drainage and to lessen the pressure within the eyeball. The actual procedure varies from case to case, depending upon whether the surgeon is dealing with an acute or a chronic glaucoma.

What anesthetic is used?

Local or general anesthesia.

How long a hospital stay is necessary?

Usually three to six days.

Are special private nurses required after surgery?

No.

Is there a visible scar after glaucoma operations?

No, except that one can see where a small piece of iris has been removed.

Does glaucoma recur after it has been operated upon?

Usually not in the acute type. In the chronic glaucoma, it may recur.

What limitations on activity are imposed after a succesful glaucoma operation?

a. Exceptional cleanliness must be maintained.
b. Water should be kept out of the eye if a *filtering* operation has been performed to cure the glaucoma.

How soon after the operation can one do the following:

Bathe:
   One week.
Walk out in the street:
   One week.
Walk up and down stairs:
   One week.
Perform household duties:
   Two weeks.
Drive a car:
   Two weeks.
Resume sexual relations:
   Two weeks.
Return to work:
   Two weeks.

Resume all physical activities:
   Four weeks.

Is it necessary to return for periodic examinations after an attack of glaucoma?

Yes. The physician will pay particular attention to the health of the uninvolved eye.

CATARACT

What is a cataract?

An opacity or a clouding of the lens.

Where is the lens of the eye?

It is located inside the eye, just behind the pupil.

What is its function?

To focus the image onto the retina in the back of the eye.

What happens when a patient has a cataract?

The opaque lens does not allow light to enter the eyeball. Vision is thereby decreased.

What causes cataract?

The cause is usually unknown. Sometimes, however, it may be due to diabetes, a glandular disorder, an infection within the eyeball, radiation, drugs, or a direct injury to the lens. The tendency to develop cataracts increases with age.

Do cataracts tend to run in families or to be inherited?

Frequently, one finds that a tendency toward cataract formation is inherited.

The Eyes

What harm results from leaving a cataract untreated?

As cataracts progress, vision decreases. If a cataract of long standing is not removed, it will become overripe, causing a severe inflammation and possible loss of the eyeball.

How can one tell if he has a cataract?

Cataracts should be suspected if there is blurring of vision that cannot be improved by glasses. In the later stages it is possible to see the cataract as a white opacity in the pupil.

Do cataracts usually affect both eyes at the same time?

Not often, but a person who has had a cataract is more prone to develop one on the other eye at some later date.

Can people who have been operated upon for cataracts tolerate contact lenses?

Yes. They are advisable in many cases rather than standard eyeglasses.

What is an intraocular lens?

It is a plastic lens that is sewn into the eyeball after the natural lens containing the cataract has been removed. The intraocular lens does away with the need for unsightly cataract eyeglasses and for contact lenses.

Are intraocular lenses used routinely after cataract surgery?

No. At the present stage of development there is too great an incidence of serious complications, including infection followed by loss of vision.

When are intraocular lenses most suitable?

a. When there is a cataract in one eye only. In such cases it does away with double vision.
b. In people in their eighties.

How much greater is the risk of serious complication when intraocular lenses are employed?

The risk is approximately ten times greater when this type of lens is used after cataract removal.

Are the new *continuous-wear* contact lenses valuable for use after a cataract removal?

Yes, although some problems still exist concerning their use by all patients. Nevertheless, they are much safer than intraocular lenses, and many patients tolerate them well.

Is there any way to prevent getting cataracts?

No.

What tests are performed to make a positive diagnosis of cataracts?

By using an instrument called an ophthalmoscope, the opacity of the lens can be seen readily.

What is the treatment for cataracts?

Surgical removal of the lens.

At what stage should a cataract be removed?

When it disables the patient. This usually does not take place until the vision in the involved eye is markedly diminished.

358

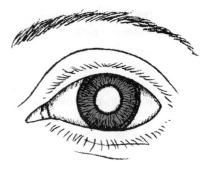

Eye with cataract

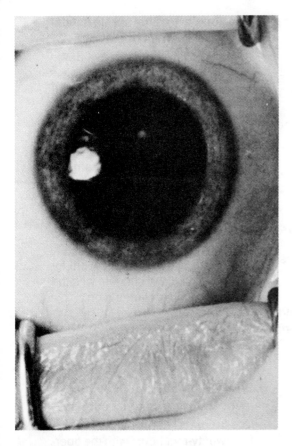

Cataract: *The opacity, or clouding of the lens, is shown in this picture of an eye with a cataract.*

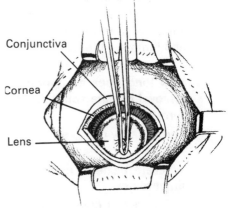

Conjunctiva

Cornea

Lens

Removing cataract

At right:
Cataract Operation. *An eye with a cataract is shown at the top. In the center, the lens and cataract are being removed through an incision made in the cornea. At the bottom, the eye, with the lens removed, has been sutured.*

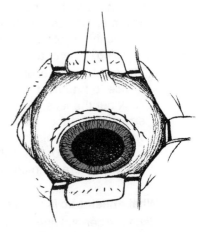

Eye with lens removed

359

The Eyes

Do cataracts ever disappear by themselves?

No.

What are the chances for recovery following cataract surgery?

In over 90 percent of cases, good results are obtained.

What kind of operation is performed?

An incision is made at the margin of the cornea and the white of the eye. Through this incision the surgeon inserts a probe, freezes it to the lens, and removes it.

How long does an operation for removal of cataracts take to perform?

Forty to sixty minutes.

What are the newer methods of cataract removal?

a. The use of cryosurgery, or lens removal through freezing. A "cryoprobe" freezes the probe to the lens, and the lens is lifted out. This method has largely replaced the technique of taking a forceps, grasping the lens, and lifting it out.

b. The employment of an ultrasound device to fragment, destroy, and suck out the lens. (Some people erroneously label this a laser device; it is not.) This method is reserved mainly for use in the treatment of cataracts in children.

What anesthetic is used?

Usually a general anesthetic, but local anesthesia can be used, too.

How long a hospital stay is necessary for a cataract operation?

In uncomplicated cases, five days.

Are special private nurses required after surgery?

No, except for patients who are unable to care for themselves.

Are special preoperative examinations necessary before a cataract operation?

It is important to know that the patient is in good general health and free from infection, diabetes, etc. Poor general health or a distant focus of infection will interfere with the result of a cataract operation.

Is the postoperative period especially painful?

No.

What is the postoperative treatment following cataract surgery?

The patient is kept on his back for the first twenty-four hours with the operated eye bandaged. After this, the patient is allowed out of bed and the bandage is removed from the operated eye.

What are possible complications of cataract surgery?

Infection or hemorrhage within the eyeball.

How are these complications treated?

Infections are treated by the use of antibiotics and by washing out the eye. Hemorrhage is treated by applying a pressure bandage to the eye ball and keeping the patient quiet in bed. Certain drugs may also help to stop hemorrhage.

How long does it take for the wound to heal after the usual cataract operation?
Six weeks for thorough healing.

What kind of scar remains?
The scar is practically invisible.

Do cataracts ever recur once they have been removed?
Occasionally a membrane may form and obscure vision. However, this can be removed by a rather simple operation, and good vision usually will result.

How soon may a patient obtain glasses after a cataract operation?
Within one month. If vision in the unoperated eye is good, it is sometimes not possible to use glasses for the operated eye as the patient may see double unless a contact lens is used.

What postoperative precautions must be followed?
The patient should not bend over or do strenuous work for about a month to six weeks after a cataract removal.

After recovery from a cataract operation, does one return to a completely normal existence?
Yes.

Surgical Microscope. This high-powered instrument is used by surgeons to magnify greatly the site of an operation in delicate eye surgery.

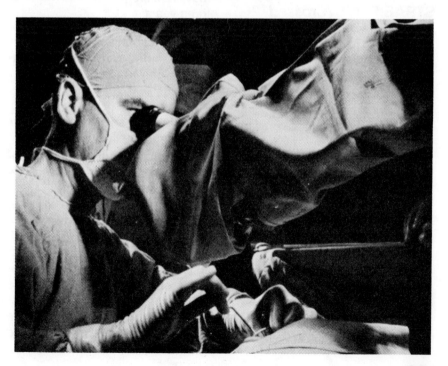

The Eyes

How soon after the cataract operation can one do the following:

Bathe:
  Two weeks.
Walk in the street:
  One week.
Walk up and down stairs:
  Two weeks.
Perform household duties:
  Four weeks.
Drive a car:
  Six weeks.
Resume sexual relations:
  Six weeks.
Return to light work:
  Two weeks.
Return to heavy work:
  Eight weeks.
Resume all physical activities:
  Eight weeks.

STRABISMUS (Crossed Eyes)

What is strabismus?

A condition in which the eyes are not straight but are crossed. One or both eyes may turn in or out. The condition may be inconstant or constant.

What causes strabismus?

When strabismus is noticed at birth, it is due either to small brain hemorrhages or to abnormal attachments of the muscles of the eyeball. When it occurs after the first or second year of life, it is usually due to a weakness of the "fusion center" in the brain. It may also be associated with a weak or paralyzed eye muscle.

Convergent strabismus, where the eye turns in, is usually associated with farsightedness. Divergent strabismus, where the eye turns out, is often associated with nearsightedness.

Does strabismus tend to run in families or to be inherited?

Yes.

What is meant by "a cast in the eye"?

This is another term for crossed eyes.

Is it more difficult to cure eyes that turn out than eyes that turn in?

Yes, but not always.

How early in life can crossed eyes be recognized?

Often at birth; definitely at some time during the first three years of life. It may, however, start after the first three years.

What percentage of crossed eyes can be cured with medical treatment alone?

About 40 to 50 percent.

What is the medical treatment for strabismus?

a. The regular performance of special eye exercises known as orthoptics.
b. The regular performance of special eye exercises known as pleoptics. The latter is used to restore vision to a "lazy" eye.
c. The wearing of corrective eyeglasses and the use of eyedrops that constrict the pupil.
d. Placing a patch over the good eye to encourage vision in the crossed eye.

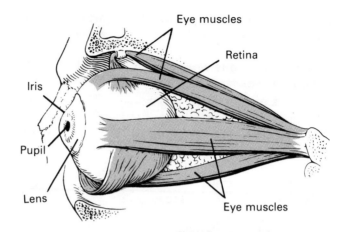

Eye muscles

Retina

Iris

Pupil

Lens

Eye muscles

Eye Muscles. *This diagram shows the muscle attachments to the outside of the eyeball. When these muscles fail to function normally, the eyes may become crossed or they may diverge. Both conditions can be helped greatly by surgery. The surgeon will either shorten or lenghten the muscles in order to bring the eyes into proper alignment. Such an operation, although delicate, is not very complicated and may be performed safely on small children.*

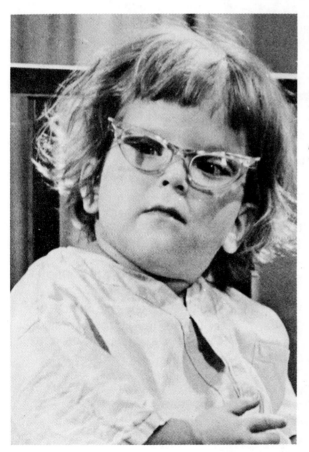

Crossed Eyes. *This child has not had beneficial results from wearing eyeglasses, and her crossed eyes will be corrected by surgery.*

The Eyes

e. The use of eyeglasses to correct farsightedness.

How long must one wear glasses before the eyes straighten?

If the eyes are going to straighten, they will straighten immediately, but the glasses will have to be worn for many years.

Why does strabismus sometimes not improve even after glasses are worn?

Because it is due to some factor other than nearsightedness or farsightedness such as faulty attachments of the muscles surrounding the eyeballs or to faulty nerves going to the muscles.

What is the earliest age at which a child will be able to wear glasses for crossed eyes?

Two years of age.

What harm results from strabismus?

It is disfiguring and can produce deep psychological harm. Convergent strabismus, if not treated, may result in poor vision or even loss of vision in the eye that turns in. This is referred to as a "lazy eye."

Is there any way to prevent eyes that turn in from developing poor vision?

Yes. The patient wears a patch over the good eye, which forces him to use the weak eye. This will very often improve the vision in the weak eye. This method of treatment must be started at a very early age. After five or six years of age, this treatment is ineffective.

Is there any way to prevent strabismus?

Yes. If the patient shows signs of developing strabismus, the wearing of proper eyeglasses will often straighten the eye.

Is surgery always necessary for strabismus?

No. If the strabismus is mild and inconstant, surgery is not necessary.

Does strabismus ever get well by itself without treatment?

Yes. A mild case may get well by itself, but this is rare.

What are the chances for a good result from surgery?

The chances for a good result are excellent, but more than one operation may be necessary to obtain the desired result.

What are the risks of surgery for strabismus?

The risks are practically nil, but failure to correct the defect sometimes occurs.

How long does it take to perform an operation for strabismus?

This will depend upon the number of muscles that have to be operated upon. The average case takes one hour.

What kind of operation is performed?

This will vary with the type of strabismus. It may be necessary to strengthen a muscle. This is done by cutting off a piece of the muscle, or shortening it, and reattaching it to its original insertion on the eyeball. It may be necessary to weaken a muscle. This is done by detaching it from its insertion and reattaching it farther back on the eyeball.

What anesthetic is used?

For children, a general anesthetic. For adults, a local or general anesthetic.

How long a hospital stay is necessary?

Two days.

Are special preoperative treatments necessary?

In certain cases, orthoptics and/or patching is advisable.

Are special private nurses required after surgery?

No.

Is the postoperative period exceptionally painful?

No.

What special postoperative procedures are carried out?

Eyedrops and cold compresses are necessary following surgery. If the eyes are not absolutely straight, it may be necessary for the patient to take special eye exercises. These exercises are known as orthoptics.

How long does it take for the wound to heal following a strabismus operation?

About two to four weeks.

Do patients ever see double after a strabismus operation?

Yes, but this condition usually disappears within three to four weeks.

What kind of scar remains after this operation?

The scar is invisible.

Does strabismus ever recur after it has been operated upon?

Yes, in some cases.

What can be done if the strabismus is not corrected by the initial surgery?

Reoperation often brings about a cure.

What postoperative precautions must be followed?

For about a week after surgery, some patients should not read or watch television. Also, dirt must be kept away from the eye to avoid infection.

How soon after a strabismus operation can one do the following:

Bathe:
  As soon as one wishes.
Walk in the street:
  Immediately.
Walk up and down stairs:
  Immediately.
Resume some physical activity:
  Immediately.
Perform light household duties:
  One week.
Perform heavy household duties:
  Two weeks.

Is it necessary for a patient to continue wearing glasses after surgery?

If the patient was nearsighted or far-

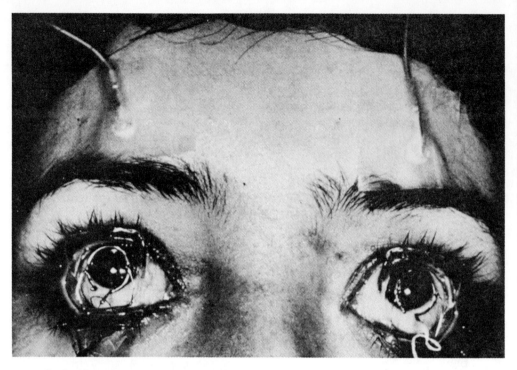

Retina Examination. *Electroretinography is a method of diagnosing disorders of the retina (above).*

The fundus, the back of the retina, may be examined through a funduscope, a special type of ophthalmoscope (below).

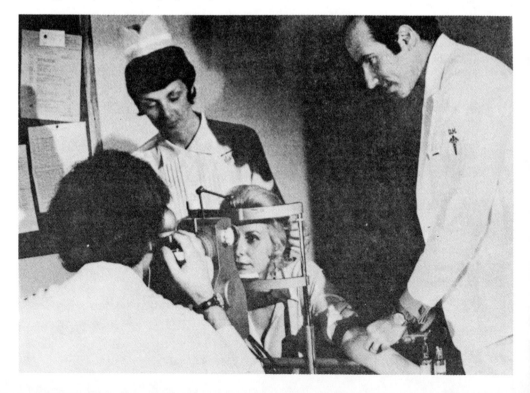

sighted before the operation, it will be necessary for him to continue wearing glasses. Strabismus operations do not cure these eye conditions.

After full recovery from a strabismus operation, can one use his eyes as much as he wishes?
Yes.

DETACHED RETINA AND RETINAL TEARS

Where is the retina located and what is its function?
The retina lines the inside of the back two-thirds of the eyeball. It is the sensitive part of the eyeball that transforms the light impulses into nerve impulses and transmits them to the brain. The retina is analogous to the film of a camera.

What is a retinal tear?
A rip in the retina, often caused by an injury.

Is a retinal tear frequently followed by detachment of the retina?
Yes.

Can retinal detachment be prevented by prompt treatment of a retinal tear?
Yes, in many cases.

What are the symptoms of a retinal tear?
Light-flashes and spots before the eyes. These symptoms are similar to those of a retinal detachment.

What is the treatment for a tear in the retina?
The tear is sealed by photocoagulation, using a laser beam.

What is detachment of the retina?
A condition in which the retina is pulled away from its attachments to the inside of the eyeball.

What causes detached retina?
It may be caused by a tear in the retina following an injury, inflammation, extreme nearsightedness, or a tumor of the choroid (a portion of the eye lying beneath the retina).

Does detached retina occur more often among men than women?
No.

Does it tend to run in families or to be inherited?
No.

What harm results from a detached retina?
A detached retina, if not treated, may result in blindness.

How can one tell if he has a detached retina?
A detached retina may be suspected if there is a veil or spots before the eyes or blurred vision in one portion of the eyeball. Light-flashes resembling lightning are a suspicious symptom.

Is there any way to prevent getting a detached retina?
Exceptionally nearsighted people should be particularly careful to

guard against injuries to the head. Also, a tear in the retina should be sealed off promptly.

What tests are performed to make a positive diagnosis of detached retina?

The eye specialist will examine the eye with an ophthalmoscope, which allows him to see the retina. In the early cases, where the detachment is slight, or where the detachment is not centrally located, several examinations may be required before a definite diagnosis can be made.

What surgical procedures are performed for detachment of the retina?

a. Light coagulation of the detached portion with the laser.
b. Freezing (cryotherapy) of the sclera over the area of the retinal detachment.
c. Shortening procedures of the eye in which portions are removed to cause buckling of the eyeball, thus allowing the retina to flop back into place against the back of the eyeball.
d. If there is a malignant tumor causing the detachment, it will be necessary to remove the eye.

What will happen if surgery is not performed?

The eye will become blind and may even have to be removed.

What are the chances of recovery of vision after surgery for retinal detachment?

This will depend upon the type of operation performed and the extent of the detachment. The recovery of vision and repair of the detachment takes place in about 90 percent of those patients who have undergone coagulation; the chances of successful results are about 75 percent when a buckling or shortening operation has been performed; with the use of the laser light coagulation, approximately 95 percent of tears in the retina can be sealed off.

How often is a detached retina caused by an underlying tumor?

In only 1 percent of cases.

How long does it take to perform an operation for detached retina?

Approximately one to three hours.

What anesthetic is used in surgery for retinal detachment?

General anesthesia.

How long a hospital stay is necessary?

One to two weeks.

Is the postoperative period exceptionally painful?

No.

What special postoperative treatments are carried out?

a. The operated eye is bandaged for a few days.
b. The patient can be out of bed in one to four days.
c. Eyedrops are used for varying periods of time.

How long does it take for the wound to heal?

Three to six weeks.

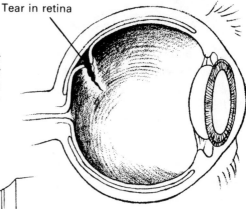

Tear in retina

Retinal Detachment and Surgery. At right, the arrow points to the detached part of the retina. In the drawing below, a cryosurgical probe has frozen the detached retina to the eyeball.

Cryosurgery probe

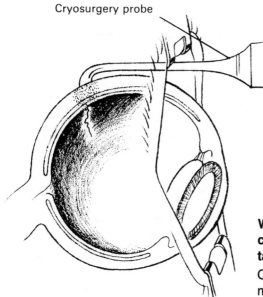

Are postoperative precautions necessary?

Yes. The patient must limit physical activity for one to two months.

Does detachment ever recur after it has once been successfully treated?

Yes. This is not an infrequent occurrence.

After full recovery from a detached retina, can one return to a completely normal existence?

Yes.

When should one return for a checkup after an operation for detached retina?

Once a month for the first three months; thereafter, every four to six months.

How soon after surgery for detached retina can one do the following:

Bathe:
   Three weeks.
Walk out in the street:
   Two weeks.
Walk up and down stairs:
   Four to six weeks.
Perform light household duties:
   Six weeks.
Perform heavy household duties:
   Eight weeks.
Resume all physical activities:
   Eight weeks.

DIABETES MELLITUS

Does diabetes affect the eyes?

Yes. Variations in the blood sugar can cause variations in vision. Diabetics who wear eyeglasses may require frequent changes in their prescriptions.

Can diabetes cause blindness?

Yes. It is one of the leading causes of blindness.

How can partial or complete loss of vision be prevented in the diabetic?

a. By regular periodic visits every four months to one's eye specialist.
b. By an immediate visit to one's eye specialist if a change in vision is noted.
c. By laser beam coagulation of areas of hemorrhage in the retina.

Does leakage of blood from tiny vessels in the retina cause loss of vision in the diabetic?

Yes, and the areas of leakage must be promptly treated with laser coagulation.

Can vision be restored by use of laser coagulation?

Yes, in a great many cases.

Can vision ever be restored to an eye that has been blind for months or years?

Yes, in some patients in whom hemorrhage has taken place within the inner gel (the vitreous) of the eye. To help these people, an operation known as a *vitrectomy* is performed in which the blood is washed out of the vitreous.

Do cataracts occur more frequently, and at an earlier age, in diabetic patients?

Yes.

TUMORS OF THE EYE

How common are tumors within the eyeball?

They are rare.

What are the common types of tumors within the eyeball?

a. Melanomas, which arise in the choroid.
b. Gliomas, which arise in the retina.

What age groups are most prone to develop these tumors?

The glioma of the retina usually occurs in children under the age of five. It occurs in one eye in most cases, but sometimes occurs in both eyes. The melanoma of the choroid usually occurs in adults between the ages of forty and sixty and involves one eye only.

What are the symptoms of glioma in children?

If the child is very young, he may not complain at all. The parent, however, may notice a peculiar yellow color in the pupil. Older children may complain of blurring of vision, and in some cases the eye may turn in or out. In adults there may be blurring of vision. However, some patients may have no symptoms, and the

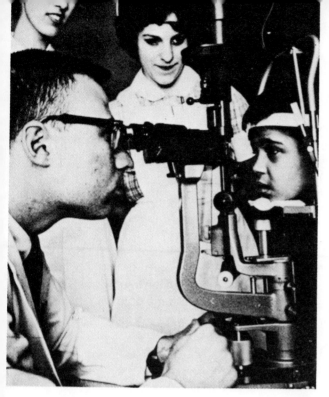

Tumor of the Eyeball.
Sophisticated equipment enables the ophthalmologist to examine the interior of the eyeball for the presence or absence of an eye tumor.

condition is recognized only on routine examination.

What is the treatment for glioma when only one eye is involved?

The eyeball should be removed as soon as possible! If both eyes are involved, the eye with the larger tumor is usually removed, and the tumor in the other eye is treated with radiation.

What will happen if the operation is not performed?

The condition will spread to other parts of the body and cause death.

What are the chances of recovery in adults?

The chances for recovery are good, especially if the tumor is treated during the early stages of its development.

What are the chances for recovery when children have eye tumors?

Eye tumors in children are very serious. However, the latest reports are encouraging, and more and more children are being saved.

RETINAL THROMBOSIS

What is retinal thrombosis?

A condition in which clots form within the retinal blood vessels. As a result, a hemorrhage of the retina takes place, and vision is blurred or lost.

What causes retinal thrombosis?

It is associated with hardening or arteriosclerosis of the blood vessels.

What are the symptoms of retinal thrombosis?

Abrupt blurring or loss of vision.

371

The Eyes

What is the treatment for retinal thrombosis?

In mild cases, rest of the eyes is all that is required. In severe cases, medication to reduce the clotting of the blood may be necessary. Laser beam coagulation is sometimes used to seal off newly formed blood vessels and thus prevent serious hemorrhage in the eye.

Does recovery take place after retinal thrombosis?

In mild cases, yes. Severe cases may result in blindness.

How long is one sick with retinal thrombosis?

Several months to years.

SYMPATHETIC OPHTHALMIA

What is sympathetic ophthalmia?

A strange inflammation that affects the healthy eye after a penetrating injury to the other eye.

What causes sympathetic ophthalmia?

The cause is unknown.

How does one know if sympathetic ophthalmia is developing?

If a patient has an injured eye that is red and painful, and he then develops redness or blurring of vision in the opposite eye, he may be developing the condition.

Is there any way to prevent sympathetic ophthalmia?

In the past, it was often necessary to remove the injured eye in order to save the vision in the opposite eye. Today the use of cortisone and the antibiotic drugs often prevents sympathetic ophthalmia in the uninjured eye.

After sympathetic ophthalmia has set in, is there any chance for complete recovery?

Yes.

Does removing the injured eye help once sympathetic ophthalmia has set in?

No.

TRACHOMA

What is trachoma?

A serious, specific chronic inflammation of the eyes. It involves the cornea, the conjunctiva, and the eyelids.

What causes trachoma?

The cause of trachoma is unknown, but poor hygiene and diet seem to play a great part in its causation.

Where is trachoma most likely to be encountered?

In eastern Europe and northern Africa. It is extremely rare in the United States.

What are the symptoms of trachoma?

In early cases, the symptoms are redness and tearing of the eyes. If the cornea is involved, there will be pain and extreme sensitivity to light.

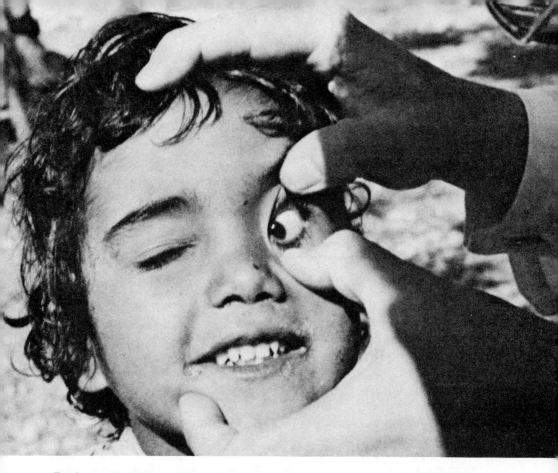

Trachoma. Nearly one-sixth of all the world's people suffer from trachoma, a painful eye disease that can cause partial or total blindness.

What is the treatment for trachoma?

The use of the sulfa drugs has proved to be effective in the early stages of the disease.

Does trachoma ever cause blindness?

In serious cases, yes.

Can trachoma be cured?

Yes, in its early stages.

How long does trachoma last?

The neglected cases may last a lifetime.

How can trachoma be prevented?

a. By proper diet and good hygiene.
b. By avoiding contact with people with trachoma.
c. By prompt medical attention to any eye irritation in those who live in an area where trachoma is prevalent.

25 THE FEMALE ORGANS

(See also Chapter 3 on Adolescence Chapter 11 on Birth Control; Chapter 15 on Breasts; Chapter 55 on Pituitary Gland; Chapter 57 on Pregnancy and Childbirth; Chapter 64 on Sex; Chapter 69 on Sterility, Fertility, and Male Potency; Chapter 77 on Venereal Disease)

THE EXTERNAL GENITALS

What is the vulva?

It is the area that surrounds the entrance to the vagina and is composed of the clitoris, the labia majora (major lips), the labia minora (minor lips), the opening of the urethra from the bladder, the hymen, the Bartholin glands, and the opening of the vagina.

What is the clitoris and what is its function?

It is a small, knoblike structure on top of the vaginal opening where the lips of the vulva join together. The clitoris is a focal point of sexual excitement and plays an important part in sexual relations. The tissue structure of the clitoris is quite similar to that of the male penis.

What is the hymen?

It is a fold of mucous membrane that partially or completely covers the vaginal opening. It is this membrane that is ruptured on first sexual contact.

Are there many variations in the structure of the hymen?

Yes. In most girls, the hymen is not a complete covering but contains perforations that permit the exit of the menstrual flow. In some rare cases, these perforations are missing, and the hymen must be incised surgically in order to permit the exit of menstrual blood.

374

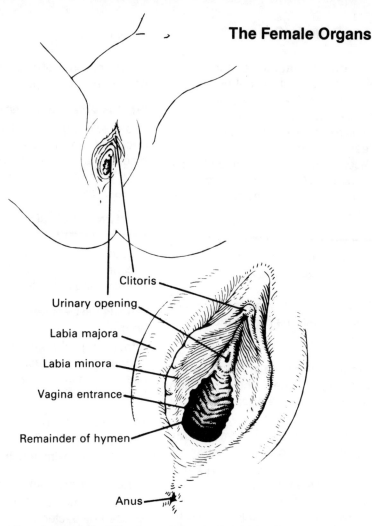

The Female Organs

Clitoris

Urinary opening

Labia majora

Labia minora

Vagina entrance

Remainder of hymen

Anus

The External Female Genitals. This diagram shows the external female genitals, including the clitoris, the lips of the vagina, and the vagina. It is amazing how few females are familiar with their own bodily construction in this region.

What is a hymenotomy?

The surgical incision of the hymen in order to enlarge the vaginal opening.

Why is hymenotomy performed?

a. For an imperforate hymen.
b. When a thickened or rigid hymenal ring makes sexual intercourse difficult or impossible.

Is hymenotomy a major operative procedure?

No. It is a simple procedure performed under light anesthesia in the hospital.

Is hymenotomy always necessary when intercourse is difficult?

No. Most cases of painful intercourse

375

are due to vaginal spasm. This spasm is brought about by tension and fear of sexual relations. By proper advice and instruction, women can overcome many of their fears, thus controlling the spasm. Also, in many cases, stretching the hymen is all that is necessary. This procedure is performed in the gynecologist's office.

Is difficulty in breaking the hymen a common occurrence?

No. It is relatively rare.

How soon after hymenotomy can sexual relations be attempted?

About three weeks.

What is the cause of painful intercourse in women who have been having normal relations for many years?

a. An emotional problem is often responsible for painful intercourse (dyspareunia) when it appears later in life.
b. Less commonly, there is an organic condition, such as an inflammation of the vagina or an inflammation of the pelvic organs, which is responsible for painful intercourse.

What are the Bartholin glands?

They are two small bulblike structures located in the lower end of the lips, one on each side of the vagina. They are connected to the vaginal canal by a narrow duct.

What is the function of the Bartholin glands?

They secrete a mucous substance, which acts as a lubricant for the inner surface of the lips of the vagina.

What is a Bartholin cyst?

It is a swelling of the duct—or the duct and the gland—caused by a blockage at the vaginal end of the duct. These cysts may be as small as a pea or as large as a plum.

What are the usual symptoms of a Bartholin cyst?

a. Pain on walking or during intercourse.
b. A swelling in the lips (labia).

What is the treatment for a Bartholin cyst?

Either surgical removal or incision into the cyst and fashioning a new opening ("marsupialization" operation).

Is hospitalization necessary for this type of operation?

Yes, for approximately three days.

What is a Bartholin abscess?

It is an infection of a Bartholin gland caused by bacteria.

What is the treatment for a Bartholin abscess?

a. Antibiotic drugs, hot soaks, and sedatives for the relief of pain.
b. In the more severe case, it will be necessary to incise and drain the abscess or to create a new permanent opening by performing a marsupialization operation.

Is hospitalization necessary for incision and drainage of a Bartholin abscess?

Yes. This procedure must be carried

out under general anesthesia and will require hospitalization for a few days. In some instances, under local anesthesia, incision and drainage are performed as an office procedure.

What is vulvitis?

It is an inflammation or infection of the area about the external genitals. It is most often associated with an infection within the vagina.

What is leukoplakia of the vulva?

It is a disease of the skin of the vulva characterized by an overgrowth of cells and a tendency toward the formation of cancer. The areas of leukoplakia look grayish white and develop a parchmentlike appearance.

What causes leukoplakia of the vulva?

The exact cause is unknown, but it is supposedly related to a decrease in the secretion of ovarian hormone, which takes place after menopause.

Who is most likely to develop leukoplakia?

Women who have passed the menopause.

Is leukoplakia of the vulva a common condition?

No. It is relatively infrequent.

What are the symptoms of leukoplakia of the vulva?

Itching is the most striking feature of this condition. Scratching will often lead to secondary infection from surface bacteria and may lead to inflammation, swelling, pain, redness, and even bleeding from the vicinity.

Does leukoplakia ever develop into cancer of the vulva?

Yes. Most cases of cancer of the vulva are preceded by leukoplakia. However, this does not mean that all women with leukoplakia will develop cancer.

What is the treatment for leukoplakia of the vulva?

a. If infection is present, antibiotic drugs should be given locally and orally.
b. If itching is severe, anesthetic ointments should be applied.

Does leukoplakia ever clear up by itself?

Temporary relief often results from medical management, but surgery is the only real cure for this condition.

How long would it take for leukoplakia to develop into cancer?

This is a very slow process, which takes place over a period of years.

Does cancer ever involve the vulva?

Yes. The clitoris, the lips, the Bartholin glands, or the opening of the urethra may sometimes be involved in a cancerous process.

What is the treatment for cancer of the vulva?

Vulvectomy. This means the surgical removal of all those structures comprising the vulva. The lymph glands in the groin are also removed in performing a radical vulvectomy for the eradication of an extensive cancer of the vulva.

Is cancer of the vulva curable?

Yes, if treated properly in its early stages by vulvectomy. It is estimated that more than 60 percent of cancers of the vulva can be cured permanently.

What is the incidence of cancer of the vulva?

It is a rare disease.

How is the diagnosis of cancer of the vulva made?

A piece of tissue is surgically removed and submitted to microscopic examination.

Who is most likely to develop cancer of the vulva?

Women beyond sixty years of age.

Is vulvectomy a serious operation?

Yes, but operative recovery takes place in almost all cases.

What is the vagina?

It is a tubelike canal approximately three to four inches in length, extending internally from its opening at the vulva to the cervix of the uterus. It is lined by a mucous membrane, which has many folds and great elasticity.

What are the functions of the vagina?

a. It is the ultimate female organ of intercourse.
b. It is a receptacle for the deposit of male sperm.

c. It is the outlet for the discharge of menstrual fluid.
d. It is the passageway for delivery of a baby.

Should women douche regularly?

Some gynecologists do advocate douching for purely hygienic purposes; others recommend it only for specific medical conditions.

What is the best solution with which to douche?

An acid douche containing white distilled vinegar or lactic acid is adequate. Other commercially prepared douches are also effective. The latter should be prescribed by a physician.

Are strong antiseptic douches harmful?

Yes. Strong chemicals can cause vaginal ulcers or burns.

Should women douche if they have a vaginal discharge or unpleasant odor?

Not without a gynecologist's specific instructions.

Should women douche following sexual relations or after the conclusion of a menstrual period?

Yes, as it will often prevent unpleasant odor or discharge. However, douching is not essential.

What is the treatment for cancer of the vagina?

Wide surgical excision of the vagina or radium implantation.

Is cancer of the vagina very common?

No. This is a very rare disease.

What other growths may affect the vagina?

a. Polyps.
b. Cysts.
c. Benign tumors, such as fibromas of the vaginal wall.

What is the treatment for benign growths of the vagina?

Simple surgical removal will bring about a cure in all of the above conditions.

What is prolapse of the uterus?

It is an abnormal descent of the uterus and cervix into the vagina. It is often associated with disturbance of the bladder and the rectum.

What causes prolapse of the uterus?

Most cases occur as a result of stretching or tears that have been incurred during labor and delivery. Women who have had several children may suffer stretching or tearing of the ligaments and muscles that ordinarily support the uterus and the vagina.

Is prolapse of the uterus caused by poor obstetrical management?

No. Tears of supporting ligaments may take place despite excellent obstetrical care.

Are there various degrees of prolapse?

Yes. There may be just slight descent of the uterus and cervix into the vagina, or the entire cervix and uterus may come down so far that they appear outside the vaginal opening.

What are the symptoms of prolapse of the uterus?

There is a feeling of fullness in the vagina and a sensation that something is falling down. These symptoms are aggravated after walking or lifting a heavy object. The prolapsed structures may interfere with sexual intercourse, and a disturbance in urination and bowel function may be present. Symptoms will depend largely upon the degree of prolapse.

Can prolapse of the uterus be prevented?

Good obstetrical care will tend to minimize the incidence of prolapse, but it often cannot prevent it.

What is the treatment for prolapse?

The treatment is surgical. It will require a plastic operation upon the vagina to reconstruct the ligaments and muscles, or, in a woman past the menopause, it may require the removal of the uterus and cervix (vaginal hysterectomy).

Are operations for prolapse serious?

They are considered major surgery, but the risks are not great and recovery will take place.

How long a period of hospitalization is necessary for prolapse operations?

Approximately ten to twelve days.

379

The Female Organs

Is there any medical treatment for prolapse?

Yes. The insertion of a pessary will help to keep the uterus and cervix in normal position. However, this form of treatment will not bring about a cure and should not be used as a substitute for surgery unless for some reason the patient cannot undergo an operative procedure.

Why isn't the use of a pessary prolonged indefinitely?

a. It does not cure the underlying deficiency.

b. It may lead to an ulceration of the vagina, an inflammation of the vaginal wall, or secondary infection.

c. The wearing of a pessary requires frequent douching and frequent visits to the gynecologist.

d. A pessary requires monthly visits to the doctor's office for removal, cleansing, and replacement.

What is a cystocele?

It is a hernia of the bladder wall into the vagina. Cystoceles may vary in degree from a mild bulge into the vagina to a maximum descent in which almost the entire bladder protrudes through the vaginal opening.

What is a rectocele?

It is a hernia of the rectal wall into the vagina. Again, the degree of herniation varies markedly from case to case.

What causes cystoceles or rectoceles?

They are caused by the same type of injury that causes a prolapse, that is,

a tear of supporting ligaments as a result of childbirth.

How often do cystocele, rectocele, and prolapse occur?

These are common conditions. The incidence is greater in women who have had many children. Also, women past forty are more likely to develop these conditions as their supporting ligaments begin to weaken and stretch.

Do cystocele, rectocele, and prolapse tend to occur together?

Yes, in a great number of instances. However, it is entirely possible to have a prolapse without a cystocele or rectocele, or to have a cystocele without a rectocele, or vice versa.

What are the symptoms of a cystocele?

The most common symptoms are frequency of urination, loss of urine on coughing, sneezing, laughing, or physical exertion. There may also be a sensation of a bulge into the vagina.

What are the symptoms of rectocele?

A feeling of pressure in the vagina and rectum, with difficulty in evacuating the bowels.

Do cystocele or rectocele and prolapse ever lead to cancer?

No.

What is the treatment for cystocele and rectocele?

A vaginal plastic operation in which the torn ligaments and muscles are

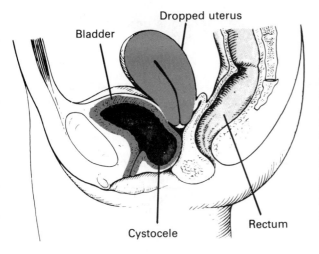

Dropped uterus

Bladder

Rectum

Cystocele

Left:
Cystocele. *Due to stresses and strains often occuring during childbirth, a tear of the muscles and ligaments that support the urinary bladder may take place and may result in a hernia of the bladder down toward the vagina. Loss of bladder control may follow, and when this happens, surgical repair should be undertaken.*

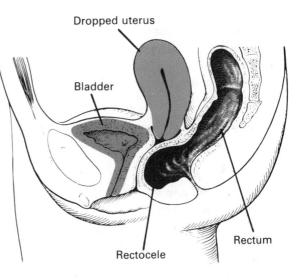

Dropped uterus

Bladder

Rectum

Rectocele

Right:
Rectocele. *When the tear in the supporting muscles and ligaments takes place in the posterior portion of the vagina, the rectum may protrude into the vagina. A rectocele is often accompanied by symptoms of marked constipation. Fortunately, this condition too can be repaired readily by surgery.*

repaired and stretched or excess tissues excised.

Are operations for cystocele and rectocele serious?

No, but they demand the attention of an expert gynecologist who understands the anatomy and function of the region.

How long a period of hospitalization is necessary following vaginal plastic operations?

Seven days.

Can cystocele, rectocele, or prolapse be corrected medically?

No, but temporary relief can be obtained with the use of rings or pes-

381

saries. Such appliances do not bring about a cure.

Are the results of operations for cystocele, rectocele, and prolapse satisfactory?

Yes. Cure can be accomplished in almost all cases.

When is surgery necessary for cystocele, rectocele, or prolapse?

When the symptoms mentioned previously are sufficient to interfere with normal happy living, or when bladder or bowel function becomes impaired.

What are the chances of recurrence after surgery?

After competent surgery, the chances of recurrence are less than 5 percent.

Are there any visible scars following vaginal plastic operations?

No.

What type of anesthesia is used for these procedures?

Spinal, epidural, or general anesthesia.

How long do these operations take to perform?

A complete vaginal plastic operation may take anywhere from one to two hours.

Are private nurses necessary after these operations?

Not usually, although they are a great comfort if the patient is able to afford them for a few days.

Are operations upon the vagina very painful?

No.

How soon after vaginal operations is the patient permitted to get out of bed?

On the day following surgery.

Are any special postoperative precautions necessary?

Yes, a catheter may be placed in the bladder for a few days to aid restoration of bladder function.

What is the effect of vaginal plastic operations upon the bladder and rectum?

Occasionally, for the first week or two, there may be difficulty in urinating. Also, in operations for rectocele, there may be difficulty in moving one's bowels for a similar period. These complications are temporary and will subside spontaneously.

Do stitches have to be removed after these operations?

No. The stitches are absorbable and do not have to be removed.

Is it common to bleed a great deal after operations upon the vagina?

No.

Do vaginal plastic operations interfere with sexual relations?

No. When the tissues have healed, intercourse can be resumed. This usually takes six to eight weeks.

Can women have babies after surgery for a cystocele or rectocele?

Yes, but delivery may have to be performed by Cesarean section, as surgery may have interfered with the ability of these structures to stretch and dilate sufficiently. Also, vaginal delivery might bring on a recurrence of the cystocele or rectocele.

Can pregnancy take place after surgery for prolapse of the uterus?

Yes, if only the cervix has been removed. Here, too, delivery should be by Cesarean section. Of course, if a hysterectomy has been performed in order to cure the prolapse, pregnancy cannot take place.

When is it best to undergo plastic repair?

After one has completed having children.

How soon after a vaginal plastic operation can one do the following:

Shower:
  One to two days.
Bathe:
  Four weeks.
Walk in the street:
  One to two weeks.
Perform household duties:
  Three weeks.
Drive a car:
  Four weeks.
Resume sexual relations:
  Eight weeks.
Return to work:
  Six weeks.
Douche:
  Six weeks.

What is vaginitis?

It is an inflammation of the vagina.

What causes vaginitis?

a. Infections such as *Trichomonas*.
b. Fungi such as *Monilia*.
c. Common bacterial infections with staphylococcus, streptococcus, etc.
d. Changes due to old age (senile vaginitis).
e. As a complication of the administration of antibiotic drugs that destroy certain useful vaginal bacteria, vaginitis is occasionally encountered.

Does the healthy vagina contain bacteria?

Yes, and most of these bacteria are beneficial and are not the cause of disease.

What causes *Trichomonas* or fungus infections of the vagina?

A change in vaginal acidity, which permits these organisms to outgrow the other organisms that are normally present.

Can *Trichomonas* infections be transmitted through sexual intercourse?

Yes. Men as well as women can have *Trichomonas* infections.

What lessens acidity of the vagina?

Menstrual blood will often lessen the acidity and allow harmful organisms to grow and multiply and produce the symptoms of vaginitis.

What are the symptoms of vaginitis?

This will depend upon the cause of the infection. Parasitic, fungus, or

The Female Organs

bacterial vaginitis usually produces the following symptoms:
a. Itching of the vulva.
b. Vaginal discharge.
c. Pain on intercourse.
d. Pain and frequency of urination.
e. Swelling of the external genital structures.

What are the symptoms of senile vaginitis?

Itching, but very little vaginal discharge. There is also pain on intercourse and, rarely, vaginal bleeding.

What tests are performed to determine the type of vaginitis that is present?

A smear of the vaginal discharge is taken and is submitted to microscopic examination. This will demonstrate whether the infection is caused by *Monilia, Trichomonas,* or bacteria.

What is the treatment for vaginitis?

This will depend upon its cause:
a. Fungus infections are now treated successfully by giving various antifungal medications by mouth as well as local applications into the vaginal canal.
b. *Trichomonas* infections are treated by giving both the female and male a drug known as Flagyl. This medication is taken orally for seven to ten days.
c. Bacterial vaginitis is treated with one of the antibiotic medications, administered orally or locally.
d. Senile vaginitis is treated by the administration of a local cream containing an estrogenic substance.

Is there a tendency for vaginitis to recur?

Yes. Many types of vaginitis do have this tendency. For this reason, treatment must be continued over a prolonged period of time. It is common for people to discontinue treatment too quickly because of early relief of symptoms.

What is the most common time for a vaginitis to recur?

Just before or after a menstrual period and during the later months of pregnancy. This strongly suggests that hormone changes in the vaginal lining play an important role in these conditions.

Does vaginitis ever occur in children?

Yes, vulvovaginitis is not uncommon in young girls from two to fifteen years of age. The infection is transmitted by poor hygiene, poor toilet habits, or by a foreign body the child might have inserted into her vagina.

What is the treatment for vaginitis in children?

Specific medications should be given for the specific infection. These may include the administration of medications orally and the application of ointments locally.

What causes gonorrhea in women?

In almost every instance it is caused by sexual intercourse with an infected male. Very rarely, gonorrhea may be transmitted from contaminated fingers or bathroom equipment.

384

What structures in the female genitals are affected by gonorrhea?

The vulva, Bartholin glands, the urethra, the vagina, and the cervix of the uterus are almost always involved in the infection. If the infection extends, it goes up through the cervix into the uterus, out into the Fallopian tubes to the ovaries, and finally to the abdominal cavity, where it causes gonorrheal peritonitis.

What are the symptoms of gonorrhea in the female?

There may be no symptoms at all, or the first symptoms might be slight discomfort in the vagina, vaginal discharge, burning, frequency of urination, and abdominal pain. These symptoms progress and become more marked for the first few days of the disease.

How is the diagnosis of gonorrhea made?

Microscopic examination reveals the specific causative germ, the gonococcus. *A definite diagnosis is never made unless the actual germ can be seen under the microscope.*

What is the treatment for gonorrhea in the female?

The administration of antibiotic drugs. *If treated promptly, all the harmful permanent effects of gonorrhea can be avoided.* All too often the shame of having a social disease restrains young women from seeking early treatment. The result is that the harmful results have taken too firm a hold before active treatment is instituted. If this has happened, infection of the tubes, ovaries, and abdominal cavity cannot be obliterated completely even with the use of the antibiotic drugs.

Does gonorrhea ever require surgical treatment?

Yes, under the following conditions:
a. When the Bartholin glands are involved, they may have to be incised or removed.
b. When the Fallopian tubes or ovaries are chronically infected, they may have to be removed.

Does gonorrhea interfere with childbearing?

Untreated gonorrhea, or chronic gonorrhea that has affected the tubes and ovaries, will definitely be a factor in the causation of sterility. There is a very high incidence of sterility in women with chronic gonorrhea.

Does complete recovery take place if treatment for gonorrhea is carried out promptly and adequately?

Yes.

How does syphilis affect the female genital organs?

A painless chancre (syphilitic sore) may appear anywhere in the vulva or vagina.

How is the diagnosis of syphilis made in a female?

It is diagnosed by direct examination of a suspicious lesion. A scraping from the sore is taken and is examined under a microscope. The diagnosis is then further confirmed by taking a blood test for syphilis.

385

The Female Organs

What is the usual method of transmission of syphilis?

Through sexual intercourse with an infected male.

What is the treatment for syphilis?

See Chapter 77, on Venereal Disease.

Can syphilis interfere with childbearing?

If the syphilis has been treated adequately and promptly, cure can be brought about so that childbearing will probably not be affected. Years ago, when syphilis was more prevalent, it caused miscarriages and stillbirths.

MENSTRUATION

What is menstruation?

It is a bloody discharge from the vagina occurring at more or less regular intervals throughout the childbearing period of a woman's life. Each month the womb (uterus) prepares itself for pregnancy by certain changes in its lining membrane. If a fertilized egg does not implant itself into the wall of the uterus, its lining disintegrates and is discharged from the uterus in the form of the menstrual flow.

When does menstruation begin?

Sometime between the ages of eleven and sixteen years. This will depend upon factors such as climate, race, and general health. In rare instances, normal menstruation may commence before the eleventh year or after the sixteenth year.

How long does menstruation last?

It usually continues until age forty-five to fifty-five.

What is the normal interval between menstrual periods?

The normal menstrual cycle occurs approximately every twenty-eight days. However, this is highly variable, and some women may develop a cycle with intervals of twenty-one, thirty, thirty-five, or even forty days. A woman who menstruates every twenty-eight days and then changes to a twenty-one-day cycle or a thirty-five-day cycle should consult her physician.

What are common conditions, other than pregnancy, that will cause a woman to miss a period?

a. A sudden change in climate.
b. An acute emotional upset.
c. An acute infection or illness.
d. Hormone imbalance or poor function of the endocrine glands.
e. A cyst or tumor of the ovary.
f. Poor nutrition or vitamin deficiency.
g. Marked anemia.
h. Chronic debilitating diseases, such as tuberculosis, cancer, etc.
i. The onset of menopause (change of life).

How soon after a period has been missed can it be determined if pregnancy exists?

A pregnancy test can give this information approximately fourteen days after a period has been missed.

Can medications, or other artificial measures, be used successfully to

bring on a menstrual period when it has been skipped because of pregnancy?

No. Hot baths, laxatives, or patent drugs will not bring on a period if pregnancy exists.

Are there harmful effects from taking medications to bring on a menstrual period when it is late?

Yes. The patient should never try to treat herself to bring on a menstrual period artificially. There is definite danger from the use of such medications. Moreover, if a pregnancy exists, the embryo may be injured.

How long do menstrual periods usually last?

Approximately four to five days. Here again, the length of time may vary from one to seven or eight days. The important consideration is a deviation from the usual duration.

What is the natural appearance of menstrual blood?

Normal menstrual blood is a pink to dark red color and does not clot. The presence of clots, or pieces of blood, or marked change in the amount of flow or the duration of the period warrants medical consultation.

Is there a detectable odor to normal menstruation?

No.

Is it normal for some women to have slight swelling of the face, neck, breasts, and abdomen during the menstrual period?

Yes. This is often due to retention of body fluids. Many physicians pre-

scribe diuretic tablets to relieve this condition.

What is the significance of scant menstruation?

a. If pregnancy is not a likelihood, then a single instance of scant menstruation should be disregarded as insignificant.

b. Repeated, persistent, scant menstruation is often due to a failure of the bleeding mechanism caused by an upset in the glands that regulate menstruation, such as the pituitary or the ovaries or the thyroid.

c. In women in their forties or early fifties, scant menstruation may be the forerunner of change of life (menopause).

What is the cause of failure of onset of menstruation?

This is almost always caused by a disturbance in glandular function. Less frequently a mechanical block, such as an imperforate (closed) hymen, may be responsible.

Should lack of menstruation in a girl in her middle or late teens warrant investigation by a physician?

Yes. Proper treatment can frequently correct this condition.

What is the treatment for scant menstruation?

During the childbearing age, scant menstruation requires no treatment if there is evidence that the woman is ovulating regularly. This means that she is producing a mature egg from an ovary each month. If ovulation is not taking place, further med-

387

ical investigation is indicated. This should include an evaluation of the activity of the various endocrine glands. Where a deficiency in the secretion of a particular hormone is discovered, specific treatment is directed toward replacing or correcting such deficiency.

Does the giving of the appropriate hormone usually correct scant menstruation or absent menstruation?

When properly administered, hormone treatments will usually bring about regulation of the normal cycle.

Does scant menstruation prevent pregnancy from taking place?

Only when it is associated with lack of ovulation. If ovulation is present, scant menstruation will not interfere with pregnancy.

Does scant menstruation often indicate the beginning of menopause in a woman in her late forties or early fifties?

Yes.

What is the significance of irregular menstrual bleeding?

Its significance varies with the type of irregularity. Most women have a slight variation of one to two days, either in onset or in length of flow. Marked changes in the time of onset, in the length of the flow, the amount of bleeding, or the presence of bleeding not associated with menstruation requires investigation by the gynecologist. The appearance of "staining" just before or just after menstruation should also be investigated.

What are some of the more common causes of irregular menstruation?

a. Infection within the female genital system.

b A benign tumor of the uterus or ovaries.

c. A malignant tumor of the uterus or ovaries.

d. Imbalance of the endocrine glands (pituitary, thyroid, or ovaries).

e. Ectopic pregnancy (a pregnancy that takes place outside of the uterus, usually in the Fallopian tubes).

f. Other nongynecological conditions, such as hepatitis, pneumonia and other infections, or stress, often affect the menstrual cycle.

What is the significance of excessive menstrual bleeding?

Excessive bleeding during the period is not normal and should be investigated. It may be indicative of infection, glandular upset, or the presence of a tumor within the uterus or the ovaries.

What is the treatment for excessive menstrual bleeding?

This will depend entirely upon the cause; each cause will be discussed separately in other sections of this chapter.

What is dysmenorrhea?

This term applies to painful menstruation.

What causes dysmenorrhea?

In some patients, particularly those who have not had pregnancies, the cause may be associated with a narrow cervical canal (mouth of the womb). Excessive fluid retention within the body is also associated with painful menstruation. Various emotional conditions are seen in conjunction with dysmenorrhea, especially in patients who have a low threshold for pain.

Organic conditions such as cysts or tumors of the ovaries, tumors of the uterus, endometriosis (see the questions on Endometriosis in this chapter), and adhesions from previous infections or surgery in the pelvic area are also common causes of painful menstruation.

What is the medical treatment for dysmenorrhea?

a. Pain-relieving and antispasmodic medications.
b. In many cases, the administration of birth control pills are very helpful.
c. Diuretic medications to get rid of excess water retention.

Will a pregnancy tend to relieve painful menstruation?

After a woman has borne a child, dysmenorrhea is often relieved.

Is surgery ever helpful in treating painful menstruation?

If the dysmenorrhea is so severe that it becomes disabling, surgery may be contemplated. This will consist of dilatation of the cervical canal to widen the opening. If the dysmenor-rhea is due to disease of the tubes, ovaries, or uterus, these conditions must be remedied surgically.

What is premenstrual tension?

It is the periodic appearance of disturbing anxieties occurring about the middle of the menstrual cycle and increasing in intensity as menstruation approaches. This tension subsides when menstruation begins.

What causes premenstrual tension?

The exact cause is unknown, but this phenomenon is attributed to a change in the amount of hormones that are secreted at various times throughout the menstrual cycle and the amount of fluids that the body retains.

What are some of the symptoms of premenstrual tension?

There may be personality changes, irritability, emotional instability, episodes of crying, etc. Physical symptoms such as backache, severe abdominal cramps, breast pain and tenderness, headaches, and swelling of the legs are some of the more definable features.

What is the treatment for premenstrual tension?

Simple measures will include:
a. Restriction of salt intake prior to menstruation.
b. The giving of medications to increase the output of urine and the reduction of tissue fluids.
c. The taking of birth control pills.

The Female Organs

Will a woman who is taking birth control pills continue to menstruate regularly?

Yes, but menstruation will not be accompanied by ovulation (the shedding of an egg by the ovary).

Are tampons that are inserted into the vagina harmful to use?

Not for the great majority of women. However, in a small number of cases, a serious infection called "toxic shock syndrome" has resulted following their use.

How common is toxic shock syndrome?

Tens of millions of women use tampons; only a few dozen cases of toxic shock syndrome have been reported.

What are the symptoms of toxic shock syndrome?

High fever, chills, nausea, and diarrhea.

How is toxic shock syndrome treated?

By intensive antibiotic therapy carried out in a hospital.

Can toxic shock syndrome be overcome?

Yes, in most instances, if treated early and intensively.

What is the cause of toxic shock syndrome following the use of tampons?

It is thought that the condition occurs because of leaving the tampons in too long, thus allowing bacteria to grow and enter the body through the uterus.

Should a young child of ten or eleven years be told about menstruation?

Yes. Preparing the girl for menstruation is a very important parental duty. Children should not be permitted to reach the age of menstruation without adequate advance information.

Is it true that if a mother has painful menstruation her child will develop it?

Painful menstruation is not inherited, but a child unconsciously tends to mimic her mother's reactions. It is wise, therefore, for the mother to minimize the discomfort of menstruation.

Can a shower be taken with safety during a menstrual period?

Yes.

Is it dangerous to go swimming or to take a bath during a menstrual period?

No.

Are sexual relations dangerous or harmful during menstruation?

No.

THE CERVIX

What is the cervix?

The cervix, or neck of the womb, is that portion of the uterus that appears in the vagina. It is a small, firm, muscular organ with a canal through its center (the cervical canal), extending from the vagina to the interior of the body of the uterus. The cervix is the only portion of the uterus that can actually be seen during the course of a pelvic examination.

How is the cervix examined?

A special instrument known as a speculum is inserted into the vagina.

What is the function of the cervix?

a. It guards the cavity of the uterus from invasion by bacteria or other foreign particles.
b. It allows for the passage of sperm into the cavity of the uterus.
c. It protects the developing embryo during pregnancy.
d. It opens during labor to allow for the passage of the baby.

What is cervicitis?

It is an inflammation of the cervix.

What are the causes of cervicitis?

a. Bacteria, fungi, parasites.
b. Injury secondary to delivery or surgery.
c. A congenital deficiency in the normal covering layer of the cervix.

What are the symptoms of cervicitis?

a. The most pronounced symptom is vaginal discharge. The appearance of the discharge may vary from a colorless mucus to a whitish or yellowish discharge.
b. Bleeding after sexual intercourse.
c. In severe cases, menstrual bleeding may be heavier than normal or may be preceded or followed by staining for a day or two.

Does cervicitis ever interfere with the ability to become pregnant?

Occasionally. In such cases it is necessary to clear up the cervicitis before pregnancy can take place.

What is the treatment for cervicitis?

a. If an infection is present, it must be eradicated by appropriate, specific medication.
b. Douching helps to keep local infection under control; an acid douche may prevent the recurrence of an infection caused by a fungus or parasite.
c. Treatment by cauterizing with silver nitrate applications or by electrocauterization.

How is electrocauterization of the cervix performed?

It is an office procedure in which incisions are burned into the cervix by means of an electrically heated, metal-tipped instrument. The burning incisions, of which many are made, cause the eroded or infected tissue to die and fall away from the underlying healthy cervical tissue. In time, the healthy tissue is able to grow again and to cover the entire cervix.

Is cauterization of the cervix a painful procedure?

No. It is accompanied by relatively little discomfort. There may be a feeling of warmth in the vagina and

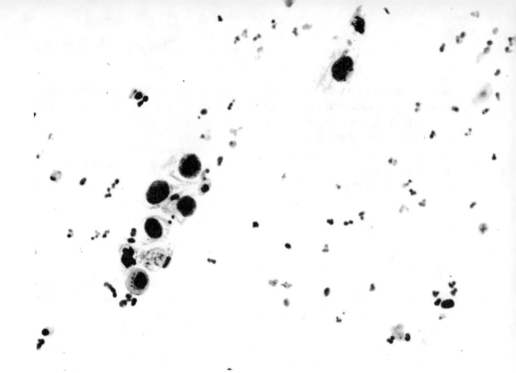

Cancer Smear. In this photomicrograph of a Papanicolaou smear, the very darkly stained cells are cancer cells, which have been extruded from the surface of the cervix. Such findings often enable the surgeon to make the diagnosis of cancer in its very earliest stage, thus increasing the chances for cure of this form of cancer. All women should have a Papanicolaou smear taken every year.

some cramps may follow, but it does not produce any disability.

How long does cauterization take to perform?

In the hands of a competent gynecologist, only a few minutes.

What precautions should be taken after cauterization of the cervix?

The patient should abstain from in-

tercourse and douches for twelve to fourteen days.

Is it necessary to take douches at any time following cauterization?

Yes. After the slough has been expelled—in about twelve to fourteen days—douches and antibiotic creams are used to prevent reinfection. These measures should be continued for approximately three weeks, except during the menstrual period.

How long does it take for healing to be complete after cauterization?

Approximately six weeks.

Is there a tendency for cervicitis or cervical erosion to recur?

Yes. If it recurs, treatment should be started again. It is not unusual for a slight recurrence to take place, but it will respond if treated promptly.

392

Does the gynecologist always examine the cervix for cancer?

Yes.

What is a cancer smear (Papanicolaou smear)?

It is a method of collecting surface cells from the vagina and cervix and examining them, with special staining techniques, for cancer. It concerns itself with examining those very superficial surface cells that are thrown off (desquamated).

Is a "Pap Smear" the same as a Papanicolaou smear?

Yes.

What is the value of the cancer smear?

It can reveal cancer cells at a *very early* stage of their development, thus allowing for extremely early treatment.

Should all women have a cervical cancer smear?

All women past the age of eighteen

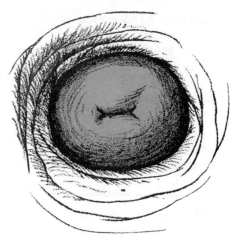

Normal cervix

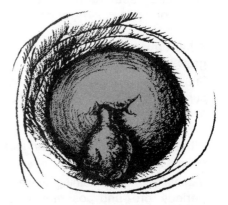

Polyp

Cervical Polyp. At the top is a normal cervix. In the middle diagram, a polyp protrudes from the cervix. In the side view at the bottom, the cervical polyp is shown protruding into the vagina.

393

years should have a routine vaginal smear taken every year. Also, a smear should be taken at any time when a lesion is suspected.

Is it painful to take a cancer smear?

Absolutely not. The entire procedure takes no more than a few seconds and is performed by merely swabbing the surface of the cervix and the vagina.

What is a cervical polyp?

It is a small benign tumor arising from the cervix. It usually has a thin stalk and assumes the size and shape of a pea, cherry, or grape.

What causes cervical polyps to grow?

The cause is unknown. They can occur at any time during the years that a woman menstruates.

What are the symptoms of cervical polyps?

Vaginal discharge, staining between periods, pre- and post-menstrual cramps. One or all of these symptoms may appear, or there may be no symptoms whatever.

What is the treatment for cervical polyps?

They should be removed in the office of the gynecologist or, under certain circumstances, in the hospital. This is considered a minor operative procedure and is accompanied by little discomfort.

Do polyps tend to recur?

Once a polyp has been removed, it will not regrow. However, women who have developed one polyp do have a tendency to form others. These, too, should be removed.

Are polyps of the cervix ever malignant?

Rarely.

Do polyps interfere with pregnancy?

Usually not.

Is cancer of the cervix a common condition?

It accounts for 25 percent of all cancer found in women!

What causes cancer of the cervix?

The exact cause is unknown.

At what age is cancer of the cervix usually encountered?

It can occur at any age, but it is seen most often in women between thirty and sixty years of age.

Who is most likely to develop cancer of the cervix?

a. Women who began sexual intercourse at an early age.
b. Women who have had many different sexual contacts.
c. Women who have had children at a very early age.
d. Women who are married to, or have frequent sexual contacts with, uncircumsized men.
e. Women who have viral infections of the genitals, such as herpes.

Can cancer of the cervix be prevented?

Cancer prevention is not actually

possible, but a *late cancer* can be avoided through early treatment. Thus, periodic examinations will uncover many cancers in their early curable stages.

Is it wise to seek early treatment for any abnormal condition of the cervix in an attempt to prevent cancer?

Definitely, yes. Many component gynecologists feel that erosion, laceration, inflammation, or benign growths of the cervix may predispose toward cancer formation.

What are the early symptoms of cancer of the cervix?

Very early cancer may cause no symptoms whatever. This is one of the main reasons for periodic vaginal examinations, including Pap smears. Later on, there may be vaginal discharge, bleeding after intercourse, bleeding after douching, or unexplained bleeding between periods.

Can early cancer of the cervix be detected by a cancer smear?

Yes.

What is noninvasive cancer of the cervix?

This is a condition, also called *in situ* cancer of the cervix, in which the cancer is limited to the most superficial layer of cells, and there is no spread to the deeper tissues. This term is used to distinguish it from invasive cancer, in which the spread has extended beyond the superficial layers of cells into the deeper tissues, including the lymph channels and the bloodstream.

How accurate is the cancer smear in diagnosing cancer?

A positive cancer smear is accurate in about 97 percent of cases.

Does a positive cancer smear consitute sufficient investigation of cancer of the cervix?

No. Whenever a cancer smear is positive, a biopsy and cutterage should be taken to make the diagnosis and location absolutely certain.

What procedures are carried out to further investigate whether a cancer of the cervix is present?

A more extensive biopsy, known as a *cone biopsy,* is taken. This involves removing the entire lining of the cervical canal (the entrance to the uterus). Examination of this large piece of tissue will not only reveal the presence of a cancer, but will show the extent of its invasiveness.

Can a cancer of the cervix ever be cured by a cone biopsy?

Yes, if it happens to be a superficial *in situ* cancer. The cone biopsy must, on microscopic examination, show that the cancer has been completely removed.

What is the treatment for cancer of the cervix?

This will depend entirely upon the stage of development of the cancer at the time it is discovered. There are three ways of treating this disease:
a. By the use of radium and x ray.
b. By wide surgical removal of the cervix, uterus, tubes, ovaries, and all the lymph channels draining the area. *(continued)*

The Female Organs

c. By a combination of radium, x ray, and surgery.

Who will determine what form of treatment should be administered?

The gynecologist will know which form of treatment to institute after the extent of the cancer has been determined.

What are the chances of recovery from cancer of the cervix?

Early cancer of the cervix can be cured in almost all cases—by either radium, x ray, or surgery. As the extensiveness of the disease increases and the operative procedures become more involved, recovery rates are lower.

Is it painful to insert radium?

No. This procedure is carried out in the hospital, under anesthesia.

Does radium remain inside the body permanently?

No. The radium is usually applied in capsules, and after a sufficient number of radioactive rays have been tranmitted, the capsule is removed.

How long does radium usually remain within the genital tract?

Anywhere from 72 to 110 hours, according to the specific dosage indicated.

How long a hospital stay is necessary when radium is inserted?

Anywhere from two to six days.

Is the application of radium followed by postoperative discomfort?

Yes, because extensive packing is inserted into the vagina when radium is being used. This is controlled by use of sedatives.

Is x-ray treatment often given after radium treatment?

Yes. This is given in the weeks after radium implantation to reach parts not reached by the radium.

Are there any postoperative symptoms following radium implantation?

Yes. Disturbance in bowel function and burning and frequency of urination are quite often complications of radium treatment of the cervix.

Does cancer ever recur after radium treatment for cancer of the cervix?

Not very often. Some cancers are resistant to radium or inaccessible to it. Recurrence will depend upon the stage of the disease at the time radium treatment was given.

Can a patient return to normal living after radium treatment for cancer of the cervix?

Yes.

Can a patient become pregnant after radium treatment for cancer of the cervix?

Because ovarian function will have been destroyed by the radium treatment, pregnancy cannot take place. Menstruation will also cease as a result of radium therapy.

What type of surgery is performed for cancer of the cervix?

a. Hysterectomy for *in situ*, or noninvasive, cancer.

b. Radical hysterectomy for most invasive cancers.

c. Exenteration for extensive and advanced cancer.

What is meant by an exenteration operation for cancer of the cervix?

This is an extremely radical operative procedure in which the entire uterus, cervix, vagina, tubes, ovaries, lymph glands, bladder, and/or rectum are removed for extensive cancer. Artificial openings are made for the passage of urine and stool. Fortunately, this procedure is not often necessary since the disease is usually detected in an earlier stage of its development.

What is the future outlook for those afflicted with cancer of the cervix?

Earlier detection can lead to a substantially higher cure rate in years to come. The advent of the cancer smear now permits the diagnosis to be made at earlier stages in the development of the disease.

THE UTERUS

What is the uterus?

The uterus, or womb, is a pear-shaped muscular organ lying in the middle of the pelvis. It is approximately three inches long, two inches wide, and one inch thick. It consists of a smooth outer covering, a middle layer composed of thick muscle tissue, and an inner cavity lined with endometrial cells. The cavity of the uterus connects with the vagina through the cervix and connects with the abdominal cavity through the Fallopian tubes. The hollow Fallopian tubes open within the abdominal cavity near the ovaries. The uterus is supported and suspended by several ligaments.

What is the exact position of the uterus?

It lies just above the pubic bones, behind the urinary bladder, in front of the rectum, and above the vagina.

What are the functions of the uterus?

a. To prepare for the reception of a fertilized egg.

b. To nurture and harbor the embryo during its development.

c. To expel the baby when it is mature and ready for delivery.

What influences the uterus to prepare for pregnancy?

Hormones that are secreted by the ovaries and the other endocrine glands. If the fertilized egg is not forthcoming, menstruation ensues, and the uterine lining is shed. This process is repeated each month, from puberty to menopause, unless there is a glandular upset or, of course, unless pregnancy exists.

What is the significance of a tipped womb?

Ordinarily, this condition has no significance.

What symptoms are caused by a tipped womb?

Usually none. In rare instances, backache and a dragging sensation in the lower pelvic region may occur with the finding of a womb that is tipped markedly in a backward direction.

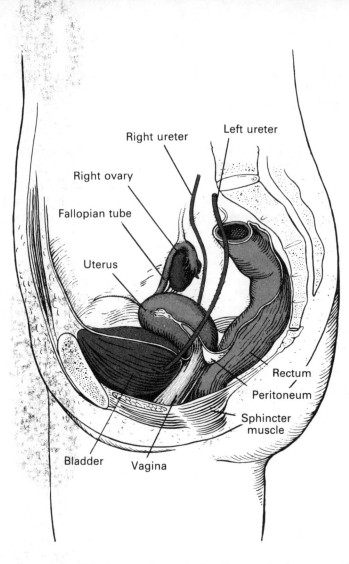

The Female Organs. *This diagram shows the female reproductive organs: the uterus, the Fallopian tubes, and the ovaries. Note the relation of the female reproductive organs to the surrounding structures in the pelvic region.*

What is the treatment for tipped womb?

The great majority of cases require no treatment whatever. (The large number of operations for "straightening out" the womb that were performed years ago have now been abandoned as unnecessary operative procedures.) In rare instances, a vaginal pessary is employed to maintain a forward position of the uterus.

Does a tipped womb interfere with pregnancy?

Definitely not.

398

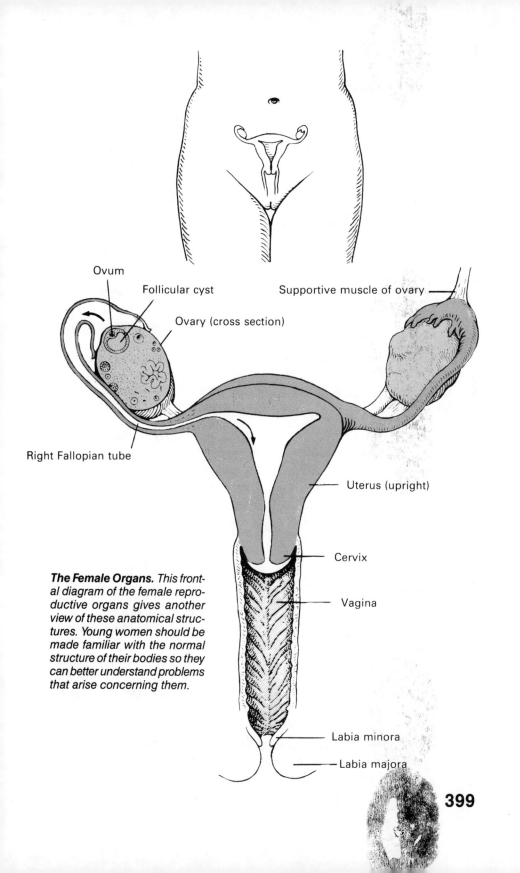

Ovum

Follicular cyst

Supportive muscle of ovary

Ovary (cross section)

Right Fallopian tube

Uterus (upright)

Cervix

The Female Organs. *This front-al diagram of the female repro-ductive organs gives another view of these anatomical struc-tures. Young women should be made familiar with the normal structure of their bodies so they can better understand problems that arise concerning them.*

Vagina

Labia minora

Labia majora

399

The Female Organs

Does a tipped womb interfere with intercourse?

No.

What is an infantile uterus?

This is a term formerly used to describe a smallsized uterus.

What is the significance of an infantile uterus?

None, providing the uterus functions normally. In other words, if menstruation is normal and pregnancy can take place, a small-sized uterus is of no significance.

Do women with an infantile uterus have difficulty in becoming pregnant?

Not if their menstrual function is normal.

What is a curettage?

This is an operation performed upon the cavity of the uterus through the vagina. It consists of scraping out the lining membrane of the uterus. Special instruments are used to dilate the cervix and to scrape out the uterine cavity.

Why is curettage performed?

a. For diagnostic purposes.
b. For therapeutic purposes.
c. A curettage is often diagnostic and therapeutic at the same time, as in cases of hyperplasia or polyps of the uterus.

When is a therapeutic curettage performed?

a. When a disorder such as a polyp of the lining membrane of the uterus has already been diagnosed, curettage may result in a cure.
b. When an overgrowth of the lining membrane of the uterus (endometrial hyperplasia) has been diagnosed, a curettage will often bring about a cure.
c. Following a miscarriage, when parts of the fetus or placenta remain behind. Curettage in such instances will clean out the cavity and thus restore normalcy.

When is a diagnostic curettage performed?

a. In cases of unexplained uterine bleeding.
b. In cases in which a polyp of the uterine cavity is suspected.
c. In cases in which a cancer of the body of the uterus is suspected.

What is another name for curettage?

It is commonly called a "D and C" operation. This stands for dilatation and curettage.

Is a D and C a painful operation?

No. It is performed under general anesthesia in the hospital.

How long a hospital stay is necessary following curettage?

Approximately one to two days.

Are there any visible incisions following curettage?

No. It is done completely through the vagina.

How soon after curettage can one return to work?

Within a week.

400

What restrictions must be followed after curettage?

Douching and intercourse must not be performed for two weeks.

Can normal pregnancy take place after a curettage?

Yes, A curettage performed by a competent gynecologist in a hospital will not interfere with subsequent pregnancies.

What is endometritis?

It is an infection of the lining of the uterus.

What causes endometritis?

a. Bacterial infections such as gonorrhea.
b. It may follow a miscarriage or abortion.
c. It may follow normal delivery where an accidental infection of the uterus has taken place.

What are the symptoms of endometritis?

Irregular bleeding, vaginal discharge, pain and tenderness in the lower abdomen, a feeling of weakness, fever, urinary distress, etc.

What is the treatment for endometritis?

The first step is to determine the exact cause. If there has been an incomplete miscarriage, the uterine cavity must be emptied by the performance of a curettage. If the endometritis has been caused by bacterial infection, antibiotic drugs should be given. If the infection has extended beyond the lining membrane into the wall of the uterus, it may be necessary to remove the uterus in order to effect a cure.

Does endometritis ever heal by itself?

Yes, in certain cases. More often, the infection will spread outward to involve the deeper layers of the uterus, the tubes, the ovaries, and even the abdominal cavity.

What is an endometrial polyp?

It is a growth arising from the lining of the uterus and extending into the uterine cavity. Often there are multiple polyps.

What are the symptoms of an endometrial polyp?

In some cases there are no symptoms. In others, there is cramplike menstrual pain, staining between periods, excessive menstrual bleeding, and vaginal discharge.

How is the diagnosis of an endometrial polyp made?

By diagnostic curettage or by the performance of a hysterogram.

What is a hysterogram?

It is an x-ray investigation of the cavity of the uterus performed by injecting an opaque dye through the cervix into the uterine cavity. When films are taken, they will show the outline of the cavity.

What is the treatment for endometrial polyps?

They are removed by curettage. When they protrude through the cervix into the vaginal canal, they can be removed with an instrument

401

The Female Organs

through the vagina. If there is any evidence of malignant change within the polyp, a total hysterectomy with removal of the tubes and ovaries must be performed.

Do endometrial polyps ever become malignant?

Yes, occasionally.

What is endometrial hyperplasia?

It is a benign overgrowth of the lining of the uterus.

What causes endometrial hyperplasia?

It is usually associated with excessive and prolonged production of female sex hormone (estrogen) by the ovaries. Frequently, an ovarian cyst or tumor is present and may be responsible for the production of excess estrogen.

What are the symptoms of endometrial hyperplasia?

It is characterized by completely irregular and unpredictable bleeding, varying from total lack of menstruation to more frequent periods than normal, and from slight staining to profuse bleeding. Characteristically, endometrial hyperplasia results in painless bleeding.

Does endometrial hyperplasia have anything to do with the inability to become pregnant (infertility)?

Yes. Women with endometrial hyperplasia often do not ovulate and therefore cannot become pregnant.

How is endometrial hyperplasia diagnosed?

By microscopic examination of tissue that is taken from the lining of the uterus by endometrial biopsy. Also, by examination of tissue removed by curettage.

Where and how is an endometrial biopsy performed?

This is an office procedure and is performed simply by the insertion of a special instrument through the vagina and cervix into the uterine cavity. A small piece of tissue is removed and is examined microscopically.

Is endometrial biopsy a painful procedure?

No. It is a simple office procedure accompanied by a minimal amount of discomfort.

Is there any connection between endometrial hyperplasia and cancer of the uterus?

In women past childbearing age, it is thought that certain types of endometrial hyperplasia may be associated with development of cancer of the uterus. For this reason, more intensive treatment is advised for older women with endometrial hyperplasia.

What is the treatment for endometrial hyperplasia?

This depends upon the age of the patient, the type of hyperplasia found on microscopic examination, and the presence or absence of accompanying ovarian growths. In young females still in the childbearing age, simple hyperplasia is treated by curettage and by use of estrogen and progesterone (ovarian hormones) to simulate the normal menstrual cycle. This is called cyclic therapy.

After menopause, and depending upon the type of hyperplasia, the treatment varies from simple curettage to hysterectomy. If the hyperplasia recurs or shows a preponderance of certain types of cells, and if the patient is past childbearing age, hysterectomy will probably be the best treatment. In the presence of an enlarged ovary, hyperplasia must be suspected as being related to a tumor of the ovary. In these cases, an abdominal operation should be performed and the ovaries and uterus removed.

Should women who have endometrial hyperplasia return for frequent periodic examinations?

Yes. Any irregularity in the menstrual cycle of a woman still in the childbearing age should stimulate a visit to the gynecologist.

What is the treatment of choice for recurrent hyperplasia in young women?

a. Repeated curettage or cyclic hormone therapy for a prolonged period.
b. If symptoms of hyperplasia cannot be controlled, it may be necessary to perform a hysterectomy even in a young woman. Fortunately, this is rarely necessary.

What is the incidence of cancer of the body of the uterus?

It is the second most common cancer of the female genital tract. However, cancer of the cervix is five times more frequent than cancer of the body of the uterus.

Who is most likely to develop cancer of the uterus?

It occurs at a later age than cancer of the cervix. It is most prevalent in women past fifty.

Is there a tendency to inherit cancer of the uterus?

No.

What is the difference between cancer and sarcoma of the uterus?

Cancer arises from the lining membrane of the uterus, while sarcoma (an equally malignant tumor) arises from the muscle layer of the uterus.

What are the symptoms of cancer of the uterus?

a. Irregular vaginal bleeding in women still having menstrual periods.
b. Bleeding after menopause.
c. Enlargement of the uterus.

How is cancer of the uterus diagnosed?

By performing diagnostic curettage. Any bleeding in a woman past her menopause must be looked upon with suspicion and must be investigated by curettage to rule out cancer.

What treatment is advocated for cancer of the uterus?

Application of radium in most cases, followed in four to six weeks by a total hysterectomy.

The Female Organs

Is this a serious procedure?

Yes, but recovery from surgery will take place in almost all cases.

What is the rate of cure for cancer of the body of the uterus?

If the cancer is detected before it has extended beyond the confines of the uterus, approximately four out of five cases can be cured. In cases where spread has already gone beyond the uterus, only about one out of eight can be cured.

Is it possible to prevent cancer of the uterus?

It cannot be prevented, but it *can* be detected earlier if women seek medical help as soon as they notice abnormal vaginal bleeding.

What are fibroids (leiomyoma) of the uterus?

Fibroids are benign tumors composed of muscle tissue. They tend to be round in shape and firm in consistency.

What is the incidence of fibroids?

Almost 25 percent of all women have fibroids of the uterus. The majority of such growths cause no symptoms and demand no treatment.

What causes fibroids?

Although the exact cause is unknown, it has been found that certain ovarian hormones play an important role in the speed of growth. Thus, after menopause, when very little ovarian hormone is being secreted, fibroids stop growing and may even shrink.

When are women most likely to develop fibroids?

During the later stages of the childbearing period, that is, between the ages of forty and fifty years. However, they may be found occasionally in women in their early twenties or in those past menopause.

Do fibroids tend to run in families?

There is no actual inherited tendency, but since one in four women have fibroids, it is not uncommon to find more than one member of a family with this condition.

What are the various types of fibroids?

a. Subserous; those growing beneath the outer coat of the uterus.
b. Intramural; those growing in the muscular layer of the uterus.
c. Submucous; those growing beneath the lining membrane of the uterine cavity.

Do fibroids vary greatly in size?

Yes. They may be as small as a pinhead or as large as a watermelon. They are almost always multiple.

What are the symptoms of fibroids?

a. Many fibroids cause no symptoms and are found inadvertently on routine pelvic examination.
b. If the fibroid is submucous in type, it may cause prolonged heavy menstruation.
c. Intramural and subserous fibroids may cause excessive menstrual bleeding but may produce no symptoms at all.

404

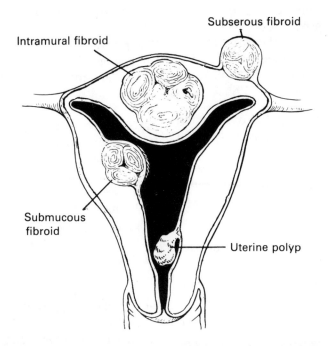

Intramural fibroid

Subserous fibroid

Submucous fibroid

Uterine polyp

Fibroids of the Uterus. *This diagram shows various forms of fibroid tumors of the uterus and where they are located. These tumors are not malignant but can cause serious symptoms, such as bleeding between menstrual periods or, if they grow large enough, pressure upon the urinary bladder or rectum. When symptoms are pronounced or when the tumors grow very large, the surgeon may recommend their removal.*

d. There may be frequency of urination and difficulty in bowel function if the fibroids grow to a large size and press upon the bladder or rectum.

e. Backache or lower abdominal pain occurs occasionally.

f. Infertility may ensue if the fibroid distorts the uterine cavity.

g. They may be the cause of repeated miscarriage.

How is the diagnosis of fibroids made?

By manual pelvic examination. Such a vaginal examination will reveal the size, shape, and other features of the tumor. A hysterogram may help to diagnose small submucous fibroids. A sonogram, too, often may reveal the presence of fibroids.

Is a fibroid of the uterus a malignant tumor?

Definitely not. Fibroids are benign growths!

Do fibroids become malignant?

Not frequently. Occasionally, cancer develops in a uterus containing

405

fibroids, but the presence of the fibroid does not predispose toward the development of the cancer. Sarcoma, a malignant growth of the uterus, may develop from a fibroid in rare instances.

Are fibroids found in association with other conditions within the uterus?

Yes. There is a high incidence of endometrial polyps and endometrial hyperplasia in those patients who have fibroids.

What is the best treatment for fibroids?

If the fibroids produce symptoms or grow rapidly, they should be removed surgically.

What operative procedures are performed for fibroids?

When only the fibroids are removed, it is called a myomectomy. When the entire uterus is removed, it is termed a hysterectomy.

How does a gynecologist decide whether to do a myomectomy or a hysterectomy?

This will depend upon the age of the patient and her desire to have children. If the patient desires children, an attempt will be made to preserve the uterus, and a myomectomy will be performed.

Are there methods of treating fibroids other than myomectomy or hysterectomy?

Yes. Some small submucous fibroids can be removed by simple curettage when they develop into polyplike growths.

Do fibroids have a tendency to recur?

Ten percent will recur following myomectomy. Of course, if the entire uterus is removed, fibroids cannot recur.

Must all fibroids be operated upon?

No. A fair proportion require no treatment whatever.

What are the indications for surgical removal of fibroids?

a. Increased, prolonged, and more frequent menstruation.
b. Episodes of severe bleeding.
c. Pressure symptoms causing continued urinary or rectal discomfort.
d. Rapid increase in the size of a fibroid.
e. Any fibroid larger than the size of a three-month pregnancy should be removed even if it causes no symptoms.
f. Acute pain due to degeneration of a fibroid or to a twist in a fibroid.
g. Repeated miscarriage or sterility.

Do fibroids ever occur during pregnancy?

Yes. When present, they may increase in size as the pregnancy grows.

Should a fibroid be treated during pregnancy?

No. It is best to postpone treatment until after the baby is born.

Can a woman become pregnant after surgery for fibroids?

If a myomectomy has been performed, subsequent pregnancy is possible. In such cases, the baby may have to be delivered by Cesarean section.

Is the surgical treatment of fibroids usually successful?
Yes, a cure is the result in almost all cases.

Is there any satisfactory nonsurgical treatment for fibroids?
No.

Is myomectomy considered a major operation?
Yes, since it involves an abdominal incision. However, recovery takes place. Hospitalization for seven to ten days is usually required.

Does menstruation return to normal after myomectomy?
Yes.

How long does it take to recover from the effects of myomectomy?
Approximately six weeks.

How long should a woman wait after myomectomy before attempting pregnancy?
Three months.

What is a hysterectomy?
An operation for the removal of the uterus.

What are the various types of hysterectomy?
a. Subtotal or supracervical hysterectomy; removal of the body of the uterus leaving the cervix behind.
b. Total hysterectomy; removal of the body of the uterus and the cervix.

c. Radical hysterectomy; this includes removal of a good portion of the vagina, the tubes and ovaries, the supporting tissues and lymph glands along with the body and cervix of the uterus.
d. Porro section; removal of the uterus at the time of delivery of a baby by Cesarean section.
e. Vaginal hysterectomy; removal of the uterus and cervix through the vagina instead of through an abdominal incision.

What are some of the indications for hysterectomy?
a. Symptomatic fibroids.
b. Chronic, incurable inflammatory disease of the uterus, tubes, and ovaries, such as gonorrhea or tuberculosis.
c. Severe recurrent endometrial hyperplasia.
d. Cancer of the uterus or cervix.
e. Cancer of the tubes or ovaries.
f. Chronic disabling endometriosis.
g. Uncontrollable hemorrhage following delivery of a baby.
h. In certain cases where the ovaries must be removed for cysts or growths, the uterus should also be removed.
i. Rupture of the uterus during pregnancy.

Is hysterectomy a major operative procedure?
Yes. However, it is not considered a dangerous operation, and operative recovery occurs in almost 100 percent of the cases.

Does a woman menstruate after hysterectomy?
No.

407

The Female Organs

Can a patient become pregnant after hysterectomy?

No.

Must the ovaries always be removed when hysterectomy is performed?

If the disease for which the hysterectomy has been performed is cancerous in nature, the tubes and ovaries must be removed. If the condition is benign and the woman is still under forty years of age, one or both ovaries may be left in place so that the uncomfortable symptoms of change of life do not ensue. Every attempt is made to leave the ovaries in place when the patient is young. They are usually removed when the patient is past the menopause. If the ovaries are inflamed or abscessed, or if endometriosis is present, the ovaries are removed when performing a hysterectomy.

A hysterogram is an x-ray of the uterus. This one reveals a bicornuate uterus, a congenital condition in which the body of the uterus is separated into two branches.

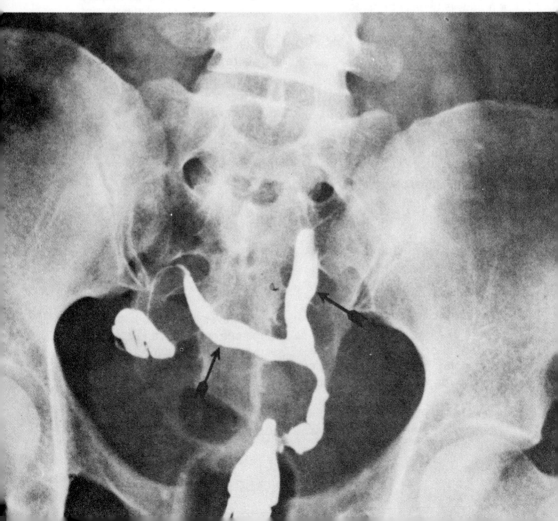

Do the symptoms of menopause (change of life) always follow hysterectomy?

No. If one or both ovaries are left behind, menopause will not follow. Menopause occurs only when both ovaries have been removed.

Can the symptoms of menopause be controlled after hysterectomy?

Yes. There are excellent means of combating the symptoms of menopause by the judicious administration of female hormones.

Does the removal of the uterus affect one's sex life in any way?

No. The removal of the uterus, with or without the removal of the ovaries, does not affect sexual ability or sexual desire. As a matter of fact, some women state that they are happier in their sexual relations after hysterectomy than before.

Are the external genitals altered during hysterectomy?

No. The vagina and other external genital structures are unaffected by hysterectomy.

Will hysterectomy cause changes in the physical appearance of a woman?

No. This is a common misconception. Women do not tend to become fat or to lose their feminine characteristics because of hysterectomy! It must be remembered, though, that most hysterectomies are performed in the fifth and sixth decades of life, when women ordinarily show signs of aging. It is the removal of the ovaries that sometimes causes weight gain.

Is the scar from hysterectomy disfiguring?

No. It is a simple line on the abdomen. If a vaginal hysterectomy has been performed, no scar will be visible.

What are the indications for the performance of a vaginal hysterectomy?

When there is prolapse of the uterus along with a cystocele and rectocele, it is sometimes advisable to remove the uterus through the vagina so that a vaginal plastic operation can be performed at the same time. This cannot be done if the uterus is enlarged to such an extent that it cannot be delivered through the vagina. Vaginal hysterectomy is not indicated when an invasive malignancy is suspected.

Is vaginal hysterectomy a dangerous operative procedure?

No. It carries with it the same risks as hysterectomy performed through an abdominal incision.

Is hysterectomy a painful operation?

There is the same discomfort that follows any abdominal operation. Most pain can be controlled readily by medication.

How long does it take to perform the average hysterectomy?

From one to two hours.

How soon after hysterectomy can a patient get out of bed?

Usually, the day following the operation.

409

The Female Organs

How long a hospital stay is necessary following hysterectomy?

Seven to ten days.

What postoperative symptoms follow hysterectomy?

There may be vaginal bleeding or discharge for a week or two. There may also be difficulty in passing urine or in moving the bowels for a week or more after hysterectomy.

How soon after hysterectomy can one do the following:

Shower:
   One week.
Bathe:
   Four weeks.
Walk in the street:
   Eight to ten days.
Drive a car:
   Four to five weeks.
Perform all household duties:
   Six weeks.
Resume sexual relations:
   Eight weeks.
Return to work:
   Eight weeks.
Resume all physical activities:
   Three months.

What is endometriosis?

A condition in which the lining cells of the uterus (endometrial cells) are found in abnormal locations. These cells may be found deep within the wall of the uterus, on the outer coat of the uterus, the Fallopian tubes, the ovaries, the uterine ligaments, bowel, bladder, vagina, or in other places within the abdominal cavity.

How do these endometrial cells exist in abnormal positions?

They implant upon the surface of other structures and grow as small nests of cells. They vary in size from that of a pinhead to the size of an orange. They often form cysts, which contain a chocolate-appearing fluid that represents old, bloody menstrualike material.

What abnormal conditions are produced by these endometrial implants?

They may cause firm adhesions between the tubes and the ovaries or the bladder, the bowel, or the uterus. They may form cysts. These cysts may twist or rupture, causing acute abdominal pain and distress.

Do these endometrial implants function like normal uterine cells?

Yes. They become distended and engorged with blood as each menstrual period approaches, and they bleed when menstruation takes place.

What causes endometriosis?

The exact cause is unknown. One theory is that the lining cells of the uterus are expelled through the Fallopian tubes by a reverse peristaltic action in the tubes during menstrual periods. Another theory is that these cells are dislodged following surgery upon the uterus.

What are some of the symptoms of endometriosis?

a. It may cause no symptoms whatever and be discovered accidentally at operation for another condition.
b. There may be marked pain before and during the menstrual period.
c. There may be marked pain on uri-

nation, defecation, or during intercourse.

d. Menstrual bleeding may be markedly increased.

e. Inability to become pregnant is a complication of extensive endometriosis.

What is the treatment for endometriosis?

a. Treatment is usually medical and will include the administration of enough female hormones to temporarily stop menstrual periods.

b. In persistent cases of endometriosis with marked symptoms, hysterectomy may have to be performed, This is reserved for women past the childbearing age or for those whose symptoms are so severe that they demand treatment.

c. In young women in the childbearing age, pregnancy causes temporary relief since the cyclic influence that causes the symptoms of endometriosis is interrupted.

Does endometriosis lead to cancer?

No.

What can happen if endometriosis is permitted to go untreated?

The symptoms may become progressive and debilitating. If the endometriosis involves the bowel or intestinal tract, obstruction of the bowel may take place. In certain cases, endometrial cysts will grow so large that they will create pressure on other organs and will demand surgery. Endometrial cysts sometimes twist or rupture, thus requiring immediate surgical intervention.

ABORTION *(Miscarriage)*

What is an abortion?

It is the expulsion of the products of conception from the uterus during the first six months of the pregnancy. Abortion applies to loss of pregnancy at a time when the fetus is unable to maintain life on its own.

Does the term "abortion" always mean the pregnancy has been artificially interrupted?

No. Among medical people, abortion refers only to the fact that the pregnancy has ended at a time when the fetus is not yet sufficiently developed to be able to maintain life.

What are the various kinds of abortion?

a. Spontaneous abortion, where no artificial means have been used to bring it on.

b. Induced abortion, where instrumentation, medication, or operation have been used to bring about the termination of the pregnancy.

Are there various types of spontaneous abortion?

Yes, They are threatened abortion, inevitable abortion, incomplete abortion, complete abortion, infected abortion, and missed abortion.

What are some of the common causes of spontaneous abortion?

a. Defects in the egg, the sperm, the fertilized egg, or the placenta.

b. Disease of the uterus, such as an infection or a fibroid tumor.

c. Upset in the glandular system as-

411

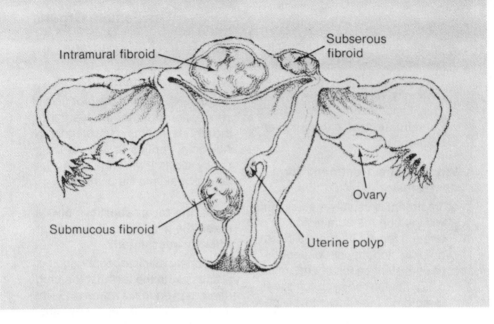

Spontaneous Abortion. *Fibroid tumors of the uterus are conducive to spontaneous abortion.*

sociated with ovarian, thyroid, or pituitary dysfunction.

d. Constitutional diseases, such as diabetes, malnutrition, syphilis, tuberculosis, etc.

e. Exposure to excessive x-ray radiation, the taking of poisons, etc.

Are there various types of induced abortion?

Yes. They are therapeutic abortion and voluntary abortion.

What is a threatened abortion?

It is a state during early pregnancy in which there are vaginal staining and abdominal cramps, but the cervix remains undilated and the products of conception are not expelled.

What is inevitable abortion?

It is a state in which bleeding and dilatation of the cervix are so advanced that nothing can be done to prevent expulsion of the fetus from the uterus.

What is incomplete abortion?

This refers to a condition in which there has been only partial expulsion of the products of conception.

What is a complete abortion?

It is a state wherein the entire fetal sac and placenta have been fully expelled from the uterus.

What are the symptoms of spontaneous abortion?

a. In the early stages of threatened abortion, staining is the only positive sign. Slight cramps or backache may then develop. This state often continues for days or even weeks.

b. In inevitable abortion, bleeding is

heavier, cramps become regular, severe, and progressive, and the cervix begins to dilate.

c. In incomplete abortion, cramps and bleeding are marked, pieces of tissue or clots are passed, and the cervix is dilatated.

d. In complete abortion, after increasingly severe cramps and passage of clots, a large mass is expelled from the vagina. On examination, it will be found to contain all the products of conception.

What is the treatment for inevitable abortion?

When it is obvious that abortion is inevitable, the uterus should be emptied. The evaluation of the inevitability of an abortion is difficult to make, but all gynecologists will give the patient every opportunity to maintain the pregnancy. When it is obvious that this is impossible, it is best to empty the uterus completely by curettage.

What is the treatment for incomplete abortion?

A curettage should be performed in order to clean out the cavity of the uterus completely. If a great deal of bleeding has been associated with the miscarriage, blood transfusions should be given.

What is the treatment for complete abortion?

No treatment is necessary unless severe blood loss has taken place. In that event, transfusions should be given. If there is evidence of infection, antibiotic drugs should be prescribed.

What is a missed abortion?

This is a state of pregnancy wherein the fetus has died and has been separated from the uterine wall but, instead of being expelled, is retained within the uterine cavity. In certain cases, medications are given to bring on the onset of labor. However, the safest course may often be to wait for the uterus to empty itself spontaneously.

What is habitual abortion?

This is a term applied to women with no children who have had four or more spontaneous abortions.

What are thought to be the causes for habitual abortion?

a. Hormonal imbalance involving the pituitary, thyroid, or ovaries.

b. Uterine abnormalities.

c. Genetic abnormalities in the chromosomes of the embryo.

Can habitual abortion ever be helped by medical treatment?

Yes, but it demands thorough investigation into all its aspects and intensive treatment by the physician.

When does abortion require hospitalization?

When the bleeding is profuse or when abdominal cramps become severe and persistent.

What are the greatest dangers associated with abortion?

a. In incomplete abortion, bleeding may be so profuse as to threaten life. In such cases, prompt transfusions are lifesaving.

b. Infection following abortion is an

413

occasional complication, especially when abortion is performed under less than ideal conditions. Infection will require active, strenuous treatment with antibiotic drugs.

What are the consequences of improper treatment of abortion?

a. Infection may set in and may necessitate removal of the uterus, tubes, and ovaries.
b. Sterility may ensue.

Can infection follow any type of abortion?

Yes, but it is rare when performed in a hospital operating room by a qualified gynecologist.

What restrictions are imposed following miscarriage?

a. Rest for one to two weeks.
b. No douches or tub baths for two weeks.
c. No sexual relations for two weeks.

What laws now govern the performance of abortion?

Up to the fourth month of pregnancy, a woman can voluntarily undergo abortion in all states. After the third month, states may regulate conditions under which abortions may be performed. These laws vary from state to state, some permitting abortion at any time up to the sixth or seventh month of pregnancy.

Does the Supreme Court ruling obligate a doctor to perform an abortion?

No. The attending physician may decide that in his opinion an abortion is not indicated. Under such circumstances, his patient's desire for an abortion may not sway him to perform the procedure. Also, some doctors do not believe in termination of pregnancy merely because the patient wishes it. A doctor may disapprove of abortion on moral and religious grounds and thus may decline to carry out the procedure.

Does the Supeme Court ruling consider the matter of termination of pregnancy during the final ten weeks?

Yes. It states specifically that a state may pass a law prohibiting termination of pregnancy during this period unless the life of the mother is seriously endangered.

Why is termination of pregnancy considered specially during the last ten weeks?

Because this is the period when the fetus is considered capable of maintaining life outside the womb.

Is there danger of sterility following abortion?

No, unless postabortion infection sets in. This is unusual today because of the new abortion laws that have resulted in most abortions being performed under sterile conditions in hospitals.

What kinds of operative procedures are used in doing an abortion?

1. Dilatation and curettage. This means dilating the cervix (the entrance to the uterus) and scraping out the interior of the uterus with a curette.

2. The suction method. This means dilating the cervix and inserting a specially designed suction apparatus that will suck out the embryo and lining of the uterus.
3. "Salting out." This method of abortion is used when the pregnancy is several months old. It involves injecting a concentrated salt solution or substances known as prostaglandins into the fluid surrounding the fetus, thus stimulating the uterus to expel it.

Are there any pills that can bring on a spontaneous abortion?

No, although there are drugs on the market that claim to be able to do so. Most of these pills contain a potentially dangerous drug called ergot. Overdose of these drugs may lead to serious, irreversible damage to blood vessels.

Will taking birth control pills for a long time make a woman more susceptible to miscarriage?

No. Statistics have shown that women who have become pregnant after long use of birth control pills have no greater tendency to miscarry.

Is there any safe method of self-abortion?

No! Attempts to produce abortion upon oneself are associated with a huge incidence of infection, hemorrhage, and fatality.

Should a couple abstain from sexual relations if there is any vaginal staining or bleeding?

Yes. If there is any evidence of a possibility of a miscarriage, sexual relations should be avoided.

Is sexual intercourse conducive to miscarriage?

No.

Does emotional shock or severe stress predispose to miscarriage?

There is no evidence that this happens.

Is work or physical activity conducive to miscarriage?

No.

Is lower abdominal pain an indication that abortion or miscarriage might be imminent?

In some instances, cramplike abdominal pains may signify that there is a possibility of miscarriage. If these pains persist, the obstetrician should be notified.

THE FALLOPIAN TUBES
(The Uterine Tubes)

What are the Fallopian tubes?

They are two hollow tubelike structures that arise at the upper end of the borders of the uterus and extend outward to each side of the pelvis for a distance of three to four inches. Each tube is the width of a lead pencil and at its most distant point is funnel shaped. The tubes are composed of an outer layer of muscle and an inner lining membrane covered with hairlike projections. These projections have a swaying, sweeping motion, which helps send

415

The Female Organs

the egg down toward the uterus and may aid the sperm in coming up through the tube to reach the egg.

What is the function of the Fallopian tubes?

To transport the egg that has been discharged from the ovary down to the uterine cavity. To permit sperm to pass from the uterine cavity up toward the egg.

What is salpingitis?

A bacterial infection of the Fallopian tubes.

What are the most common causes of infection within the Fallopian tubes?

a. Gonorrhea, which has ascended via the vagina, cervix, and uterus.
b. Staphylococcus, pneumococcus, or streptococcus infections.
c. Tuberculosis, usually secondary to a primary infection elsewhere.
d. The presence of an intrauterine device (IUD).

Is salpingitis a common condition?

Yes, but with the advent of the antibiotic drugs and the discovery of medications to control tuberculosis, inflammation of the tubes is much less frequently encountered than it was ten, twenty, or more years ago.

What harm may result from an infection within the Fallopian tubes?

a. Sterility.
b. Tubal pregnancy (ectopic pregnancy).
c. The formation of a chronic abscess involving the ovary as well as the tube.

d. Spread of the infection out into the abdominal cavity, thus causing peritonitis.

What treatment must often be instituted in order to cure chronic infection of the Fallopian tubes?

Surgery, with removal of the uterus, tubes, and ovaries.

What are the symptoms of acute salpingitis?

Lower abdominal pain, fever, chills, difficulty on urination, nausea and vomiting, vaginal discharge, increased menstrual bleeding, vaginal bleeding between periods, pain on intercourse, etc. Some or all of these symptoms may be encountered in salpingitis.

What is the best way to prevent salpingitis?

Of course, women should avoid contact with infected men. However, whenever vaginal discharge develops following intercourse, it should be treated promptly by a gynecologist. This can, in the great majority of cases, prevent the spread of the infection through the uterus into the Fallopian tubes.

What is the treatment for salpingitis once it has developed?

Acute salpingitis is treated with antibiotics. The patient is put to bed and given medications to relieve pain. If an abscess has formed and it persists, surgery, with removal of the tube, may be necessary.

Is surgery usually performed during the acute phase of salpingitis?

No. The gynecologist will make every attempt to bring the inflammation under control by medical means. Immediate surgery may be necessary when an abscess within the tube is threatening to rupture and produce peritonitis.

Is hospitalization necessary for all cases of salpingitis?

No. In the early stages of the disease, treatment can be carried out at home with safety. However, if response is inadequate, hospitalization is indicated.

Does salpingitis ever clear up by itself?

No. All cases must be treated intensively.

What are the chances of recovery from salpingitis?

Very few women die of salpingitis, but the chronic form of the disease can be cured only by removal of the tubes. In the acute stage, salpingitis can be cured if treatment is started quickly and is pursued vigorously.

Can the antibiotics cure a chronic or persistent abscess within the Fallopian tubes?

Usually not. Once a chronic abscess has formed, the only satisfactory method of treatment is the removal of the tube.

What kind of surgery is performed for salpingitis?

In disease restricted to one tube, simple removal of that tube is carried out. In more advanced disease, it may be necessary to remove both tubes, the tubes and the ovaries, or both tubes along with the ovaries and the uterus.

Is operation for the removal of an inflamed tube a major operative procedure?

Yes. It is performed through an incision in the lower abdomen under general or spinal anesthesia.

How long a hospital stay is necessary after an operation upon the tube?

Approximately five to nine days.

How soon after an operation upon the tubes can a patient get out of bed?

The day following surgery.

How long does it takes these wounds to heal?

Approximately ten days.

Does recurrence of salpingitis ever take place after surgery?

Where surgery has been performed with the removal of the tubes, a recurrence will not take place. Where only one tube has been removed, it is possible for inflammation to return and involve the adjacent ovary or the other tube and ovary.

Is there a tendency for salpingitis to recur when it is treated medically?

Yes.

How often is salpingitis limited to one tube?

This situation occurs infrequently. In the majority of cases, the inflammation affects both tubes. However,

417

The Female Organs

removal of both tubes is not always necessary, as it is sometimes possible to salvage one tube.

Will removal of the Fallopian tubes interfere with normal sexual relations?
No.

Does removal of the Fallopian tubes cause change of life (menopause)?
No. It is only when the ovaries are removed along with the tubes that menopause follows.

How soon after an operation for the removal of one or both tubes can a patient do the following:
Shower:
  One week.
Bathe:
  Four weeks.
Perform household duties:
  One week.
Drive an automobile:
  Six weeks.
Resume sexual relations:
  Six weeks.
Douche:
  Six weeks
Return to work:
  Six weeks.

What is an ectopic (tubal) pregnancy?
It is a condition in which a fertilized egg implants in the wall of the Fallopian tube and starts to grow.

What causes tubal pregnancy?
a. Previous inflammation of the tube is by far the most common cause of ectopic pregnancy. Approximately 25 percent of all cases occur in women who have had previous salpingitis.
b. Infection following abortion or infection following the delivery of a child.
c. Ovarian or uterine tumors that have produced mechanical compression, distortion, or blockage of a tube.
d. Previous peritonitis (inflammation of the abdominal cavity), which has created adhesions of a tube and has distorted its channel.
e. A birth deformity of the tube.
f. Unknown causes in women who are otherwise perfectly normal.

How often does tubal pregnancy occur?
In approximately one out of every three to four hundred pregnancies.

How soon after the egg is fertilized can a tubal pregnancy occur?
Two to four days after fertilization.

How soon after a tubal pregnancy has taken place can a diagnosis be made?
Usually within four to six weeks.

What are the symptoms of a tubal pregnancy?
In the early stages of an unruptured tubal pregnancy, the patient usually misses a menstrual period but does have slight vaginal staining. Some pain develops in the lower abdomen, particularly after intercourse. All of the signs seen during early pregnancy, including morning sickness, breast enlargement, etc., may be present.

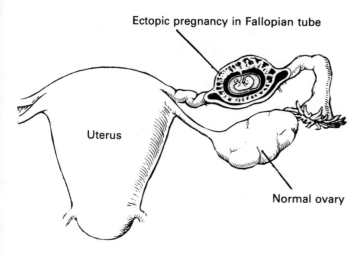

Ectopic pregnancy in Fallopian tube

Uterus

Normal ovary

Ectopic Pregnancy. An ectopic, or tubal, pregnancy usually lasts only a few weeks, terminating in rupture of the tube and severe hemorrhage, which will require immediate emergency surgery. When ectopic pregnancy is diagnosed before rupture, the surgeon will operate and remove the involved Fallopian tube.

When an ectopic pregnancy ruptures, the above symptoms may be followed by severe shock, fainting, marked pallor, abdominal pain, pain in the shoulder region, and pressure in the rectum.

What causes the symptoms when a tubal pregnancy ruptures?

There is actual rupture of the tube accompanied by great loss of blood into the abdominal cavity.

What is meant by the term "tubal abortion"?

This is a situation in which the fertilized egg or young embryo is expelled from the end of the tube into the abdominal cavity. In many of these cases, the symptoms are not as severe as in a ruptured ectopic pregnancy, for the tube itself does not rupture, and there is much less blood loss and shock.

Is a pregnancy test always positive in tubal pregnancy?

No. There are many cases in which

the pregnancy test will be negative. This will depend upon whether the pregnancy is still viable (alive).

How does the gynecologist make the diagnosis of tubal pregnancy?

a. By noting the appearance of the symptoms described above associated with the presence of a pelvic mass in the region of the Fallopian tube. A positive pregnancy test will also help to establish a diagnosis.

b. In suspected cases, a needle may be inserted into the pelvic cavity through the vagina to note the presence of blood within the pelvic cavity. Or an instrument can be inserted from the vagina into the pelvic cavity to visualize the tubes.

c. A sonogram will often demonstrate the presence of a tubal pregnancy.

What is the best method of treatment when a tubal pregnancy is suspected?

If the diagnosis cannot be determined positively, the safest procedure is to operate and examine the tubes under direct vision. Although this involves an abdominal operation, it is much safer to follow this procedure than to permit a patient to progress to a stage where the tube will rupture.

Is there any known method of preventing tubal pregnancy?

No, except to treat all disease within the pelvis prior to permitting the patient to become pregnant.

What is the treatment for tubal pregnancy?

a. When a definite diagnosis has been made, the patient should be operated upon immediately and the tube removed.

b. Blood transfusions should be given rapidly if there has been marked blood loss.

c. Suspected cases should be watched carefully and advised to call the physician should there be any change in their condition.

Are the ovaries removed when operating for tubal pregnancy?

No, unless they are found to be diseased.

What is the greatest danger in tubal pregnancy?

Hemorrhage!

Is the operation itself a serious operation?

No more serious than the removal of a tube for any other reason.

What are the chances of recovery following tubal pregnancy?

When modern facilities are available and prompt surgery is performed, practically all cases recover.

What anesthesia is used?

General anesthesia.

How long a hospital stay is necessary after an ectopic pregnancy?

Seven to nine days.

What treatments are given prior to operating upon a patient with a ruptured tubal pregnancy?

Transfusions are given to get the patient out of shock and thus permit surgery.

Is it possible for someone to have a normal pregnancy after a tubal pregnancy?

Yes. The removal of one tube or ovary does not prevent a subsequent pregnancy, nor does it necessarily mean that another tubal pregnancy will occur.

Are women who have had one tubal pregnancy more prone to develop a second ectopic pregnancy?

Yes.

How soon after operation for a tubal pregnancy can one become pregnant again?

Two months.

How soon after a tubal pregnancy will menstrual periods return?

Usually in six to eight weeks.

Does cancer ever take place within the Fallopian tubes?

Yes, but it is an extremely rare condition.

What is the treatment for cancer of a Fallopian tube?

It is treated like any other pelvic cancer, by complete removal of the uterus, tubes, and ovaries.

Can a cure take place after cancer of a tube?

Yes, provided the disease has been eradicated before it has spread to other organs.

THE OVARIES

What are the ovaries?

They are a pair of almond-shaped glandular structures about one and a half inches by one inch in diameter. They are located in the pelvis on either side of the uterus and are suspended from the posterior wall of the pelvis in close proximity to the funnel-shaped openings of the Fallopian tubes. Each ovary consists of an outer capsule, which is grayish white in color, a cortex, or main substance, and a hilum, or stalk, through which the blood vessels enter and leave.

What are the functions of the ovaries?

a. The periodic production and discharge of a mature egg. The cortex of each ovary contains several thousand immature eggs, one of which matures and is discharged into the funnel-shaped opening of a Fallopian tube each month. *This process is called ovulation.* If the egg is fertilized by the male sperm, the process halts. If fertilization does not take place, menstruation follows. The interval between ovulation and menstruation is approximately fourteen days.

b. The ovaries manufacture and secrete sex hormones into the bloodstream. These hormones are called estrogen and progesterone. They regulate ovulation and menstruation, help to maintain pregnancy when it exists, and are responsible for the development of female characteristics. Thus they are responsible for breast development, the female distribution of hair, the female figure, and the feminine voice.

Are both ovaries necessary for normal ovarian function?

No. Only one ovary, or part of an ovary, is necessary to maintain normal function.

At what age does the ovary begin to function?

From the onset of puberty, at approximately twelve to fourteen years of age.

Is the ovary ever the site of inflammation or infection?

Yes. Because of its close proximity to the Fallopian tube, disease of that structure will frequently spread to the ovary.

421

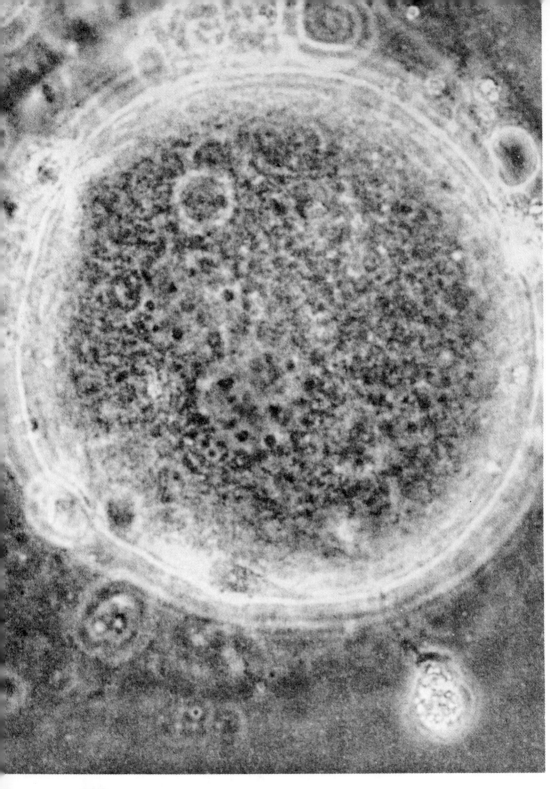

422

What are the symptoms of an inflamed or infected ovary?

They are the same as those involving disease of the Fallopian tube (salpingitis).

What is meant by the term "ovarian dysfunction"?

It is a state in which there is disturbed ovarian hormone production or imbalance, characterized by upset in the menstrual cycle and in the ability to become pregnant or maintain pregnancy. Such disorders may originate within the ovary or they may be secondary to disturbed function within other endocrine glands, such as the pituitary or thyroid.

What are some of the symptoms that may develop with prolonged dysfunction of the ovaries?

a. Complete upset in the menstrual cycle and in the character and nature of menstruation.
b. Obesity.
c. The development of extra hair upon the body (hirsutism).
d. Overgrowth of the lining membrane of the uterus (endometrial hyperplasia).
e. Infertility (inability to become pregnant).

What is the treatment for ovarian dysfunction?

First, the exact cause of the imbalance must be determined. Hormone studies of the blood and urine are carried out in an attempt to find the seat of the difficulty and to determine whether it originates in the ovary, the thyroid, or the pituitary gland. Endometrial biopsy and vaginal smears are also performed as an aid to a precise diagnosis.

a. When cysts accompany ovarian dysfunction, an operation with removal of a wedge-shaped section from each ovary often helps correct the disturbance.
b. When thyroid or pituitary gland dysfunction is found to be the cause of the ovarian disorder, the condition must be remedied by appropriate medication before the ovarian dysfunction can be corrected.
c. Cyclic therapy, the giving of regulated doses of estrogen and progesterone hormones, in a manner simulating the normal cycle, may prove beneficial.
d. More recently, cortisone has been found successful in certain cases in restoring normal ovarian function.

Does disturbed ovarian function ever subside by itself?

Yes. This occurs frequently without any treatment whatever.

At what age may ovarian dysfunction occur?

It can take place at any age from pu-

Opposite page:
Human Egg. *The human egg (shown here greatly magnified) is actually about the size of the period at the end of this sentence.*

berty to menopause but is seen most often during the first years of adolescence or early adulthood.

Can pregnancy follow ovarian dysfunction?

If ovarian dysfunction is accompanied by lack of ovulation, pregnancy will not take place. However, once the dysfunction is corrected, pregnancy may take place.

Are there medications that can help a woman who fails to ovu late?

Yes. There are several medications that can correct this condition. In some instances, these drugs have not only encouraged ovulation and pregnancy but have been associated with multiple births such as twins, triplets, quadruplets, etc.

What are follicle cysts?

These are small, fluid-filled sacs appearing on the surface of an ovary. They arise from the failure of the egg-producing follicle to rupture. Thus, the cyst persists instead of being absorbed.

To what size do follicle cysts grow?

They may vary from the size of a pea to that of a plum.

What are the causes of follicle cysts?

a. Previous infection that has produced a thickening of the outer coat of the ovary.
b. Disturbance in ovarian function.

What symptoms do follicle cysts cause?

They may cause no symptoms, or they may result in ovarian dysfunc-

tion as described above. The larger, solitary follicle cysts sometimes cause lower abdominal pain, urinary distress, pain on intercourse, and menstrual irregularity.

Do follicle cysts ever rupture?

Yes. When this happens, it may be accompanied by severe pain in the lower abdomen, tenderness on pressure, nausea, vomiting, or even a state of shock. It is often difficult for the gynecologist to distinguish a ruptured follicle cyst from appendicitis or from a tubal pregnancy.

What is the treatment for follicle cysts?

Treatment is seldom required for the simple, small, or multiple cysts that are associated with no symptoms. Multiple cysts that cause symptoms and are associated with ovarian dysfunction should be treated by surgery with the removal of wedge-shaped sections of the ovaries. If rupture or twist of a solitary cyst takes place and the symptoms do not abate within a day or two, surgery may be necessary.

Do follicle cysts of the ovaries ever disappear by themselves?

Yes.

Is there a tendency for follicle cysts to recur?

Yes. Patients who have had follicle cysts require periodic observation by their gynecologists.

How is the diagnosis of an ovarian cyst or tumor made?

a By pelvic examination.
b. By sonography (ultrasound test).

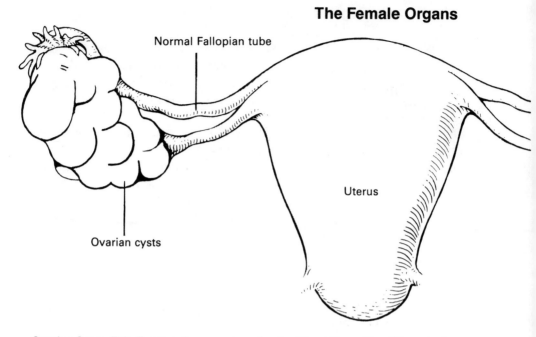

Normal Fallopian tube

Uterus

Ovarian cysts

Ovarian Cysts. This diagram shows an ovary involved in cyst formation. When ovarian cysts become larger than the size of a lemon or an orange and persist for any length of time, they are best treated by surgical removal. If the opposite ovary is normal, completely normal menstrual and reproductive functions will be maintained. A pathological enlargement of an ovary can be felt on pelvic examination.

c. By laparoscopy (the insertion of a metal tube, with a light at the end, through the navel and into the abdominal cavity).

What is a corpus luteum cyst of the ovary?

After the egg has broken out of the ovary, the follicle is supposed to undergo shrinkage and disappear. In some cases, instead of disappearing, the follicle develops into a cyst (sac). Such a cyst may be filled with blood and may enlarge to the size of a lemon, orange, or even larger.

What are the symptoms of a corpus luteum cyst?

It may cause no symptoms, or if it is large, it may cause pain, delay in menstruation, or painful intercourse. If the cyst ruptures, there may be acute onset of pain, nausea, vomiting, urinary disturbance, and severe pain in the lower abdomen. This may give the appearance of an acute surgical condition such as appendicitis or ectopic pregnancy and may demand surgery.

When is it necessary to operate upon a ruptured corpus luteum cyst?

If the symptoms persist or if there has been a great deal of blood loss.

Are there other types of ovarian cysts?

Yes. There are many types, including

425

simple solitary cysts and cystic tumors.

Are tumors of the ovary very common?

Yes.

Do these cysts ever grow to a large size?

Yes. Some of them may fill the entire abdominal cavity and reach the size of a watermelon.

What is the treatment for these cysts?

Surgical removal as promptly as possible.

What types of tumors affect the ovary?

a. Benign solid or cystic tumors.
b. Malignant solid or cystic tumors.
c. Hormone-producing tumors.

Why is the ovary so often the seat of tumor or cyst formation?

The eggs within the ovaries contain all the basic primitive cells that go into the formation of a new human being, and it is not surprising that some of these may undergo abnormal growth. Also, the ovary itself is subject to so many wide and varied fluctuations in function that it is not difficult to appreciate that things might go wrong and lead to tumor growth.

Do tumors of the ovary occur in women at any age?

Yes. They occur from earliest childhood to the latest years of life.

What is a dermoid cyst of the ovary?

This is a tumor occurring in women usually between the ages of twenty and fifty. It is frequently found in both ovaries and may grow to be as large as an orange. It is composed of many types of cells and may even include hair, bone, and teeth. Dermoid cysts have also been found to contain other tissues that resemble organs in a primitive stage of development.

Are dermoid cysts malignant?

The great majority are not malignant, but some will become malignant if they are not removed.

How is the diagnosis of a dermoid cyst made?

By pelvic examination, sonography, and laparoscopy.

What is the treatment for a dermoid cyst of the ovary?

In the childbearing age, resection of the dermoid cyst. Past the childbearing age, removal of the ovary, or ovaries, and uterus.

Opposite page:
Dermoid Cyst. *This x-ray shows an ovarian dermoid cyst (arrows) which contains teeth.*

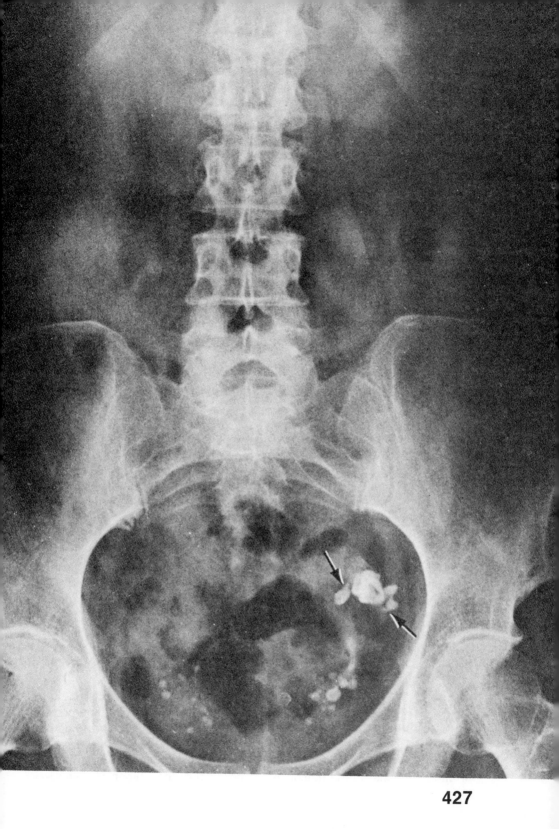

427

The Female Organs

What are hormone-producing tumors of the ovaries?

These are tumors that manufacture either female or male sex hormones in great excess. Thus, a tumor of the ovary that produces a male-type hormone will cause the patient to assume male characteristics, such as growth of hair on the face and chest, deepening of the voice, and loss of feminine appearance.

Are hormone-producing tumors of the ovary very common?

No.

What is the treatment for hormone-producing tumors of the ovary?

Age plays an important role. Surgical removal of the diseased ovary is indicated in some cases; in older women, the uterus should also be removed.

Will altered characteristics disappear after removal of a hormone-producing ovarian tumor?

Yes.

What are fibromas of the ovary?

These are solid tumors constituting about 5 percent of all ovarian growths. They are commonly associated with fluid secretion in the abdominal cavity, and, because of their similarity to certain malignant growths of the ovary, they must be very carefully analyzed after being removed.

Does endometriosis affect the ovary?

Yes. In about one out of eight cases of endometriosis, the condition is found in the ovary. It is almost always associated with endometriosis elsewhere.

Is cancer of the ovary a common condition?

Unfortunately, yes. Cancers will appear as either solid or cystic growths, and they may arise from one or from both ovaries. Cancer of the ovary may also develop from benign tumors of the ovaries, such as dermoid cysts.

Does secondary cancer ever affect the ovary?

Yes. This is quite common and occurs from the spread of a cancer of the stomach, bowel, breast, or uterus.

At what age does cancer most commonly affect the ovary?

The highest incidence occurs in the years between thirty-five and forty-five, although it is sometimes found in young girls and in elderly women.

How does one make the diagnosis of cancer of the ovary?

By pelvic examination, sonography, and laparoscopy. Fluid in the abdominal cavity is a frequent finding suggestive of an ovarian malignancy.

What is the treatment for malignant tumors of the ovary?

The present mode of treatment involves surgery with total and complete removal of the uterus, both tubes, both ovaries, and the ligaments and tissues surrounding these structures. Surgery is often followed by chemotherapy and, in some instances, by radiation.

What are the possibilities of cure of cancer of the ovary?

If the patient is operated upon early—before there has been spread to other structures or organs—the chances are fairly good. Surgical recovery takes place in almost all cases, as these operations are not excessively dangerous.

What is the best method to prevent cancer of the ovary?

Frequent, periodic pelvic examinations will reveal the presence of abnormality in the ovary and alert the patient to the need for possible surgery. If surgery is performed early for suspicious tumors, many patients can be saved before the tumor has become malignant or before it has spread to other structures.

What is the best treatment for any ovarian cyst or tumor?

If it persists or shows signs of growth an operation should be performed to evaluate the exact nature of the lesion. In this way, many ovarian tumors can be removed that might have become malignant at some future date. Also, early removal of a persistently cystic or enlarged ovary will prevent it from twisting or rupturing.

Is medical treatment ever preferred to surgical treatment in tumors of the ovaries?

No.

What are some of the exact criteria for advising surgery for ovarian conditions?

a. Any ovarian mass more than two inches in diameter that persists on repeated examination should be removed.
b. Any rapid growth of an ovarian tumor should be operated upon.
c. The presence of free fluid within the abdominal cavity in the presence of an ovarian tumor should indicate surgery.
d. The appearance of weight loss, anemia, and weakness in the presence of an ovarian tumor should warrant surgery.

Is it possible to determine while the patient is on the operating table whether a tumor of the ovary is malignant?

Yes. A pathologist will take a frozen section of a tumor and examine it under the microscope while the patient is on the operating table. This will determine whether or not the tumor is malignant and will suggest to the surgeon how extensive his operative procedure should be.

Do ovarian tumors ever occur during pregnancy?

Yes. Cysts of the ovary occasionally occur during pregnancy.

Do cysts that occur during pregnancy harm the embryo?

No.

Do ovarian cysts or tumors ever create an acute abdominal condition?

Yes, there is a great tendency for

429

cysts or tumors of the ovary to twist upon their stalks. This will cause all of the signs of an acute abdominal condition and will require immediate surgery.

Do cysts of the ovary ever rupture?
Occasionally this happens, and when it does, emergency operation is indicated.

Does the removal of the ovaries alter one's sexual desires?
Not in the slightest.

How soon after operations upon the ovaries can one do the following:
Shower:
  One week.
Bathe:
  Two weeks.
Drive an automobile:
  Four weeks.
Resume household duties:
  Six weeks.
Return to work:
  Six weeks.
Resume sexual relations:
  Six weeks.
Douche:
  Six weeks.

Can a woman become pregnant after the removal of one ovary?
Yes. This does not reduce her chances for pregnancy at all.

Does a patient with only one ovary menstruate regularly?
Yes.

Does removal of both ovaries al-ways bring on change of life (menopause)?
Yes, unless the woman has already passed the menopause.

THE MENOPAUSE
(Change of Life)

What is the menopause?
It is that period in a woman's life during which ovulation (the production of mature eggs) and menstruation come to an end. It is commonly called the "change of life." In other words, menopause represents the natural aging process.

When does menopause occur?
In most women between the ages of forty-five and fifty, but it may occur as early as thirty-five and as late as fifty-five years of age.

What is meant by the term "artificial menopause"?
It is a state created by the surgical removal of the ovaries or by x-ray treatments to the ovaries that cause them to cease ovulating.

What produces menopause?
A decrease and eventual stoppage in the secretion of hormones by the ovaries.

What are the reactions to menopause?
These vary widely. They may be absent or minimal; they may be marked and disabling. The most important

factor in menopause is a woman's psychological attitude toward it. Women who for one reason or another wish to suffer, may unconsciously have severe menopausal symptoms. It is not uncommon for a woman to mimic her mother's reaction to menopause. If women are properly oriented and informed as to the menopause, and if they are emotionally stable, they will probably react mildly.

What are the usual general symptoms of menopause?

a. Hot flashes.
b. Cold sweats.
c. Headaches.
d. A feeling of fatigue.
e. Nervousness and a feeling of emotional strain and tension.
f. Depression and a feeling of inadequacy.

What are early specific symptoms of menopause?

Irregularity of menstrual periods and a diminished flow.

How can one distinguish between irregular bleeding due to menopause and that which is due to a tumor or other disorder within the pelvic organs?

If there is any doubt as to the cause of the irregularity of the menstrual flow, the gynecologist will investigate it by doing vaginal smears or by taking a biopsy of the tissue from the uterus or cervix. Frequently, the doctor will recommend a curettage in order to determine the exact nature of the condition.

What is the usual duration of menopause?

It may last anywhere from a few months to a few years.

What is the treatment of menopause?

a. The most important step in the treatment of menopause is to reassure the patient and to inform her fully as to the nature of the condition.
b. If the symptoms are not severe, the best treatment is no treatment.
c. Hormone replacement is often administered when symptoms are severe. Such therapy should not be given longer than necessary, as it increases the chances of developing cancer of the uterus.
d. Tranquilizing drugs and sedatives have proven helpful in relieving symptoms in some instances.

Can relief from the symptoms of menopause be obtained by the giving of ovarian hormones?

Yes. This form of treatment, however, should be carried out only under the constant supervision of a gynecologist.

Is there a changing attitude toward giving hormones to women who are past the menopause?

Yes. Formerly, continued ovarian-replacement therapy was advocated by many gynecologists. Today this is not advised routinely because there is a suspicion that it increases the chances of developing cancer of the uterus.

431

The Female Organs

Are the tranquilizing drugs efficient in relieving the symptoms of menopause?

Yes, but in mild cases only.

Do the symptoms of menopause always subside after the passage of time?

Yes, within a few months to a few years.

Is it natural for emotionally disturbed women to have more severe and longer menopause?

Yes.

Does the desire for sexual relations change with the menopause?

No. After cessation of menstruation, sexual desire continues as previously.

Should there be any change in a woman's personal feminine hygiene after menopause?

No.

Is it natural for the voice to deepen and for hair to grow on the face and body with menopause?

Absolutely not.

Can pregnancy occur after the menopause?

No. When ovulation and menstruation have ceased, pregnancy will not take place.

For how long a period after the onset of menopause can pregnancy take place?

It is possible for pregnancy to take place during the first six months to one year of menopause.

Are there any structural changes in the appearance of the ovaries or uterus following menopause?

They tend to undergo slight shrinkage in size, but this change is not significant.

What is the significance of vaginal bleeding after the menopause has been well established?

Bleeding that occurs a year or more after the periods have stopped should always be looked upon as possible evidence of a tumor within the cervix or uterus. This must be investigated thoroughly.

Are a woman's abilities to think clearly and to be mentally alert just as great after the menopause as they were before?

Yes.

Is it common for women to lose their youthful appearance after the menopause?

No, except that one must realize that the menopause occurs at an age when the youthful appearance tends to wane. The loss of female hormone secretions, however, has very little to do with the physical appearance of a woman.

Will the giving of ovarian hormone drugs restore the youthful appearance of a patient past menopause?

No, despite many reports to the contrary.

432

Is there a tendency to inherit early menopause or late menopause?
No.

Can ovarian hormones delay the aging process in menopausal women?
They may, but only to a limited extent and for a limited period of time. The aging process, unfortunately, is inevitable.

Does an early menopause indicate that the life span will be short?
Definitely not. The menopause is no indication whatever of a woman's ability to live a long life.

26 FIRST AID IN EMERGENCIES

(See also Chapter 2 on Abscesses and Bacterial Infections; Chapter 14 on Bones, Muscles, Tendons, and Joints; Chapter 29 on Heart; Chapter 71 on Throat)

BITES

Animal or Human Bites

What is the first-aid treatment for animal or human bites?

These injuries usually consist of puncture wounds, jagged lacerations, or bruises. They should be treated quickly and thoroughly in the following manner:

a. Scrub and cleanse the wound with water and any mild soap for a period of five to ten minutes.

b. Apply a sterile bandage, or if this is not immediately obtainable, a clean handkerchief.

c. Any animal bite that has punctured the skin should be treated immediately by a physician so that he may give tetanus antitoxin and antibiotics and recommend antirabies injections if indicated.

Are human bites particularly dangerous?

Yes, because the germs in the human mouth frequently produce very severe infections, often much worse than those caused by animal bites.

Should antiseptic solutions, such as iodine, be used in the first-aid treatment of animal or human bites?

No. Strong antiseptics may damage the tissues further and should not be used.

Are bites always sutured (stitched) by the physician?

No. In some instances, for fear of infection, such wounds are left wide

Scorpion. This photograph shows the type of scorpion found in this country. Although the sting of a scorpion can be very painful, it does not cause death.

open to drain and are not sutured until several days later. Wounds of the face are usually sutured after thorough cleansing.

Insect Bites

Are bites dangerous from such insects as fleas, sandflies, mosquitoes, wasps, hornets, bees, or chiggers?

If someone is allergic to the sting of these insects, such bites can be serious injuries requiring immediate treatment with antivenin.

What is the first-aid treatment for insect bites?

a. If a sting has been left in place, it should be gently plucked out. It is important not to break it in attempts at removal.

b. If a person is known to be allergic to a particular type of bite and is bitten on an extremity, it might be well to place a tourniquet above the bite on the extremity so that the absorption of the poison will take place more slowly. It is important not to allow a tourniquet to remain in place for more than twenty minutes at a time. Release it for ten minutes and then reapply.

c. Medical advice should be obtained if a great degree of swelling takes place. The physician will give an antiallergic medication or will take other measures to counteract the effect of the bite. Antivenin extracts are available in many hospitals for those who are extremely allergic to insect bites.

d. It is important not to scratch a bite, as this will cause secondary infection and will lead to greater absorption of the poison.

Is a bite from a black widow spider a serious injury?

Yes, particularly when it affects young children. Occasional fatalities have been reported. Bites from these spiders are characterized by severe abdominal pain and board-like stiffness of the abdominal muscles.

How can one recognize a black widow spider?

It has a rounded, jet black body with a red marking on its belly in the shape of an hourglass. This is the female of the species and the one to be avoided. The black widow male does not bite.

What is the first-aid treatment for a black widow spider bite?

a. It should be treated just like a snake bite, by making a crossed incision over the bite and sucking out the poison.

b. A tourniquet should be applied above the bite just tight enough to cut off the return circulation. The pulse should still be obtainable.

c. Medical consultation should be sought quickly as there are counteracting medications to the bite of a black widow spider.

d. Physical exertion should be avoided as much as possible.

What should be done for the bites of other spiders, poisonous centipedes, scorpions, or tarantulas?

These should be treated similarly to a black widow spider bite.

Are the stings of centipedes, scorpions, or tarantulas very serious?

Usually not. The only time a sting from these insects endangers life is when it happens to a young infant or when the bite is on the face or neck. However, stings from these insects may produce severe temporary symptoms and great discomfort.

Snake Bites

What is the first-aid treatment for a snake bite?

Since it is not always possible to tell whether the snake is poisonous, precautions should be taken in all cases of snake bite. The following procedures should be carried out:

a. A tourniquet should be placed just above the site of the bite. This should be only tight enough to stop venous flow and must not cut off the pulse. Anything, such as a handkerchief, tie, or belt, can be used as a tourniquet. The tourniquet must be released every twenty minutes for a ten-minute interval.

b. A crossed incision should be made over the site of the bite, and the bite should be sucked out.

c. The patient should be put at absolute rest and should undergo as little physical exertion as possible.

d. Have the patient transported to the nearest hospital and, if possible, ascertain the type of snake that caused the bite.

What are some of the poisonous snakes commonly found in the United States?

The coral snake, the rattlesnake, the copperhead, and the moccasin.

Is alcohol a good remedy for a snake bite?

Absolutely not.

Are the bites of poisonous snakes always fatal?

On the contrary, the majority of adults recover from snake bites. This is especially true if they can be admitted to a hospital promptly for the administration of the appropriate antivenin. The danger is greater in children, as the snake poison is apt to be more overwhelming.

BURNS AND FROSTBITE

How are burns usually classified?

a. First-degree burns. These involve only the superficial layers of the skin and evidence themselves by mere reddening. Most sunburns are first degree.

b. Second-degree burns. These burns involve not only the superficial layers but also the deeper layers of the skin. They are characterized by blisters and by the discharge of serum. Severe sunburns may fall into this category.

c. Third-degree burns. These burns involve all of the layers of the skin and usually have caused complete skin destruction. *(continued)*

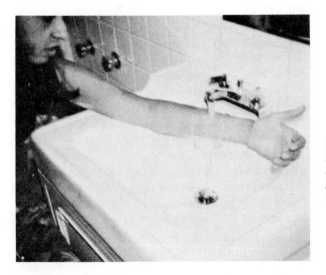

Superficial Burns. Immediate first aid for a superficial burn should consist of placing the burned area under cold, running water for 10 to 15 minutes.

437

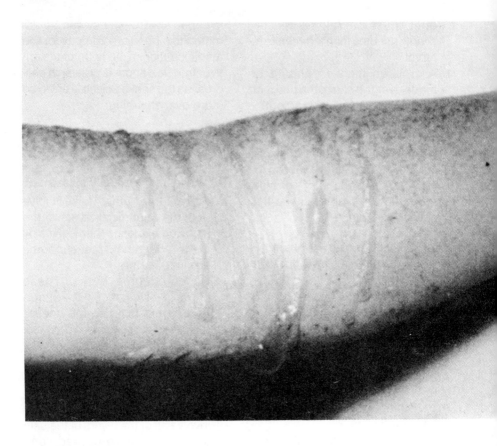

d. Fourth-degree burns. These burns not only destroy all layers of the skin but involve the tissues beneath the skin, such as the subcutaneous tissues, muscles, tendons, blood vessels, bone, etc.

Are all burns caused by excessive heat?

No. There are many other types of burns, such as those caused by chemicals, alkalis, extreme cold, or strong acids. Also, some burns are caused by electricity or radiations such as x ray, radioactive substances, etc.

438

What is the proper first-aid treatment for burns?

a. First-degree burns can be treated by any of the usual ointments that relieve pain and prevent the skin from drying or cracking. Most first-degree burns can be self-treated and do *not* require the advice of a physician unless the general health of the patient is also affected.

b. Second-degree burns must be treated by a physician. First-aid measures will include:

1. Immersing the burned area in

(continued)

Second-Degree Burns. *The photograph on the opposite page shows a second-degree burn of the arm. Such burns will usually heal within a period of a few days to a few weeks and will not require the application of skin grafts.*

Burns. *Photo at right shows an arm with healed second- and third-degree burns.*

Burns. *The photograph below shows an arm burn that has both second- and third-degree areas. A third-degree burn goes through all the layers of the skin, and if the area involved is extensive, it may require grafting.*

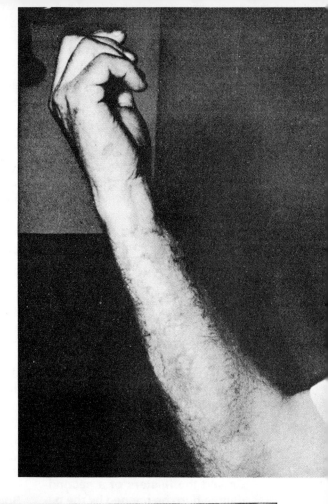

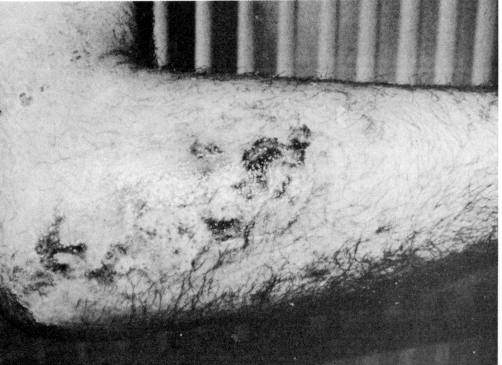

running cold water for approximately ten minutes.
2. Covering the area with a sterile dressing.
3. Seeing that the patient maintains a large intake of fluids.
4. Cleansing the burned areas with large quantities of water and a mild soap.
5. Avoiding the use of ointments.
c. Third-degree burns should never be self treated. As a preliminary measure, dirt should be gently washed off with water and a clean dressing applied. Large quantities of fluids should be given by mouth, and if the patient is in shock, he should be immediately transported to a hospital on a stretcher. Ointments should *not* be applied to the burned area.
d. Fourth-degree burns should be treated in the same manner as third-degree burns.

Should the blisters of a second-degree burn be opened by the patient himself?

No. A physician should treat these blisters. Some physicians open them while others allow them to dry up by themselves.

Should people apply ointments to burns?

It is perhaps best not to apply an ointment to anything but a mild first-degree burn. There are various ways of treating a burn, and many physicians do not believe in the appliction of ointments. Furthermore, the ointment that the patient prescribes for himself may not be the one the doctor may want used. It then becomes

difficult to remove it in order to apply the proper medication.

Do chemical burns require special treatment?

Yes. It is wise to wash any chemically burned area thoroughly with large quantities of water in order to dilute the chemical and eliminate that which may still be in contact with the skin.

What should be done about the shock that accompanies burns?

Shock demands immediate treatment. (See the section on Shock in this chapter.)

Is any special first-aid treatment indicated for burns of the eye?

Yes. These burns should be irrigated thoroughly with water to dilute the agent that has produced the burn. Medical care should then be sought immediately.

Should butter or homemade remedies or greases be used on burns as a first-aid treatment?

No.

Frostbite

What is frostbite?

It is a burn caused by exposure to excessive cold.

What is the first-aid treatment for frostbite?

a. Treat the general condition of the patient by warming him and by giving him warm foods to eat and warm liquids to drink.

b. The patient must be thawed out gradually and not suddenly placed from a very cold into a very warm atmosphere.

c. Give medications to relieve any pain that may exist. Tylenol or similar medications are usually adequate.

d. The affected part should be brought back to use slowly and should be exercised, but should in no event be vigorously massaged or rubbed.

e. The frostbitten part should be covered with a dry, clean dressing.

How warm should a frostbitten part be made?

Immerse the part in lukewarm water (100° to 103°F.).

Should snow be rubbed into a frozen part?

No.

Are any medications helpful in aiding a part to return to normal circulation?

Yes, but they must be administered by a physician.

Should antiseptics be applied to frozen areas?

No. They may cause further burn.

Can one determine the extent of the damage resulting from frostbite soon after it has occurred?

No. It may take several days to several weeks to discover the full extent of the damage.

CHOKING

Do some people have a greater tendency to choke than others?

Yes. People who eat rapidly and those who talk with food in their

Choking. A not infrequent cause of choking in children is the swallowing or aspirating of foreign bodies. This coin was stuck in the back of a child's throat and was removed in the hospital.

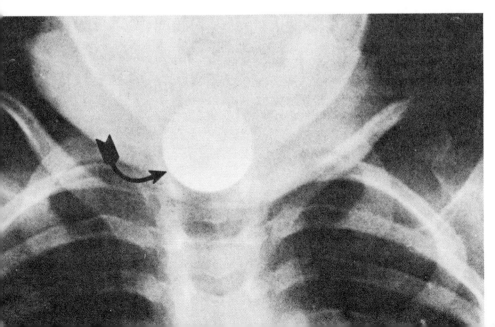

First Aid in Emergencies

mouths are much more likely to choke than those who eat slowly and keep their mouths closed while chewing.

Are children particularly prone to choking?

Yes, because they do not observe the cautions described above. Also, they frequently put coins or other foreign bodies in their mouths.

Do elderly people have a tendency toward choking on food?

Yes, because the swallowing mechanism in older people doesn't often work as well as it does in younger people.

What normally prevents choking on food?

The epiglottis in the throat moves to close over the entrance to the trachea (windpipe) during the act of swallowing. This prevents liquids and solids from gaining access to the trachea, bronchial tubes, and lungs.

What are common causes of the epiglottis not working during the swallowing process?

A sudden cough or sneeze may prevent the epiglottis from shutting off the trachea, thus allowing food or liquid to enter it.

Do most people recover spontaneously from choking?

Yes. In the great majority of instances they cough out the liquid or food that has "gone down the wrong way."

What first-aid measures should be given someone who is choking on food or some other ingested object?

a. Strenuous coughing should be encouraged.
b. A few sharp slaps on the back of the chest may aid in the expulsion of the food.*
c. If the victim is a child, hold him upside down and give him a few sharp slaps on the back.*
d. If the obstructing object is not expelled, place an index finger in the back of the victim's mouth and sweep it around the back of the throat. This frequently dislodges the foreign body.
e. If the above measures fail, the Heimlich maneuver should be carried out promptly. Time should not be wasted in repeating the above measures if they are not immediately successful.

How is the Heimlich maneuver performed?

a. The victim is raised to his feet.
b. The first-aider stands behind him and places both arms about the victim's waist at a level just below the rib cage.
c. The right fist is placed high up in the abdomen, just below the breastbone.
d. The right fist is firmly grasped with

*Although the Red Cross recommends sharp slaps on the back, Dr. Henry J. Heimlich (the originator of the Heimlich maneuver) believes this is of no value and may even be harmful.

442

the left hand. The victim is held tightly.

e. With a sudden inward and upward thrust, the grip on the victim is tightened as forcefully as possible. This will cause a sudden, tremendous increase of pressure within the victim's chest cavity and will force air—along with the foreign body or food—out of the windpipe.

f. If the first thrust fails to clear the windpipe, repeat the maneuver. Remember, the thrust must be a quick, instantaneous one. Release your grip once the thrust has been carried out.

Does the Heimlich maneuver work?

Yes, in the vast majority of cases.

Is a tracheotomy ever indicated if all other methods fail to relieve the choking?

Yes, but it should not be done by an inexperienced layman. If a physician is available, or an experienced paramedic is the only one available, it may be performed on a victim who is obviously choking to death.

How can one tell if a victim is choking to death?

If he is unable to breathe at all, has turned blue, and his heart action becomes irregular, he will probably die within a few minutes.

What is done when the patient *can* breathe but has not expelled the obstructing food or other object?

He should be transported as soon as possible, in a semisitting position, to the nearest doctor or hospital.

CONVULSIONS AND "FITS"

What is the first-aid treatment for someone who has had a convulsion or "fit"?

a. See that the patient does not further injure himself by striking his head or other parts of his body against hard objects.

b. Allow the patient to lie down and give him plenty of freedom. Do not attempt to restrain him.

c. Open a tight collar at the neck to allow easier breathing.

d. Lift up the chin to improve the breathing airway.

e. If it can be done easily, place a folded handkerchief between the patient's teeth to prevent tongue biting. (Do not place your fingers between the patient's teeth, as you may be bitten.)

Do most people recover from convulsions or fits?

Yes, particularly if the convulsions are epileptic in origin. Convulsions due to a brain hemorrhage or tumor may lead to death.

Should small children with convulsions be immersed in water?

No. It is much better to allow these children to remain comfortably in bed.

Should cold water be thrown on people who are having convulsions or fits?

No. This is improper treatment.

Should a parent pick up a child having a convulsion and run with him to a physician?

No. Recovery takes place in almost

all cases of childhood convulsions. The best treatment is to allow the child to lie in bed unmolested.

Is there any way to find out how to aid a person having a convulsion?

Yes. In many instances people subject to convulsions will carry instructions in their clothing concerning their condition. Diabetics may carry instructions on what to do for them if they go into insulin shock. Epileptics often carry explicit instructions as to how they should be treated if they have a seizure.

What aftertreatment is necessary for people who emerge from a convulsion or fit?

It usually takes quite a little time before they reestablish their normal thinking processes. Therefore, they should not be abandoned as soon as the convulsion has subsided. Many of these people will need quite a few minutes to know where they are and to realize what has happened. Stay with them until they regain their normal state completely.

DROWNING

What are the first-aid measures to be taken in cases of drowning?

After the patient has been removed from the water, he should be given artificial respiration if he is not breathing. The mouth-to-mouth breathing method is advocated and should be used instead of other methods.

444

How does one carry out mouth-to-mouth artificial respiration?

a. Stretch out patient on his back; loosen any tight clothing around the neck, chest, or waist.

b. Lift up chin and tilt head back as far as possible. (This straightens out the windpipe and improves the airway to the lungs.)

c. With your fingers, pinch the patient's nostrils so that they are closed.

d. Place your mouth tightly over patient's mouth and blow as hard as you can.

e. Take your mouth away to permit air to be expelled from the lungs.

f. Repeat this every five to six seconds.

g. Continue this maneuver so long as there is any pulse or heartbeat. It may take as much as several hours to revive someone.

h. When you tire, have someone substitute for you.

i. If the patient seems to have water or mucus in his throat or chest, tilt him on his side to permit such fluid to run out the mouth.

j. Wipe out patient's mouth with your fingers if mucus or other material collects there. (A nonbreathing person will never bite.)

k. If you are squeamish about direct mouth-to-mouth contact, you may blow through an opened handkerchief. (This may not prove to be as effective as direct contact.)

l. Discontinue artificial respiration only when you are certain there is no pulse or heartbeat for several minutes. Listen carefully with your ear to patient's left chest region and feel for pulsations in the neck.

(continued)

MOUTH-TO-MOUTH ARTIFICIAL RESPIRATION

Three Basic Techniques

Below:
Mouth-to-nose breathing *(top). Inflate lungs by holding victim's mouth tightly closed and blowing hard into his nostrils. In* **mouth-to-mouth breathing** *(center) hold nostrils closed and blow air into mouth.* **Nose-and-mouth breathing** *(bottom) is useful on children. Place mouth firmly over victim's nose and mouth and blow gently.*

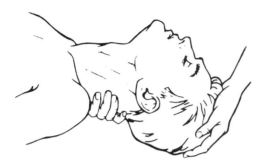

Tilt head far back and elevate the chin *before beginning mouth-to-mouth breathing. This will straighten the windpipe and will provide a good air passage. If foreign matter is present in victim's mouth, it should be removed.*

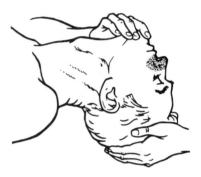

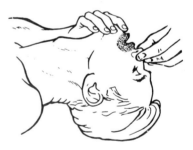

Pinch nostrils shut with one hand *and keep the chin elevated with the other. Place mouth directly over victim's mouth and blow air until his chest rises. Repeat about twelve to twenty times a minute until spontaneous breathing resumes.*

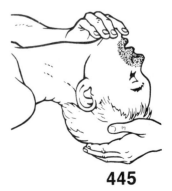

445

m. If patient is revived, keep him warm and do not move him until the doctor arrives, or at least for a half hour.

Should mouth-to-mouth artificial respiration be used in all cases where breathing has stopped— whether due to drowning, suffocation, poisoning, electric shock, etc.?

Yes.

Is the mouth-to-mouth breathing method of artificial respiration beneficial in cases of drowning?

Yes, but it is easier for the victim to expel water from the lungs when he is in a prone position. After water has been expelled, mouth-to-mouth breathing can be started.

Is drowning always caused by too much water in the lungs?

Not always. Many cases of drowning are caused by spasm of the larynx and can be relieved by overcoming the spasm. There are many cases on record in which life has been saved by the performances of a tracheotomy below the point of the laryngeal spasm.

Should a tracheotomy be performed by a first-aider?

No, unless it is almost certain that medical attention cannot be obtained or that the patient will die before it arrives.

Does it help to turn a drowning person upside down and to hold him in this position?

Usually not. He will bring up water from his lungs if merely permitted to lie in a prone position.

When should artificial respiration be abandoned?

When the patient no longer has a heartbeat and is obviously dead.

ELECTRIC SHOCK

What is the first-aid treatment for electric shock?

Do not touch a person who is still in contact with an electric wire! This may cause your death as well as his. The patient should be removed from electric contact as quickly as possible. This may be accomplished by cutting off the current that is going to the patient or by disconnecting the patient from the wire contact by use of a dry stick or rope that is thrown around him. An axe may be available to cut the wire that is causing the contact with the patient. When using an axe, be sure that your hands are dry and that the wood handle of the axe is dry.

What treatment should be carried out for electric shock after the patient has been disconnected from electric contact?

a. Artificial respiration should be instituted as soon as possible.
b. The patient should be kept quiet and warm and supplied with oxygen if this is available.
c. The burned area, which is often present at the site of contact, must be treated in the same manner as any burn.

446

FAINTING, DIZZINESS, AND VERTIGO

What is the first-aid treatment for fainting, dizziness, or vertigo?

a. Place the patient in a lying-down position with his face up and his head at body level or slightly lower than the level of the rest of his body.
b. Raise the legs slightly above the level of the rest of the body.
c. If there is a tight collar or tie, loosen it so that the patient can get plenty of air.
d. If breathing is shallow, it can be improved by artificial respiration.

How long should a patient be kept in a supine position after he has fainted or after an attack of vertigo has taken place?

Until he is fully recovered and feels himself again.

Is it common for people to faint a second time soon after they have recovered?

No, but they should be observed for a considerable time before being permitted to proceed on their own.

Fainting. *This photograph shows the proper position in which to place someone who has fainted. By slightly elevating the legs, blood from the lower extremities can be made to gravitate back toward the head, where it is needed. Fainting is thought to be caused by constriction of the blood vessels which go to the brain. By keeping the head at the level of the rest of the body or slightly below it, blood will flow in larger quantities toward the brain and consciousness will be restored.*

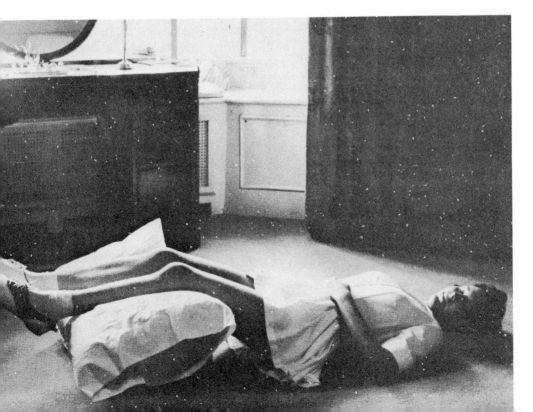

First Aid in Emergencies

Do people ever die in a faint?

This almost never takes place unless a person has struck his head violently in the process of fainting and has sustained a fatal head injury.

Should cold water be thrown upon people who have fainted?

No.

Do people who faint or who have attacks of dizziness or vertigo usually recover by themselves?

Yes, without any treatment other than being permitted to lie down for several minutes.

FOREIGN BODIES

What should be done in the way of first-aid treatment for foreign bodies?

a. Eyes. Only the most superficial foreign bodies should be removed from the eyes by nonphysicians. If medical care is not readily available, the eye should be irrigated with lukewarm water, or a moist piece of cotton can be used to brush out the foreign body. A little bit of mineral oil instilled into the eye will relieve most of the irritation. Avoid rubbing the eye and avoid trying to scrape out a foreign body with any hard object.

b. Nose. If one can get the patient to sneeze, the foreign body will often be extruded. This can be accomplished by having him inhale some pepper through his nostrils or by tickling the opposite nostril.

c. Ears. Foreign bodies in the ear should not be attacked by lay people, as damage may result to this delicate structure. The best first aid is to place some olive oil, mineral oil, or castor oil into the ear and let it stay there for a few minutes. This will usually bring out the foreign body. No great harm will result from a foreign body remaining in the ear until medical attention is obtained.

d. Splinters. Only those splinters that can be grasped firmly by a protruding end and can be gently withdrawn should be attacked by laymen. Soft splinters or broken-off splinters should be treated by physicians. If a piece of a foreign body is allowed to remain in the skin, it will usually become infected. If medical care is not available, warm soaks for a period of a few days will often bring a splinter to a position where it can be withdrawn with a pair of tweezers.

e. Stab wounds (knives, shrapnel, or other weapons). Protruding objects of this type should usually be left in place until medical care can be obtained. Removal by nonphysicians may result in severe hemorrhage. The best first aid is to place a sterile dressing over the area and transport the patient to the nearest hospital.

What should be done about pieces of clothing or dirt that have gotten into an abrasion or laceration?

Thorough washing with soap and water will usually dislodge such foreign bodies. This should be done as soon as possible after the injury. The injured area should then be covered with a clean dressing, and medical attention should be obtained.

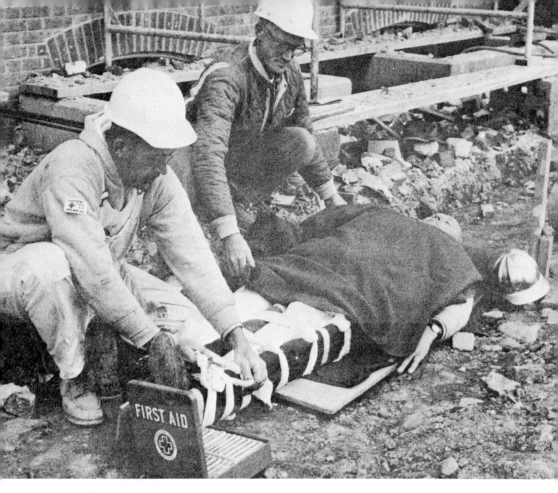

First Aid. Injured people should be given first aid at the site of the accident, whenever possible. They should then be kept quiet as they await the arrival of medical assistance.

FRACTURES, DISLOCATIONS, SPRAINS

What is the first-aid treatment for fractures?

a. Keep the patient quiet and do not move the injured part until the extent of the injury has been determined.

b. Immobilize or splint the damaged extremity before moving the patient.

c. Always move the patient to a hospital in a lying-down position. Never sit the patient up or bend or move the injured part any more than is absolutely necessary.

What should one do if a splint is not available?

There is always a piece of wood or a stick or some straight, firm object that can be used as an improvised splint. Furthermore, a fractured arm can be splinted against the body, and a fractured leg can be splinted against the other leg.

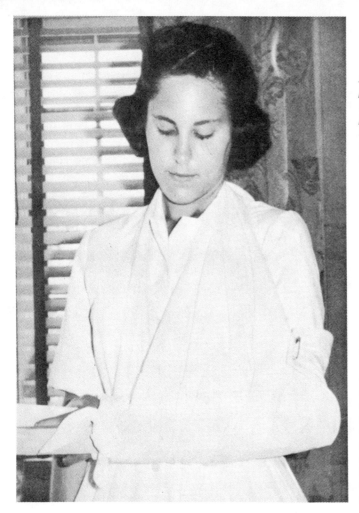

At left, a sling is being placed over an arm splint. It is usually best to transport the patient with his arm in a sling, so that the dead weight of the arm does not cause added pain.

Fracture Splint.
The photograph below shows a makeshift splint for a fractured arm. The only materials required are two pieces of wood, two ordinary towels, and two ordinary handkerchiefs. Such splints will prevent the fracture fragments from moving until definite care can be given by the orthopedist.

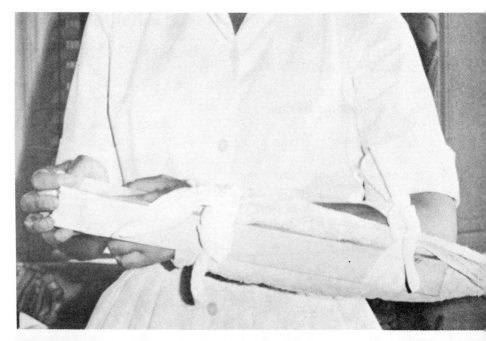

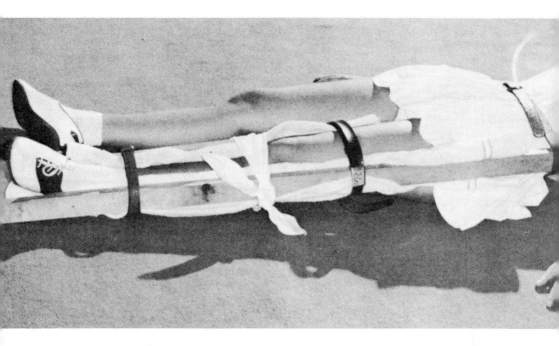

Fracture Split. Here is a makeshift leg splint made with two pieces of wood, two towels, three ordinary belts, and a handkerchief. A blanket or overcoat makes an excellent make-shift stretcher on which to carry a patient with a fractured leg.

Should the splint be padded before being placed alongside a fractured extremity?

Yes. A piece of clothing placed between the injured extremity and the splint will prevent injury from undue pressure.

How should a splint be kept in place?

By tying handkerchiefs at various places along the splint or by tearing up a shirt and using it as a bandage.

Before applying a splint, what should be done with the fractured limb?

Try to place it in as straight a position as possible. Do it gently so as not to hurt the patient.

What are the best positions in which to splint an arm?

In a straight position; or the arm can be strapped to the side of the body. In this way, the body itself acts as a splint.

What is the best way to splint a leg?

The opposite leg can be used as a splint so that the injured leg can be straightened and attached to the other leg. This will form an excellent splint in most instances.

Are special first-aid measures

451

First Aid in Emergencies

needed in the treatment of compound fractures?

a. Yes, the wound must be covered with a clean dressing or, if none is available, a clean handkerchief.

b. If there is severe hemorrhage from a compound fracture, it may be necessary to apply a tourniquet temporarily. If bleeding can be controlled by direct pressure over the wound, a tourniquet should not be applied.

c. The limb should be splinted, but no attempt should be made to alter the position of the broken fragments.

How long can a tourniquet be safely left in place?

A tourniquet should be released every twenty minutes for a few minutes to restore circulation. During this time, pressure with one's fingers should be applied over the bleeding artery.

What special first-aid treatment is necessary for a fractured skull?

a. The patient should be placed on his back with his head flat.

b. The patient should be kept still and not allowed to move about.

c. The patient should be kept warm

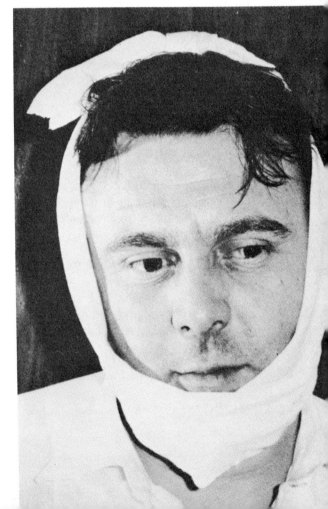

Fractured Jaw. This picture demonstrates how to apply a splint for a fractured jaw. Two handkerchiefs or towels or bandannas are the only materials required. The jaws should be kept together and the patient should do as little talking as possible, in order not to disturb the fracture fragments.

452

and transported to the hospital as soon as possible.

Should whiskey or pain-killing drugs be given to a patient with a possible fractured skull?

No. This may do definite harm.

Should fractures of the bones of the face be treated as potential fractured skulls?

Yes. A fractured bone in the face is often accompanied by a fractured skull.

What is the best first-aid treatment for a fractured jaw?

a. Close the mouth so that the teeth come together as closely as possible.
b. Tie a handkerchief so that it circles the head from under the chin to the top of the head.
c. Allow the patient to remain in a sitting-up position.

What is the best first-aid treatment for a fractured shoulder or a fractured collarbone?

Place the hand on the chest in a comfortable position and tie a shirt or necktie around the entire body, keeping the arm and hand close to the chest wall. This will act as a splint and prevent motion in the fractured area.

Is it safe to immobilize a fractured limb in the position that is most comfortable for the patient?

Yes. This is safer than forcibly attempting to straighten out an extremity.

Should people with severe injuries to a lower extremity be permitted to walk or bear weight on the extremity?

No. When in doubt as to whether a fracture exists, do not put weight on the extremity.

How can one distinguish between a severe sprain and a fracture?

It is not always possible to make this distinction. It is wisest, therefore, to treat all severe injuries as if they were fractures.

What is the first-aid treatment for a dislocation?

Nonphysicians should not try to correct dislocations but should immobilize the affected part and take the patient to a hospital as soon as possible.

Is it safe to pull or stretch a dislocated shoulder or finger?

This should be done only if medical attention is unavailable.

What special first-aid treatment is indicated for neck injuries?

If there is a severe neck injury, the patient should be transported, flat on his back, on a board, to the hospital. It is important to avoid twisting the body or bending the neck.

Is it necessary to keep the head rigid and not allow flexing of the neck if there is an injury in this area?

Yes. This is absolutely essential in order to prevent movements of the vertebrae. Movement may press

Shoulder Splint. *This photograph shows the type of bandage used for a fractured shoulder or collarbone. Such a bandage will be effective for several hours, allowing time for the patient to be taken to a hospital or to an orthopedist.*

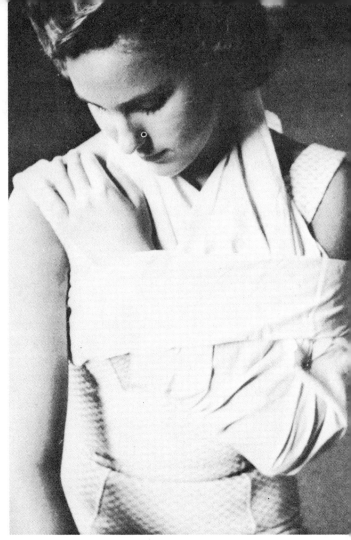

Neck Fracture. *Splinting a patient with a possible fractured neck, before taking him to a hospital. As little movement as possible is advocated for people who have a possible fracture of the neck or back, so as to avoid any unnecessary injury to the delicate nerves within the spinal cord. If there is doubt as to the extent of injury in this type of case, it is better to wait until experts arrive on the scene, rather than to move people in a manner that may produce further damage to the spinal cord.*

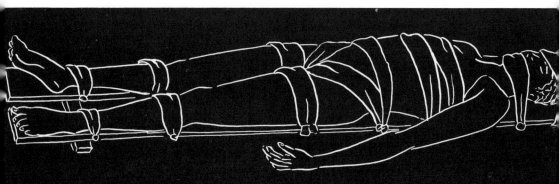

upon the nerves in the spinal cord and cause paralysis.

What is the best way to avoid neck movement?

Someone should hold the head rigid by placing the palms of his hands firmly against the sides of the injured person's face and head.

What special first aid is required for a possible fracture of the back?

People with back injuries should be transported to a hospital lying flat, face downward. A board should be obtained, or a blanket can be used as a stretcher.

Is it safer to keep a patient at the scene of an accident until medical attention arrives, or should immediate transportation to a hospital be attempted in the case of a severe fracture?

If possible, wait for medical help before moving the patient, as serious damage can result from improper methods of transportation.

GAS POISONING

What is the first-aid treatment for gas poisoning?

a. Shut off the gas and open the windows.
b. Get the patient out into the open where he can breathe fresh air.
c. Mouth-to-mouth breathing should be applied if the victim is not breathing on his own.
d. Loosen any tight collars or tight clothing.
e. Call for an emergency squad so that pure oxygen can be administered.

For how long a period should artificial respiration be continued if the victim is not breathing?

For as long as there is the slightest evidence of a pulse or heartbeat. Feel for the pulse in the neck.

Do people who recover from gas poisoning require careful observation?

Yes. There may be serious mental disturbance as a consequence of the effect of the gas poisoning upon the brain cells.

HEAT STROKE AND HEAT EXHAUSTION

What is heat stroke?

It is sunstroke, caused by overexposure to sun and extremely high temperatures.

Who is most likely to be affected by heat stroke?

Older people and those who are not in good health; men seem to be more readily affected than women.

What are the characteristic symptoms and results of heat stroke?

The patient runs an extremely high fever, which may cause extensive damage to important structures such as the brain, the liver, or the kidneys.

What is the first-aid treatment for heat stroke?

a. Place the patient in a tub of cold water, preferably containing ice.

455

First Aid in Emergencies

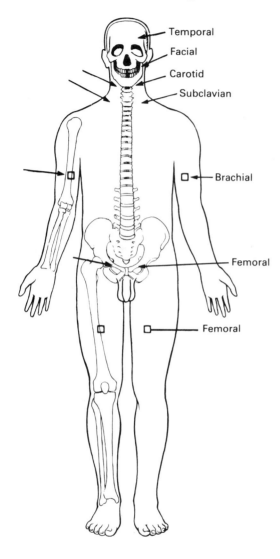

Temporal

Facial

Carotid

Subclavian

Brachial

Femoral

Femoral

Rectangles = *Points of application of tourniquets*

Arrows = *Digital pressure points*

Pressure Points to Stop Bleeding from Major Arteries. *These pressure points can be located by noting the pulsations of the arteries at various spots throughout the body.*

456

This will reduce the body temperature.

b. Wrap the patient in cold, wet sheets or towels.

c. Give an enema containing iced water.

d. Summon the doctor as quickly as possible. People whose temperatures remain much above 106° F. for prolonged periods usually do not recover.

What is heat exhaustion?

This is a condition caused by excessive exposure to heat, not necessarily in the sun, in which the patient perspires, becomes weak, and may faint or lose consciousness. Heat exhaustion is more common in women than in men.

What is the first-aid treatment for heat exhaustion?

a. People suffering from heat exhaustion should be cooled quickly by being placed into a tub of cold water.

b. Salt tablets should be given. Ten grains three times a day is sufficient. (Heat exhaustion is always accompanied by free perspiration and loss of body salt.)

c. The patient should be kept in bed and allowed to rest until body fluids and salt have had time to be absorbed.

HEMORRHAGE

What is the best first-aid treatment for hemorrhage?

This will depend on the type of hemorrhage. If there is severe inter-

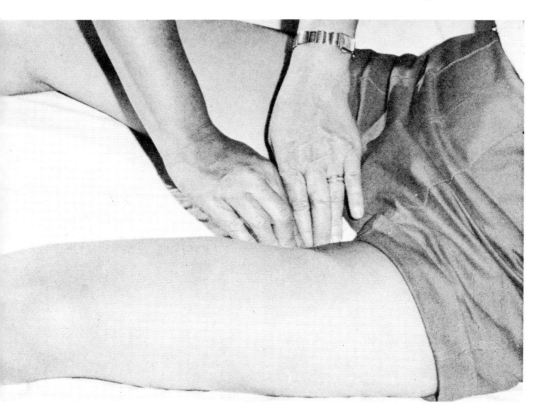

Application of direct pressure over a bleeding point in the upper thigh.

nal bleeding, such as may occur from an ulcer or tumor within the intestinal tract or hemorrhage secondary to the coughing up of large quantities of blood, the patient should be placed in a lying-down position and transported as quickly as possible to a hospital.

Are there any medications that should be given to a patient to stop bleeding from the intestinal tract or from the lungs?

This does not constitute first-aid treatment. Such people should re-

ceive expert medical care, and it is perhaps best not to attempt to treat them before such care can be obtained.

What is the best treatment for external hemorrhage?

a. Place pressure directly on the wound! This can be accomplished by placing a sterile gauze dressing or a clean handkerchief on the bleeding points and pressing firmly with the flat of one's hand or with one's fingers.

b. If the bleeding is secondary to a

457

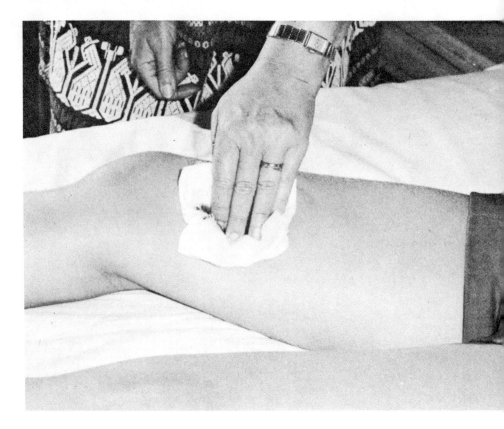

very severe laceration in the arm or in the leg, a tourniquet may be required. This should be applied only as a last resort if the bleeding cannot be controlled by direct pressure. The tourniquet is placed just above the site of the injury. It should be remembered that tourniquets must be loosened every ten minutes to allow the circulation to return.

How near to a wound should a tourniquet be applied if it is needed?

As close as possible and just tight enough to stop the bleeding. If a tourniquet is applied too loosely, it

Direct pressure is being applied to a bleeding point on the lower thigh.

will increase the amount of bleeding. If applied too tightly, it may unnecessarily damage tissues.

Does bleeding always start again after a tourniquet has been loosened for a few minutes?

No. It is often found that when a tourniquet has been in place for some minutes, it can be removed permanently without resumption of hemorrhage.

458

Direct Pressure for Bleeding. *This photograph shows the application of direct pressure over a bleeding point in the forehead. Most bleeding can be checked temporarily by putting direct pressure over the spot which is bleeding. Note that a clean gauze bandage has been placed between the fingers and the bleeding point. If no bandage is available, a clean handkerchief may be used.*

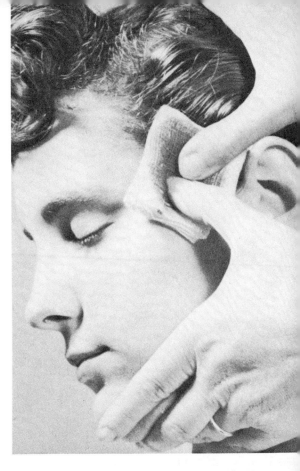

Direct Pressure for Bleeding Point in Neck. *Life can often be saved by placing direct pressure upon a bleeding jugular vein. It is important, however, that the pressure be localized merely to the bleeding point and that pressure not be placed on the windpipe, which is in the midportion of the neck.*

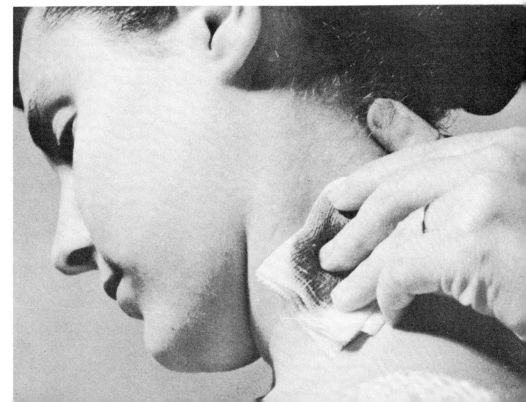

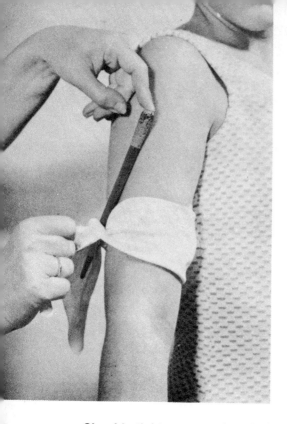
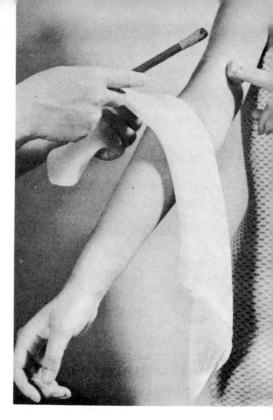

Should a tight pressure dressing or tourniquet be applied in the region of the neck?

No. The best way to stop bleeding from the neck is to constrict the bleeding vessel with one's fingers.

Do people often bleed to death from external wounds?

No. Hemorrhages from the scalp, the face, or from one of the extremities usually look much worse than they are. It is rare for someone to bleed to death from the ordinary scalp or extremity wound, and most of these lacerations will stop bleeding by themselves within a few minutes.

In what position should people who have hemorrhaged be transported?

Usually lying flat or with the feet

elevated. This will tend to combat shock by causing blood to gravitate toward the head.

Should alcohol or coffee be given to people who have had a severe hemorrhage?

It is perhaps best not to give any stimulants to those who have hemorrhaged. All efforts should be concentrated on getting the patient to the hospital.

LACERATIONS, ABRASIONS, AND CONTUSIONS

What is the first-aid treatment for lacerations, abrasions, and contusions?

a. Thorough cleansing of the wound

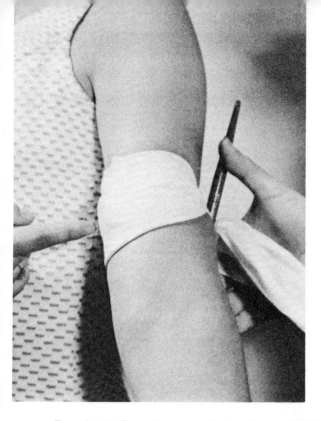

Tourniquet. *Opposite page and above from left to right: All the material required to make a tourniquet. A handkerchief, a penholder (or small stick), and an eraser are placed above a bleeding artery.*
The handkerchief is tied loosely over the eraser and the penholder inserted into the knot. The tourniquet is tightened until the flow of blood is stopped. Tourniquets should be loosened every twenty minutes in order to permit blood flow to the rest of the extremity.

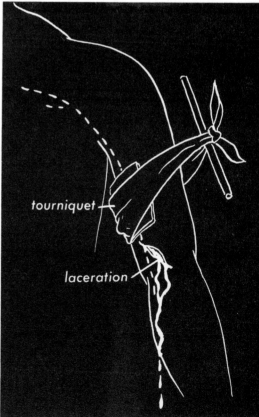

tourniquet

laceration

This diagram at right *shows the proper distance between the placement of the tourniquet and the bleeding laceration.*

with soap and water for five to ten minutes.

b. Direct pressure with a clean dressing to stop bleeding.

c. The application of a clean dressing and transportation of the patient to the nearest hospital or physician.

Should antiseptics such as alcohol, iodine, etc., be poured over abrasions, contusions, or lacerations?

No. It has been found that these substances do more harm than good. The best insurance against infection is a thorough cleansing for a period of five to ten minutes with ordinary soap and tap water.

Will the application of ice to a bruise or contusion tend to lessen the amount of hemorrhage into the tissues?

Yes, but it should be remembered that damage can result if the ice is applied for too long a period of time. Ice should be applied for no longer than twenty minutes at one time and then discontinued for a similar period.

POISONS

What are the best first-aid treatments for swallowed poison?

a. Call the Poison Control Center in your area. The number is in the front of the telephone book. Give them all the details, including the name of the poison or drug, if known, and the quantity you believe has been swallowed. The Control Center will instruct you on how to obtain medical help quickly. If you can't locate the Poison Control Center, call 911 or dial 0.

b. If the swallowed poison is an overdose of a medication or drug, vomiting should be induced.

c. If the swallowed poison is a petroleum product such as gasoline, kerosene, or oil, or if it is a strong acid or alkali, vomiting should *not* be induced.

d. If vomiting is not being induced, the poison should be diluted by giving the victim a glass of water or milk. Repeat this, but if nausea ensues, discontinue the process.

e. If the victim vomits, save the vomit for subsequent analysis.

f. If respirations cease or are shallow and irregular, give the victim mouth-to-mouth artificial respiration.

g. If the heart stops, give the victim CPR (cardiopulmonary resuscitation).

Why is it bad practice to cause vomiting when someone has swallowed a petroleum product or a strong acid or alkali?

a. When one vomits a petroleum product, some of it may get down into the lungs and cause pneumonia.

b. When one vomits a strong acid or alkali, the substance may result in further burning of the esophagus (foodpipe) and mouth.

What are the best ways to cause vomiting?

a. Tickle the back of the throat with your finger.

b. Give the victim a glass or two of

462

warm water containing salt, soap, or mustard.

c. If you have syrup of ipecac on hand, give the victim a tablespoonful.

If vomiting is indicated, is it advisable to cause more than one episode?

Yes. The stomach may not completely empty itself the first time one throws up.

After the stomach has been emptied, what should be given to drink?

Tea, milk, or the whites of several eggs. These will act as antidotes to many poisons.

Should activated charcoal be given to one who has swallowed a poison?

Yes. This is a good substance to have on hand in the household as it tends to bind (deactivate) the poison.

How can one tell whether a strong acid or alkali has been swallowed?

In many cases there will be obvious burns around the lips or in the mouth.

How can one tell whether a petroleum product has been swallowed?

Often one will be able to smell gasoline, kerosene, or oil on the victim's breath.

What poisons are most apt to interfere with breathing?

One of the most common causes of depressed breathing is an overdose of barbiturates or other sleeping pills.

Also, morphine and heroin cause deep depression of respirations when taken in large doses.

RADIATION EXPOSURE

What are the chances of being overexposed to nuclear radiation?

Although one or two accidents have threatened people living in the vicinity of nuclear plants, governmental authorities are moving toward minimizing possibilities of the release of radioactive substances. To date, there are no proven cases of harmful effects to people living near nuclear plants.

What would be the first-aid treatment should radiation exposure actually take place?

a. People threatened with radiation exposure should evacuate the area in a quick, orderly manner. Local authorities will give specific instructions on how best to do it.

b. People already exposed should remove and discard all clothing that was worn at the time of the exposure and should wash their bodies thoroughly for a prolonged period of time in a shower.

c. Medical advice should be sought promptly. Evacuation and admission to a hospital out of the area of radiation may be advised.

SHOCK

What are the symptoms of shock due to injury?

a. There may or may not be loss of consciousness.

b. The skin becomes a dull gray color and is cold and clammy to the touch.

c. The patient's body is covered with a fine perspiration.

d. The pulse is weak and rapid.

e. The pupils of the eyes are dilated.

f. Respirations are rapid and shallow.

g. The patient is apprehensive and complains of weakness and excessive thirst.

What is the first-aid treatment for shock?

a. Place the patient on his back with his feet higher than his head.

b. If there is any active bleeding contributing toward the shock, it should be stopped. (See the section on Hemorrhage in this chapter.)

c. The patient should be kept warm. Supply him with adequate blankets or other covering.

d. If there is severe pain that can be relieved by the first-aider, this should be done immediately. Pain is one of the strongest contributors toward the development of shock. If a fracture is present, it should be splinted.

e. If it can be determined that there is no injury or wound to the abdomen, the patient may be given warm fluids to drink.

f. The patient should be transported to a hospital as soon as possible.

Should tea or coffee be given to people who are in shock?

No. In the time it takes to obtain tea or coffee, the patient should really have had provisions made for transportation to a hospital where specific treatment can be instituted.

Should alcohol be given as a stimulant to patients who are in shock?

No. This will only serve ultimately to increase the state of shock.

SUFFOCATION OR STRANGULATION

(See also the section on Choking in this chapter)

What is the best first-aid treatment for suffocation or strangulation?

a. The patient should be placed in the open air.

b. If there is anything about the neck that might obstruct breathing, it should be loosened immediately.

c. Elevate the chin; this will give the patient a better airway.

d. If strangulation is due to a foreign body that has lodged in the windpipe, grasp the victim around the waist from behind with both hands and tighten your grip with a sudden, forceful inward and upward thrust. This will usually cause him to cough up the foreign body.

CPR *(Cardiopulmonary Resuscitation)*

What is CPR?

CPR is an abbreviation for cardiopulmonary resuscitation, a series of maneuvers to bring back to life a person whose heart has stopped beating. It is a combination of closed cardiac massage and mouth-to-mouth artificial respiration.

What is cardiac arrest?

Heart stoppage.

Can a patient ever be saved once the heart has stopped beating?

Yes. Although the majority of people whose heart has stopped beating do die, it is possible to save a considerable number of them if prompt CPR is instituted.

How soon after cardiac arrest must CPR be started?

It must be begun *immediately*. Unless CPR is instituted within a few minutes, the patient will succumb.

How can a first-aider know that CPR should be carried out?

a. He notes an unconscious patient.
b. He feels for a pulse in the neck and does not find it.
c. He listens with his ear over the heart and hears no beat.
d. He looks for respirations and finds none.

Is CPR indicated when there is a heartbeat but no obvious breathing?

No. In such cases only mouth-to-mouth artificial respiration is indicated.

Does the heart ever stop beating and respirations continue?

No. Once the heart stops, breathing stops.

Can anyone carry out CPR?

Yes, but it is much better if a trained person does it. Civilians are being trained all over the country in the techniques of this lifesaving procedure.

What is closed cardiac massage?

The pumping of blood throughout the body by intermittent thrusts upon the breastbone (sternum) overlying the heart. By pushing down every second against the breastbone, it is possible to expel blood from the heart so that it will circulate throughout the body. Closed cardiac massage is an essential part of CPR.

How hard should one press against the breastbone in performing CPR?

Sufficiently enough to depress the breastbone about one to two inches.

What steps should be carried out after it has been definitely determined that cardiac arrest exists?

a. The first-aider kneels alongside the head of the victim.
b. The left hand is placed under the victim's neck, thus raising his chin and opening the air passage.
c. The right hand pinches off the victim's nostrils.
d. The first-aider then places his mouth firmly against the victim's mouth and artificial respiration is begun. The first-aider blows hard into the victim's mouth twice.
e. The first-aider then locates the lowest extent of the sternum (the xiphoid process), measures up about one-and-a-half inches, places the heel of one hand on the breastbone and his other hand over it, and begins the intermittent thrusts in a downward direction. The thrusts are continued for fifteen strokes, after which the first-aider again pinches off the nostrils and blows hard once into the victim's mouth.

465

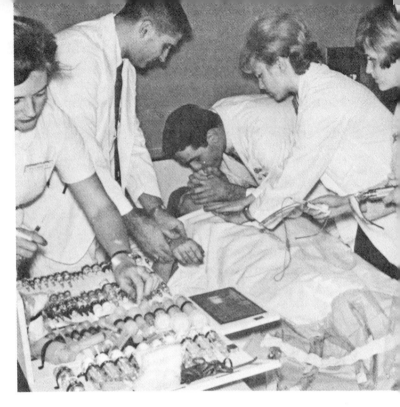

CPR. For patients in shock, hospital personnel institute immediate first-aid measures including cardiopulmonary resuscitation.

f. Cardiac massage is resumed for fifteen more strokes and then mouth-to-mouth respiration is given again.

g. These maneuvers are continued indefinitely until the first-aider notes the resumption of a heartbeat and spontaneous respirations.

Is CPR best carried out with two first-aiders?

Definitely, yes! One will concentrate on the cardiac massage; the other on mouth-to-mouth artificial respiration. The cardiac massage should consist of a downward thrust upon the breastbone every second. The person giving artificial respiration should employ it after every five thrusts of the person performing the cardiac massage.

466

Should the two first-aiders change places when doing CPR?

Yes. Usually the person performing the cardiac massage tires first. He should then exchange duties with the one performing the mouth-to-mouth breathing.

How long should CPR be continued?

At least a half hour. By this time, some kind of heartbeat should be restored if the first aid is going to be successful.

Should CPR be continued indefinitely if the slightest evidence of an occasional heartbeat is noted?

Yes. Occasional heartbeats often signify that a rhythmic beat can be restored.

Does regular breathing come back before a heart beat is restored?

No. Heart actions come before resumption of breathing.

How long does it take to learn CPR?

The average intelligent individual can learn the technique in several hours of instruction.

Where can one get instruction in CPR?

Call your local Red Cross.

BANDAGING

The Anchor: Below left, starting the bandage. Below right, the bandage is rolled around the wrist. Bandages should be apllied snugly, but never so tightly that they act as a tourniquet or cut off circulation.

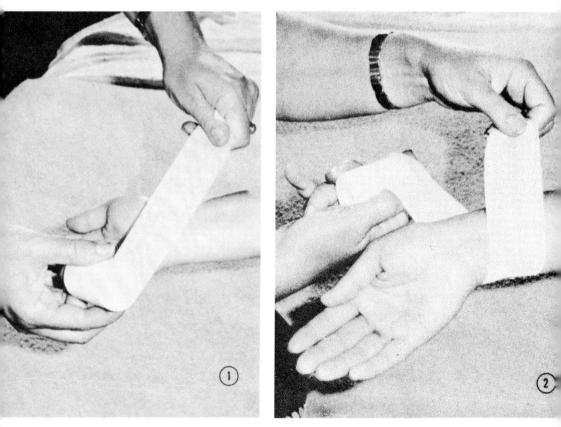

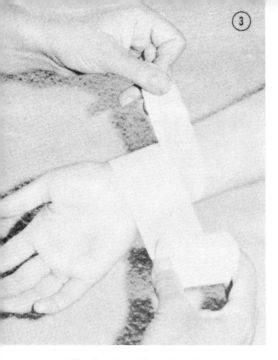

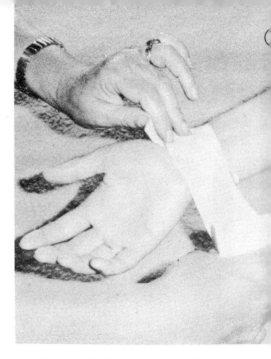

The Anchor: *The offset first turn is bent or twisted over the second turn.*

The Anchor: *A third turn locks the bent-over end firmly in place.*

The Anchor is completed *and the "roller" begun.*

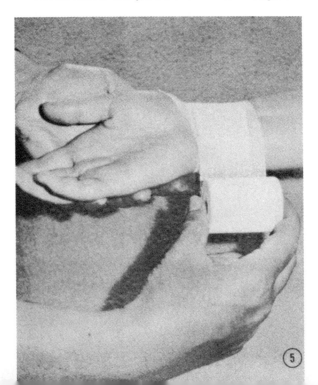

468

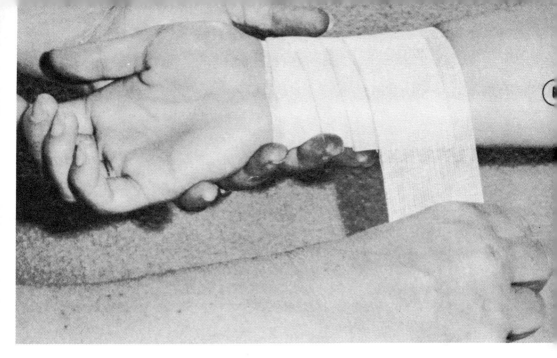

When the part of the body being bandaged is approximately uniform in size and shape, a simple roller bandage is used. Each turn should cover about two-thirds of the previous turn.

When the size or shape of the part is not uniform, the bandage is bent back on each turn so as to make it cling more tightly. This type of bandaging is called "the spiral reverse."

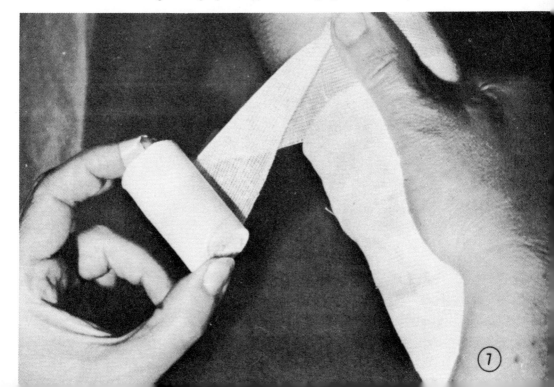

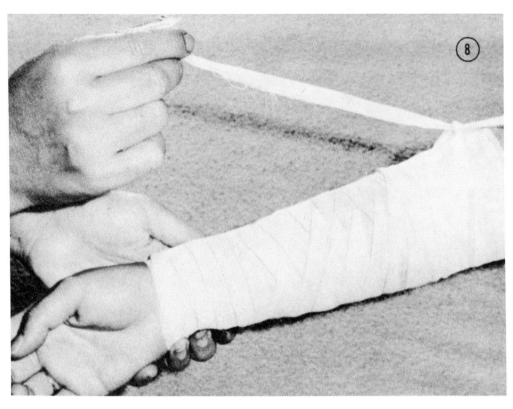

Bandages may be completed and fastened in place with adhesive tape or by splitting the bandage down the middle and tying it in a knot or bow.

This photograph shows a completed bandage about to be tested for tightness.

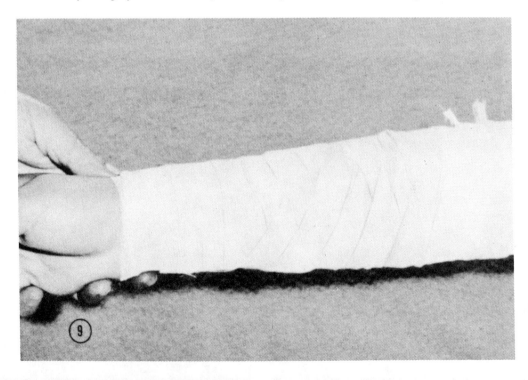

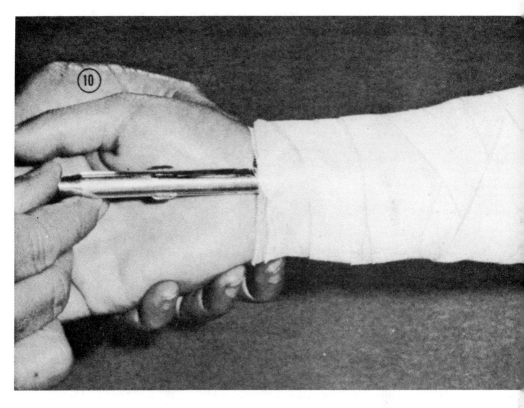

No bandage should ever be considered finished until it has been determined that it is not too tight. This test can be carried out by placing a pen or pencil under the bandage next to the skin so as to make sure that circulation is not being impaired.

CHAPTER 27

GALL BLADDER AND BILE DUCTS

(See also Chapter 40 on Liver; Chapter 70 on Stomach and Duodenum)

Where is the gall bladder and what is its function?

The gall bladder is a pear-shaped sac attached to the underside of the liver beneath the ribs in the upper right part of the abdomen. Its function is to receive bile produced and secreted by the liver and to store and concentrate it for use when needed in the processes of digestion.

For what types of food is bile particularly necessary for digestion?

Bile is essential for the digestion of fats and fat-like substances.

How does bile reach the intestinal tract?

Through a system of ducts or tubes. The cyctic duct leads from the gall bladder into the common bile duct. The common bile duct is the result of the joining of the two hepatic ducts, which originate in the liver. Bile from the liver and the gall bladder travels down the common bile duct and enters into the intestine at the ampulla of Vater in the second portion of the duodenum.

If the liver produces and secretes bile, what is the special function of the gall bladder?

To store and concentrate bile so that an additional supply can be secreted into the intestine when it is needed after the eating of a meal.

What foods often disagree with the individual who has a gall bladder disorder?

Any fried and greasy foods, French fried potatoes, heavy sauces, gravies, chicken or turkey skins, eggs

472

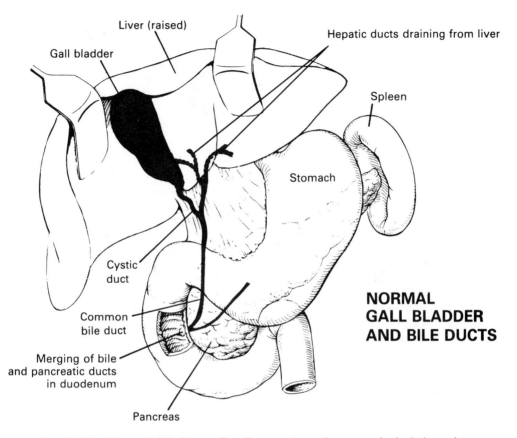

Liver (raised)

Gall bladder

Hepatic ducts draining from liver

Spleen

Stomach

Cystic duct

Common bile duct

Merging of bile and pancreatic ducts in duodenum

Pancreas

NORMAL GALL BLADDER AND BILE DUCTS

The Gall Bladder and Bile Ducts. The diagram shows the anatomical relations of a normal gall bladder and bile ducts. It is seen that the bile ducts and gall bladder are connected to the liver and to the intestinal tract.

fried in lard, turnips, cabbage, cauliflower, sprouts, radishes, certain raw fruits, etc.

Are disorders of the gall bladder and bile ducts very common?

It is generally agreed that disease of the gall bladder and malfunction of the sphincter at the end of the common duct constitute the most common causes of indigestion.

Is it necessary to operate upon the gall bladder very often?

Surgery for removal of a diseased gall bladder is the most frequently performed abdominal operation in people past middle life and is one of the most common indications for surgery in all age groups.

What causes gall bladder disease?

a. Infection with bacteria. This may

473

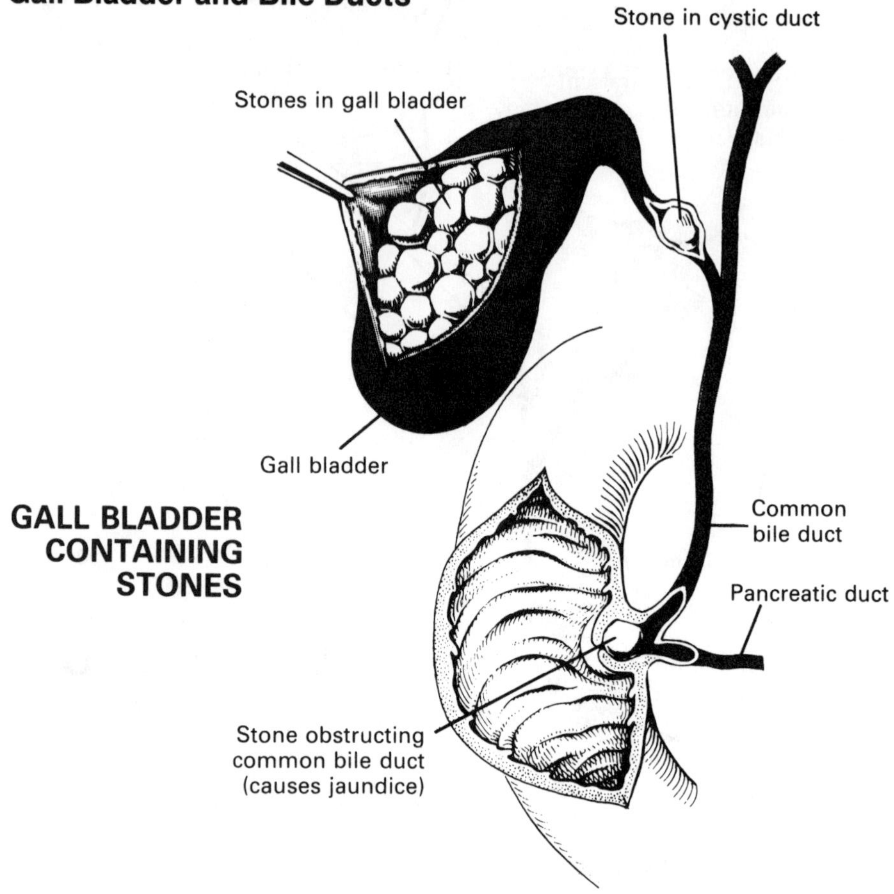

Gall Bladder and Bile Ducts

Stone in cystic duct

Stones in gall bladder

Gall bladder

GALL BLADDER CONTAINING STONES

Common bile duct

Pancreatic duct

Stone obstructing common bile duct (causes jaundice)

Gall Bladder Containing Stones. The diagram shows a gall bladder containing stones, a stone jammed in the cystic duct, and one in the common bile duct leading into the intestine. When a stone obstructs the common bile duct, jaundice ensues. People with gallstones should have them removed surgically since they never dissolve by themselves.

result in an acute or chronic inflammation in the same manner that infection involves the appendix, tonsils, or any other organ.

b. A functional disturbance in which the gall bladder fails to empty when it is called upon to secrete bile.

c. A chemical disturbance causing stones to precipitate out from the bile. These stones may create an obstruction to the passage of bile along the ducts and into the intestinal tract.

Are gallstones always caused by an upset in chemistry within the gall bladder?

No. Gallstones may result from a chemical disturbance, or they may form as a result of infection within the gall bladder.

How prevalent are gallstones?

It is estimated that approximately one out of four women and one out of eight men will develop gallstones at some time before reaching sixty years of age.

Is there a special type of person who is most likely to develop gall bladder disease?

Yes. It is thought that the heavyset type of person who eats a large amount of fats and greases is most likely to develop gall bladder disease. However, the condition is seen in all ages and in all types of people.

At what age does gall bladder disease usually develop?

In the thirties and forties, although it is occasionally seen in younger people.

Does childbearing predispose one to the formation of gallstones?

Yes. Pregnancy often produces a disturbance in fat and cholesterol metabolism. This is often followed by stone formation within a few months after the pregnancy has terminated.

Does gall bladder disease often take place *during* pregnancy?

Not very frequently. (It is seen most commonly in women who have had one or two children.)

Does gall bladder disease tend to run in families or to be inherited?

Only insofar as there is a tendency to inherit the type of body configuration, the type of chemical metabolism, and the type of eating habits that one's parents maintain.

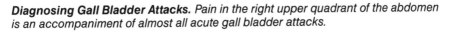

Diagnosing Gall Bladder Attacks. Pain in the right upper quadrant of the abdomen is an accompaniment of almost all acute gall bladder attacks.

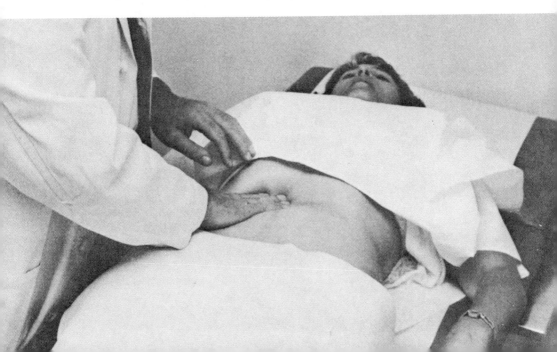

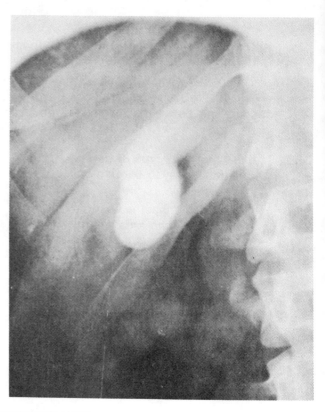

X-ray of a Normal Gall Bladder. In order to determine more accurately the presence of gall bladder disease, x-rays are taken after the giving of a medication which functions as a dye and, in the x-ray, lights up the interior of the gall bladder. If the gall bladder fails to light up or visualize, it indicates the presence of disease. Most stones appear as negative shadows in the x-rays.

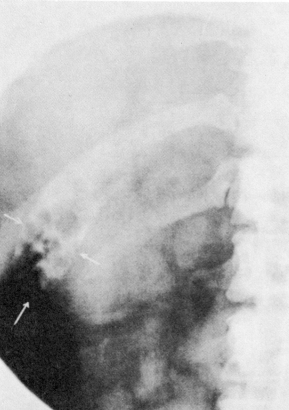

X-ray of a Gall Bladder Containing Stones. The stones in this x-ray show up as negative shadows surrounded by dye. Such a finding is a clear-cut indication for surgical removal of the gall bladder. This procedure (cholecystectomy) is safe and effective.

What takes place when the gall bladder becomes acutely inflamed?

The blood supply to the wall of the gall bladder may be interfered with, and the gall bladder may become filled with pus, or its walls may undergo gangrenous changes as the result of inadequate circulation.

What causes most acute inflammations of the gall bladder?

A stone blocking the cystic duct, the outlet from the gall bladder.

What takes place when there is a chronic inflammation of the gall bladder?

Stones, resulting either from previous inflammation and infection or from an upset in chemistry within the gall bladder, will be associated with a thickening and chronic inflammation of the gall bladder wall. This will lead to poor filling and emptying or even to nonfunctioning of the gall bladder.

What takes place when there is a functional disorder of the gall bladder or bile ducts?

This condition is characterized by failure of the gall bladder to empty and secrete bile when it is called upon to do so. Or there may be spasm at the outlet of the common bile duct, which interferes with the free passage of bile into the intesti-

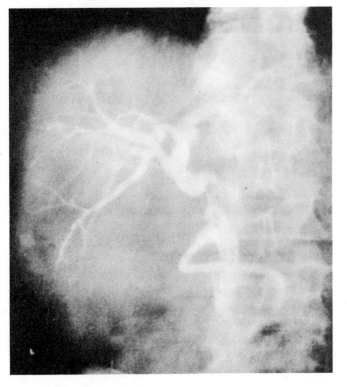

X-rays Showing the Outline of the Normal Bile Ducts Leading from the Liver into the Intestinal Tract. When the dye is injected into the veins, it travels to the bile ducts, and x-rays taken shortly thereafter show the lighting up of these structures. The outlines shown above would be distorted with negative shadows if gallstones were present.

Gall Bladder and Bile Ducts

nal tract. The patient has indigestion, heartburn, and an inability to digest fatty foods, greases, and certain raw fruits and vegetables.

Are functional disorders of the gall bladder usually accompanied by the formation of gallstones?

Not necessarily.

Is there any way to prevent gall bladder disease or the symptoms of a poorly functioning gall bladder?

Moderation in one's diet—with the eating of small quantities of fats, fried foods, and greases—will cut down on the demands made upon the gall bladder and may lessen the chances of symptoms due to inadequate function.

How can one tell if he has gall bladder disease?

a. Acute gall bladder disease (acute cholecystitis) is accompanied by an elevation in temperature, nausea, and vomiting, along with pain and tenderness in the upper right portion of the abdomen beneath the ribs. An x ray or sonogram (see Chapter 67, on Sonography) of the gall bladder may reveal a nonfunctioning organ or may demonstrate the presence of stones. A blood count may show the presence of an acute inflammation.

b. Chronic gall bladder disease (chronic cholecystitis) when accompanied by stones may cause excruciating attacks of colicky pain in the upper right portion of the abdomen. This is usually due to a stone being stuck in the cys-

tic duct or bile duct. The pain often radiates to the right shoulder or through to the back. There is nausea, vomiting, and tenderness in the abdomen, which may cease abruptly within a half hour or so if the stone drops back into the gall bladder or passes through the obstructed duct. X-ray studies in chronic gall bladder disease usually show a nonfunctioning gall bladder and sometimes demonstrate the presence of gallstones.

c. Functional disturbances of the gall bladder evidence themselves by chronic indigestion, inability to digest fats, greases, and certain raw fruits and vegetables, and heartburn. X-ray studies in these cases may show poor filling and poor emptying of the gall bladder.

Are there tests that can make a diagnosis of gall bladder disease?

Yes. An x-ray test known as a cholecystogram. This is done by giving the patient a specific dye in the form of pills. Some hours later, x rays of the gall bladder are taken, and if the organ is normal, the dye will fill it up and outline its contours smoothly. The x ray will also show emptying after the ingestion of a fatty meal. Sometimes, instead of giving the dye by mouth, it is injected into the veins prior to taking the x ray. Failure of the gall bladder to show upon x ray usually indicates the presence of disease. In other instances, stones are seen as negative shadows on the cholecystogram x rays.

A sonogram is also a good test to show presence or absence of gall bladder disease. This test is carried out by recording ultrasound waves that echo over the region of the gall bladder. Irregularities in the recording of the waves may demonstrate the presence of gallstones.

What is the significance of a gall bladder not showing on gall bladder x-ray film?

Almost invariably this shows that the gall bladder is not functioning. Often, if the gall bladder fails to visualize with the dye, a second and larger dose of dye is given. Should the gall bladder not show with a double dose of dye, it is clearcut evidence that the gall bladder is diseased or, in rare instances, that advanced liver disease is present.

Do gallstones always show on x-ray examination?

No. In some cases there may be many stones present, and still they will not show on x ray.

Can x rays show stones in the bile ducts?

Yes. A new diagnostic process called intravenous cholangiography will demonstrate stones in the bile ducts. This is performed by injecting the dye directly into a vein of the patient's arm and taking x rays immediately thereafter.

Is this type of test dangerous?

No, except in the very rare case where an allergy to the dye exists.

Is the medical management for functional disorders of the gall bladder very helpful?

Yes, when the patient cooperates by adhering closely to a sensible diet and when medications are taken as advised.

How does a physician decide whether to advise medical or surgical treatment for gall bladder disease?

The functional disorders of the gall bladder, when not accompanied by stone formation, are best treated medically. All other disturbances of the gall bladder are best treated surgically.

Does a patient with gallstones always have to be operated upon?

Not in all instances. There are many people who have stones in their gall bladder that produce no symptoms. However, if gallstones cause any symptoms whatever, it is safer to operate than not to operate.

When is a gall bladder operation mandatory?

a. When the organ is acutely inflamed.
b. When the patient is suffering from repeated attacks of severe colicky pain due to the presence of stones.
c. When the gall bladder is known to have stones and the patient is suffering from chronic indigestion, nausea, flatulence, and occasional pains in the abdomen.
d. When jaundice (yellow discoloration of the skin) occurs as a result of a stone obstructing the bile ducts.

What is the medical management for gall bladder disease?

a. The avoidance of those foods that

produce indigestion, such as fats, greases, sauces, stuffings, and certain raw vegetables and raw fruits.

b. The eating of a bland, well-rounded diet, with no large meals.

c. The use of certain medications to relieve spasm of the bile ducts and to reduce excess acidity in the stomach.

Does surgery always relieve the symptoms caused by a functional disorder when the gall bladder is known to be free of stones?

Although a certain percentage of these patients are benefited by gall bladder removal (cholecystectomy), others are not.

What can happen if an operation upon the gall bladder is not performed when indicated?

a. An acute inflammation of the gall bladder may progress to gangrene, with rupture of the organ. This may lead to peritonitis and possible death.

b. Recurring attacks of colic due to an obstructing gallstone may lead to the stone being passed into the common bile duct, where it will obstruct the passage of bile and cause jaundice.

c. If jaundice takes place because of an obstructing stone and surgery is not performed, the patient may die from liver damage and the toxic effects of prolonged bile obstruction.

Is jaundice always produced by gallstones?

No. There are many other causes for jaundice. The most common is hepatitis, an inflammation of the liver.

How can one tell whether jaundice is caused by an obstructing gallstone or some other cause?

There are many tests that help make a conclusive diagnosis as to whether the jaundice is obstructive or is inflammatory in nature. A thorough history and physical examination, x-ray examinations, and several blood chemical tests will usually reveal the correct diagnosis.

Do stones predispose toward the formation of cancer in the gall bladder?

Yes. Approximately 1 to 2 percent of those who have stones in the gall bladder will eventually develop a cancer. This is an important reason for advocating surgery upon gall bladders containing stones, regardless of the presence or absence of symptoms.

Is removal of the gall bladder (cholecystectomy) a dangerous operative procedure?

No. It is no more dangerous than the removal of an appendix.

Can gallstones be dissolved with medications?

Recently, the administration of concentrated bile salts over a period of many months has resulted in dissolving some gallstones. However, this method of treatment is still in the experimental stage and is not a substitute for surgical removal of the stones.

When operating upon the gall bladder, does the surgeon remove the entire organ or just the stones?

In almost all cases, the gall bladder is removed. However, there are occasional cases where the organ is so acutely inflamed and the patient so sick that the surgeon may decide merely to remove the stones and place a drain into the gall bladder. This procedure takes less time to perform and carries with it less risk.

Are the bile ducts removed when operating upon the gall bladder?

No. There must be a free passage of bile from the liver into the intestines. The bile ducts are therefore left in place.

How does the surgeon remove stones from the bile duct?

He makes a small incision into the duct, picks out the stone or stones with a specially designed instrument, and then drains the duct with a rubber tube (T tube). This tube is removed anywhere from a few days to a few weeks later, depending upon the subsequent tests and x-ray findings.

How long does it take to perform a cholecystectomy?

From three-quarters of an hour to one and a half hours, depending upon the severity of the inflammatory process.

What type of anesthesia is used for gall bladder operations?

A general inhalation anesthesia.

Is it common practice to remove the appendix while operating primarily for a gall bladder condition?

This used to be done quite often, but since appendicitis has become so rare, the practice has been discontinued by most surgeons.

What special preparations are necessary prior to gall bladder surgery?

Usually none for the patient being operated upon for a simple chronic inflammatory condition without jaundice. However, patients who have acute inflammation or who are suffering from jaundice require considerable special preoperative preparation.

What are the special preoperative measures used in these cases?

a. The passage of a tube through the nose to make sure the stomach is empty at the time of surgery.
b. The giving of intravenous medications before operation in the form of fluids, glucose, and certain vitamins, particularly Vitamin K in the presence of jaundice to protect against possible postoperative hemorrhage.
c. The giving of antibiotics to the patient who has an acutely inflamed gall bladder or an inflammation of the bile ducts.

Are blood transfusions given in gall bladder operations?

Not usually; only in the most seriously sick and complicated cases.

Are private nurses necessary after gall bladder operations?

If the patient can afford it, a private

Gall Bladder and Bile Ducts

nurse for two or three days will add greatly to his comfort.

How long a hospital stay is required?

Approximately nine days.

How soon after surgery can the patient get out of bed?

For the ordinary case, on the first or second postoperative day.

Where are the incisions made for gall bladder disease?

Either a longitudinal incision in the upper right portion of the abdomen or an oblique incision beneath the rib cage on the right side is carried out for a distance of five to seven inches.

Are drains usually placed in gall bladder wounds?

Yes. One or two rubber drains will be inserted following surgery. These will stay in place anywhere from six to ten days.

Are gall bladder operations especially painful?

No. There may be some pain on deep breathing or coughing for a few days after surgery, but the operative wound is not exceptionally painful.

What special postoperative measures are carried out?

a. In the ordinary operation for a chronically inflamed gall bladder with stones, there are few special postoperative orders. The patient may eat the day after surgery, but fats, greases, raw fruits and vegetables should not be included. Antibiotics may be given if there is fear of infection. A stomach tube is passed through the nose and kept in place for the first day in order to avoid discomfort from distention.

b. The patient operated upon for an acute gall bladder inflammation or for jaundice will probably receive intravenous solutions, drainage of the stomach through a tube inserted through the nose, medications with Vitamin K to counteract jaundice, and large doses of antibiotics for a few days. Occasionally, blood transfusions are also given.

How long does it take the average gall bladder wound to heal?

Anywhere from twelve to fourteen days.

Can a patient live a normal life after removal of the gall bladder?

Yes.

What takes over the function of the gall bladder after it has been removed?

Bile continues to flow from the liver directly into the intestinal tract. The bile ducts take over many of the duties of the gall bladder.

Is it common for indigestion to persist for several weeks after removal of the gall bladder?

Yes.

Should a woman whose gall bladder has been removed allow herself to become pregnant again?

Yes, if she so desires.

Is it necessary to follow dietary precautions after gall bladder removal?

Yes. The patient should stay on the same kind of diet he followed before surgery, that is, a bland, low-fat diet.

How soon after the removal of a stone from the common bile duct will jaundice disappear?

Within several weeks.

Do symptoms of gall bladder disease ever persist or recur after surgery?

Yes. Approximately 10 percent of patients who have been operated upon for gall bladder disease will continue to have symptoms after surgery. These symptoms are thought to be caused by spasms of the lower end of the common bile duct (biliary dyskinesia).

Do patients ever form stones again after they have once been removed?

If the gall bladder has been removed, they cannot re-form stones in the gall bladder. However, a very small percentage of patients may re-form stones in the common bile duct or in the stump of the cystic duct that has been left behind.

What treatment is carried out when stones are inadvertently left behind in the common bile duct or when stones re-form in the common bile duct after initial surgery?

Attempts are made to remove left-behind stones in one of the following ways:

a. A specially designed metal instrument with a basket attached to its end is passed through the channel leading from the skin into the bile duct. When this instrument, as determined by x ray, has gone beyond the stone in the common bile duct, the basket is opened and the instrument is withdrawn. As the instrument is withdrawn, the stone is snared by the basket and comes out of the body with the instrument.

b. By endoscopy. This entails passing a specially designed tube through the mouth and down through the stomach into the duodenum. The opening of the bile duct into the duodenum is then dilated, thus permitting the stones to fall out into the duodenum where they will do no harm.

c. If the above methods fail, reoperation to remove the stones is necessary.

Can any doctor pass a tube down into the duodenum to retrieve stones from the bile duct?

No. This is a very specialized procedure carried out by highly trained physicians known as *endoscopists.*

Is there any way to prevent stones from reforming?

Not really, except that one should guard against infection and follow a sane, sensible, bland, lowfat diet.

Does gall bladder removal affect the life span?

Not at all.

What are the chances of recovery from a gall bladder operation?

The mortality rate from gall bladder

483

Gall Bladder and Bile Ducts

surgery is less than 1 percent. A fatality occurs mainly in the very complicated case or in people who have neglected to seek treatment early.

How soon after a gall bladder operation can one do the following:

Bathe:
   In about eleven to twelve days.
Walk out in the street:
   Two weeks.
Walk up and down stairs:
   Ten to twelve days.
Perform household duties:
   Four weeks.

Drive a car:
   Six weeks.
Resume sexual relations:
   Four to five weeks.
Return to work:
   Five to six weeks.
Resume all physical activities:
   Six weeks.

How often should one return for a checkup after a gall bladder operation?

About six months after surgery and then again a year after surgery.

CHAPTER  **THE HAND**

(See also Chapter 10 on Arthritis; Chapter 14 on Bones, Muscles, Tendons, and Joints; Chapter 26 on First Aid in Emergencies; Chapter 62 on Rheumatic Fever)

How common are hand injuries and other conditions affecting this vital structure?

Approximately a third of all accident victims suffer from hand-related injuries, and millions of others are afflicted with painful arthritis and inflammatory disorders of the hand. The importance of normal hand function cannot be overstated. Deformities and impairment cause enormous socioeconomic and psychological problems for all peoples and age groups. Due to the magnitude of the problem and the need for expert care, hand surgery has now evolved into a comprehensive medical specialty. The hand, a magnificently designed organ, is extremely complex in structure, function, and repairs. The hand surgeon requires special training in order to afford proper treatment.

What is the most common hand injury?

The fingertip injury.

Is this a minor injury?

No. There is no such thing as a minor injury to the hand. Without proper treatment, poor healing, painful scars, swelling, loss of sensation, joint stiffening, and infection may lead to a severe disability of the entire hand.

What are common problems with fingertip injuries?

a. Loss of the skin and the fingertip pad.
b. Loss of the nail and damage to the nail bed.
c. Fractures of the bone and joint.

All of the above may require surgical treatment. Skin grafting, repair of the nail bed, and reduction and fix-

485

The Hand

ation of the fracture are frequently necessary.

Do amputated fingertips grow back?

No. However, young children have the peculiar ability to heal and remodel tissues in a way that can compensate for small losses.

Are nerve and tendon injuries common?

Yes, particularly with deep cuts in the wrist, palm, and finger.

With a nerve injury, is the finger always completely numb?

No. There are two nerves in each finger. If only one is injured, some feeling is still present.

With a tendon injury, is all finger motion lost?

No. There are two flexor tendons and one extensor tendon in each finger. If only one tendon is cut, some movement will still be present.

Can nerves be repaired?

Yes. Using microsurgery, the nerves may be accurately repaired. However, under the best circumstances, the nerves may not regenerate, or heal, completely.

When should a tendon be repaired?

Formerly, flexor tendons cut in the finger were not repaired immediately. Most hand surgeons now feel that better function will result if the

Ultrasonic therapy is used to hasten the pace of recovery of an injured hand.

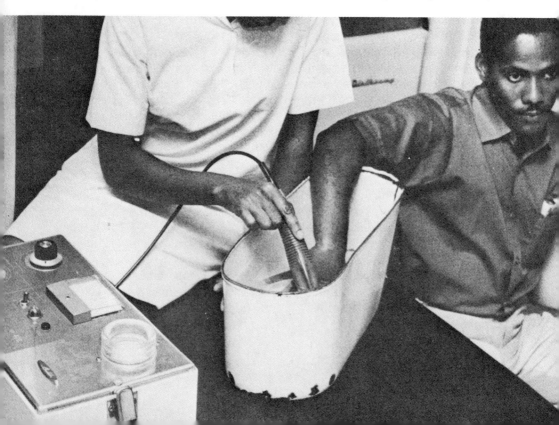

tendons are repaired soon after injury.

What is the major problem following tendon repairs?

Scar tissue that binds the tendon and prevents its movement.

What is required for successful tendon repair?

Delicate surgery and a cooperative patient pursuing a carefully planned postoperative hand therapy program. By special exercises and splinting, the patient must actively break up the scar tissue to regain good tendon function.

What is tendon grafting?

A surgical technique in which a "spare" tendon is taken from another part of the body and is used to replace a damaged tendon in the hand.

What is a "jammed" finger?

This is a nonspecific term that refers to a joint, bone, or tendon injury of the fingers. These are often neglected and lead to permanent and disabling finger deformities. Each injury should be carefully examined with x rays. Examples of the jammed finger are the baseball finger, boutonniere finger, and the skier's thumb.

What is a "baseball" finger?

A bent fingertip, which results from a tendon rupture. This is also called a "mallet" finger and is usually caused by a direct blow to the fingertip from a baseball, football, volleyball, etc.

What is a boutonniere, or buttonhole, deformity?

This is a bent finger caused by a tendon rupture. Here the middle finger joint buttonholes through the ruptured tendon.

How does one treat the mallet and boutonniere deformities?

By splinting for about six weeks.

Is a dislocated finger a minor injury?

No. The dislocation is often "popped" in by the patient with no further treatment. However, this is frequently followed by prolonged pain, swelling, and stiffness. Each injury requires followup, evaluation with x rays, and, in most cases, the finger is splinted.

What is a skier's thumb?

This is a torn ligament of the thumb, which can happen to anyone but is particularly common among skiers. A completely torn ligament requires surgical repair.

What is a fracture?

A fracture, crack, or chip all mean a broken bone. The hand is the most common site for fracture in the entire body.

What are the common signs of a fracture?

Painful swelling and deformity in the region of the bone.

What is a "boxer's" fracture?

This is a fracture near the knuckle of the little finger. It usually results from the fist striking a hard object.

The Hand

How are fractures treated?

Most should be splinted or placed in a cast for three to four weeks. If the fracture is out of place, the bone fragment must be accurately placed in proper position.

Do most fractures heal rapidly?

Yes, with one exception: fractures of the scaphoid bone. This is a small bone in the wrist located deep in the anatomical snuffbox on the thumb side of the hand. It is possibly the most difficult bone in the body to heal and usually requires three to four months of casting. Some cases may require surgery.

Is the anatomical snuffbox area in the wrist a common area for pain?

Yes. Arthritis, fractures, and tendon inflammations frequently cause pain in this area.

What is de Quervain's disease?

A painful tendon inflammation in the anatomical snuffbox. The tendons that straighten the thumb are caught or squeezed in a narrow tunnel at the side of the wrist.

What is a "trigger" finger?

Painful clicking or snapping occurs when the finger moves. The flexor tendons are caught or squeezed in a narrow tunnel at the base of the finger.

Is there effective treatment for de Quervain's disease and trigger finger?

Yes. Local injections may give some relief. Surgical unroofing of the tunnel gives permanent relief. These are simple operations followed by good results.

What is the most common cause of pins and needles or numbness in the fingers?

The so-called carpal tunnel syndrome.

What is the carpal tunnel syndrome?

It is a condition in which there is numbness and weakness of the thumb, index, and middle finger along with pain, especially at night. The condition is caused by a pinched nerve in the wrist.

What causes the pinching of the nerve in the carpal tunnel syndrome?

A tightness of the carpal ligament, which stretches across the front of the wrist. This tightness presses upon the median nerve as it courses through the narrowed tunnel from the wrist to the hand.

What is the treatment for the carpal tunnel syndrome?

An incision is made on the anterior surface of the wrist, and the carpal ligament is cut. This enlarges the tunnel and takes the pressure off the pinched nerve.

Are operations to relieve the carpal tunnel syndrome very successful?

Yes.

What is the most common cause of numbness in the little finger?

A pinched nerve at the elbow.

Are there other causes for numbness and pain in the hand?

Yes. Neck and shoulder problems, as well as diseases such as diabetes, may cause these symptoms.

How does one diagnose a pinched nerve?

By examination and special electrodiagnostic tests.

Is surgery necessary for a pinched nerve?

Yes, if the pain and numbness are progressive or constant and if there is evidence of nerve damage.

Is nerve surgery safe?

Yes. It is delicate, but with little risk to the patient. In most cases, the severe pain is relieved almost immediately.

What is Dupuytren's contracture?

Thickening of the tissue beneath the skin of the palm. This tissue is called fascia. The thickened tissue may cause the finger to contract toward the palm.

Is medication helpful in preventing Dupuytren's contracture?

No. The only treatment of value is surgery.

Is surgery necessary for all cases?

No. Surgical excision of the fascia is reserved for those cases in which deformities are present.

Is the hand a common site for tumors?

Yes. However, the vast majority are benign and do not threaten either life or function. Surgery is necessary only if the tumor is painful, enlarging, or interferes with function.

What is a ganglion?

It is a benign tumor or cyst usually arising on the back of the wrist.

Where do infections commonly occur in the hand?

At the fingertips and along the tendons. A paronychia is an abscess around the nail, and a felon is an abscess in the pad of the fingertip.

What is the proper care for infections?

Antibiotics, elevation of the infected part, rest, saltwater soaks, and incision and drainage if an abscess is present. Infections of the hand tend to be underestimated and neglected. Unless properly treated, they may rapidly spread and destroy normal tissues.

Are human bites serious injuries?

Yes. These often lead to extremely serious infections in the knuckle joints. The most common cause of human bites is a fight in which a fist strikes an opponent's mouth. Hospitalization is generally required for proper care.

What is the cause of birth deformities of the hand?

In most cases, the cause is unknown; in others, a family history of such deformities can be elicited. (See Chapter 35, on Genetic Medicine.)

What are the common birth deformities of the hand?

Webbing of the fingers, called syn-

489

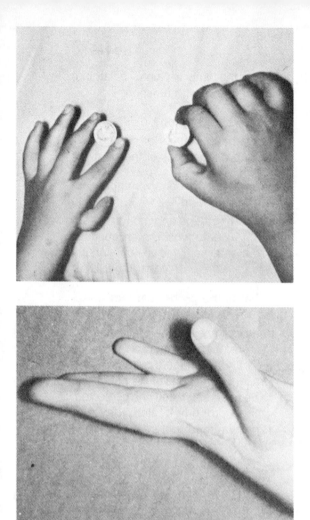

Birth Deformities. *A rudimentary thumb is a birth deformity. To remedy this condition the useless thumb is amputated and the index finger is pollicized, or transposed, to create a new thumb. The operation results in a four-fingered but useful hand.*

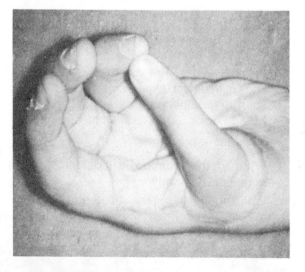

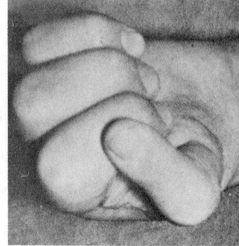

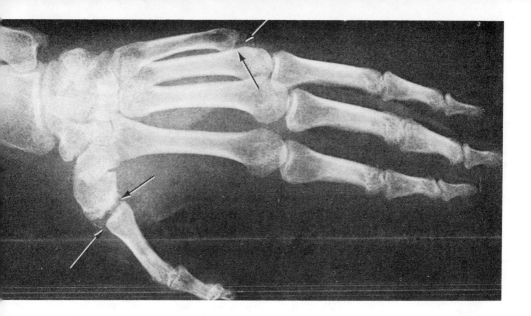

dactyly, and extra fingers, called polydactyly. With surgery, the webbed fingers can be separated and the extra fingers removed.

When should surgery be performed?

Generally anytime after one year of age. It is wise to complete all surgery during the preschool years.

Can absent fingers be replaced?

There are no normal substitutes for missing fingers. Unrealistic surgery should be avoided. In most cases the child will adapt quite well to an

Birth Deformities. Sometimes a little finger is transposed to replace a useless thumb. The arrows in this x-ray point to the sutures which unite the transposed finger to the metacarpal bones of the thumb and to the place where the little finger was amputated.

absent finger. However, when a thumb is missing, it is frequently beneficial to fashion a thumb from one of the other fingers. This is a major operative procedure (pollicization), but results are often very rewarding.

491

CHAPTER 29 THE HEART

(See also Chapter 5 on Aging; Chapter 13 on Blood Vessels and Blood Vessel Surgery; Chapter 62 on Rheumatic Fever; Chapter 73 on Transplantation of Organs)

What is the structure of the heart?

The heart is a hollow, globular, muscular organ composed of four compartments. It is divided into a left side and a right side, each of which has two connecting chambers—an atrium and a ventricle.

The right atrium receives blood supplied to it by two great veins—the inferior and superior vena cavas. These vessels carry to the right atrium the blood from all the veins of the body. This venous blood is dark red in color, having a low proportion of oxygen and a high proportion of waste carbon dioxide and other products absorbed from the intestinal tract or manufactured by the tissues. From the right atrium, passing through a valve called the tricuspid

valve, this blood travels to the right ventricle. From there blood passes through another valve called the pulmonic valve and then enters the blood vessels of the lungs. Here the oxygen supply of the venous blood is replenished, and the waste carbon dioxide is passed out into the exhaled air. From the lungs, the reoxygenated blood passes on to the left side of the heart, first entering the left atrium. From there it passes through another intervening valve called the mitral valve and enters the powerful and muscular left ventricle. The left ventricle contracts forcefully and expels this fresh blood through the aortic valve into the largest artery of the body—the aorta. From there on, the reoxygenated blood is distributed to

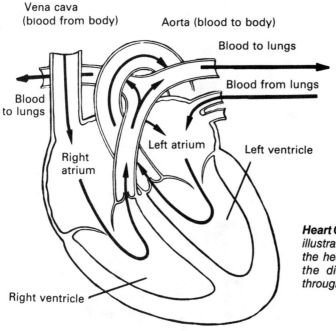

Vena cava
(blood from body)

Aorta (blood to body)

Blood to lungs

Blood from lungs

Blood
to lungs

Left atrium

Left ventricle

Right
atrium

Right ventricle

Heart Chambers. *This diagram illustrates the four chambers of the heart; the arrows indicate the direction of blood flow through the heart.*

all the blood vessels and tissues of the body.

What is the function of the heart?

The heart is the motor, or main source of energy, that supplies the propelling force to keep the bloodstream in motion through all the blood vessels of the body. This organ, hardly larger than a fist, pumps an average of six thousand quarts of blood a day and can multiply its efforts manyfold when necessary. It beats incessantly during life, contracting at an average rate of seventy-eight times per minute, or approximately a hundred and ten thousand times daily.

Poor heart action leads to poor circulation, which in turn leads to de-rangement and impairment of the function of the vital tissues of the body.

How can a doctor tell if a patient has a "good heart"?

He evaluates the heart on the basis of the patient's clinical history, the physical examination, and by other tests, such as fluoroscopy, x ray, and electrocardiography, which are carried out when additional investigation is indicated.

What is meant by the expression a "strong heart"?

Any heart that is normal in structure and that functions efficiently can be "strong."

493

The Heart

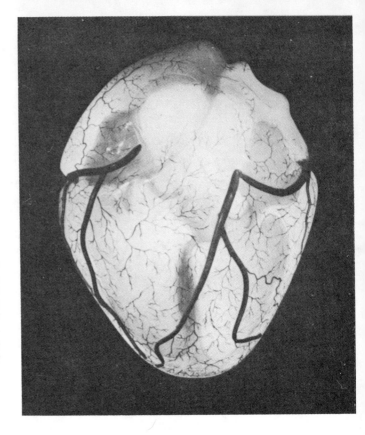

The Heart Muscle. The heart is a hollow muscular organ with a network of arteries that supply blood to its muscle tissue. A powerful pump, the heart contracts and expands approximately 70 to 80 times a minute to keep blood flowing through the body's circulatory system.

What is meant by the expression a "weak heart"?

A heart that functions inefficiently because of underlying disease or defect in structure.

Does heart trouble tend to be inherited or to run in families?

While certain conditions that attack the heart may tend to run in families, heart disease, by and large, is *not* inherited. The fact that one member of a family suffers from a heart ailment should not alarm related individuals about the condition of their own heart. However, it should serve as an additional incentive for these individuals to visit their physician regularly so that he may outline a preventive program if indicated.

Does a patient with a "poor heart" ever develop a "strong heart"?

This depends upon the age of the individual as well as the primary cause of the heart condition. Many types of heart trouble can be treated effectively, and in certain cases complete cure can result.

Do children with heart trouble ever outgrow it?

The term "outgrow" is one that physicians no longer use. The thought that a condition will clear up without treatment often encourages a negligent attitude rather than a positive approach to a heart problem. Strictly speaking, heart trouble is not outgrown.

The popularity of this term had its

494

origin in the fact that some heart murmurs heard in childhood were found to disappear later on in life. In actuality, these murmurs were not really indicative of true heart disease but were innocent, atypical heart sounds. A true murmur indicative of an actual organic heart disease almost never disappears spontaneously.

Is strenuous physical exertion bad for someone with a normal heart?

Strenuous physical exertion probably has no significant harmful effect upon a normal heart.

Is strenuous physical exercise dangerous for someone with a "weak heart"?

Patients who suffer from heart disease should not indulge in strenuous physical exercise! This does not mean that such patients should make complete invalids of themselves. Rather, they should function within the range of limitations dictated by their own particular heart condition. The specific advice of their physician should be followed carefully.

What effect does smoking tobacco have upon the heart?

It is now generally agreed among most doctors that smoking is harmful to the heart. It causes constriction of small and large arteries, which supply the muscle of the heart, and thus deprives the heart of much-needed oxygen. In some patients, smoking manifests itself by causing spasms of the coronary artery, by creating irregularities in the rhythm of the heart, or by elevating the blood pressure. It is estimated that heart attacks are much more common among smokers than among non-smokers. Certainly, people with heart disease should discontinue smoking.

Is drinking of alcohol bad for the heart?

Not particularly, unless drinking is excessive and prolonged. Recent studies have shown that under the latter conditions, definite injury to the heart muscle can occur.

Is it harmful to the heart to take aspirin?

No.

What medications in common usage are harmful to the heart?

Most of the commonly prescribed medications have no effect at all upon the heart.

Is excessive emotional strain bad for the heart?

Yes, but the normal heart tolerates acute emotional, as well as physical, strain remarkably well. Chronic emotional strain may eventually cause heart disease. Also, exceptional strain caused by a life crisis may precipitate an acute heart attack in an otherwise normal heart. Clearly, prolonged emotional strain is deleterious to a heart whose function is already impaired by primary, underlying disease.

How can one tell if pain in the heart region is due to a heart condition or is due to trouble in some other organ?

Heart pain is an extremely variable

symptom. It requires the skill of an experienced physician to evaluate whether a particular ache or pain actually arises from the heart. Frequently, he must resort to procedures such as electrocardiogram or x ray to reinforce his clinical opinion.

Is there such a thing as a "broken heart"? In other words, can the heart be affected by grief or disappointment?

The term "broken heart" is, for all practical purposes, a purely poetic expression.

Do people with normal hearts tend to outlive those who have heart trouble?

Other things being equal, yes.

How often should people have their heart examined?

People without a specific history of heart disease should not think in terms of having their heart checked. Rather, they should think in terms of a periodic, comprehensive physical examination.

The patient with heart disease should have his heart examined at regular intervals, as advised by his physician. These intervals may vary greatly from patient to patient.

Do men have heart trouble more often than women?

Men have a much greater tendency toward diseases of the coronary arteries and therefore are more prone to develop angina pectoris or coronary thrombosis. Other forms of heart disease are equally distributed between the sexes.

496

Do thin people tend to get heart conditions less frequently than obese people?

Statistically, the incidence of coronary artery disease is definitely greater among overweight people. Other forms of heart disease do not appear to be appreciably greater among the obese. But it should be remembered that obesity places an additional burden upon an already weakened or impaired heart.

Can doctors predict length of life by listening to the heart and making heart tests?

No. A doctor can merely determine whether a heart is functioning properly or whether it is diseased. However, in spite of all modern medical advances, it is impossible to make more than a rough guess as to the life span of the patient with a diseased heart. Certainly, there is no basis whatsoever for predictions of longevity in the patient with an apparently normal heart.

IMPAIRED HEART FUNCTION AND HEART DISEASE

What are some of the common causes of impaired heart function and heart disease?

a. The heart muscle itself may be weakened so that it cannot contract with sufficient force. This may be caused by poor nourishment to the heart muscle tissue (as in disease of the arteries supplying the heart). Also, infection, inflamma-

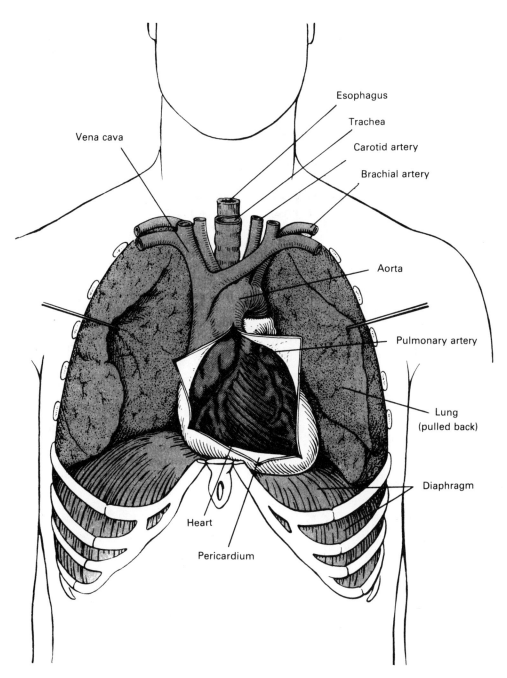

Esophagus

Trachea

Carotid artery

Brachial artery

Vena cava

Aorta

Pulmonary artery

Lung
(pulled back)

Diaphragm

Heart

Pericardium

Position of Heart in Chest Cavity. *The normal heart is shown in relation to surrounding organs. Contrary to popular belief, the heart tends to be more in the middle of the chest than on the left side, and a part of it actually extends over into the right chest cavity.*

497

tion, toxins, hormonal disorders, or blood-mineral imbalance may weaken the muscle tissue of the heart.

b. The heart valves may not function properly—either because they do not open and close adequately or because they were defectively formed or absent as a result of a developmental birth deformity.

Heart valve disorders may also be caused by acquired disease, the most common of which is rheumatic fever. Other less common causes of heart valve dysfunction are syphilis, bacterial infection, or diseases of the cell-cementing substance.

c. The heart muscle may be weakened if it has been overworked because of high blood pressure, chronic lung disease, endocrine gland disorders, anemia, abnormal connections between arteries and veins, or the above mentioned valvular disorders.

d. Congenital (inborn) defects in the wall dividing the right and left side of the heart, as well as a great variety of bizarre inborn abnormalities of the heart and connecting great blood vessels. Fortunately, these birth deformities are quite rare.

e. Inflammatory diseases of the heart muscle and sheath of the heart may be caused most likely by viral infections known as myocarditis and pericarditis.

f. Structural abnormalities of the chest cage and spine.

g. Disorders of the rhythmicity of the heart. Instead of beating regularly, the heart may adopt any of a variety of disorderly or abnormal rhythm patterns. As a result of these rhythm disorders, the heart is sometimes unable to pump blood efficiently.

h. Tumors of the heart may seriously interfere with good heart function. These tumors may arise in the heart tissue itself, or they may spread to the heart from other organs. (Such tumors of the heart are a rare cause of cardiac impairment.)

What are the more common causes of heart disease?

a. Coronary artery disease. (The coronary arteries are the blood vessels supplying the blood to the heart muscle.)

b. High blood pressure.

c. Chronic lung disease.

d. Congenital (inborn) heart abnormalities.

e. Rheumatic fever.

HEART FAILURE

What is heart failure?

Heart failure, medically known as cardiac decompensation, may be caused by one or more of the conditions enumerated above. The term is applied when the heart is no longer able to accommodate to the normal circulatory requirements of the body.

Ordinarily, the human heart has

sufficient reserve strength to compensate for most ordinary handicaps in the course of the above-mentioned disorders. However, as the disorder increases in severity and as the heart muscle becomes more and more fatigued, the heart becomes increasingly incapable of meeting its obligations.

What are the symptoms of heart failure?

a. Easy fatigability.
b. Shortness of breath, increased by mild exertion.
c. Swelling of the feet, ankles, and legs, usually increasing toward the end of the day and improving overnight.
d. Inability to lie flat in bed without becoming short of breath, thus requiring several cushions to prop up the head and chest.
e. Blueness of the lips, fingernails, and skin.
f. Accumulation of fluid in the abdomen, chest, and other areas of the body.
g. Sudden attacks of suffocation at night, forcing the patient to sit up or get out of bed and gasp for air.
h. Distention of the veins of the neck.

Acute Heart Attacks. More and more people who suffer acute heart attacks are being placed in intensive cardiac care units, where these patients are monitored 24 hours a day, and are cared for by nurses and physicians specially trained in treating cardiac emergencies.

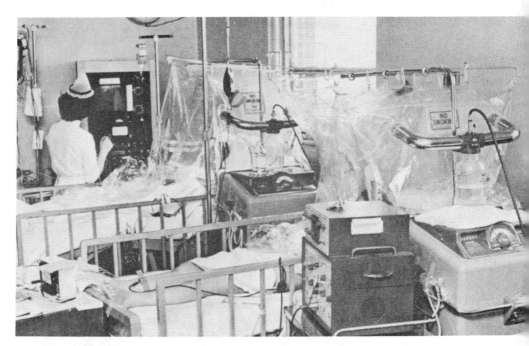

The Heart

How long does it take a damaged or strained heart to go into failure?

The time required is extremely variable from patient to patient. The heart has an amazing capacity to do its work under great handicaps for a period of many years and will continue to do so provided the obstacles do not become overwhelming.

Once the heart begins to decompensate (fail), does it mean the patient will die?

No. A decompensating heart may be bolstered for many years with proper care such as limitation of activity, salt restriction, digitalis therapy, diuretics (drugs that increase the elimination of water and salt by the kidneys), or surgery in specially indicated instances.

How does a physician evaluate the cardiac status of a patient?

a. By taking a careful history of symptoms and past illnesses.
b. By listening to the heart through a stethoscope.
c. By fluoroscoping or x raying the heart.
d. By taking an electrocardiogram.
e. By other, more exhaustive tests, such as the stress test.

What is an electrocardiogram?

The heart muscle generates a feeble, though characteristic, electrical current when it contracts and

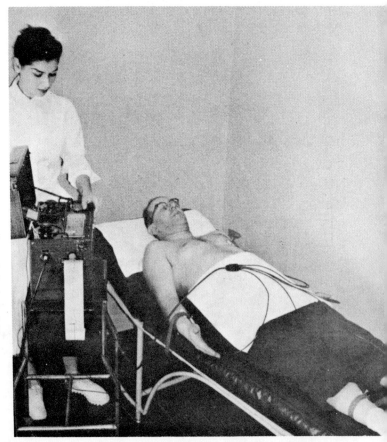

A Patient Having an Electrocardiogram Test Performed.
This is a painless procedure which indicates whether the heart is functioning normally. However, not all heart diseases can be diagnosed through this test.

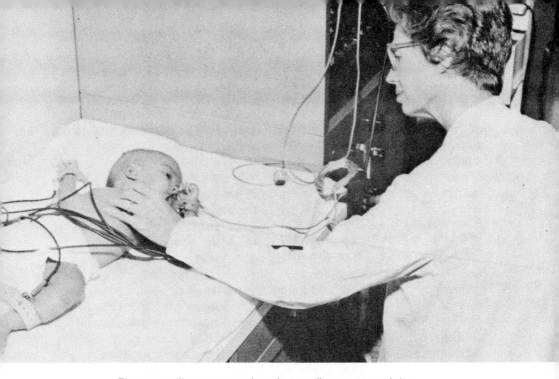

Electrocardiograms can be taken easily even on an infant.

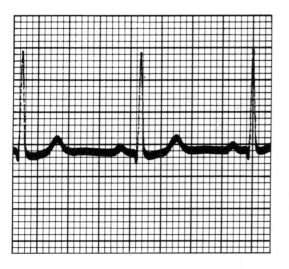

Left:
Normal Electrocardiographic Tracing. *Cardiologists interpret variations from normal tracings and thereby diagnose heart disease.*

Below:
Coronary Thrombosis. *This electrocardiographic tracing shows that the patient has had an acute cornonary thrombosis. It is not difficult to note the variation in this tracing from the normal electrocardiographic tracing shown at left.*

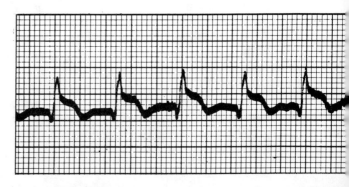

The Heart

relaxes. This current can be picked up and recorded on paper by a very sensitive instrument known as an electrocardiograph. Variations in amplitude and direction of the current may give important information concerning the heart's function and state of health.

Are electrocardiographic findings in themselves sufficient to establish a patient's cardiac status?

No. They give only supplementary information. The electrocardiogram may be completely normal in the presence of a serious heart disorder. On the other hand, it may demonstrate abnormalities at a time when the physical examination is essentially normal.

What is an exercise *stress test*?

For certain patients, heart function is normal at rest but not during exercise. The response of the heart rate and electrocardiogram to measured exercise will help find those patients whose activities must be limited.

What is an echocardiogram?

It is a test in which sound waves are directed at the heart, and echoes reflected from these waves are recorded. The pattern seen on the recording gives important information on the health of the heart muscle and heart function. The test is completely without risk.

What are radionucleotide studies of the heart?

Radioisotope substances are injected into the patient's arm vein, and energy emitted from these radioactive isotopes is measured. From these measurements one can obtain information about damage to the heart muscle and heart function. This test can be performed easily and without risk.

What is cardiac catheterization?

There are a number of situations in the evaluation of a patient's heart in which the methods listed above do not yield enough information. In such instances, cardiac catheterization may be performed. This consists of passing and threading a long, narrow, hollow plastic tube into the blood vessel of one of the extremities until it reaches one or more chambers of the heart. Pressure recordings are made through the tube, and blood samples are withdrawn. This is not a routine procedure and requires the skill of a specially trained physician. (Cardiac catheterization has become an important research tool, adding immensely to our knowledge concerning the working of the heart.)

What is angiocardiography?

Primarily, angiocardiography is used for the same reasons as cardiac catheterization and under similar circumstances. However, it does impart a somewhat different type of information. It consists of injecting a chemical into the bloodstream that is opaque to x rays. X rays of the heart are taken in rapid progression as this chemical passes through the various chambers. Like cardiac catheterization, this procedure is not employed routinely and requires specialized skills and training. However, in recent years, it has contributed greatly to our knowledge of heart function.

BLOOD PRESSURE

What is blood pressure?

Blood pressure is the force created by the contracting heart to keep the blood circulating adequately and constantly through the blood vessels of the body. In order to overcome the resistance that is present in miles of narrow blood vessels, and in order for the blood to finally arrive at the tissues with enough residual pressure to effect an interchange of chemicals, the heart must maintain a certain minimal level of pressure within the circulatory system.

How is blood pressure measured?

A tubular rubber cuff is strapped around the upper arm. The cuff is connected to an apparatus that measures pressure, and it is inflated with air while the physician listens to the arterial pulse in the crook of the elbow. The air pressure in the cuff is raised until the pulsation can no

Taking a Blood Pressure Reading. Blood pressure is the force which the heart exerts in pumping the blood through the blood vessels out to the tissues of the body. When blood pressure is high, it means that the heart is pumping with extra force. Prolonged over many years, this serious strain may eventually lead to heart failure.

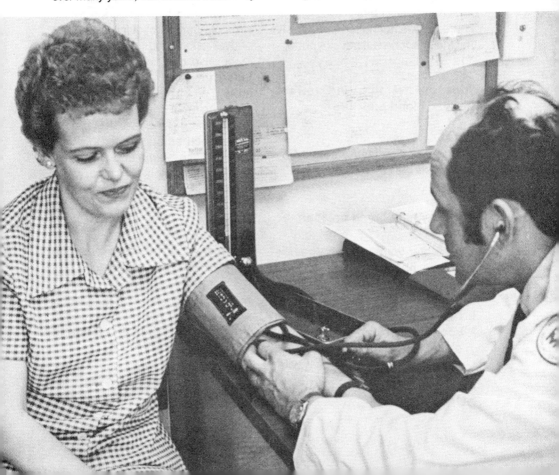

The Heart

longer be heard. After this the cuff is deflated until the physician begins to hear the pulse beat return. This is known as the systolic pressure. The cuff is gradually deflated further until the pulse beat again disappears. The pressure at this point is called the diastolic pressure.

What causes high blood pressure?
It is thought that narrowing of the smaller arteries throughout the body causes the heart to pump harder to get the blood to the various tissues. When the heart pumps harder, blood pressure is elevated.

Is there a hereditary tendency toward high blood pressure (essential hypertension)?
Yes, but it should be stated that the presence of high blood pressure in a parent does not necessarily imply that the offspring will have hypertension.

Does overweight tend toward elevated blood pressure?
Yes.

Is high blood pressure caused by eating red meat, salt, or spices?
No.

Why may high blood pressure be harmful?
a. A greater-than-average strain is placed upon the heart. If it is prolonged, the heart may become enlarged and damaged.
b. Greater wear and tear is placed upon all the blood vessels since blood courses through them at greater pressure. Eventually, vital damage may be inflicted upon

vessels. This in turn causes impairment of function of the tissues and organs that they supply. Organs particularly susceptible to such damage are the heart, brain, kidneys, and eyes.

Is there a variation in the way different individuals react to high blood pressure?
Yes. Females are able to withstand continuous high blood pressure levels much better than males. Also, there is a great variation in reaction among different people.

Is high blood pressure curable?
Not really, but modern methods of medication make it possible to keep the pressure under control, thereby minimizing serious potential injury.

In addition to medication and a sensible pattern of living, reduction of overweight and constant surveillance also contribute substantially toward the control of high blood pressure.

On the other hand, there are other less common causes of hypertension—such as certain tumors, kidney diseases, and endocrine disturbances—which can actually be cured, providing the underlying cause is detectable and can be eradicated.

Can high blood pressure (essential hypertension) be prevented?
No, but the above measures can in many instances lead to its control.

Do emotion and temperament affect the blood pressure?
Yes. Imprudent living and extravagant emotional excesses can raise

blood pressure. Such extremes of conduct are thought not to be the basic cause for hypertension but, rather, aggravating influences.

Can a patient with high blood pressure feel healthy and be unaware of its presence?

Many people have high blood pressure for years without being aware of it.

What are the usual symptoms of high blood pressure?

Actually, there are none specifically attributable to the elevated pressure. The headaches and hot flashes complained about are usually due to other conditions.

What is the normal blood pressure level?

There is no such thing as a set, normal blood pressure. There is a wide range of pressures considered normal for the average adult. The upper limit of normal systolic pressure is about 150 to 160mm. of mercury, and the upper limit for the diastolic pressure is from 90 to 100mm.

What is low blood pressure?

The common or garden variety of low blood pressure is not a disease. It refers to a state in which blood pressure readings are found to be in the lower level of the normal range. This is usually a healthy situation for it means that the heart and blood vessels are not being put to undue strain.

Is low blood pressure ever an evidence of true disease?

In certain rare diseases, persistent low blood pressure is found as a constant sign.

Does the common form of low blood pressure give rise to symptoms such as fatigue or lethargy?

Only rarely. Unfortunately, low blood pressure has become a psychological hat rack upon which many individuals hang a variety of unrelated complaints.

Does low blood pressure require treatment?

Rarely, if ever.

Can one have "temporary" high blood pressure?

Yes. Often the excitement of an examination or the circumstances surrounding an examination may give rise to abnormally high pressure readings. Later examination under more relaxed conditions may yield a perfectly normal result. Also, exceptional emotional stress may cause elevated blood pressure for a period of several days or weeks. This will usually return to normal when the strain is eased.

CONGENITAL HEART DISEASE

What types of congenital heart conditions are there?

a. Abnormal communications between the right and left sides of the heart, so that blood from the veins passes into the arterial circulation.
b. Abnormalities in the structure and function of the heart valves, which

505

separate the various chambers of the heart.

c. Abnormalities in the heart muscle itself.

d. Abnormalities in the inner and outer linings of the heart.

What causes congenital heart conditions?

Defects in prenatal development due to a variety of causes not yet fully understood. Recent evidence has illustrated that the incidence of congenital heart disease is much greater if the mother has contracted German measles in the first three months of pregnancy. Other viral diseases during this stage of pregnancy have been suspected but not yet substantiated. Certain drugs (such as thalidomide) have been shown to have the potential to develop cardiac as well as other abnormalities in the embryo. It is therefore advisable to avoid any and all drugs in the first three formative months unless recommended by the physician. Also, a variety of poorly understood changes in the genes have been shown to lead to congenital heart abnormalities.

Are congenital heart conditions hereditary?

Most often, no. However, in a small but definite percentage of cases, certain heart abnormalities have been shown to be hereditary.

Can abnormalities of the heart be detected immediately after the child is born?

Some may be detected by listening with a stethoscope at birth or noting the blue color of the baby. Other con-

ditions remain obscure until much later in childhood or even until adulthood.

How common are congenital heart conditions?

They occur approximately three times in every thousand births.

Are congenital heart conditions serious?

Yes, because they often lead to impairment of heart function and circulation and produce situations in which the tissues receive an insufficient quantity of oxygen.

What is a "blue baby"?

A baby born with a condition in which oxygen-poor blood from the veins passes directly from the right side of the circulatory system to the left, or arterial, side. This blood bypasses the lungs and is therefore deficient in oxygen.

Can congenital heart abnormalities be cured?

In the past few years tremendous strides have been made surgically in the treatment of these conditions. Some abnormalities can be cured completely through surgery; others may be helped considerably. (See the section on Heart Surgery in this chapter.)

CORONARY ARTERY DISEASE

What are the coronary arteries?

They are the blood vessels that course through the wall of the heart and nourish the heart muscle. They are the first blood vessels to branch off from the aorta as it leaves the heart.

What is coronary artery disease?

Since the heart muscle expends a huge amount of energy in its ceaseless work, it naturally demands a good supply of blood. Any impairment of these blood vessels that interferes with adequate blood flow is known as coronary artery disease.

What is the most frequent cause of coronary artery disease?

Arteriosclerosis (hardening of the arteries).

What is coronary insufficiency and angina pectoris?

If the blood flow through the coronary arteries is significantly diminished, the heart cannot function at maximum efficiency. The heart then signals its plight by registering pain or discomfort in the chest—usually under the breastbone. Often, however, the discomfort or pain may be manifest in more remote regions of the body, such as in the back, arms, neck, jaw, or upper abdomen. The registering of such pain, with or without exertion, is called angina pectoris. The pain subsides when the patient rests and stops any physical exertion.

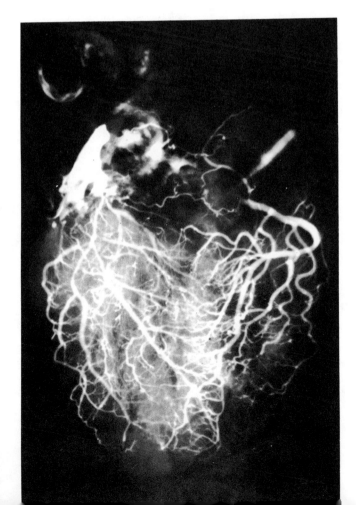

The Coronary Arteries. This illustration shows a heart specimen in which the coronary arteries have been injected with dye. It demonstrates that the coronary arteries supply blood to the wall of the heart itself. Blockage of these arteries causes serious heart damage and may result in sudden death.

507

The Heart

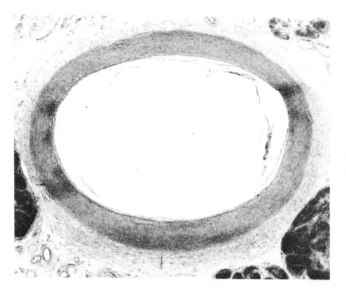

Normal Coronary Artery.
This photomicrograph shows a cross section of a normal coronary artery. Note how wide and open the passageway is in the middle of the vessel.

Coronary Thrombosis. This photomicrograph shows a cross section of an arteriosclerotic coronary artery in which thrombosis (a clot) has taken place. Naturally, no blood can flow through such an artery, and the heart muscle wall supplied by such an artery will be severely damaged from lack of circulation.

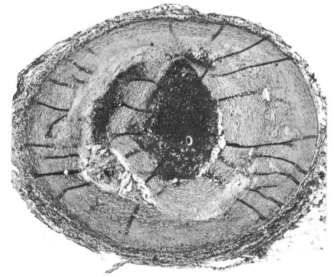

What is coronary occlusion?

It is the complete interruption of blood flow through one of the branches of the coronary artery. As a result, a portion of heart muscle may be destroyed from lack of nourishment. This is called myocardial infarction. If a large main artery is blocked, a large portion of heart muscle is damaged. If a small subsidiary branch is blocked, a smaller portion of muscle is damaged. The term "heart attack" is commonly used to allude to this sequence of events.

What is the cause of coronary occlusion?

The most common cause is the blockage of the coronary arteries by the formation of a blood clot. This is termed coronary thrombosis. It usually occurs at a site where the artery was previously damaged by arteriosclerosis.

What are some of the factors that govern the outcome of a heart attack?

a. The amount of previous heart damage.
b. The size of the area of heart muscle damaged by the particular attack.
c. The amount of remaining normal heart muscle.
d. The degree to which the coronary obstruction spreads toward other branches of the artery.
e. The occurrence or absence of disorders in the rhythm of the heart.
f. The presence or absence of blood clots on the inner wall of the heart that may break off and travel to other parts of the body.
g. The possibility of rupture of the weakened heart wall.

What are the chances of recovery from an initial coronary thrombosis?

Approximately four out of five people recover.

What is the significance of coronary insufficiency or angina pectoris?

Angina pectoris is a term applied to the chest pain caused by coronary insufficiency. There are many degrees of angina pectoris and many degrees of coronary insufficiency. Mild degrees are compatible with all but the most strenuous activity. Severe degrees may completely incapacitate a patient.

Can attacks of angina pectoris be prevented?

To a certain extent; that is, a more orderly, regulated life with the deletion of excessive work and excitement, plus the taking of certain medications, may control attacks of angina pectoris. In some cases, they can be avoided completely.

Do all people with angina pectoris eventually develop coronary occlusion?

No, though it is true that such patients are definitely more prone to such heart attacks.

Is angina pectoris compatible with a normal life span?

Yes. However, the individual outlook depends on many factors that vary from patient to patient.

Is surgery helpful in coronary artery disease?

Yes. The coronary bypass operation has helped a considerable number of people with coronary disease. Also, an operation in which the passageway of the coronary artery is restored by removing obstructing arteriosclerotic plaques of tissue gives promise of being helpful.

What is the treatment for coronary thrombosis?

The mainstay of treatment is careful monitoring, twenty-four hours a day, for cardiac arrhythmias (heartbeat irregularities) and prompt treatment should they arise. Oxygen is administered for several days following onset of an attack. Formerly, anticoagulant drugs were given during the acute phase of a coronary attack, but now these medications are reserved for long-term use after the acute attack has subsided. Drugs to strengthen the heart, such as digitalis, may at times be given, and drugs to correct irregular heart rhythm may be prescribed. Medications to relieve pain are also of considerable benefit.

Why are bed rest and limited physical activity important?

The less active the individual, the less the heart has to work to supply the necessary circulatory support. It may not seem so, but there is a tremendous difference in the amount of energy expended by the heart during absolute rest and ordinary activity.

How long must a patient with coronary thrombosis stay in bed?

This depends upon the extent and progress of the illness. If there is no shock, heart failure, or serious irregularity of the heart, patients are gotten out of bed in a week.

How long must a patient with coronary thrombosis stay in the hospital?

The average hospital stay in uncomplicated acute cases is approximately three weeks.

How long must a patient who has had a coronary occlusion stop working?

On the average, most patients may return to work two to three months after the onset. It is wise that these people increase their activity in a gradual fashion rather than plunge right in. It is also important that the patient provide for modification in his occupation if it is unduly taxing. Most patients who have had a heart attack *can* and *should* return to work, but they must avoid emotional as well as physical strain.

What percentage of people who have had coronary thrombosis can make a good recovery and return to work?

Statistics show that most patients who have had a heart attack make an excellent recovery and return to their usual occupation.

What are anticoagulant drugs?

They are chemical compounds that decrease the normal clotting ability of the blood. (Heparin and dicumarol are two of the most frequently used.)

Why are anticoagulant drugs used in treating coronary thrombosis?

a. To prevent the clot in the artery from spreading, thus further impairing the blood supply to the heart muscle.

b. To prevent clots from forming on the inner lining of the heart and in the leg veins, since the clots may break loose and travel in the bloodstream (embolism).

Is it possible to predict the onset of a heart attack?

Not always. It often occurs without warning to people who have been in apparent good health and who may have had a normal electrocardiogram just prior to the attack. There are instances, however, where warning signs—such as chest pains—may have occurred for weeks or months prior to an acute attack.

Can periodic electrocardiograms give advance information as to the possibility of a future heart attack?

Only to a very limited extent.

What age group is most susceptible to a heart attack?

People between forty and sixty years of age.

Can a patient who has had a heart attack look forward to many years of life?

Yes. Patients who have had serious heart attacks often live twenty-five to thirty or more years thereafter.

Are men more susceptible to heart attack than women?

Yes. They are approximately three times more prone to coronary artery disease. However, after fifty years of age, the incidence of coronary

thrombosis increases markedly in women.

Is there a hereditary susceptibility to coronary artery disease?

There sometimes appears to be a hereditary predisposition, but this is not an exclusive determining factor in the causation of the disease.

How important is emotional strain in the production of a heart attack?

It is thought to be a contributing factor, although it is usually not the sole, or the main, causative agent.

What influence does physical exertion have upon the immediate or future occurrence of coronary heart disease?

Generally speaking, physical exertion is not a highly significant factor in the cause of heart attacks. However, there have been instances of heart attacks having occurred concomitantly with, or shortly after, severe physical exertion. The consensus is that most of these people had quiescent underlying disease of the coronary arteries, which predisposed them to attacks.

What conditions predispose one toward the development of coronary artery disease?

Diabetes, high blood pressure, excessively high cholesterol levels in the blood, obesity, and heavy smoking.

What is the influence of diet on coronary artery disease?

A number of factors in the diet have

511

been indicted as contributing to coronary artery disease, e.g., saturated fatty acids derived from animal meats and dairy foods such as milk and cream; common table sugar, known as sucrose; and foods with a high cholesterol content.

What is the influence of smoking upon coronary artery disease?

At the present time it is the consensus of opinion that the more one smokes, the more likely is coronary artery disease to develop, all other factors remaining equal. Certainly, an individual who already has coronary artery disease should not smoke at all.

HEART IRREGULARITIES
(Cardiac Arrhythmia)

What is cardiac arrhythmia?

An irregularity in the rhythmic beat of the heart.

What causes cardiac irregularity?

Some cases are caused by true heart disease; others are associated with normal hearts that for one reason or another go "off beat." The physician can usually distinguish between the various causes for such irregularities.

Do irregularities of the heart interfere with its function?

An occasional extra beat or skip (extrasystole) has little effect upon heart function. Other cardiac arrhythmias may seriously interfere with circulation.

Can cardiac irregularities be treated successfully?

In the great majority of cases, cardiac irregularities will respond to treatment with certain heart drugs.

What is a skipped beat or premature beat?

This is an occasional irregularity of the heart in which the patient is aware of a peculiar ("butterfly") sensation in the chest or a fleeting, sinking, or empty sensation in the chest. Technically, it is known as an extrasystole.

What is the significance of a skipped beat?

In the vast majority of cases, there is no serious significance to this, although at times it may be annoying.

What causes skipped beats?

A variety of conditions, among which are exhaustion, the unwise taking of drugs, nervousness, irritability, an acute infection, etc. Less commonly, the cause may be underlying heart disease.

Is the use of tobacco ever a cause for extrasystoles?

Yes, this is one of the commonest causes for cardiac irregularity.

ATHLETE'S HEART

What is "athlete's heart"?

This term has been used erroneously in most instances to refer to enlargement of the heart in people who had overexerted themselves during days of strenuous athletics. At present it is felt that these hearts were, in

512

The Heart

effect, basically unsound to begin with. There is no sure evidence that indulgence in athletics produces heart disease in a normal heart.

PALPITATION OF THE HEART

What is meant by "palpitation of the heart"?

This is a nonmedical expression often used to denote consciousness of a rapid and exceptionally forceful heartbeat. Occasionally this feeling of palpitation is associated with irregularities of the heartbeat.

Does palpitation denote heart disease?

Usually not. It occurs most often in people who are suffering from undue tension and anxiety.

PAROXYSMAL ARRHYTHMIA

What is paroxysmal arrhythmia?

This is a condition in which the heart suddenly and abruptly goes into another rhythm, often becoming extremely rapid. These attacks may come on suddenly, at frequent or infrequent intervals, without warning.

How long do attacks of paroxysmal arrhythmia last?

Anywhere from a few minutes to a few days.

Do these attacks occur only in diseased hearts?

No. Often the heart is completely normal.

What causes episodes of paroxysmal arrhythmia?

a In organic heart conditions, it is usually a disease of the "rhythm centers."

b. In normal hearts, the cause is usually unknown.

What is the treatment for paroxysmal arrhythmias?

In most cases, these episodes can be controlled by medications such as quinidine. Occasionally, the treatment of choice is the use of electronic heart-shocking devices.

HEART BLOCK

What is heart block?

Complete heart block is a condition in which the electrical impulse from the atrium (which initiates heart contractions) is not transmitted to the ventricle. As a result, there can be complete cardiac standstill, cessation of heartbeat, and death, or there can be temporary cardiac standstill with loss of consciousness and strokelike manifestations. On the other hand, the ventricles can set up their own focus of activity and operate independently of the atrium. Another type of heart block is known as incomplete heart block, where every second or third beat may not be transmitted from the atrium to the ventricle. The manifestations of this phenomenon are not as dramatic as complete heart block.

Is heart block usually associated with a disease of the heart?

Yes.

How is the diagnosis of heart block usually made?

By physical examination corroborated by electrocardiographic study.

Is heart block compatible with life?

This depends on the severity of the condition. Such a patient is constantly threatened with the possibility that the ventricles may cease to beat at all or react in such a way as to be life threatening.

What can be done when heart block becomes a life-threatening situation?

Either temporary or permanently implanted electronic devices can be instituted surgically. These devices electrically stimulate the ventricles of the heart to beat regularly and effectively. These devices are known as pacemakers.

FIBRILLATION OF THE HEART

What is auricular atrial fibrillation?

It is a condition in which there is complete disorder, originating in the auricles, in the rhythmic beat of the heart.

What causes auricular atrial fibrillation?

It is commonly seen in long-standing rheumatic heart disease, arteriosclerotic heart disease, and in hyperthyroidism (a disease in which there is overactivity of the thyroid gland).

What is the significance of auricular atrial fibrillation?

An irregularly beating heart is usually not as efficient as one that beats regularly, and it therefore pumps blood to the tissues in an inefficient manner.

What complications may occur with chronic auricular atrial fibrillation of the heart?

a. Because of too rapid and irregular contractions, the output of the heart may be inadequate and may lead to heart failure or decompensation.

b. A fibrillating heart may develop clots of blood on its inner wall. If these should break off and travel to other organs of the body, they can cause severe damage (embolization).

Can a fibrillating heart be brought back to normal rhythm?

In many instances this can be accomplished by either medication or by electronic heart-shocking devices. Very often the results are temporary, and the heart reverts to auricular fibrillation.

HEART MURMURS

What is a heart murmur?

An abnormal sound produced by the beating heart.

How can a physician make a diagnosis of a heart murmur?

By listening with a stethoscope.

Do heart murmurs cause symptoms?

No. The patient is usually unaware that a murmur exists.

Do all murmurs indicate heart disease?

No. A high percentage of murmurs are produced by normal hearts and are of no clinical significance.

What is a functional heart murmur?

One not associated with heart disease.

What is an organic murmur?

A murmur associated with heart disease.

Can a doctor tell the difference between an organic and a functional murmur?

Usually it is quite simple for the physician to determine the difference by the location and position of the murmur, by the heartbeat cycle, and by other distinctive features. A small percentage of murmurs remain in question, and diagnosis is quite difficult.

HEART VALVE INFECTION
(Bacterial Endocarditis)

What is bacterial endocarditis?

Heart valves previously damaged by rheumatic fever, congenital heart disease, or other pathology, are particularly susceptible to bacterial infection. This is called bacterial endocarditis. This complication is an extremely serious one and unless promptly treated causes irreparable destruction of the valves. In addition, bacteria are carried by the bloodstream to other organs of the body, which in turn may also be seriously damaged.

Is bacterial endocarditis curable?

At the present time, successful treatment is available for the majority of these cases.

What is the treatment for bacterial endocarditis?

The prolonged and intensive administration of antibiotics.

Is bacterial endocarditis preventable?

To a degree, yes. Any infection in the body should be promptly and vigorously treated lest bacteria break through the tissue barriers, enter the bloodstream, and become implanted upon a heart valve.

What other measures should be taken to prevent the onset of bacterial endocarditis?

All people suffering from rheumatic heart disease should be particularly careful about surgical procedures. For instance, the extraction of a tooth should be preceded and followed by antibiotic therapy.

HEART SURGERY

What conditions can be helped through heart surgery?

a. Congenital heart conditions:
    1. Patent ductus arteriosus—the

515

HEART DEFECTS THAT CAN BE CORRECTED SURGICALLY

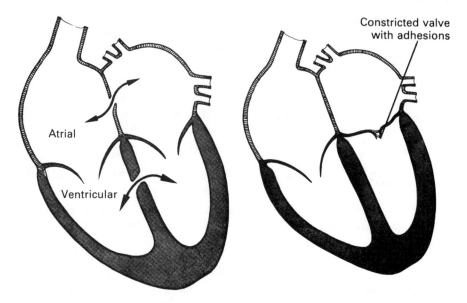

Above left:

Septal Defects. *This diagram shows defects in the walls between the various heart chambers. newer advances in heart surgery have made it possible to open the heart and repair septal defects. During the operation the patient's circulation is conducted with the help of a heart pump so that the heart is bypassed until the surgical repair is completed.*

Above right:

Mitral Stenosis. *This illustration shows one of the most common of all heart conditions, mitral stenosis. This disease is characterized by a narrowing of the valve between the left atrium and the left ventricle of the heart. Mitral stenosis is the end result of a severe attack of rheumatic fever.*

persistence of a blood vessel that ordinarily closes by the time the child is born.

2. Septal defects—abnormal opening and connections between the various chambers of the heart.

3. The condition that causes blue babies, the tetrology of Fallot—

abnormal position and connections of major blood vessels leading to and from the heart.

4. Pulmonic stenosis—a condition in which there is either an underdeveloped pulmonary artery leading from the heart to the lungs or a constricted pulmonary valve opening. *(continued)*

516

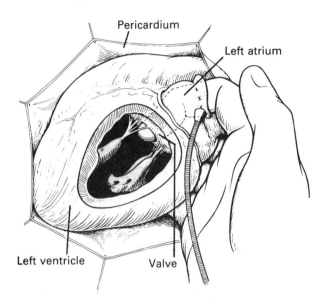

Pericardium

Left atrium

Left ventricle

Valve

Clockwise:
Mitral Commissurotomy. *Overgrowths and adhesions on the constricted mitral valve are freed by finger in this operation. This is usually done by sight during open heart surgery.*

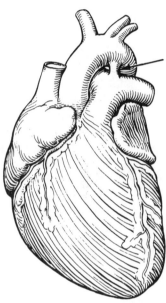

Patent Ductus Arteriosus. *This diagram shows a common congenital heart deformity known as patent ductus arteriosus. This can be surgically corrected by tying off the artery. People born with this abnormality can now be cured by a simple, safe heart operation.*

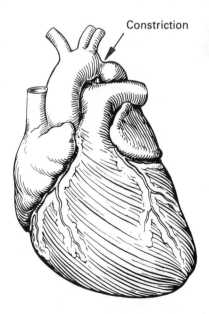

Constriction

Coarctation of Aorta. *This diagram shows a birth deformity of the vessels of the heart known as coarctation of the aorta. With newer surgical techniques, it is now possible to remove this constricted portion of the aorta and to reshape it to allow for normal circulation.*

The Heart

5. Coarctation of the aorta—a narrowing of the aorta in the chest.
b. Acquired heart conditions:
1. Rheumatic heart disease—a condition in which there is constriction or other deformity of the heart valves secondary to rheumatic fever.
c. Coronary artery disease.
d. Pericarditis—an inflammatory condition of the sheath (pericardium) that surrounds the heart.
e. Heart injuries:
1. Stab wounds or gunshot wounds.
2. Aneurysm of the heart—in which there is a bulge of the muscle wall secondary to damage caused by a previous coronary thrombosis.
f. Heart block due to inadequate transmission of impulses from the atrium to the ventricle.

Are operations upon the heart dangerous?

Refinements in the techniques have reduced the dangers of heart surgery remarkably, so that it is fast approaching the degree of safety obtained in some of the other major fields of surgical endeavor.

Can all people with heart disease be operated upon?

No. Only certain types of heart conditions lend themselves to surgical help.

Is it difficult to approach the heart surgically?

No. Incisions into the chest cavity make the heart readily available to the surgeon.

How successful are heart operations for congenital defects?

Almost all of those suffering from a patent ductus arteriosus can be cured; approximately 85 to 90 percent of those with coarctation of the aorta can be cured; and approximately 75 percent of the blue babies can be cured. Septal defects, utilizing a heart pump and open heart surgery, can be controlled either by patching the defects with a Dacron graft or, if the hole is very small, by direct suturing. These operations are successful in well over 90 percent of cases.

Can patients with congenital heart defects that have been successfully operated upon look forward to a more normal life?

Yes. Many children who were labeled heart cripples can now look forward to near-normal lives after heart surgery.

Do congenital defects often come back once they have been corrected?

No.

Is surgery for rheumatic heart disease successful?

Yes. Most of those who have defects of their valves can be helped tremendously through surgery. There are many cases now on record in which the heart valve has been repaired surgically through open heart surgery or has been replaced by an artificial valve.

What percentage survive of those

518

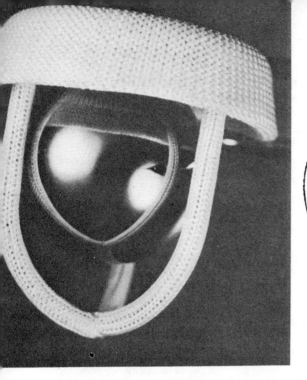

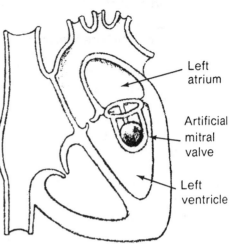

Left
atrium

Artificial
mitral
valve

Left
ventricle

*Mitral Valve Replacement. The artificial valve, shown here (left), is the most common-
ly used replacement for an aortic or mitral valve damaged by rheumatic fever. In the past,
the biggest drawback of this replacement had been blood clots forming on valve sur-
faces, especially on the metal struts of the cage. Covering these struts with a loose-weave
synthetic fabric has significantly reduced clotting complications following installation
of this valve.*

operated upon for rheumatic heart disease?

Approximately 90 to 95 percent.

What percentage are benefited by such surgery?

Almost all of those who are operated upon.

Do all patients with rheumatic heart disease require surgery?

No. Surgery is limited to those whose lives are severely handicapped by the disease.

Is life expectancy improved by

operations upon hearts that have been affected by rheumatic fever?

Yes.

Do these patients often return to normal living?

Yes.

What operations are performed upon those with coronary artery disease?

Several operations have been devised, but the most popular procedure involves using a patient's leg
vein as a graft to bypass coronary artery obstruction. This is known as a

519

coronary bypass operation. Another one consists of transplanting the internal mammary artery from beneath the breastbone into the heart muscle. An older procedure, in which talcum powder was instilled into the sac surrounding the heart, has been discarded.

What is the benefit of a coronary bypass operation?

It carries the blood, through the vein graft, from the aorta (the large artery leading away from the heart) back to the heart muscle at a point *beyond* the obstruction in the coronary artery. As a result, the heart muscle receives blood that would otherwise not be able to pass through the obstructed, arteriosclerotic portion of the coronary artery.

Are coronary bypass operations done very frequently?

Yes. It is estimated that more than a hundred thousand such operations are performed every year in this country.

Are coronary bypass operations carried out with the use of only one graft from the aorta to the coronary artery?

Ordinarily, several grafts are used, thus bypassing several obstructed areas in the various branches of the coronary arteries. As many as five grafts are not unusual.

Does the bypass operation often relieve the angina pectoris (heart pain) suffered so often by people with coronary artery disease?

Yes. The great majority are relieved of their pain.

Will the performance of a coronary bypass operation prolong one's life span?

Most specialists in the field believe

Coronary Bypass Operation. This diagram illustrates how the narrowed arteriosclerotic segment of the coronary artery is bypassed by placing a vein graft from the aorta to a normal portion of the artery.

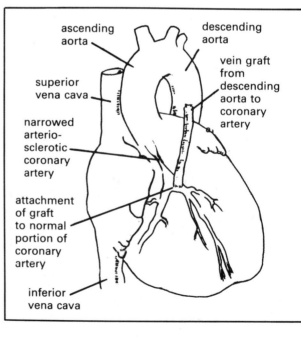

ascending aorta

descending aorta

superior vena cava

vein graft from descending aorta to coronary artery

narrowed arteriosclerotic coronary artery

attachment of graft to normal portion of coronary artery

inferior vena cava

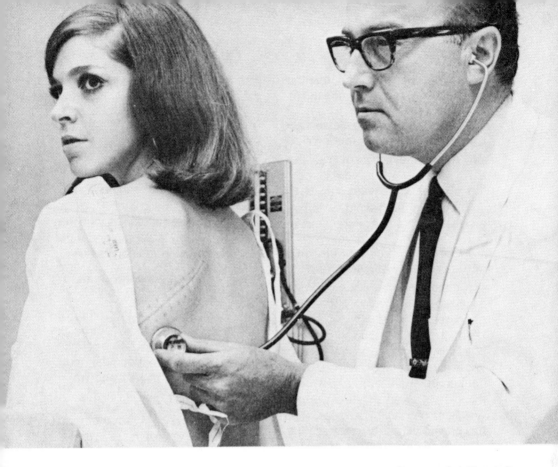

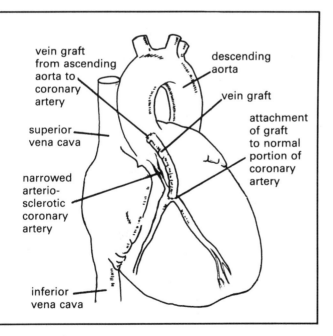

vein graft
from ascending
aorta to
coronary
artery

descending
aorta

vein graft

superior
vena cava

attachment
of graft
to normal
portion of
coronary
artery

narrowed
arterio-
sclerotic
coronary
artery

inferior
vena cava

Successful Heart Surgery. *The scar extending from the back to the front is an indication that heart surgery was performed (photo above).*

The Heart

that the life span is extended by this operation.

Can one do physical exercise after a coronary bypass operation?

Yes. As a matter of fact, it is advisable to exercise as this increases the flow of blood to the heart muscle. Of course one should avoid violent exercise and other stressful situations.

Are there any other operations for coronary artery disease?

Yes, although some of them are still in an experimental stage. Some surgeons have cored out the narrow channel of the diseased coronary artery in an attempt to restitute its passageway. This operation is quite dangerous and is carried out while the patient is on the heart pump. Also, the coronary bypass operation has proved helpful to some patients with acute coronary thrombosis, if performed within six to eight hours after the onset of the acute attack.

Where is the incision made for heart operations?

Between the ribs that overlie the left side of the chest.

What anesthesia is used for heart operations?

An inhalation anesthesia given through a tube placed in the trachea.

Are the results of surgery for coronary artery disease satisfactory?

The bypass operation has had remarkably satisfactory results in the great majority of cases. However, many people who have had coronary thrombosis do not, at the present time, lend themselves to this surgical procedure.

Have methods been devised that permit bypassing of the heart during surgery?

Yes, there are heart pumps that can take the place of the heart during the time that it is undergoing surgery. This permits the surgeon to open the heart and operate upon it under direct vision and in a bloodless field.

What is meant by "hypothermia" in heart surgery?

This means cooling the patient's body so that his heart action is slowed down markedly. This permits the surgeon to work upon the heart while it is more at rest and when blood flow is greatly curtailed.

When will physicians recommend heart surgery?

a. When it is felt that the ultimate chances for survival are greater with surgery than without surgery.
b. When a person is leading an invalided, useless life and desires the chance for more normal living through heart surgery.
c. When a reasonable chance for cure or improvement exists through heart surgery and when the patient or his family fully understands the risks involved.

Are heart operations lengthy?

Yes. Some heart operations take several hours to perform.

Are heart operations painful?

No. Patients are usually quite comfortable during recovery from a heart operation.

Do heart conditions tend to recur once they have been benefited by heart surgery?

No. The majority of successful results in heart surgery are of a permanent nature.

Do all of the heart valves lend themselves to surgical repair?

Yes. Formerly, only the mitral valve was operated upon when it was found to be damaged. Now the other major valves—such as the pulmonic, aortic, and the tricuspid valves—have been repaired or replaced successfully through surgery.

Does the surgeon ever purposely stop the heart from beating while it is being repaired?

Yes. This procedure can be carried out only when the patient is on the heart-lung pump so that there can be continued circulation of blood. The heart is sometimes stopped temporarily to allow more rapid and accurate repair of defective structures.

Can people who have undergone successful heart operations return to a completely normal life?

It may be necessary for some to restrict their physical activity even though the operation may have been extremely successful.

Is it ever possible to reoperate upon a patient who has had a poor result from heart surgery?

Yes. Many of those who underwent mitral valve surgery for rheumatic fever in the early days of this type of treatment have developed recurrences of their disease. These pa-tients can now be successfully re-operated on, and the damaged valve can be repaired under direct vision with the heart open, or the valve can be replaced with an artificial valve. Patients whose coronary bypass grafts have closed down can frequently be reoperated with successful results.

Are heart transplants practicable?

The actual technique of heart transplantation is not very difficult and has been performed several hundred times at various cardiac surgery clinics throughout the world.

Are heart transplants usually successful?

Because of the rejection phenomenon most patients who have successfully undergone a heart transplant operation have not survived more than a few months or a year to two. However, better matching procedures and methods of combating the rejection reaction have been found. As a consequence, much better results have been achieved.

Are heart transplants being done at the current time?

Yes, but only upon patients who would not survive more than a few weeks or months unless they were operated. There are a few surgical clinics throughout the world where encouraging results are now being attained.

What are the chances of surviving a heart transplantation?

In one of the most expert cardiac surgical clinics, 50 percent of those

523

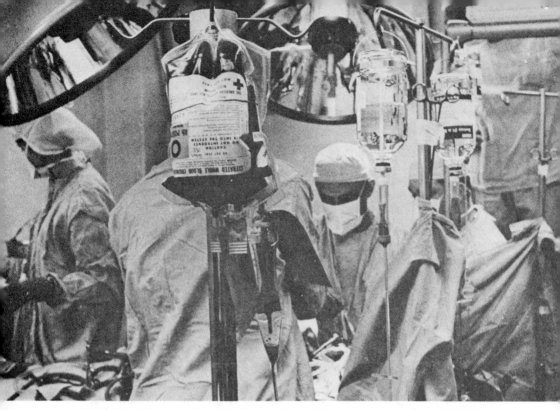

Open-Heart Surgery: *A surgical team gets ready to perform a complex open-heart operation. Essential to the operation's success is blood, one unit of which is shown ready for transfusion.*

Inhalation anesthesia, given through a tube and passed into the trachea, is used in heart operations.

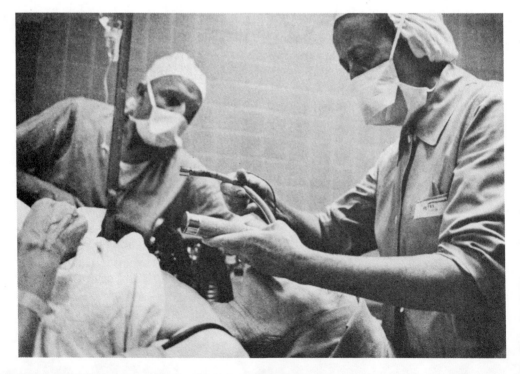

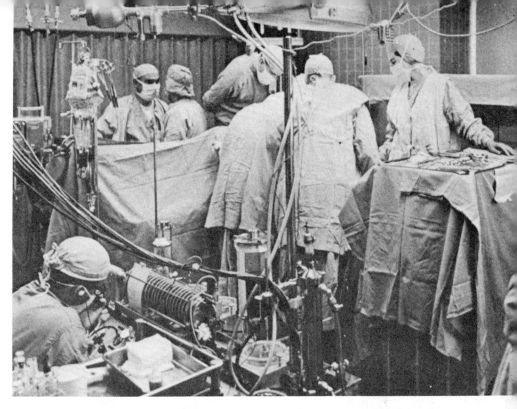

Open-heart surgery is carried out while the patient is on the heart-lung pump which substitutes for the heart's action during the operation.

In open-heart surgery, the heart tissue is sutured and closed much like tissue in any other part of the body.

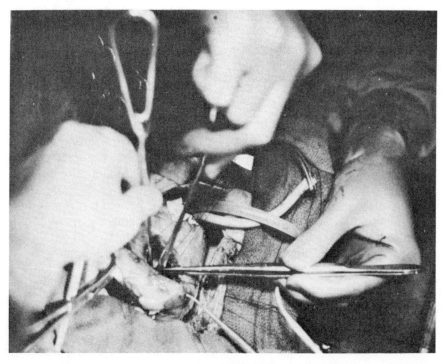

operated upon have survived for a year, and some have lived for more than five years. It must be remembered, however, that *none* would have lived for more than a few weeks or months had they not received a new heart.

CCU *(Cardiac Care Unit)*

(See also Chapter 36 on ICU)

What is a CCU?

A CCU is essentially an Intensive Care Unit (ICU) for patients with acute, serious heart ailments. In many hospitals, the CCU is located adjacent to the ICU, and some of the staff, especially nurses and technologists, serve both units. In most large hospitals, however, the units are separate.

Do CCUs usually serve all types of cardiac patients who have acute problems?

Yes, but by far the greatest number are those who have experienced an acute coronary thrombosis. Most of the other patients suffer from various degrees of heart failure.

What are some of the other heart conditions that might be treated in a CCU?

a. Pericarditis, an inflammation of the outer covering of the heart.
b. Acute myocarditis, an inflammation of the muscle wall of the heart.
c. Heart valve disease.
d. Endocarditis, an inflammation of the inner lining of the heart.
e. Injuries to the heart.

f. Uncontrollable irregularities in the heartbeat.

How many beds are in a CCU?

This will depend upon the size of the hospital and whether it has a large heart surgery service. Naturally, the larger the hospital and the more cardiac surgery that is performed, the more beds will be needed for the CCU. A general hospital of five hundred beds will probably have six to eight beds in its CCU.

What are the advantages of a CCU over ordinary hospital care?

In no other illness is it more essential to monitor patients constantly. Changes in heart action are so abrupt that response on the part of the medical and nursing staff must be instantaneous. Such a response is not possible except in a unit staffed twenty-four hours a day by specially trained personnel.

Should a physician always be on duty and physically present in a CCU?

Yes.

What special equipment is in a CCU?

a. An apparatus that connects the patient to a cardiogram and constantly records the electrical impulses on a video screen. The slightest change in these electrocardiographic tracings will be noted immediately by the physician and nursing staff so that immediate corrective treatment can be started.
b. An alarm system that alerts the

CCU staff to changes in the patient's heartbeat or in the transmission of electrical impulses through the heart.

c. Electrical equipment to "shock" the heart back to a normal rhythm should a dangerous irregularity, or even cardiac arrest, develop.

d. Equipment and medications to combat sudden heart irregularities or cardiac arrest. This will include respirators, endotracheal tubes, apparatus for instituting cardiac massage, etc.

e. An intravenous line is always kept going in a patient in a CCU so that medications can be given directly into the bloodstream at anytime without waiting.

f. Catheters for insertion into veins, arteries, or even into the heart itself.

g. Apparatus to measure the *cardiac output.* (A failing heart is unable to pump sufficient blood through the body.)

h. Apparatus to take samples of blood for laboratory testing. This is important so that the blood gases and body chemistries can be monitored, and treatment can be begun for abnormalities if present.

Have many lives been saved through establishment of the CCU?
Yes. Tremendous numbers of cardiac patients owe their lives to their sojourn in a CCU.

What determines when a patient may be transferred from the CCU to an ordinary hospital room?
When the physicians responsible for the patient's care decide that his condition is *stable* and that he can sustain life without minute-to-minute monitoring and support. Stability would include a satisfactory blood pressure, a regular heartbeat, and evidence that the heart is mending. However, before the decision to transfer is made, the patient must maintain a satisfactory condition for a few days *without* the supportive measures that are available only in the CCU.

CHAPTER 30 HERNIA

What is a hernia?

A hernia is a defect in a body compartment (cavity) that permits a structure to leave its normal confines and extend into a region where it does not belong. As an example, in a hernia of the diaphragm, the stomach may leave the abdominal cavity and enter the chest cavity through the diaphragmatic defect.

What other name is used for hernia?

The word "rupture" is frequently used to denote a hernia.

What causes hernias?

The great majority of hernias are caused by defects or weaknesses in the muscular and connective tissue structures that separate the various compartments or cavities of the body, such as the chest from the abdomen, or the abdomen from the limbs. Other hernias result from an injury that tears the muscular or connective tissue barriers at various exit points of the body compartments.

Are many hernias present at birth?

Yes. A sizable number of children are born with hernias because of defects in development. These are commonly noted in the region of the navel (umbilical hernia) or in the groin (inguinal hernia).

At what specific areas in the body are hernias most likely to occur?

At the various points where large structures—such as blood vessels or portions of the intestinal tract—

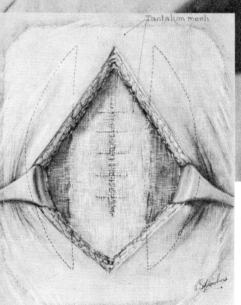

Surgical Repair of Hernia. *This little boy was born with an umbilical hernia which was corrected by surgery. In operations to repair hernias, a tantalum-wire mesh, shown in the drawing at the left, is sometimes used to reinforce the weakened tissues.*

529

Hernia

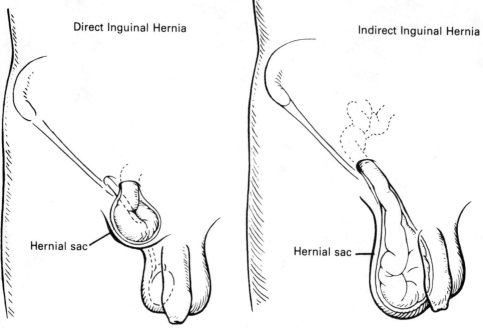

Direct Inguinal Hernia

Indirect Inguinal Hernia

Hernial sac

Hernial sac

leave or enter the various body cavities. At these sites there are loose tissues that, when placed under great strain, may separate and tear.

What types of strain or injury are most likely to lead to a rupture?

a. Lifting heavy objects.
b. Sudden twists, pulls, or muscle strains.
c. Marked gains in weight, which cause an increase in intraabdominal pressure.
d. The growth of a large abdominal tumor, which displaces the organs.
e. Pregnancy, with its accompanying increase in intraabdominal pressure.
f. Chronic constipation, with its associated straining at stool.
g. Repeated attacks of coughing,

which create sudden increases in intraabdominal pressure.

How common are hernias?

Hernias are one of the most common of all conditions requiring surgery.

Are men more prone than women to develop hernias?

Yes, if it is the type that results from physical strain and effort, such as hernia in the groin (inguinal hernia). Women are more likely to get hernias of the umbilical region (navel) as a result of pregnancy.

Do hernias tend to run in families or to be inherited?

No, but the kind of muscular development that one possesses does tend to be inherited.

530

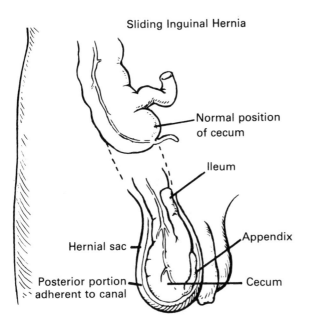

Sliding Inguinal Hernia

Normal position of cecum

Ileum

Hernial sac

Appendix

Posterior portion adherent to canal

Cecum

Inguinal Hernia. The accompanying diagrams on this and the opposite page show various types of inguinal herniae, or hernias, which are located in the groin. If the patient is in satisfactory general health, surgery should be performed for their repair. Failure to undergo surgery may result in a loop of bowel becoming caught within the hernial sac, thus producing bowel strangulation, a very serious condition.

What are the most common types of hernia?

a. Inguinal hernia. This is the most prevalent type of hernia. It occurs in the groin, often developing on both sides of the body. Such ruptures are called bilateral inguinal hernias.

b. Femoral hernia. This type is located just below the groin and occurs alongside the large blood vessels that extend from the trunk into the lower limbs.

c. Ventral hernia. This type usually occurs in the midline of the abdomen below the navel and often takes place as a result of the separation of the muscles of the abdominal wall following pregnancy.

d. Epigastric hernia. This type is located in the upper midline of the abdomen above the navel. Such hernias probably exist from birth but only become apparent in adult life.

e. Umbilical hernia. This is one of the most common forms of hernia and takes place in the region of the navel. Newborns and women who have had many pregnancies appear to be particularly prone to develop umbilical hernias.

f. Incisional hernia. This type of hernia occurs through an operative scar, either because of poor healing power of the wound or because infection has caused the tissues to heal inadequately. A hernia of this type can be located anywhere on the abdominal wall.

g. Recurrent hernia. About one in ten hernias will recur after surgical repair. This is called recurrent hernia. *(continued)*

Hernia

h. Diaphragmatic hernia. This is an extremely common defect and takes place most frequently alongside the point where the esophagus (foodpipe) passes through the diaphragm from the chest into the abdomen. Other diaphragmatic hernias result from lack of development of the diaphragm or from rupture of the diaphragm due to an injury. These hernias of are characterized by abdominal organs—such as a portion of stomach, small intestine, or large bowel—entering the defect and lodging in the chest cavity. Hernias alongside the entrance of the esophagus into the abdominal cavity are known as *hiatus hernias*.

i. Internal hernia. This is an unusual type of rupture in which an internal abdominal organ, usually the small intestine, enters crevices or subdivisions of the abdominal cavity where it does not belong.

j. Gluteal and lumbar hernias. These hernias are extremely rare and are due to defects in the musculature of the buttocks or back. The herniated organs will appear as bulges posteriorly in either the buttocks or the back.

When is medical, rather than surgical, management advocated in the treatment of hernias?

a. If a hernia has recurred two or more times after surgery and the patient's tissue structures appear to be poor, it is probably best not to attempt surgical repair a third or fourth time, as it will be met with failure in a large percentage of cases.

b. Patients who are markedly overweight should not be operated upon until they reduce, as repairs

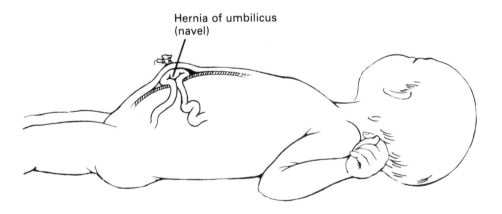

Hernia of umbilicus (navel)

Umbilical Hernia or Hernia of the Navel. *Many children are born with small umbilical hernias. The majority of these will heal by themselves within the first year of life. If the hernia persists, it is advisable to have it repaired surgically. The operation for repair of an umbilical hernia is a simple, safe procedure.*

in these people are notoriously unsuccessful.

c. People with serious medical conditions, such as active tuberculosis or serious heart disease, are probably best treated without surgery.

d. People with small hernias who are in their seventies or eighties are perhaps best treated medically unless the hernia causes severe symptoms.

What is the medical treatment for hernias?

The wearing of a support or truss to hold the hernial contents within the abdominal cavity.

As a general rule, should trusses be worn for prolonged periods of time before surgery is carried out?

No. Trusses tend to weaken the structures with which they are in constant contact. Therefore they should not be worn for more than a few weeks prior to surgery.

Why isn't the wearing of a truss advised—rather than surgery—in all hernias?

Because trusses do not cure hernias. They merely hold the hernial contents in place. As people get older and hernias enlarge, trusses work less satisfactorily.

Are any dangers involved in neglecting to operate upon hernias?

Definitely, yes. The chance of strangulation of bowel is always present, and such a situation is dangerous to life.

Is the injection treatment satisfactory in the treatment of hernias?

No. This method has been abandoned as dangerous and ineffectual.

Do hernias tend to disappear by themselves?

No. The only hernias that ever disappear by themselves are the small hernias of the navel seen in newborns, and an occasional small inguinal hernia in a newborn.

How effective is surgery in the treatment of hernias?

The vast majority of hernias can be repaired successfully by restoring and reinforcing the torn structures, replacing the extruded structures into their normal anatomical location, and by removing the outpouching of abdominal tissue (peritoneum), which makes up the hernial sac.

When is the best time to operate upon hernias?

Hernia operations are usually elective procedures, and the time for their repair can be chosen by the patient to suit his convenience. It must be remembered, however, that most hernias tend to enlarge; the larger the hernia, the more difficult it is to repair and the greater the chance of subsequent recurrence.

When is a hernia operation an emergency procedure?

When the hernia strangulates, a condition in which an organ such as the intestine or bowel is caught in the hernial sac and its blood supply is interfered with. Under such circum-

Hernia

stances, the patient must be operated upon immediately! Failure to do so will lead to gangrene of the strangulated hernial contents and possible death from peritonitis.

Will surgeons delay operations in elective cases if the patient is overweight?

Yes. If the patient is too stout, the repair of the hernia is similar to an attempt at stuffing too much clothing into a small valise. If such a valise does close, the great pressure from within is likely to pop it open!

Are hernia operations dangerous?

No. They are rarely followed by complications, except when the operation has been carried out for strangulation. In such cases, gangrenous bowel or intestine may be encountered, and this will entail extensive serious surgery for removal of the gangrenous portions.

What procedure is carried out when gangrenous intestine or bowel is found in a hernia?

The gangrenous portions of bowel are removed. This is a most serious and complicated operation with many dangers. The mortality rate in these cases has been lowered remarkably by improved surgical techniques and the use of antibiotic drugs, but the procedure still constitutes one of the most formidable in abdominal surgery.

Are hernia operations particularly painful?

No, except for pain in the operative region for a few days after the surgery has been performed.

Are operations for diaphragmatic hernias particularly dangerous?

No, but these are more extensive procedures than those for hernias in the abdominal region.

Opposite and below:
Hernia of the Diaphragm with Organs from the Abdomen Ascending into the Chest Cavity. *This is a serious type of hernia, but it can be repaired effectively by surgery. In most cases the surgery is performed by opening the chest cavity and closing the hole in the diaphragm from above. A popular term for a diaphragmatic hernia is "upside-down stomach."*

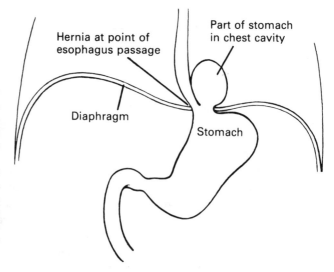

Hernia at point of esophagus passage

Part of stomach in chest cavity

Diaphragm

Stomach

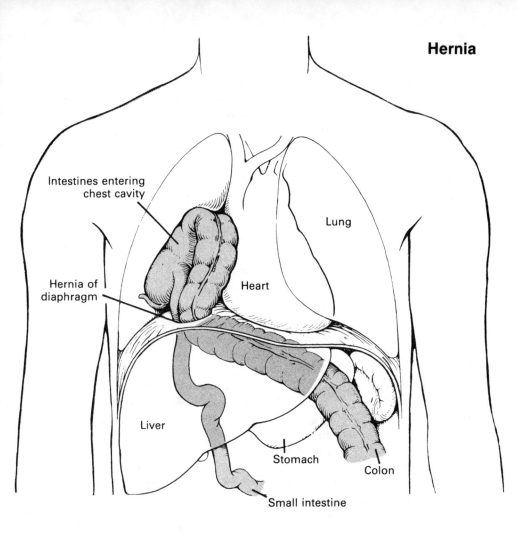

Intestines entering
chest cavity

Lung

Hernia of
diaphragm

Heart

Liver

Stomach

Colon

Small intestine

How are diaphragmatic hernias repaired?

Through an abdominal incision, one of three procedures may be carried out:

a. Closure of the opening of the diaphragm with sutures.

b. Wrapping the fundus (top portion) of the stomach around the lower end of the esophagus. This is known as fundal plication.

c. Insertion of a silicone ring, shaped like a doughnut, around the lower end of the esophagus so as to plug the opening in the diaphragm.

Is repair of a diaphragmatic or hiatus hernia usually successful?

Yes, in the great majority of cases.

How long do hernia operations take to perform?

The simple inguinal hernias can be repaired in a half to three-quarters of an hour. The more extensive hernias, such as the diaphragmatic or the incarcerated ones, in which the herniated organs are firmly attached to

535

Hernia

the sac wall, may take several hours to repair.

What kind of anesthesia is used?
For hernias below the level of the navel, general, epidural, local, or spinal anesthesia is most often employed. Diaphragmatic hernias and hernias in the upper abdomen are operated upon only under general inhalation anesthesia.

How soon after the operation can the patient get out of bed?
In most cases, the patient can get out of bed on the day of, or the day following, surgery.

How long does one have to stay in the hospital following an ordinary hernia operation?
Approximately four days. However, it is possible for some patients to leave the hospital a day or two after surgery; others who are older or who had a complicated hernia repair may require seven to ten days of hospitalization.

What is the "Canadian" method of hernia repair?
It is a slight variation in the technique used in numerous other types of hernia repair.

Are results of the "Canadian" operation superior to other methods?
The results are excellent provided the repair is carried out on an appropriate patient and that it is done carefully. Other methods, performed carefully on appropriately selected patients, obtain the same good results.

How soon after the "Canadian" type of hernia repair can the patient leave the hospital?
In many cases, the day following surgery. However, it must be kept in mind that if a patient has heart disease, difficulty with his respiratory tract, problems in urinating postoperatively, or other complications, he may have to be hospitalized for several days or longer.

Can coughing or sneezing cause a recurrence of the hernia?
No, despite the fact that patients often feel as though they have ripped open all of their stitches when they cough.

What are the chances of recurrence following surgery?
More than 90 percent of hernias are cured permanently after surgery. Most recurrences are seen in elderly people or in those who have particularly fragile muscle and connective tissues.

How long does it take for the average hernia wound to heal?
Seven days.

What precautions should be taken to prevent hernia recurrence?
a. The patient should not permit himself to gain a large amount of weight.
b. Pushing, pulling, or lifting heavy objects (those over forty to fifty pounds) should be avoided whenever possible.
c. All strenuous exercise should be avoided for a period of four to six months.

536

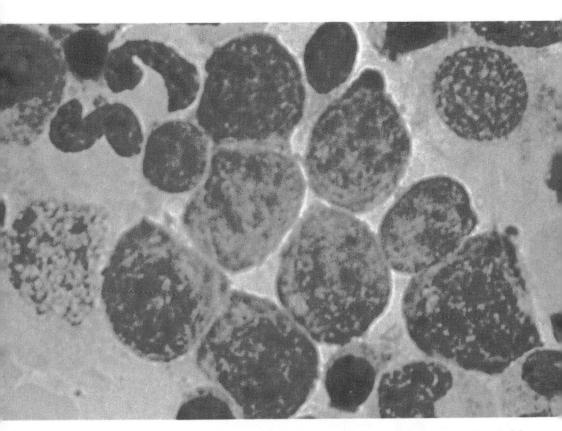

Blood cells are formed in the bone marrow, and diseases of the blood can often be diagnosed by studying a bone-marrow smear. The one above reveals an iron-deficiency anemia, the most common form of anemia.

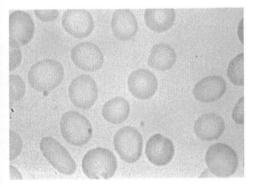

Iron-deficiency anemia is revealed by this smear of the circulating blood. The light-staining quality of the blood cells denotes lack of iron.

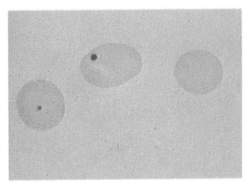

The red blood cells in a patient with pernicious (primary) anemia are few in number, larger than normal, and often contain the small black dots known as Howell-Jolly bodies.

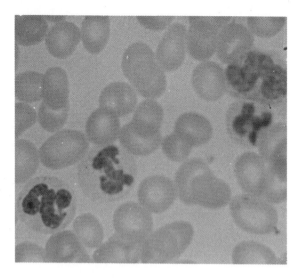

The white blood cells stain a characteristic bright pink in pernicious anemia, in which a gastric imbalance eventually prevents normal blood-cell formation.

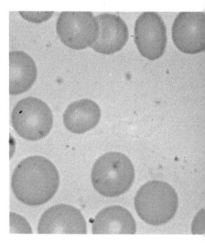

In cases of aplastic anemia, caused by a defect in the bone marrow, the red blood cells (*above*) are low in hemoglobin and fewer than normal in quantity.

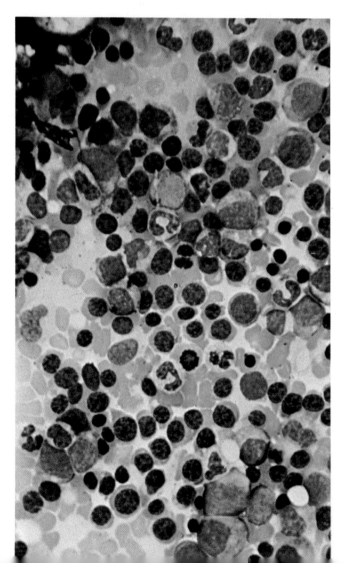

The bone marrow smear at the left is typical of hemolytic anemia, in which there is abnormal destruction of red blood cells.

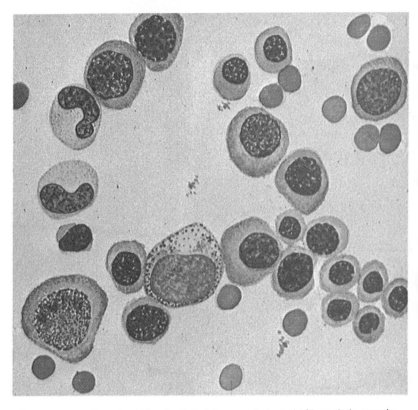

The sparse number of red blood cells in this smear is typical of hemolytic anemia; it can be due to an inherited defect in the blood as well as a destructive agent.

The smear below is from the circulating blood of a patient with hemolytic anemia; the destruction of red blood cells is usually caused by an infection, a toxin, or a poison.

In sickle-cell anemia, an inherited condition, some of the red blood cells are sickle-shaped instead of round, and some contain small specks of dark-staining material known as inclusion bodies.

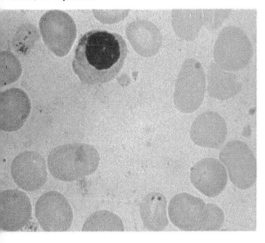

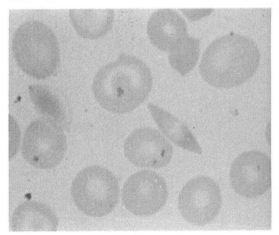

HEMANGIOMAS

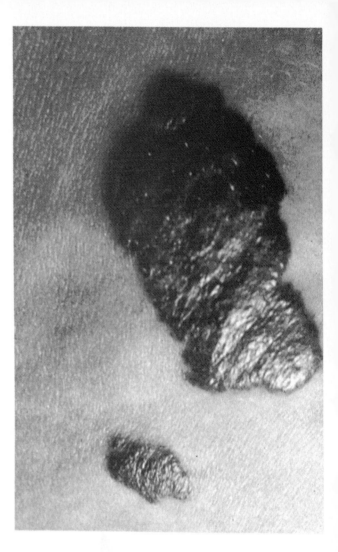

Hemangiomas which have a knobby appearance rather than the usual smooth surface are called tuberous hemangiomas.

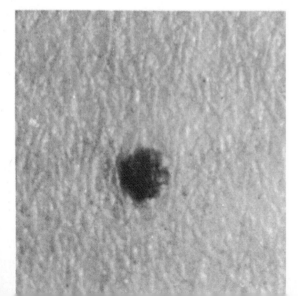

Small, discrete blood vessel tumors, known as senile angiomas, sometimes develop on the skin of elderly people.

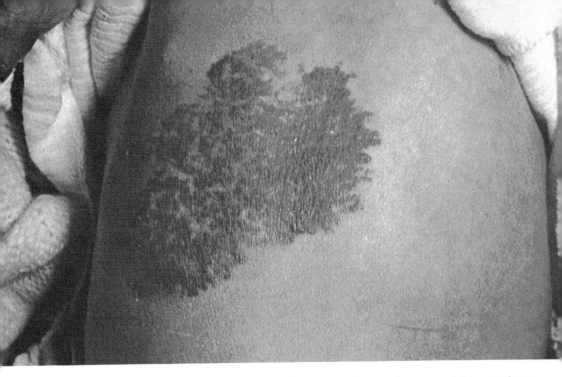

When hemangiomas are almost flush with the skin surface, they are known as flat hemangiomas.

The lips and gums are common locations of hemangiomas. These benign tumors, composed of dilated blood vessels, often occur in young children as well as in adults.

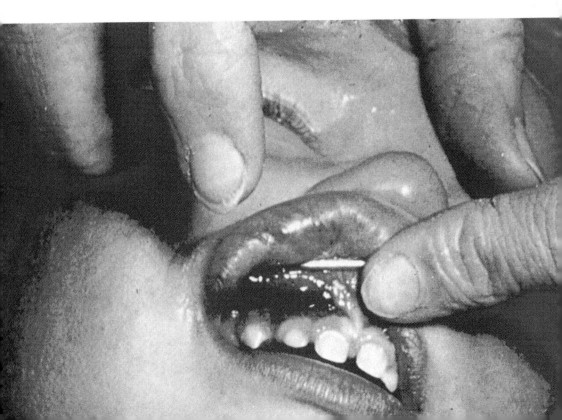

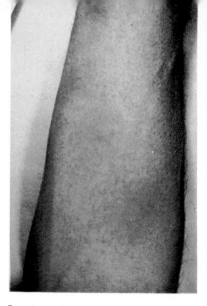

People can be allergic to many different things; the rash shown above is a reaction due to a caterpillar that walked along the patient's forearm.

Hypersensitivity to metal is a common cause of contact dermatitis. The wrist of the allergic patient has broken out in a rash owing to direct contact with the metal watch and watchband.

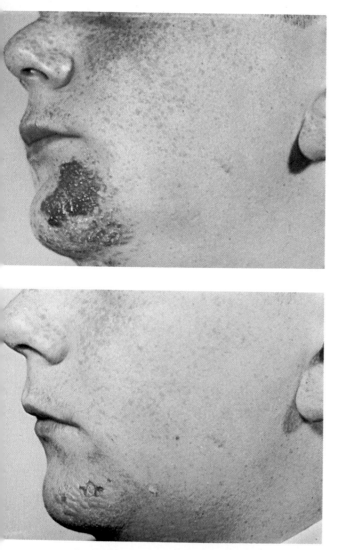

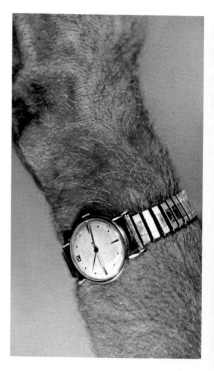

Contact dermatitis, one of the most common allergic reactions, caused by exposure of the skin to a substance to which one is hypersensitive, often resembles herpes, with its characteristic oozing, swelling blisters and crusts (seen in two typical stages of this condition, *above*).

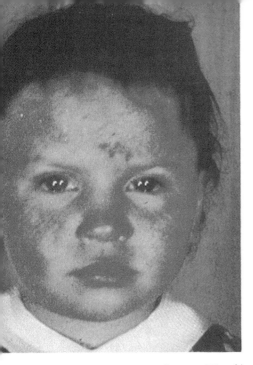

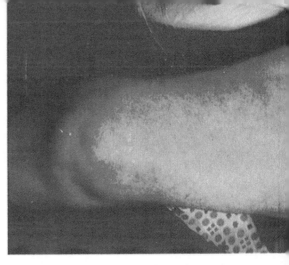

Certain materials, particularly wool or nylon, may produce contact dermatitis in people who are sensitive to them. The rash on this patient's thigh is due to the wearing of nylon stockings.

Atopic eczema, an inflammatory disease of the skin, frequently occurs in infants and small children as a result of a food sensitivity. It appears often in children with family histories of allergy.

The characteristic rash, swelling, and itching following insect bites have affected the face of the child below. Such a reaction is actually a form of allergic response.

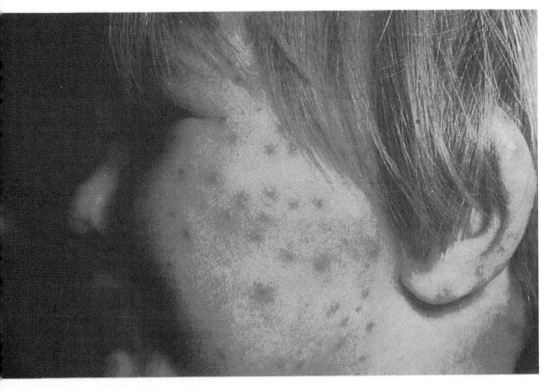

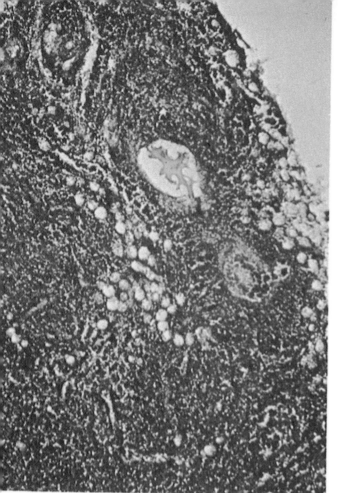

Lymphocytic leukemia is a type of leukemia characterized by enlargement of the lymph glands and by a large number of lymphocytes in the circulating blood. The microscopic appearance and the gross appearance of lymph glands involved in this condition are shown here.

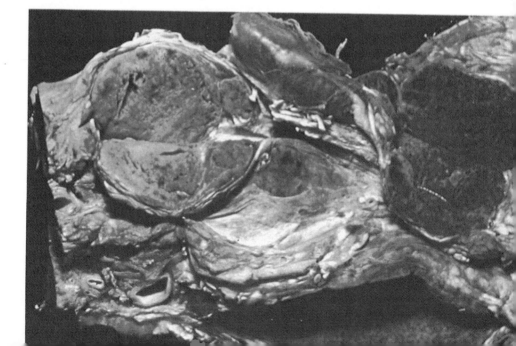

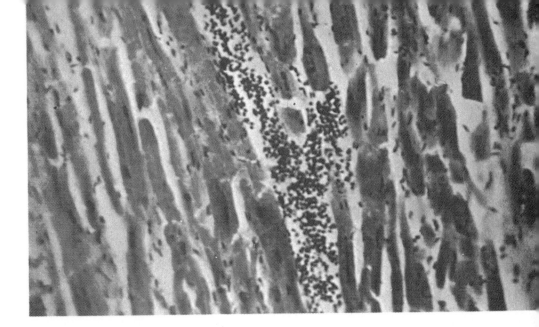

The spreading nature of lymphocytic leukemia may be observed in this photomicrograph of heart muscle which shows the invasion by the leukemic cells, the dark-stained material.

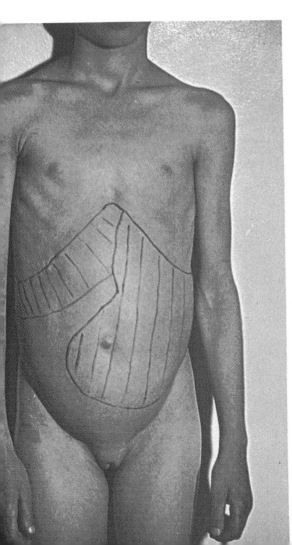

Myelocytic leukemia commonly involves the liver and spleen, as well as the lymph glands. The drawing on this patient's abdomen outlines the area of liver and spleen enlargement.

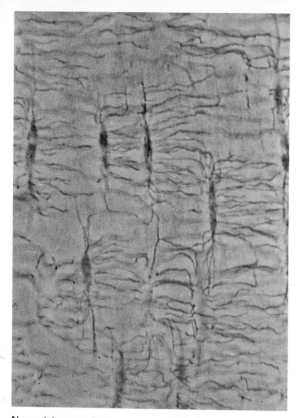

Normal bone cells appear as elliptical, nucleated structures in this microscopic lateral section of bone substance.

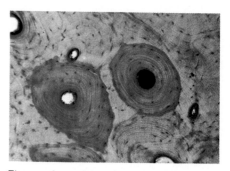

The conformation of compact bone with nourishing blood vessels and connective-tissue cells appears in this cross section.

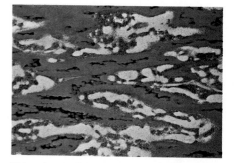

This photomicrograph (*above*) shows the microscopic structure of spongy bone. The spaces in between the bone tissue are occupied by bone marrow.

This photomicrograph (*below*) shows blood vessels and bone-forming cells beginning to form new tissue in areas which were originally cartilaginous.

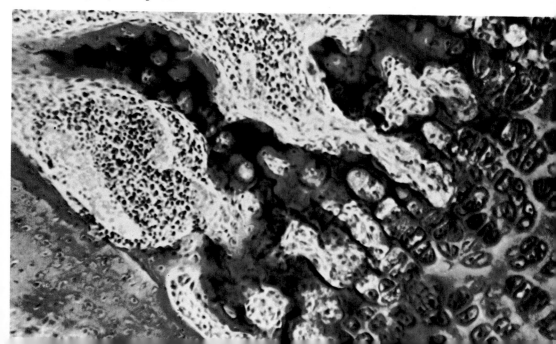

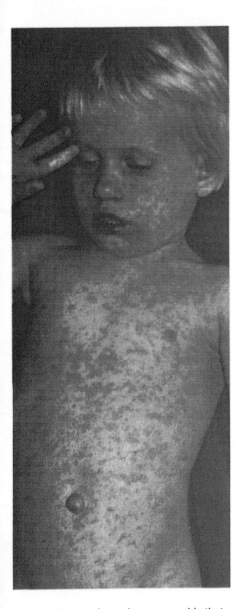

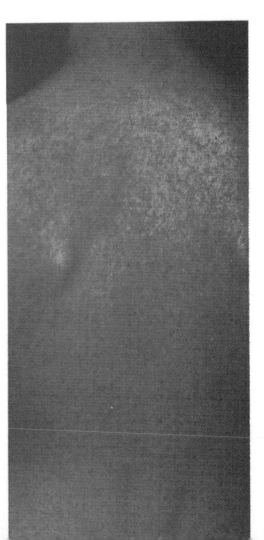

Although the measles rash may resemble that of German measles or scarlet fever, the generalized symptoms of the disease differ considerably. Measles is accompanied by typical Koplik spots in the mouth, a high fever, and by an inflammation of the mucous membranes of the eyes, nose, and throat. The diffuse nature of the German measles rash is shown at the right. This disease is much milder than measles and rarely causes a high temperature or toxicity.

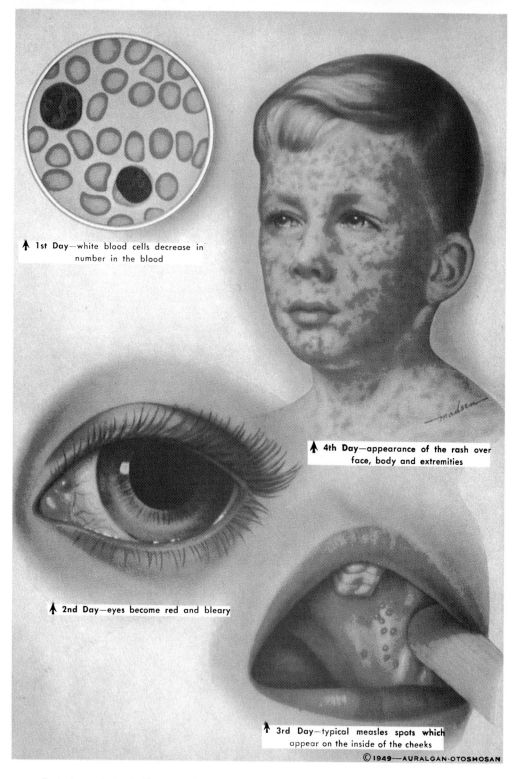

1st Day—white blood cells decrease in number in the blood

4th Day—appearance of the rash over face, body and extremities

2nd Day—eyes become red and bleary

3rd Day—typical measles spots which appear on the inside of the cheeks

© 1949—AURALGAN·OTOSMOSAN

Typical measles rash. The rash of measles is usually much more pronounced than that of German measles. Measles can be a severe disease, so the child should be kept in bed and watched carefully until temperature and all other symptoms have subsided. In occasional cases measles may affect the brain, causing encephalitis. This is a serious condition, although recovery takes place in the great majority of instances.

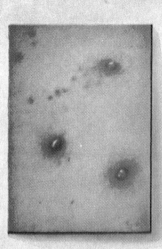

1st Day—tear-drop appearing rash over body

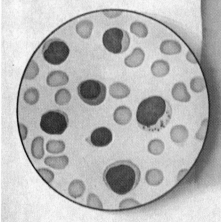

3rd Day—increased number of white blood cells appear in blood smear

2nd Day — appearance of rash over face and body

4th Day—spots begin to form crusts and dry up

© 1953—AURALGAN·OTOSMOSAN

Typical chickenpox rash. Although chickenpox is by no means a dangerous disease of childhood, it can often cause disfiguring scars if the child is permitted to pick at the scabs. During the period when scabs have formed, it is important to keep the child's fingernails clipped, and if he is old enough to understand, he should be urged not to to scratch the pockmarks.

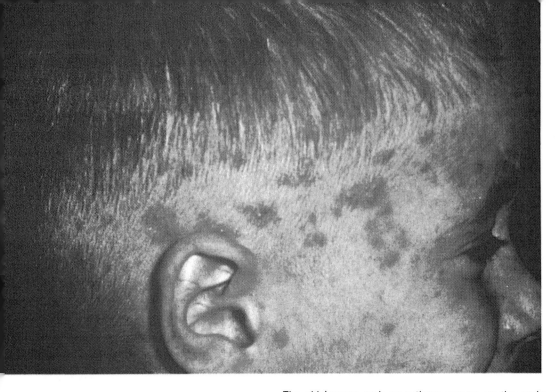

The chickenpox rash sometimes occurs on the scalp where it causes a good deal of itching and discomfort.

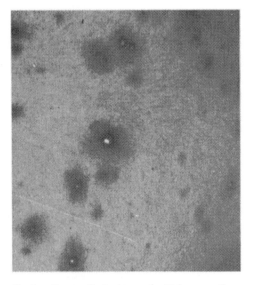

During the earliest stage of chickenpox there may appear on the body an area of diffuse, flat redness. Within 24 to 48 hours thereafter, the typical rash of raised pustules (*above*) will appear over the entire body (*right*). Although the pox are isolated and sharply demarcated, scratching may cause the area of redness to extend beyond the area of the individual pustule.

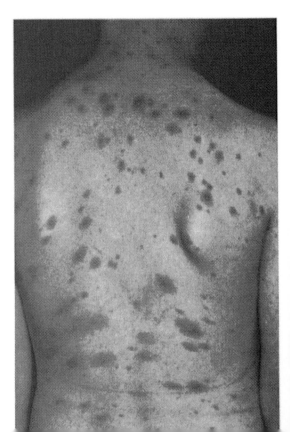

NORMAL VACCINATION REACTIONS showing typical "take"

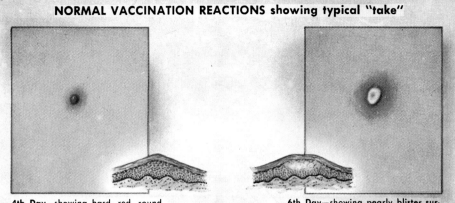

4th Day—showing hard, red, round, raised area

6th Day—showing pearly blister surrounded by red area

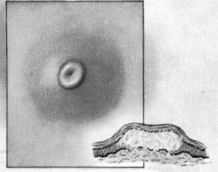

8th Day—showing larger blister and wider area of redness

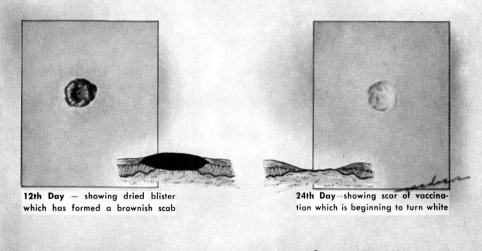

12th Day — showing dried blister which has formed a brownish scab

24th Day—showing scar of vaccination which is beginning to turn white

Smallpox vaccination reactions. It is a common misconception that only young children need to be vaccinated against smallpox. Before traveling to areas where smallpox exists, it is wise to be re-vaccinated. Many adults will have positive reactions if they have not been vaccinated for many years.

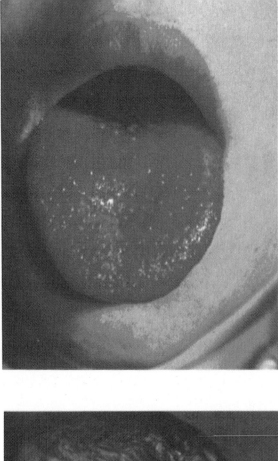

The tongue in patients with scarlet fever has a characteristic strawberry-red appearance. Fortunately, this serious disease is much milder today than it was a few decades ago.

Erysipelas is an acute inflammatory condition of the skin, caused by a streptococcus germ. It is accompanied by high fever and signs of great toxicity. Fortunately, the disease can be controlled by intensive antibiotic therapy.

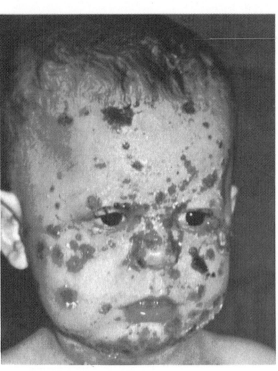

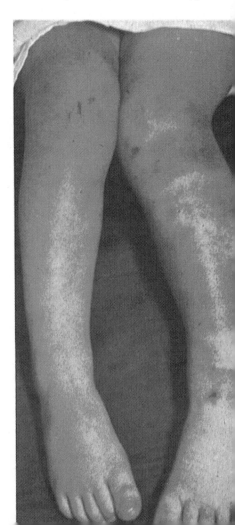

Impetigo is a highly contagious pustular condition resulting from a staphylococcal or streptococcal infection. It occurs most often on the faces of young children, although older children and adults are not immune.

If hernias do recur, what procedure is indicated?

About four out of five recurrent hernias can be cured by reoperation.

Should patients who have been operated upon for hernias wear trusses or abdominal supports?

No. Surgical repair is sufficient protection.

Is it common for patients to have slight pain, numbness, or tingling in the wound or along the scrotum for several weeks or months after hernia operations?

Yes. This happens occasionally but will disappear spontaneously.

Is sex life affected by the repair of an inguinal hernia?

No. The testicles and the other genital structures are not interfered with when hernia repair is carried out.

How soon after birth can an infant have a hernia repaired?

Newborns withstand surgery exceptionally well. If the hernia is large or if there is a danger of bowel strangulation, it is preferable to operate upon these children during the first few weeks or months of life.

Do hernias in the newborn tend to occur in both groins?

Yes. It is a common practice to operate upon both sides in these children, even though a hernia may be felt on only one side. Two out of three infants who have a hernia on one side will also have one on the other, though the second hernia may not be discovered on physical examination.

Will operating on both sides increase the risk of surgery?

No.

Can normal physical activity ever be resumed by someone who has undergone a hernia repair?

Most certainly, yes!

Can a woman permit herself to become pregnant after a hernia operation?

Yes, within a few months after surgical recovery.

How soon after a hernia operation can one do the following:

Bathe:
  Seven days.
Walk out on the street:
  Seven days.
Walk up and down stairs:
  Seven days.
Perform household duties:
  Three to four weeks.
Drive a car:
  Five to six weeks.
Resume sexual relations:
  Four weeks.
Return to work:
  Six to eight weeks.
Resume all physical activities:
  Three to six months.

How often should one return for a checkup following a hernia operation?

Approximately every six months, for a period of two years.

CHAPTER

31

IMMUNIZATIONS AND VACCINATIONS

(See also Chapter 7 on Allergy; Chapter 18 on Contagious Diseases; Chapter 34 on Infectious and Virus Diseases; Chapter 38 on Laboratory (Pathology) Tests and Procedures; Chapter 74 on Tuberculosis)

What is active immunity?

It is the protection afforded by having the disease or by receiving an injection of a substance that stimulates the body to produce long-lasting, protective antibodies.

What diseases afford permanent immunity after one has had them?

Measles, scarlet fever, diphtheria, German measles, mumps, chickenpox, and whooping cough. Typhoid fever, smallpox, and poliomyelitis also give permanent immunity if one has had them.

What is meant by passive, or inherited, immunity?

This is the type of immunity one inherits at birth if the mother has had

the disease sometime previously. The immunity is passed through the placenta and into the child's bloodstream. This type of immunity lasts only a few months. Passive immunity can also be accomplished by the injection of convalescent serum from someone who has just recently had the disease or by the injection of gamma globulin for selected illnesses. Breast milk also confers limited passive protection against certain conditions.

Is gamma globulin effective in preventing measles, German measles, infectious hepatitis, or polio if one has been exposed to these diseases?

Unfortunately, gamma globulin does

not often give protection, but it may cause the disease to be milder if it is contracted.

How long does passive, or inherited, immunity usually last?

About three to six months. In some instances, as long as nine months.

What is the reason for creating passive immunity if it lasts for only a short time?

It will tide the patient over a period when an epidemic may be in progress and thus spare him from contracting the disease.

Are convalescent serums useful in treatment of contagious diseases?

In general, no. However, convalescent serum does have some effectiveness in the treatment of whooping cough.

What is the best immunization schedule for infants?

It is best to give the triple vaccine (DPT) against diphtheria, whooping cough, and tetanus at the second, fourth, and sixth month; polio oral vaccine also at the second, fourth, and sixth month; and measles, mumps, and German measles vaccines at fifteen months. Smallpox vaccination is no longer advocated or required.

Can this immunization schedule be changed without adversely affecting the child?

Yes. It is often varied at the doctor's discretion.

What are so-called "booster shots?

These are additional injections given

a year or two after the original immunization in order to maintain immunity.

Is the effectiveness of these injections lost if the interval is prolonged because of an illness the child may have?

In general, no. The intervals may be prolonged for several weeks or even months without affecting the value of immunizations.

Should inoculations against disease be given if the child is sick from another cause?

No. Injections should be postponed when the child has another illness.

What are the reactions to injections against these contagious diseases?

Usually there are none, or they are very mild. Occasionally, one notices irritability, fever, restlessness, lack of appetite, or vomiting. These symptoms do not last for very long.

Are there any local reactions in the area where injections are given?

In some cases, there is redness and swelling in the area, but this usually passes within a day or two.

Is it common for a small lump to appear at the site where an injection was given?

Yes, but this has no significance and will disappear within a few days.

What is the treatment for reactions to immunization in children?

A small dose of aspirin or similar medication as prescribed by your doctor.

539

Immunizations and Vaccinations

On what part of the body are injections usually given?

In young infants, on the outer thigh; in older children, on the upper arm.

Who usually gives immunization injections?

Your physician or his regular nurse-assistant.

If there is a marked reaction to an injection, is it wise to inform your physician?

Yes. This information may influence him to reduce the dose of the next injection or to spread the series of injections over four to five injections instead of the usual two or three.

Is it ever necessary to discontinue immunization injections entirely?

If the child is highly allergic to the material on which the live virus is grown, it is wise to skin test the child before administering the virus.

Are there ever any harmful effects from immunization injections?

Just one or two patients among millions may have a serious reaction. The beneficial effects far outweigh any possible harm that may come from immunization injections.

Can allergic people be given immunization injections?

Yes, but smaller amounts may have to be given at each injection.

Is there any modification of this schedule for older children or adults?

Yes. In older children, a special vaccine containing only the diphtheri-

540

aand tetanus vaccine is used instead of the DPT vaccine. Also, when boosters are given to older children who have already had DPT vaccine, the boosters should contain only DT vaccine, with no pertussis.

THE SCHICK TEST

What is the Schick test?

This is a test to determine whether a child is immune or has developed an immunity (by injections) to diphtheria. The Schick test is rarely done nowadays.

How is the Schick test done?

A small amount of toxin is injected into the skin of the forearm, and the reaction is noted two to four days later. If nothing appears on the arm, the test is called negative, and the child is judged to be immune to diphtheria.

What is a positive Schick test?

If there is an area of redness and thickening of the skin the size of a dime, it is called a positive Schick test and shows that the child is not immune.

Does the Schick test cause the child to become sick in any way?

No.

What should be done if there is a positive Schick test?

The child should be given the complete course of injections against diphtheria.

THE TUBERCULIN TEST

What is the tuberculin test?

It is a test done to find whether the child has any tuberculosis germs in his body.

What tuberculosis tests are available?

a. The intradermal, or Mantoux, test.
b. The tine test.
These tests determine sensitivity to the germ of tuberculosis. They tell whether there have been any germs in the body, not necessarily whether they have done any damage. Only a chest x ray can do that.

How is the tine test done?

With a small instrument consisting of a plastic handle that has four small points, or tines, coated with testing material. These points are pressed against the forearm for a second or two. A few days later the doctor will

Smallpox. A positive reaction to smallpox vaccination may cause the arm to become red and tender, and to swell considerably. The inflammation will subside within a few days.

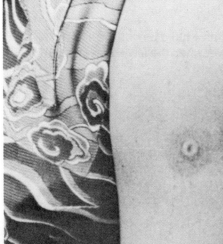

look at the arm to see if there is swelling where the test was given.

Is this test painful?

No.

What does the test show?

If the test is negative, there will be no swelling. This means there are no tuberculosis germs in the child's body.

What if the test is positive?

Then a chest x ray should be taken to show whether or not the tuberculosis germs have done any harm to the body. In a very young child, a positive test usually means active tuberculosis requiring treatment. This is not so in an older child.

At what age should the test be done?

The first test may be done at twelve months of age, then every year or two thereafter. It is important to recognize the disease early, when it can be cured and prevented from spreading to other parts of the body.

What about the family of a child with a positive test?

The other members of the family should be checked to make sure no one has tuberculosis.

SMALLPOX VACCINATION

Should all children in this country be vaccinated against smallpox?

No. Smallpox vaccinations are no longer recommended, as the risk of complications from the vaccine has

541

become greater than the risk of contracting smallpox. The disease has been almost eradicated from the earth. Of course, vaccination should be carried out if an outbreak of smallpox occurs in the vicinity.

Where is smallpox vaccine best given?

It is best to vaccinate on the outer surface of the upperarm, usually the left arm, near the shoulder.

Can people be vaccinated on the thigh?

Yes, but there is more danger of contamination by stool or urine in that area.

Is there any immediate reaction to smallpox vaccination?

No.

When does the positive reaction to smallpox vaccination set in?

In four to five days a red spot will appear and become larger and will form a blister. At about the eighth to ninth day, the blister is quite large and is surrounded by an area of redness the size of a quarter or half-dollar. Thereafter the blister dries up, leaving a crust, and the redness begins to subside and disappear within about two weeks after the original vaccination.

Is smallpox vaccination accompanied by fever and other signs of illness?

Yes, during the second week, when the vaccination reacts and is at its height. Temperatures as high as 103° to 104°F. may be recorded.

What is the treatment for the vaccination reaction?

It is wise to give aspirin in doses recommended by your doctor. Cool sponges to the body may be given if the temperature is high.

Are there any other signs of severe vaccination reaction?

Yes. There may be swelling in the armpit near the site of the vaccination. This does not necessarily indicate that an infection has set in.

If the vaccination seems to be exceptionally red, swollen, and painful, should the patient see his doctor?

Yes.

Does the patient ever develop a rash from smallpox vaccination?

In a small percentage of cases, a mild rash may appear. This will disappear as the reaction subsides.

Is it necessary to keep a dressing on the vaccination?

No. In fact, it is preferable not to have a dressing.

Should a vaccination shield be used?

Definitely not.

Can a child be bathed and the arm wet when the scab on a vaccination is dry?

Yes.

Should the vaccination area be bathed?

No. It is preferable to keep the area dry until the inflammation has subsided completely and a firm crust has formed.

Does one ever encounter secondary vaccinations?

Yes. Sometimes there may be a small blister near the original large vaccination. This will cause no harm.

How long does it usually take for the scab to fall off?

Between two and three weeks. It is best to allow it to fall off by itself.

Does it do any harm if the vaccination scab is rubbed off accidentally?

No.

Does the vaccination usually leave a large scar?

No.

What should be done if the smallpox vaccination does not "take"?

It should be done over again, after a wait of two to four weeks from the original vaccination.

Is it necessary to continue vaccinations until there is a positive "take"?

Yes, if vaccination is a requirement for travel.

Should a baby be vaccinated when he has a cold?

No.

Should a baby with eczema be vaccinated?

No. Even if the child has had a rash or a skin condition for a period of months or years, the vaccination

should be delayed. *Never* vaccinate a child while he has a rash!

Should a baby be vaccinated if another child in the family has eczema?

No. It is easy for the virus to be transmitted from the baby to the other child, with possible serious consequences.

Do vaccinations often become infected?

No. This is a common misconception.

Are there ever any convulsions from vaccination?

Rarely. They are caused by the high fever accompanying some vaccinations.

What are the chances of encephalitis (inflammation of the brain) from smallpox vaccination?

This is extremely rare, occurring perhaps once in 500,000 vaccinations.

Does this encephalitis occur in young infants?

Not usually. It occurs more often in children who are vaccinated for the first time after they are five years of age.

Do adults ever get encephalitis as a result of smallpox vaccination?

No.

Should schools permit children to enter who have not been vaccinated?

In this country, schools no longer require vaccination prior to admission.

543

Immunizations and Vaccinations

This, however, is not the case in certain other countries.

How effective is smallpox vaccination?

If there has been a positive "take," it will protect completely against this disease.

POLIOMYELITIS VACCINATION

Should polio vaccination be given if a patient is ill?

No. It is best to wait until he has recovered from any illness.

Is polio vaccine safe?

Yes. It is completely safe.

Can polio vaccine produce poliomyelitis?

No!

How effective is polio vaccination?

It is considered to be tremendously effective and will prevent the disease in more than 95 percent of those vaccinated. Those who may get it despite vaccination will get a very mild form of the disease, often without paralysis.

Can allergic people be given polio vaccine?

Yes. There have been no serious effects in allergic patients.

Are there usually reactions to polio vaccination?

No.

Oral polio vaccine can be swallowed in just a second or two. No reactions to this form of vaccination are encountered.

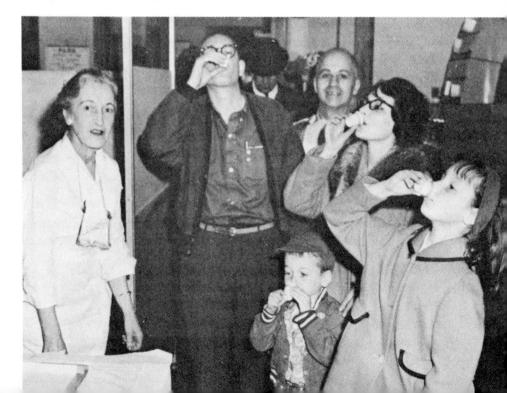

Are any special precautions necessary after polio vaccination?

No.

Does polio vaccine contain penicillin?

No. The Salk-type vaccine used to, but the Sabin oral vaccine does not. Today the Sabin vaccine is used almost exclusively.

Should people who are sensitive to penicillin be given the oral polio vaccine?

Yes.

Is it permissible to give polio vaccine at the same time as other vaccines?

Yes.

Is it permissible to vaccinate against polio at any time of the year?

Yes.

How soon after a full course of oral polio vaccine does immunity develop?

Within a period of several weeks.

Is it necessary after the three oral doses of polio vaccine to repeat the course within the next year or two?

No. It is thought that the full course of oral vaccine will produce a permanent immunity. However, just to be safe, some pediatricians do prescribe a second course of vaccine a year or two after the original one.

Should older children and adults be given the polio vaccine?

Yes. Only in this way can the disease be totally and permanently eradicated as an epidemic menace.

If a person has already had polio, will he benefit from vaccination?

Yes. The vaccine will increase his immunity. Also, he may also have immunity to only one strain of the polio virus; the vaccine will give him immunity to other strains as well.

Should polio vaccination be withheld if the child is going to have his tonsils removed?

No.

Is there any way to tell if someone is immune to polio before the vaccine is given?

Yes, but the procedure is not practical for everyday use. It is a very expensive test and takes a long time to perform. Also, there are only a few laboratories in the country equipped to perform such a test.

MEASLES VACCINATIONS

Are there satisfactory methods of immunizing against measles?

Yes, measles vaccine is effective in well over 90 percent of cases.

At what age should measles vaccination be carried out?

When the child is about fifteen months old. Older children who have never had measles should receive the vaccine no matter what their age.

How long does the immunity to measles last?

Permanently.

545

Producing Measles Vaccine. Large quantities of virus are needed to make measles vaccine and, since the viruses will grow only in living animal cells, these cells are grown under the strictest conditions of sterility. In the picture at left, a technician stacks bottles in which cells are developing. In the picture below, another technician examines them to see if they are growing normally and free of invading organisms.

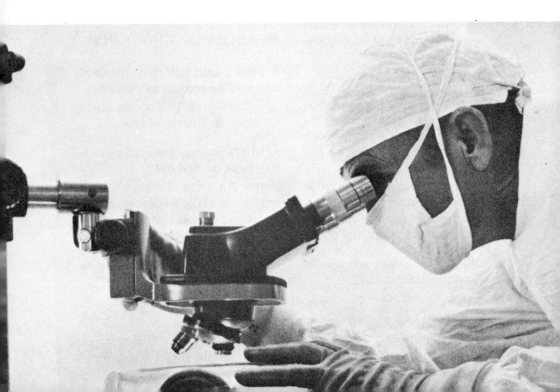

How is measles vaccination carried out?

By injection of a weakened (attenuated) live virus.

What is the reaction to measles vaccination among children?

In about one out of ten cases, a fever, upper respiratory congestion, and a slight rash appear within seven to twelve days after vaccination. Recovery is prompt within two to three days.

Are there any children who may not be suitable for measles vaccine?

Yes. Those who are allergic to egg may develop a severe reaction. They should undergo skin testing before attempting vaccination.

What should be done if a child does have a reaction to the measles vaccine?

Small doses of aspirin or a similar medication may be given for a day or two.

Is it necessary to give measles vaccine to a child who has had measles?

No. If you are sure the child has had the disease, he is permanently immune. However, if there is any doubt, there is no harm in giving him the measles vaccine.

May the vaccine be given when a child who has not had the disease is exposed to a case of measles?

Yes. It would be wise under such circumstances to give the live vaccine along with the gamma globulin. In that way the attenuated virus may give immunity and prevent the growth of the virus caught from the other child. In any event, the gamma globulin would insure that the disease would be very mild even if the active caught virus did gain the ascendancy.

GERMAN MEASLES IMMUNIZATION

Should people be vaccinated against German measles?

Yes. German measles vaccine is very effective. It should be given to all children and to women of child-bearing age who have not had the disease. Women must not be pregnant at the time of vaccination, and they must be warned to avoid becoming pregnant for two months after being vaccinated with the German measles vaccine. The main purpose of immunization is prevention of birth defects in the unborn child.

MUMPS IMMUNIZATION

Is there any vaccine against mumps?

Yes. A very effective mumps vaccine is available and should be given to all children who are not allergic to eggs.

TYPHOID FEVER VACCINATION

When is typhoid fever immunization given?

When the child or adult is going into an area where there is danger of exposure to typhoid fever. This applies particularly to certain foreign countries.

547

Immunizations and Vaccinations

What is the routine immunization against typhoid fever?

A series of three injections into the skin or beneath the skin, given one to two weeks apart.

What vaccine is used?

Usually a vaccine containing the dead typhoid and paratyphoid germs.

Are injections against typhoid fever effective?

Yes.

Are there any reactions to typhoid immunization?

Yes. The arm may become very red and swollen, and there may be fever for a few days.

What is the best treatment for the reaction to typhoid immunization?

Aspirin and bed rest.

Are booster injections necessary after typhoid immunization?

Yes. One injection a year of a small dose of the vaccine should be given if a patient is again going to an area where there is danger of contracting typhoid.

OTHER IMMUNIZATIONS

Are there any effective immunizations against the common cold?

No.

Is there any immunization against tuberculosis?

Yes, there is a vaccine called BCG. (See Chapter 74, on Tuberculosis.)

Is vaccination against tuberculosis effective?

There is great controversy on this subject; the vaccine is not generally used in this country.

When is tuberculosis vaccination advised?

In certain situations when the individual has been exposed for long periods of time to a known case of tuberculosis, it will be advised.

Is there an effective immunization against rabies?

Yes.

When is vaccination against rabies given?

When an individual has been bitten by any animal that is suspected of being rabid, such as a dog, cat, fox, squirrel, rabbit, rat, wolf, etc.

Are rabies immunization injections given in every case of a dog bite?

No. They are given when the dog is known or suspected of being diseased. The dog must be sent to a place where he can be held and examined for a few days to note whether he develops rabies. If the dog is found to be healthy, no immunization is necessary.

If the animal that has caused the bite cannot be found, should the injections be given?

Yes, as a safeguard.

How is rabies inoculation carried out?

By daily injections for fourteen days.

Is there any effective treatment for rabies once it has developed?

No. There is a very high mortality rate once a child or adult has developed the disease.

What is the best local treatment for a dog bite?

Thorough washing of the area with soap and water for at least five to ten minutes.

If the skin has not been broken by a dog bite, is there any danger of infection?

Not usually, but the area should still be washed thoroughly with soap and water for ten to twenty minutes.

Should a dog bite be reported to the authorities?

Yes. In almost all communities, it is the law that such bites be reported to the police or to the board of health.

Does it make any difference where the animal has bitten the patient?

Yes. The closer to the head the bite is, the more serious it is.

Are there any dangers from giving rabies inoculations?

No, but it is a painful process to have to endure.

Are there any effective vaccinations against typhus fever, cholera, yellow fever, and the plague?

Yes. There are very effective vaccinations against all of these diseases.

When should vaccinations against typhus fever, cholera, yellow fever, or the plague be given?

Only when one is traveling to an area where there is danger of contracting these diseases.

What immunization procedures are necessary for travel to foreign countries?

If one is traveling to Europe or well-developed countries in the Orient such as Japan, no special immunization procedures are now mandatory. Formerly, it was necessary for a traveler to be vaccinated against smallpox, typhoid and paratyphoid fever, and tetanus prior to departure for a foreign land. However, the general level of public health in most developed countries today is as high as it is in the United States. Therefore these vaccinations are not essential. To be perfectly safe, however, it is wise to check with the local department of health for the most recent requirements. And in terms of reentry, the United States no longer requires a smallpox vaccination unless one is returning from an area where cases of smallpox have been reported.

Where can one get additional information on immunizations necessary for foreign travel?

The United States Department of Health and Human Services and the Public Health Service issue a booklet giving exact details of immunization procedures advisable for travelers. The World Health Organization issues a standard certificate that can be filled in by your physician. It lists the injections and the dates on which they have been given.

IMMUNIZATION AND VACCINATION CHART

Disease	Material Used	When Given	Number of Injections	Spacing of Injections
MUMPS	Mumps vaccine	15 months of age	1	
CHICKENPOX	None			
INFECTIOUS HEPATITIS	Gamma globulin	Exposure to case of infectious hepatitis	1	
SCARLET FEVER	Penicillin	Exposure to case of scarlet fever	Oral medication	
RABIES	Rabies vaccine	Following suspicious animal bite	14	Daily
CHOLERA	Cholera vaccine	*For foreign travel	2–3	1 week
TYPHUS FEVER	Typhus vaccine	*For foreign travel	2–3	1 week
YELLOW FEVER	Yellow fever vaccine	*For foreign travel	1	
PLAGUE	Plague vaccine	*For foreign travel	2–3	1 week
INFLUENZA	Influenza vaccine	During epidemics	2	1 week
ROCKY MOUNTAIN SPOTTED FEVER	Rocky Mountain spotted fever vaccine	For persons exposed to tick in suspicious areas	3	1 week
DIPHTHERIA	Diphtheria fluid toxoid	Infancy and childhood, or upon exposure	3	1 month apart
WHOOPING COUGH	Pertussis vaccine	Infancy and childhood, or upon exposure	3	1 month apart
TETANUS	Tetanus fluid toxoid	Infancy and childhood, or after injury	3	1 month apart
SMALLPOX	Cowpox virus	Infancy, childhood and adulthood	1	
POLIOMYELITIS	Sabin polio vaccine	2, 4, and 6 months of age	No injections; 3 oral doses	2 months apart
TYPHOID FEVER	Typhoid, paratyhoid vaccine	At any age when traveling to suspicious area	3	1–4 weeks
MEASLES	Measles vaccine	9–12 months, or any time thereafter	3 of killed virus—1 of live virus	1 month apart
GERMAN MEASLES	German Measles vaccine	Childhood, and adulthood for females of childbearing age	1	

*Needed only in traveling to countries where these diseases are present—as in Asia, Africa, and some parts of Europe, Central and South America.

550

Reactions	Duration of Immunity	"Recall" or Booster Injections	Remarks
**Not to be given to egg-sensitive people	Probably lifelong		
None	4–6 weeks	None, except where exposure is prolonged	
None		Same procedure if re-exposed	May give penicillin only in adequate dosage
Slight	3–6 months	If bitten again after 3 months	May not need full series if dog is found not infected
Slight	Short	Every 6–12 months	
Slight	Short	Annually	
**May be moderate	Long	Every 6 years	
Slight	Short	every 6–12 months	
Slight	Short		
**Moderate	Short	Annually	
None to slight	Varies	First booster—after 1 year; second booster at 4–6 years; then every 10 years.	All three (diphtheria, tetanus, and whooping cough) may be combined in a single injection— in young children only. After 6 years of age, only diphtheria and tetanus (DT) are given
Slight to moderate	Varies		
None to slight	Varies		
Moderate	Several years	Every 5 years for foreign travel	Smallpox vaccination no longer required in most countries
None		Not necessary	
Moderate	1–3 years	Every 1–3 years	
None, or very slight	Long	None	May be given with or without gamma globulin
None	Probably lifelong	None	Females of childbearing age must not be pregnant or become so for 2 months after vaccination.

**Must be careful of reactions in allergic people sensitive to eggs.

Immunizations and Vaccinations

IMMUNIZATION CHART

Present accepted ideal schedule for infants and children

2–3 months First DPT (diphtheria, pertussis, tetanus) and Sabin oral vaccine

4–5 months Second DPT and second Sabin vaccine

5–6 months Third DPT and third Sabin vaccine. If desired, the DPT may be given along with the polio vaccine, or the polio vaccine may be given separately

12 months Tuberculin test

15 months Measles, mumps, and German measles vaccinations

18 months DPT, polio vaccine boosters

4–6 years DPT booster and tuberculin test

Additional boosters: Tetanus— after injury from rusty object or one contaminated by dirt. Such additional boosters may be advisable for any suspicious injury causing a puncture wound if the last tetanus immunization is more than three years old.

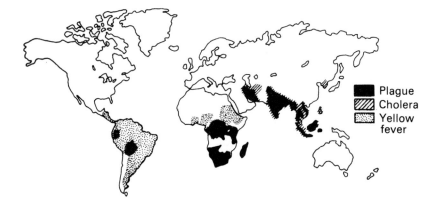

Plague
Cholera
Yellow fever

Areas of Plague, Cholera, and Yellow Fever.
If one intends traveling to places where these diseases are prevalent, it is necessary to be immunized against them. Statistics were unavailable for the People's Republic of China at the time this chart was prepared.

CHAPTER **32**

INFANT AND CHILDHOOD DISEASES

See also Chapter 17 on Child Behavior; Chapter 18 on Contagious Diseases; Chapter 33 on Infant Feeding; Chapter 47 on the Newborn Child)

What is croup (catarrhal laryngitis)?

It is an inflammatory disease of the respiratory passage involving the larynx, or voice box, and occurring mostly in children between the ages of one and five.

What causes croup?

It is caused by a virus infection in most cases. Bacterial organisms also may be the causative agent.

Does diphtheria cause croup?

Yes. There is a type of diphtheritic croup in which a membrane is formed in the larynx and trachea.

How can croup be recognized?

The first symptoms are difficulty in breathing, hoarseness or loss of voice, coughing, crowing, and a barking sound similar to that made by a seal. There is a slight elevation of temperature in the average case, but it may be considerably elevated in the severe case.

When does croup usually start?

At night. It tends to subside during the day and then to become worse again the next night.

How long does the average case of croup last?

About one to three days.

What is the treatment for croup?

a. Steam inhalations or a cold mist vaporizer.
b. Keeping the room moist with a vaporizer.

Is there any way to prevent croup?

No.

Does croup tend to recur?

Yes. Children who have once had an

553

attack of croup may have repeated attacks with each respiratory infection during the next two to three years.

Do the severe forms of croup require special treatment?

Yes. It is imperative that children with severe croup be seen by a doctor immediately, because in the severe case there is a great tendency toward obstruction of breathing.

What should be done in severe cases of croup?

Where there is obstruction to the breathing that is not relieved by mist, it may be necessary for the doctor to admit the child to the hospital for an immediate tracheotomy.

What is a tracheotomy?

It is an opening made into the windpipe to allow the child to breathe.

Is there any other treatment for severe croup?

Yes. Many cases will be benefited by giving oxygen.

What special diet should be given to a child with croup?

It is preferable to give increased fluids and soft foods.

Steam Inhalation for Croup. The old-fashioned croup kettle is still effective but has been replaced by an apparatus of the type shown below, which can be purchased at almost any drugstore. Electric steam inhalators benefit children with croup by moistening and warming the air.

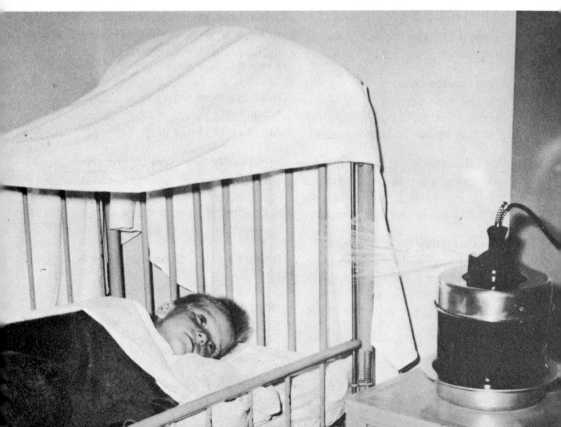

Are antibiotics effective against croup?
No.

Is there any effective vaccine against croup?
No.

Are there permanent aftereffects of croup?
Usually not. The great majority of cases make a complete recovery.

Is it necessary to quarantine a child with croup?
No, but the disease is somewhat contagious, and the same precautions should be taken as for any ordinary upper respiratory infection.

Does croup tend to occur more often in allergic children?
Yes.

Does it occur more often during ons particular season?
Yes. It occurs more frequently in the winter and fall months.

When may the child be allowed out of doors after recovery from croup?
When fever abates and the child returns to his usual level of activity.

CELIAC DISEASE

What is celiac disease?
It is a disturbance of the digestive system chiefly involving the digestion of starches and fats.

What causes this disease?
A failure or deficiency of some of the enzymes involved in the digestive process. It has been found that the digestion of gluten products is impaired, particularly the gliadin protein. This is found in wheat and rye products.

How often does celiac disease occur?
About one in a hundred children has this condition.

Does it tend to run in families?
Yes.

Is there any relationship to allergies?
Yes. We seem to find more of these cases in families that have a history of allergies. Some of the children with this condition later manifest allergic symptoms as well.

When does celiac disease become evident?
Usually during the first year of life. The baby may appear to be normal at first and then begin to show signs of this condition between six and eighteen months of age.

How does this condition manifest itself?
By alternate periods of diarrhea and constipation, with large, bulky, foul-smelling stools. The infant fails to gain weight and may even lose weight. The abdomen becomes large and distended, the buttocks become small and flabby. The appetite is poor, and occasionally there may be some vomiting. Also, the infant is subject to frequent colds and bronchitis and may have a chronic cough.

555

Infant and Childhood Diseases

Are there varying degrees of severity of celiac disease?

Yes. There are very mild cases, which are difficult to diagnose, and severe forms, which can be easily recognized.

What tests can be done to make a positive diagnosis?

The stool is examined for the presence of undigested fats and starches and for the presence of trypsin, one of the digestive enzymes. There are also certain tests to determine the absorption of Vitamin A, gelatin, and glucose into the blood from the stomach and duodenum.

Will x rays help in the diagnosis of this condition?

Yes, sometimes gastrointestinal studies will help in the diagnosis.

What is the treatment for celiac disease?

The child must be kept on a special diet for a long time. The diet will be high in proteins, low in fat, with no starches or sugars (other than natural fruit sugar). No wheat or rye products are to be given. These are the greatest offenders in causing a flare-up of the disease as they contain a large amount of gluten.

What milk is used?

Ordinary cow's milk is usually well tolerated.

What solids are tolerated by the child with celiac disease?

All foods except those containing gluten (gliadin).

Can the baby have the usual vitamins?

The water-soluble multivitamin preparations are given, usually in increased amounts because of the difficulty in absorption.

How long does the infant stay on this diet?

About six months to two years, until gliadin is tolerated.

Is recovery usually complete in celiac disease?

Yes.

Can the child take a full diet later in life?

Yes, most can. Some children may still require a gliadin-free diet.

Are there any setbacks during the treatment?

Yes, when offending foods are eaten.

How does this diet affect the child's disposition?

Some children take the diet well and eat avidly without any disturbance. Others seem to get bored by the diet, so the mother must use her ingenuity to get the child to eat the foods prescribed.

Can celiac disease be treated satisfactorily at home?

Yes. Hospitalization may be necessary only in the beginning of the disease or for thorough investigation and diagnosis.

Does the baby have to stay in bed with this condition?

No, except during an acute illness.

Will celiac disease clear up without treatment?

No. If the baby stays on a full diet, the stools become worse, weight loss increases, and severe infections are more apt to occur.

Does celiac disease tend to recur?

In some cases it may be necessary to continue modified dietary care for several years. Otherwise there may be relapses or recurrences, especially when infections occur.

Is the pancreas involved in this condition?

No.

CYSTIC FIBROSIS

What is cystic fibrosis?

It is a disease somewhat similar in its manifestations to celiac disease, but it is more severe in nature and tends to have more complications, such as lung infections.

How often does it occur?

About one in five to six hundred babies has this disease.

When does it start?

It starts earlier than celiac disease, usually from birth to six months of age.

Does it tend to run in families?

Yes.

Does heat affect these children inordinately?

Yes. They lose a great deal of salt in the sweat secretions and may go into collapse on a hot summer's day.

Do some children die with cystic fibrosis?

Yes. Some children may die during a heat spell, others may die of pulmonary complications, and still others from malnutrition. About 50 percent die before the age of five.

What is the treatment for cystic fibrosis?

Diet similar to that in celiac disease, adequate salt intake, large amounts of vitamins, constant use of antibiotics to prevent infections, and the giving of pancreatic extracts.

How long does treatment have to be continued to maintain these children?

For several years, and often through adolescence.

What causes cystic fibrosis?

The exact cause is not known, but investigations have shown that there is a basic defect in the function of many organs of the body, such as the pancreas, the liver, the lungs, and the intestinal tract. There seems to be an underlying disorder in the production of enzymes and in the mucous production of the various organs.

Was it formerly thought that cystic fibrosis was a disease limited primarily to the pancreas?

Yes. This concept has been discarded within recent years as it has become evident that the organs mentioned above are also involved in the disease process.

557

Infant and Childhood Diseases

Is cystic fibrosis often associated with excess mucous production and excess viscosity (thickness) of mucus that is secreted in the lungs and in the intestinal tract?

Yes, this is one of the most characteristic findings in cystic fibrosis.

If there is a case of this disease in the family, should the parents plan to have other children?

Yes. They may have additional children, but they should be told that there is a one in four chance that another child will have the same condition.

Are there any special tests for this disease?

Tests of the sweat to determine the salt content are specific for this condition. Recently, other tests of saliva, nails, and hair show this same particular increase in sodium.

Is it easy to differentiate this condition from celiac disease?

In very frank cases, the two can be differentiated, but in mild ones it may be difficult to tell them apart.

What is the outlook for a child with cystic fibrosis?

The outlook is improving as more and more is being discovered as to the cause of this condition. Also, the protection of the child against frequent upper respiratory infections has been shown to reduce the chances of permanent damage to the lungs. Finally, many children are now being saved by the continued use of various antibiotics, both prophylactically and in the treatment of infections.

HIRSCHSPRUNG'S DISEASE *(Megacolon)*

(See also Chapter 66 on Small and Large Intestines)

What is Hirschsprung's disease?

It is a disease present from birth involving the large intestine, in which there is a contracted segment in the sigmoid colon on the left side with tremendous dilatation and enlargement of the remainder of the bowel above the constricted portion.

How common is Hirschsprung's disease?

It is a relatively rare condition, seen more often among males, and constitutes about one out of every ten thousand hospital admissions.

What causes Hirschsprung's disease?

It is thought to be due to a developmental deformity in which certain nerves are lacking in the contracted portion of the bowel (sigmoid colon). This lack prevents the involved segment of bowel from relaxing and dilating. In order to propel the feces forward, the bowel above the constriction enlarges, and because it is difficult to get gas and feces beyond the contracted area, the bowel above dilates tremendously.

How is the diagnosis of Hirschsprung's disease made?

By characteristic findings on x-ray examination with the giving of barium to outline the bowel. Also, a biopsy of a small portion of the rectal muscle may show the absence of nerve cells.

What is the course and treatment of this condition?

Mild cases tend to improve and get well with medical management over a period of years. The majority of severe cases will require the surgical removal of the constricted portion of large intestine.

Is surgery successful in curing Hirschsprung's disease?

Yes. Modern techniques have improved greatly, and the surgical treatment of this condition is now safe and can promise an extremely high rate of cure.

NEPHROSIS

(See Chapter 37 on Kidneys and Ureters)

RHEUMATIC FEVER

(See Chapter 62 on Rheumatic Fever)

ERYTHROBLASTOSIS

What is erythroblastosis?

Erythroblastosis, also called Rh-factor disease, is a condition in which the red blood cells of the embryo or newborn are destroyed because of an incompatibility between the mother's and the child's blood.

What are other names for erythroblastosis?

a. Rh-factor disease.

b. Erythroblastosis fetalis.
c. Severe jaundice of the newborn.
d. Severe anemia of the newborn.
e. Hemolytic disease of the newborn.

What is meant by the "Rh-factor"?

All people are either Rh-positive or Rh-negative. This means that the blood contains a substance (Rh substance) in Rh-positive people that is not present in Rh-negative people.

What percentage of people are Rh-positive?

Eighty-five percent. The other 15 percent are Rh-negative.

Are these blood factors transmitted from parent to child?

Yes.

Under what circumstances will an embryo or newborn have no Rh problem?

a. If the mother is Rh-positive.
b. If the father and mother are both Rh-negative.

Will all babies born of an Rh-negative mother and an Rh-positive father develop erythroblastosis?

No, only a small percentage will develop it.

What brings about this condition?

An Rh-negative mother carries an Rh-positive baby in her uterus. Some of the Rh-positive baby blood substance gets into the mother's circulation and produces Rh-positive antibodies. These antibodies in turn will later get into the baby's circulation and destroy the baby's own blood cells.

Infant and Childhood Diseases

How does this affect the newborn infant?

By producing anemia due to destruction of the infant's red blood cells, thus producing jaundice (yellow skin and eyes).

How is the jaundice produced?

The infant's liver is unable to clear all the destroyed cells from the circulation, causing an overflow of bile into the circulation.

How can this condition be recognized?

The infant becomes pale and jaundiced during the first twenty-four hours of life. In addition, the liver and spleen are found to be enlarged. Blood tests will show the presence of the antibodies in the infant's blood.

How does the jaundice in the Rh-factor disease differ from normal newborn jaundice?

By its very early development, in the first twenty-four hours, and its severity.

Is there any way to determine during the pregnancy whether the baby may have this disease?

Yes. Every mother should be tested in advance to determine whether she is Rh-positive or Rh-negative. If she is Rh-negative, her blood should be tested frequently during the latter weeks and months of her pregnancy for the presence and amount of these specific antibodies. If they are present, the baby may develop this disease.

What is the treatment for erythroblastosis?

As soon after birth as possible, an exchange transfusion should be done. More recently, children with erythroblastosis have been subjected to special lights to reduce jaundice. This treatment is called *phototherapy.*

What is meant by an "exchange transfusion"?

An attempt is made to remove all, or nearly all, of the baby's blood and replace it with blood from a donor—blood that does not contain these dangerous antibodies. This procedure will require the services of an expert in the field.

Is it ever necessary to give more than one exchange transfusion?

Yes. In some cases, the jaundice may reappear in two to three days, necessitating a second and, in rare cases, even a third exchange transfusion.

Can an exchange transfusion cure erythroblastosis?

Yes. If done early enough, it will cure almost every case.

What can happen in an untreated case of erythroblastosis?

The baby may die in a few days because of the extreme blood destruction, or the intense jaundice may permanently injure certain parts of the brain.

What is the nature of this brain injury?

It may produce spasticity or extreme

drowsiness in the baby and may later be the cause of mental retardation, convulsions, and a form of cerebral palsy.

Can an exchange transfusion prevent brain injury?

Yes. By removing the antibodies and the jaundice producing substance, it will prevent brain injury. It must be done very early, however, and may need to be repeated if jaundice recurs.

Does Rh-factor disease ever produce stillbirths before the baby is delivered?

Yes. In some cases it is a cause of death in the uterus or just before birth. In some Rh-negative women, there may be a history of repeated stillbirths due to this disease. Physicians are now trying to prevent such stillbirths by giving the baby a transfusion through the mother's abdomen before the baby is born.

Is there any way to treat an unborn child who is being carried by an Rh-negative mother and is therefore more likely to be born with Rh-factor disease?

Yes. It is possible to give such a child blood transfusions while still in the mother's womb.

Is it possible to have a live baby in such cases?

Yes. If the condition is recognized during pregnancy, the live infant may be taken prematurely by Cesarean section or by prompting premature labor. An exchange transfusion is done immediately after birth, or the prenatal transfusion may be used if it is expected that the baby will be stillborn.

Is there any way to prevent the development of sensitizing antibodies in an Rh-sensitive mother so that subsequent pregnancies will not result in erythroblastosis?

Yes. It is now possible to immunize an Rh-negative mother against the Rh-positive factor of the embryo. A substance known as RhoGAM can be injected into an Rh-negative mother within seventy-two hours after a child is born. Mothers so injected prior to a second pregnancy will not have subsequent children born with Rh-factor disease.

May a child who has recovered from erythroblastosis be breast-fed?

Yes. There was a time when the possible introduction of these antibodies (some of which may be present in the breast milk) into the baby's stomach was feared. It is now known that they cause no harm when introduced in that manner.

Are firstborn babies ever affected with erythroblastosis?

Not ordinarily. It usually affects later pregnancies. It may affect a firstborn infant if the mother has been given a transfusion or blood injection with Rh-positive blood some time prior to her first pregnancy. Then her blood may contain the dangerous antibodies as a result of the previous blood injection.

561

Is there any other mechanism that can produce erythroblastosis besides the Rh-factor?

Yes. In a number of cases of so-called ABO incompatibility, in which the mother's blood group is "O" and the baby's group is "A" or "B," a form of this disease may be produced.

What proportion of cases is caused by ABO incompatibility?

About 5 to 10 percent.

How long does the baby have to stay in the hospital after an exchange transfusion?

For about a week, to make sure that there is no recurrence of anemia or jaundice. No other special treatments are required.

AMAUROTIC FAMILIAL IDIOCY
(Tay-Sachs Disease)

What is amaurotic familial idiocy?

It is a fatal disease of young infants associated with blindness and mental retardation.

What are the manifestations of this disease?

A baby will progress normally until about six months of age, then he will stop in his develop about six months of age, then he will stop in his development and regress. He will show signs of blindness, apathy, weakness of his muscles, and later spasticity and convulsions.

What causes this condition?

The infant is unable to utilize certain fatty substances in his food. These substances then accumulate in the brain, causing destruction of the normal brain cells.

What is the nature of the deficiency?

It has recently been found that certain enzymes are missing in the baby's blood. These enzymes act on one of the forms of sugar in its metabolism.

How is the diagnosis of this condition made?

By examination of the eyes with an opthalmoscope, A characteristic abnormal "cherry-red spot" will be seen on the retina.

Does this disease run in families?

Yes. If a family has one baby with this condition there is a one in four chance that another baby born to these parents will have the same condition. We have also found that the parents may have a partial deficiency of the enzyme. If both parents have a partial deficiency, then there is a one in four chance that they will have a baby with this condition.

Does amaurotic familial idiocy occur only in Jewish families?

Almost exclusively. About 95 percent of the cases occur in Jewish families. This condition occurs in about 1 in 6,000 Jewish births and in about 1 in 600,000 non-Jewish births.

Is there any way of preventing Tay-Sachs disease?

Yes. It is now possible to test the parents for a tendency toward passing on this condition to an offspring. If one parent has a deficiency of the enzyme that is associated with this disease, then one in four children may be born with the condition. If both parents are found to have a deficiency of the enzyme, the chances are even greater that another offspring will be born with the condition.

If both parents have a deficiency of the enzyme, should they risk having a child?

No, because the chances of the child having this fatal disease are too great.

How long can a baby live with this condition?

About two to three years. The baby's nutrition goes steadily downhill, there is loss of weight and increasing spasticity, until the baby eventually dies.

Is it necessary to put a child with this condition in a hospital?

No, as there is little that can be done in a hospital that cannot be done at home. However, in certain instances, it may be wiser to place the baby in a chronic-disease hospital or institution so as not to excessively encumber the home environment. The presence of such a baby in a home may have a bad psychological effect upon the parents and other children.

NIEMANN-PICK DISEASE

What is Niemann-Pick disease?

It is similar to Tay-Sachs disease, with the added element of a large spleen and liver. It, too, involves blindness, the cherry-red spot in the eye, and mental retardation.

Is this also familial, and does it tend to occur in Jewish families?

Yes.

Is this also fatal before three years of age?

Yes.

DOWN'S SYNDROME
(Mongolism)

What is mongolism?

It is a form of mental retardation occurring in three out of every thousand newborns. It is properly called Down's syndrome.

How is Down's syndrome recognized?

By the appearance of the child. In Down's syndrome, the head is usually small, the muscles are flabby, and the face has a characteristic appearance: eyes slanting upward and outward, a wide nasal bridge, and a protruding tongue. The hand is broad and spadelike, the palmar creases are not normal, the neck is short and broad, and there may be an abnormal heart condition present.

What causes Down's syndrome?

It is due to a defect in the chromosomes. The normal infant has forty-six chromosomes. An infant with Down's syndrome has forty-seven chromosomes.

Down's Syndrome. *A psychologist is testing a little girl to determine her intelligence level so as to plan a learning program for her.*

Is Down's syndrome hereditary?

No.

Does it occur more often with older mothers than with younger ones?

Yes.

Does it occur more often after several normal babies than as a first baby?

Yes.

Is there any special test that will make the diagnosis?

Yes. Chromosome studies will show the presence of this condition.

Can Down's syndrome be diagnosed before the child is born?

Yes, by performing amniocentesis.

This involves withdrawing some fluid from the pregnant uterus.

Is there any treatment for Down's syndrome?

No.

Is there any way of preventing it?

No.

Do children with Down's syndrome grow to maturity?

Yes.

What level of intelligence do these people reach?

They usually require supervision all their lives. However, the range of disability ranges from mild to severe, with some Down's syndrome people being able to work at simple jobs.

564

What is the usual disposition of children with Down's syndrome?

There are many stereotypes, but personalities vary widely, as in normal children.

Can children with Down's syndrome be cared for at home?

Yes, in most cases. Institutionalization should be avoided whenever possible. When home care is not possible because of parental objection, foster care in a family setting should be found.

Can children with Down's syndrome be educated?

Yes. It is a federal law that they must be educated.

Can they be taught a trade?

Yes. Most can be taught tasks and simple occupations.

Can they be made self-supporting?

Rarely, though many can be taught an occupation and can become useful citizens, though requiring support.

Why was this condition formerly called mongolism?

Because of the facial appearance and the upward slant of the eyes.

Does Down's syndrome occur only among Caucasians?

No. It occurs in all races.

RETROLENTAL FIBROPLASIA

What is retrolental fibroplasia?

This is a form of blindness which used to occur in very small premature babies who developed lung problems and required large amounts of oxygen.

What causes this disease?

Until recently, the cause was unknown. It has now been ascertained that retrolental fibroplasia was caused by *oxygen poisoning!*

Oxygen is a beneficial, lifesaving gas; how can there be "oxygen poisoning"?

Too much oxygen, when given to very small premature babies, interferes with normal eye development and can lead to blindness in some cases.

How much oxygen is used now for premature babies?

Enough to support life, but not excessive quantities.

Do all premature babies require extra oxygen?

No, only those who appear to have difficulty in breathing.

HYALINE MEMBRANE DISEASE
(Respiratory Distress Syndrome)

What is hyaline membrane disease?

It is a disease of premature babies and some Cesarean babies in which there is an interference with the normal breathing mechanism. It is also called the Respiratory Distress Syndrome.

Infant and Childhood Diseases

When does it develop?
Usually within six to twenty-four hours after birth.

Are babies born with hyaline membrane disease?
It is difficult to tell at birth. These infants seem normal at birth and for several hours thereafter. Then they start having difficulty in breathing.

What are the manifestations of this disease?
The baby's breathing becomes labored and grows progressively worse until death from suffocation ensues in about one to three days.

What causes this condition?
The cause is unknown, but it is suspected that changes in the surface tension overlying the air cells of the lungs may prevent oxygen from gaining ready access to the bloodstream.

Does this disease always terminate fatally?
No, a considerable number of infants can be saved.

What is the treatment for hyaline membrane disease?
Oxygen inhalations and increased moisture in the incubator. Some cases may require assisted breathing.

Does the oxygen act in a harmful way in these cases, as in retrolental fibroplasia?
Not necessarily, because the oxygen concentration is not too high. In any event, the eyes are examined closely.

If an infant recovers from this condition, can it be normal?
Yes, especially when it has been cared for in a modern neonatal care center.

Is there any way to prevent this disease?
The best preventive is to try to avoid a premature birth. Recently it has been discovered that the giving of cortisone to a mother who may give birth to a premature baby will prevent the onset of hyaline membrane disease.

ATELECTASIS OF THE NEWBORN

What is atelectasis of the newborn?
This is a failure of expansion of some parts of the baby's lungs. These areas contain no air or oxygen and do not function properly.

What is the cause of atelectasis?
It may be due to obstruction by mucus or amniotic fluid in the respiratory passages, or it may be caused by an immaturity of the lung tissue with failure of this tissue to develop the ability to expand.

What are the manifestations of atelectasis?
The infant will have rapid, shallow breathing, may have a grunt while breathing, may become bluish because of lack of oxygen, and may display a pulling-in of the chest wall at its ribs and near the neck when attempting to breathe in.

Is there any way to make a definite diagnosis of this condition?

Examination of the chest will reveal that air is not entering certain parts of the lungs. In addition, an x ray of the chest will show that air has not entered these areas.

What is the treatment for atelectasis of the newborn?

If there is any obstructive fluid in the respiratory passages, it must be sucked out. Sometimes, bronchoscopy is necessary in severe cases to remove any obstruction. In addition, the infant is kept in an incubator with high humidity and high oxygen content. It is important to stimulate the baby to breathe deeply by making it cry frequently, every few minutes, if necessary.

What is the outcome in these cases?

If the atelectasis is mild, it will clear up in a few days with normal lung expansion. If it is extensive, it may cause lack of oxygen to the brain and damage to the brain cells. In very severe cases, it may be fatal in one to two days.

HEMORRHAGIC DISEASE OF THE NEWBORN

What is hemorrhagic disease of the newborn?

This occurs about the second to fifth day of life and is manifested by bleeding into the skin, the mucous membranes, the navel, and occasionally by bleeding from the rectum or vagina. There may be blood in the urine or in the vomit.

What causes this type of hemorrhagic disease?

It is believed to be caused by a deficiency of one of the components in the blood-clotting mechanism and by a deficiency of Vitamin K.

What is the treatment for hemorrhagic disease of the newborn?

Vitamin K is given by injection to all newborns to prevent the condition.

TETANY OF THE NEWBORN

What is tetany of the newborn?

It is a condition that occurs during the first week or two of life, associated with irritability, extreme restlessness, twitchings, and occasionally convulsions.

What causes tetany?

It is caused by a diminished amount of calcium in the blood. It may be brought on by impaired function of the parathyroid glands or the kidneys, or by feeding the child milk that has a higher proportion of phosphorus to calcium than is normal.

What test can help to make a positive diagnosis?

A blood test for determination of the amount of calcium in the blood.

Does tetany occur in breast-fed infants?

It occurs less frequently in breast-fed than in bottle-fed infants, because breast milk has the proper proportions of phosphorus and calcium.

What is the treatment for tetany of the newborn?
Calcium solution is given intravenously, followed by the addition of a calcium-containing solution to the formula.

What can happen if the treatment is not given?
The infant will become more restless and will develop convulsions. These may be serious if calcium is not given quickly.

Can tetany be prevented?
Yes, by feeding breast milk or by putting calcium into each bottle the infant takes.

SEPSIS OF THE NEWBORN

What is sepsis of the newborn?
It is a bloodstream infection or poisoning occurring usually during the first week of life.

What is the cause of sepsis in newborns?
Bacteria entering the blood by way of the skin, mucous membranes, nose, mouth, or by way of the umbilicus.

Do these germs enter before birth or after birth?
The bacteria may enter the body at either time and then gain access to the bloodstream.

What are the manifestations of this sepsis?
Failure to take feedings, vomiting, diarrhea, loss of weight, restlessness, high fever, and occasionally convulsions.

How can the diagnosis be established definitely?
Blood cultures are taken to determine whether bacteria are present in the bloodstream.

What is the treatment for sepsis of the newborn?
Prompt administration of the appropriate antibiotic in adequate doses.

Are there any complications of sepsis (blood poisoning)?
Yes. Pneumonia, meningitis, peritonitis, abscesses of various organs, or skin abscesses may appear.

What is the outlook in this condition?
With prompt and early recognition and treatment, the outlook is good. If not recognized early or if the infection is a severe, overwhelming one, it will lead to death of the infant within a short period of time.

Can sepsis be prevented?
If there is any evidence of infection in the mother before or during delivery, the baby should be given antibiotics prophylactically. If the baby shows any evidence of skin or navel infection, treatment with antibiotics should be instituted promptly.

THRUSH

What is thrush?
It is a disease of the tongue and

mouth, usually occurring toward the end of the first week of life.

What is the cause of thrush?
It is caused by a yeast organism.

Where does this organism come from?
Usually from the mother, who may have a mild yeast infection of her vagina. During the birth passage, the infant becomes infected with this same yeast. It takes about a week for the yeast to grow. It may also come from contamination by rubber nipples and other equipment that may have been in contact with another infant who has thrush.

What are the manifestations of thrush?
There is a heavy whitish coating on the tongue, which may spread to the gums, lips, and mucous membranes inside the mouth.

Is thrush serious?
No, and it is quite common.

What is the treatment for thrush?
The use of an antibiotic called nystatin. It is applied locally to the infected areas and is also given to the infant to swallow.

Does it take long to clear up thrush?
No. In about a week to ten days the condition will have cleared.

Can thrush be prevented?
If the mother is known to have a vaginal infection with discharge, she should be treated for it during pregnancy.

In the nursery, should an infant with thrush be isolated?
Yes. In this way the spread from one infant to another can be prevented. The isolation should apply to all utensils used in the care of the infant.

OMPHALITIS

What is omphalitis?
It is an infection in the region of the navel (umbilicus) occurring during the first week of life.

Is omphalitis a serious infection?
Usually it will clear up promptly with adequate treatment. It may be serious if it spreads to a bloodstream infection.

What is the treatment for omphalitis?
a. Local applications to control the infection.
b. Antibiotics in adequate doses given internally.

CONGENITAL LARYNGEAL STRIDOR

What is congenital laryngeal stridor?
It is a noisy breathing, usually on inspiration, and especially pronounced with crying.

What is the cause of this condition?
It is usually caused by a flabbiness of the tissues around the larynx, particularly the epiglottis.

569

Infant and Childhood Diseases

Are there ever any more serious causes for congenital laryngeal stridor?

Yes. In some cases there may be a malformation of the larynx or structures adjacent to it. Foreign bodies that have been inhaled, growths on the larynx, or an abnormality of the aorta that may be pressing on the trachea—all may be the underlying cause for this condition.

When is congenital laryngeal stridor first noticed?

Usually at birth—and it may persist until the child is about twelve to eighteen months of age, when it gradually disappears.

Is any treatment necessary in the usual case of congenital laryngeal stridor?

No. It is a self-limited condition. As the infant grows older, the flabbiness of the laryngeal tissues disappears.

How are the more serious deformities in this region recognized?

By looking into the larynx with a laryngoscope. If the physician finds a cyst or web or other cause for obstruction, he will treat it at that time.

Is there need for special care in feeding infants with congenital laryngeal stridor?

Yes. These infants must be fed more slowly and carefully to prevent aspiration of the food into the windpipe. Sometimes these babies may find difficulty in sucking from a nipple and may need spoon-feeding.

Is the usual case of congenital laryngeal stridor serious?

No. It may sound very annoying to the parents, but it is usually not serious. It is important that the parents be reassured that the condition will eventually clear up spontaneously.

CHAPTER  33

INFANT FEEDING AND BOWEL FUNCTION

(See also Chapter 15 on Breasts; Chapter 17 on Child Behavior; Chapter 47 on Newborn Child; Chapter 78 on Vitamins)

BREAST-FEEDING

Is breast-feeding preferable to bottle-feeding?

Yes.

Why is breast milk best for the newborn child?

It has all the proper elements for the baby's best growth and development; it is clean and sterile; it is of the proper temperature. Also, immune substances are contained in the mother's milk, which help protect the newborn child against disease.

Are there psychological advantages to nursing?

Yes, for both the mother and the child. The closeness, the cuddling, etc., are important for both the baby and the mother.

Does a nursing mother require any special diet?

She should eat a full, balanced diet, being sure to include plenty of fluids, milk, eggs, meat, fruits, vegetables, and cereal.

Should the nursing mother avoid certain foods?

No. However, she may want to avoid gassy foods such as cabbage, broccoli, rhubarb, garlic, etc.

Do nursing mothers supplement their diet with vitamins?

Yes. Most nursing women take supplemental vitamins and calcium.

571

Infant Feeding and Bowel Function

Do drugs or medications that the mother takes affect her milk?

Consult your physician on this matter. Most medicines do show up in the mother's milk but do not affect the baby.

What general precautions should the nursing mother take?

She should:
a. Get plenty of rest.
b. Get plenty of relaxation.
c. Avoid tension and anxiety.
d. Avoid excessive smoking.
e. Avoid excessive drinking of alcoholic beverages.

Will nursing adversely affect the mother's teeth?

No. However, she should take an adequate supply of calcium in her diet every day.

Is nursing ever harmful to the mother?

Only if she is emotionally disturbed by the act. Those women who become tense or who find nursing exceedingly disagreeable should not be forced to nurse.

If the mother is ill or has a chronic debilitating disease, should she nurse?

No.

When is it wisest not to breast-feed a child?

When the child is very small or weak, or is premature, or has a cleft palate or harelip.

How soon after birth can nursing be started?

The very first day.

Is there any milk in the mother's breast during the first few days after delivery?

No, but the nursing child does obtain a substance known as colostrum.

What is colostrum, and what is its value?

Colostrum is a substance secreted by the breasts before the milk fully comes in. It contains many immune substances, which may help to protect the baby during its first few days of life.

Does the nursing child obtain sufficient nourishment the first two or three days of life, before breast milk begins to flow?

Yes.

When does real milk start to flow?

About the third or fourth day after birth, but this varies from the second to the fifth or sixth day.

What starts the flow of milk into the mother's breast?

Certain hormones in the mother's body. Also, the baby's sucking will accelerate the flow of milk.

At what intervals should the baby breast-feed?

Normal healthy babies may nurse every two and a half to three hours.

What should be done if the baby falls asleep during nursing?

Gentle stimulation may help to wake him. He should be permitted a rest of five minutes during nursing, but no longer. Following such a rest he may resume sucking at a normal rate.

572

If the baby seems to need it, is it permissible to nurse more often?

Yes, but not more often than every two hours. Consult your doctor about frequency of feedings.

Should the baby nurse on one or both breasts?

In general, it is best to nurse at both breasts.

How long should each nursing last?

Starting slowly, about five minutes on each breast. As the infant gets larger, each feeding can take up to fifteen to twenty minutes on each breast.

In what position should the mother nurse the baby?

In any comfortable position that avoids strain on the mother's elbow or shoulder.

Should water be given to the baby between nursings?

This is not necessary in most instances, but if the baby seems to be thirsty and cries, he may be given a few ounces of water.

Is it permissible to skip nursings if the child has not awakened?

Within the first few days it is best not to skip nursings. Later on the baby may be permitted a longer sleep and have a bottle to substitute for a nursing during the middle of the night.

What is the treatment for "cracked" nipples?

A mother with cracked nipples should skip a few nursings or alternate breasts. The use of a nipple shield helps protect the breast and helps it to heal more quickly. A soothing ointment may be applied after each nursing, but it must be washed off before the baby is again put to the breast.

What special care should be given the nipples?

Cleanliness is the most important objective. The nipples should be washed before and after each nursing. A comfortable, well-fitting uplift brassiere should be worn.

What is the treatment for "caked" breasts?

A good supportive brassiere and medicines to relieve pain.

Should nursing be stopped if an infection of the breast occurs?

Only if it is too painful or if an abscess must be drained.

If it is necessary to stop nursing because of a breast condition, can nursing be resumed at a later date?

Yes, but only if the breasts have been pumped regularly and the milk flow has continued to flow.

How long should breast-feeding be continued?

As long as a woman wishes to continue.

Can a woman stop breast-feeding after three to four months?

Yes, or at any time she wishes to stop it.

Is weaning a difficult process?

No. Most babies are given a supplementary bottle during the early months of life and therefore will not resist the change to bottle-feeding later on. Some babies are weaned directly to a cup.

How soon can a supplementary bottle be started?

Whenever one wishes.

What can be done if the mother must be away from the child for two or three days?

The breasts can be pumped so that the milk supply will not diminish. This will enable the mother to resume nursing when she returns.

If the mother and child are to be separated for more than a few days, is it wiser to discontinue nursing completely and to start bottle-feeding?

Yes.

Is sudden, abrupt weaning harmful?

No. Most children take the change from breast-feeding to bottle-feeding without difficulty.

Are vitamins and solid foods given to children who are breast-fed, just as they are given to bottle-fed children?

Yes. There is no variation in these supplementary substances.

What does the mother do when she stops nursing?

She usually wears a tight breast binder or brassiere. It is also advisable to limit her intake of fluids for several days. If breasts are not emp-

tied periodically, they will not refill. The baby's sucking and breast emptying are the greatest impetus to milk formation.

Is it permissible for the mother to take pain-relieving medications when she stops nursing?

Yes.

BOTTLE-FEEDING

If the mother cannot nurse, is bottle-feeding almost as satisfactory?

Yes. There are many excellent preparations of formulas that give the newborn child all he needs in the way of nourishment.

How soon after birth can a child start getting his formula?

Within eight to twelve hours.

How much formula is given at first?

About a half-ounce during the first day, increased to an ounce at each feeding the second day, one and a half to two ounces on the third day, and increased gradually as the baby needs it thereafter.

How can a mother know what equipment is needed to prepare a formula?

Your child specialist (pediatrician) will supply you with this information. Also, many hospitals give lectures to mothers about formula preparation before they leave the hospital.

From whom will a mother receive

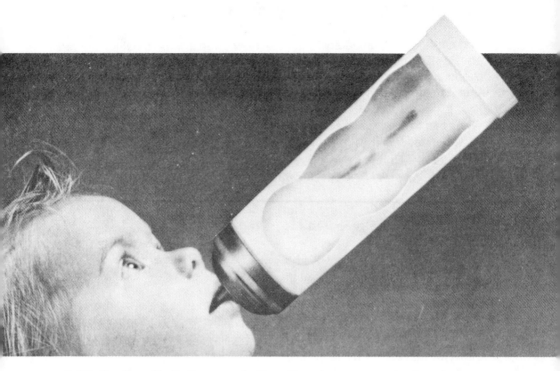

Bottle-Feeding. *Plastic throwaway bottles, although more expensive than glass ones, are preferred by some mothers.*

instructions about methods of sterilization?

a. From the pediatrician or physician.

b. From the hospital.

c. From the baby's nurse or from a nursing agency.

What types of bottles and nipples should be used?

There are many excellent ones on the market. It makes very little difference which kind is used, as long as it functions well. The small or large nipples are equally effective.

Is it safe to use plastic bottles?

Yes.

How can a mother tell if the nipple is good?

Turn the bottle upside down; the milk should come through the nipple openings freely, a drop at a time.

Is it permissible to enlarge nipple openings?

Yes, with a sterile needle.

What should be done if too much milk flows through the nipple?

Discard that nipple and use another one.

What are the basic ingredients of most baby formulas?

Most formulas are manufactured

575

with care from modified cow's milk protein. It is not necessary to use evaporated milk formula. Consult your pediatrician.

When can the formula be changed to whole milk?
When the child is about five to seven months of age.

Is it necessary to add any other substances to the prepared formulas?
No. They are usually made with adequate amounts of all necessary ingredients. Also, these preparations come with complete and simple instructions.

Can it harm the baby if the proportions of the various ingredients are varied slightly?
No.

How many bottles are made from the formula?
In the beginning, divide the formula into six or seven bottles of three and a half or four ounces each. Later, four to six ounces are put into each bottle. As the baby grows older and takes fewer feedings, the thirty-two-ounce formula may be divided into five bottles.

Should the baby be made to adhere to a rigid feeding schedule?
No, especially in the beginning. It is best to feed the baby as often as he needs it. This is called the "self-demand schedule." As he grows older, he will adopt a more definite pattern.

How often should a baby be given his bottle?
Most pediatricians recommend a modified demand approach, that is, a baby is fed whenever hungry with variable intervals, usually totaling six to eight feedings a day.

What should be done if the baby wants to be fed every two hours?
Let the baby have his formula every two hours.

How soon after birth do children start regulating their own schedule?
Most babies will develop a fairly regular schedule at about four to six weeks of age, some a little earlier, some later.

Should a baby be forced into a rigid schedule?
No. Let the baby, within reason, decide his own schedule. Gentle persuasion into a regular schedule can be carried out. However, much depends on the mother's time schedule as well as on the baby's requirement.

Should milk or formulas be heated before being given to an infant?
No. Infants adapt readily to milk or formulas whether they are cold, room temperature, or heated.

Is there any harm in letting the baby's feedings go beyond the four-hour interval?
No.

Should the baby be awakened for a night feeding?
No. It is preferable to wait until he

576

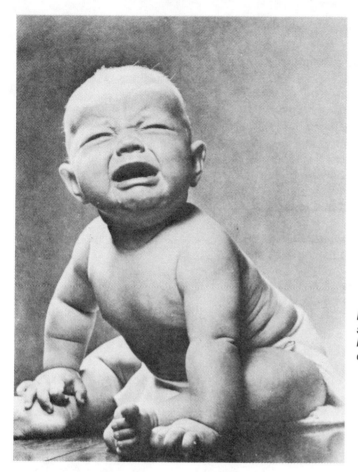

Feeding Time. Infants should be permitted to cry a little for their food. It will not do them any harm.

awakens. However, if the baby tends to awaken at an inopportune hour, such as 4:00 or 5:00 A.M., it may be wiser to awaken him earlier. Some mothers find it best to wake the baby between 11:00 and 12:00 P.M. while they are still awake, so that the baby will sleep through until 6:00 or 7:00 A.M.

How soon do most babies skip their night feedings?

Many babies skip the 2:00 A.M. feeding when they reach two to three months of age. There are great variations, all of which fall into the category of normal.

What are the best hours for feeding the baby?

This depends on the family pattern of living. Some babies will thrive on a 6:00 A.M., 10:00 A.M., 2:00 P.M., 6:00 P.M., 10:00 P.M., 2:00 A.M. schedule. In other families, the hours can be varied to 7:00 A.M., 11:00 A.M., 3:00 P.M., etc.

How much of the formula should the baby take?

This will vary according to each baby's needs. In the early months, he will take two to four ounces, later on, four to six ounces, and still later six to eight ounces at each feeding. The

577

Infant Feeding and Bowel Function

average total daily intake during the first month of life will be twenty to twenty-five ounces; later it increases to twenty-five to thirty-two ounces, and in some instances the baby may require as much as forty ounces of formula. As solid foods are added, most babies will take less formula.

Do most babies take the same amount at each feeding?

No. There may be great variations from feeding to feeding.

Should each bottle contain the same amount of formula?

Yes. However, it is usually best to let the baby set his own pattern, as he may develop the habit of taking more at one feeding than at another.

Should the baby be expected to drain each bottle?

No.

Can the amounts in the bottles be varied?

Yes, if the mother gets to know how much the baby takes at certain feedings.

What should be done with the milk the baby does not take?

Discard it.

What should be done when the baby takes only an ounce of milk at one feeding and wants more an hour later?

For a time it is permissible to allow this habit to develop. In such instances, the formula should be put into the refrigerator and rewarmed for the remainder of the feedings.

How long should it take for a baby to drain his bottle?

Most babies will fulfill their requirements within ten to fifteen minutes. If the baby dawdles, discard the remainder of the bottle, for he has probably finished feeding.

Should a baby be permitted to spend an hour at his feeding?

No. Some babies develop the dawdling habit; this should be discouraged.

Should the baby be permitted to cry for his feeding if he awakens too early?

On the self-demand schedule, the baby is usually permitted to eat whenever he wishes. However, sometimes it is necessary to vary that procedure, and it does no harm to permit a baby to cry for a little while before he gets his feeding. It is never necessary to rush to feed the baby when he cries. It should also be remembered that sometimes he may only want water.

Should babies be given water between feedings?

Most infants won't require extra water. However, one to three ounces may be given occasionally, especially in warm weather.

Do babies often take too much of their formula?

In general, babies stop when they are satisfied. Occasionally, a baby will take too much and will usually vomit the excess. There is no harm in this.

When are vitamins added to the diet?

Vitamins are usually present in prepared formulas. Breast-fed babies start vitamins at one month of age.

What vitamin preparations are usually used?

A multivitamin drop, usually one that contains Vitamins A, B_1, B_2, B_6, B_{12}, C, D, and E. Most vitamin preparations on the market contain all of these vitamins.

How are these vitamins given?

Practically all of these preparations are soluble in water, milk, or fruit juices. They can either be dissolved in these liquids, or they may be dropped directly on the infant's tongue.

How much of the vitamins is given?

Start with one to three drops for the first few days and then increase gradually up to fifteen drops a day. Most vitamins come with medicine

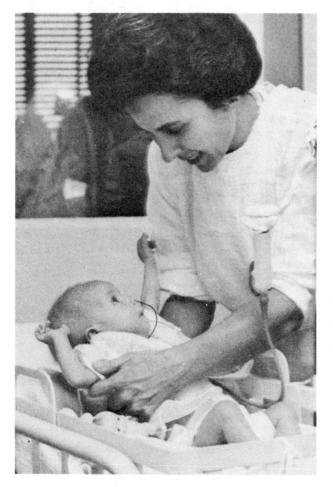

Debilitated infants who are too weak to suck a nipple can be fed by passing a tube through the nose into the stomach.

579

droppers that are marked with accurate instructions on how much to give.

Can the droppers hurt the baby's tongue?

No. Today most droppers are made of plastic material.

What is the maximum amount of vitamins to be given each day?

Fifteen drops, or 0.6cc. This amount should be given every day.

Should vitamins be given in the summertime?

Yes, in the same amounts as during the other months.

Is there any great harm if the child doesn't finish the bottle into which the vitamins have been dissolved?

It is not harmful if the child skips an occasional feeding in which the vitamins are given.

Is it possible to give too much of a particular vitamin?

Not ordinarily. There is a great deal of leeway in the amount the body can tolerate. However, on occasion, an excess has been given with harmful results. This is a rare occurrence.

Can the vitamins occasionally cause a rash?

Yes.

What is done for rashes caused by vitamins?

It may be necessary to stop giving the vitamins entirely for a while or to substitute a preparation containing only Vitamins A, C, and D. Some physicians prefer to start with an A, C, and D preparation.

At what age is orange juice started?

Usually at about six months of age.

How is orange juice given?

Start with a teaspoonful, dilute it with an equal quantity of boiled water. Increase gradually up to one ounce each of juice and water.

Is it necessary to use fresh orange juice?

No. Frozen or canned orange juice is adequate.

Do all babies tolerate orange juice?

No. Some babies will vomit or develop a rash from orange juice. In that event, do not give it.

Is there any harm if the baby does not tolerate orange juice?

Not if the baby is getting a multivitamin preparation containing Vitamin C.

Can juices other than orange juice be added?

Yes, but be sure they have an adequate supply of Vitamin C.

Can cod-liver oil be given instead of vitamin drops?

Yes, but only to supply Vitamins A and D. In that case, it is essential to add Vitamin C in the form of orange juice or Vitamin C drops.

Can various fish-liver oil preparations be used?

Yes, but again it is necessary to add Vitamin C.

Is it necessary to add Vitamin B when giving drops other than the multivitamin preparations?

Yes. It is advisable to add a Vitamin B preparation when using cod-liver oil or fish-liver oil only.

When may the baby be given solid foods?

Solid foods are not necessary for the first four to six months. However, some physicians start the baby on solid foods considerably earlier.

Which solids are given first?

Either cereal or fruit. Rice or barley cereals are excellent, too. Applesauce and mashed ripe banana are also frequently given as first foods.

How much of these foods is given?

Always start with a teaspoonful of a new food and increase the amount gradually, depending on how well the baby takes to it, until half a jar or several tablespoons of each food can be given.

Should solid foods be given before or after the formula?

In the beginning, it may be necessary to give a few ounces of the formula first and then introduce the solid food. Later on, it is better to give the solid food first and allow the baby to take the milk later.

At what feeding should the solids be given?

This does not matter. In general, cereal may be given at the 10:00 A.M. and 6:00 P.M. feedings; fruit at the 2:00 P.M. feeding.

Do all babies readily take solid food?

No. If the baby spits out the solid food, try it again and again, until he gets used to it. If the baby definitely cannot manage solid foods, stop attempts at giving them for a week or two and then start over.

How should solids be fed?

With a small spoon.

Can solids ever be given through a bottle?

Yes, but this is not recommended.

What cooked cereals can be used?

Farina, Cream of Wheat, or oatmeal may be used well cooked. This usually means cooking for twenty to thirty minutes. Precooked cereals now on the market are much easier to prepare.

When can any cereal be given?

At two to four months of age.

Can prepared fruits out of cans be given?

Yes. These preparations are all adequate.

How are solids usually added to diets?

This varies widely according to each physician's custom and also according to the child's individual taste. The following schedule is often utilized:

Age	Add
4 months	Cereals (barley and rice). Fruits (applesauce and mashed banana).
5 months	Other cereals and fruits.
6 months	All foods eaten by adults in proper consistency and quantity, either from jars or home prepared.

What are good diets for children of eight, ten, twelve, and twenty-four months of age?

SAMPLE DIET SCHEDULE FOR BABY: *EIGHT MONTHS OLD*

On Arising:
Vitamin drops and orange juice.

Breakfast:
Cereal — any cooked or precooked cereal with milk.
Egg — coddled, soft-boiled, or hard-boiled.
Bottle.

Noon Meal:
Vegetables — all prepared, strained vegetables or combinations.
 Fresh vegetables, cooked and strained.
 Potato, baked or boiled with butter added.
Meats — chicken liver, broiled and mashed or strained.
 Chicken, minced or shredded.
 Beefsteak patty, finely ground and broiled.
 All strained meats.
Desserts — any prepared fruits or fruit combinations.
Bottle — if baby wants it.

3:30 P.M.
Bottle, with arrowroot cracker or cookie.
(Some babies prefer a morning bottle on arising. In that case give vitamin drops and orange juice at this time.)

Evening Meal:
Cereal — as at morning meal — or
Baby soup — any of the prepared baby soups mixed with a little milk.
Egg — if not given in the morning.
Dessert — banana or any of the baby fruit combinations with a little milk or cream. Jello, junket, custard, chocolate, or tapioca pudding.
Bottle.

NOTE: The baby may not take all these foods. This is a menu from which to select the foods. Do not insist upon giving the baby any food not desired. Feeding, diets, and menus are highly individual. The main thought should be *not to overfeed*. Fat babies are not necessarily healthy babies.

NEW FOODS THAT MAY BE ADDED TO DIET LIST: *AT TEN MONTHS*

STARCHY FOODS: Spaghetti, noodles, pastina.
(These may be well cooked and strained.)
Rice, sweet potato.
CREAM: Sweet or sour cream.
CHEESE: Cream cheese, cottage or pot cheese. (These may be mixed with a little cream or milk.)
BACON: Crisp.
JUICES: Other fruit juices, in addition to orange juice.

NOTE: At this age the baby may refuse certain foods, or may refuse milk. This is not unusual. He may even go on jags—all milk, no solids, or the reverse, for periods. Do not be disturbed by this.

DIET LIST: *ONE YEAR OLD*

Breakfast:
Any cooked or precooked cereal with milk.
Egg—coddled, poached, soft-boiled, or hardboiled.
Strip of bacon may be added.
Bread or toast. Milk.
Vitamin drops and orange juice may be given during the morning or at mealtime.

Noon Meal:
Meats—chicken, chicken liver, calf's liver, lamb chop, lamb stew, beefsteak patty, chopped meats.
Fish—broiled or boiled. No mackerel, salmon, or salty fish.
Vegetables—all the prepared, strained vegetables or combinations of them. Strained, cooked fresh vegetables. When the baby is ready for chopped foods, these may be used.
Dessert—all prepared baby fruit desserts.

Midafternoon:
Milk with crackers, cookies, or toast and butter.

Evening Meal:
Any one of the baby soups, plain or creamed.
Spaghetti, noodles, or pastina.
Cheese—cream, cottage or pot cheese. Sweet or sour cream.

Raw vegetables—chopped carrot or tomato.
Dessert—banana and sweet cream, junket, Jello, custard, chocolate or tapioca pudding; fruit desserts.
Milk.

Occasionally egg or cereal may be omitted from the morning meal and given in the evening. Other fruit juices may be substituted for orange juice.

DO NOT FORCE THE BABY TO TAKE ANY FOOD OR MILK NOT DESIRED.

DIET LIST: *TWO YEARS OLD*

Breakfast:
Fruit—orange, grapefruit, apple, prunes, cooked pears, peaches, or apricots; any fruit juice.
Cereal—any cooked or dry cereal with milk or cream.
Eggs—may be given in any form.
Bacon may be added.
Bread or toast and butter.

Noon Meal:
Soup—any clear broth or creamed vegetable soup.
Meat—chicken or chicken liver, beef or calf's liver, lamb chop or lamb stew, ground beefsteak patty or roast beef, diced meats.
Fish—any fresh fish, broiled, baked, or boiled.
Vegetables—all cooked vegetables, preferably fresh or frozen. Prepared, chopped vegetables may be used. Raw vegetables occasionally.
Potato, rice, spaghetti, macaroni, or pastina. *(continued)*

583

Infant Feeding and Bowel Function

Dessert—any raw or cooked fruit, custard, junket, Jello, puddings, ice cream.

Midafternoon:
Milk with crackers, cookies, or toast and jam.

Evening Meal:
Any fruit or vegetable juice, or soup if not given at noon.
Salad of cooked or raw vegetables.
Cheese—cream, cottage or pot, Swiss, or American.
Sour cream.
Spaghetti or noodles.
Eggs—if not given at breakfast.
Dessert—banana or berries and cream or other desserts as listed above.
Bread and butter. Milk.

NOTE: The vitamin drops may be given at any mealtime.
Do not give any fried or canned fish; no salted, pickled, or smoked foods; no highly seasoned sauces or gravies; no pastries or rich cakes.
The above list does not represent all the foods that must be given. It is only a suggested list from which to start the menu for the day.

NEVER FORCE THE CHILD TO EAT ANY FOOD OR TO DRINK MILK.

Is it harmful if the baby tends to take too much solid food and cuts down on his liquids?
No. It is common for the child to drink less formula or milk as he takes more solids. This will vary from child to child.

584

Does the amount of solids in the formula the child takes vary from day to day?
Yes.

How should new foods be introduced into the diet?
Always try to introduce one new food at a time. Always start new foods with a very small amount and increase gradually on successive days.

Can babies eat the foods safely from a jar or can?
Yes. Foods as they are processed today do not spoil as long as the container is unopened.

How long can leftover foods in a jar or can be used?
After opening, they can be kept in a refrigerator for about a day or two without spoiling.

Is it necessary to use canned foods?
No. Many mothers prefer to prepare their own fruits, vegetables, soups, or meats. They should be well cooked, well pureed, and put through a strainer so they may be digested easily.

Can small amounts of salt or sugar be added to the foods for seasoning purposes?
Yes.

Which should be the heaviest meal of the day?
Preferably the noon meal.

When can the child be permitted to feed himself?
Some babies will start finger-feeding

at nine to eleven months of age. This may be quite messy, but the child should be allowed to do it. It represents a step toward self-sufficiency.

When are chopped or junior foods introduced into the diet?

When the baby is about ten to twelve months of age.

When should cup training be started?

When the baby is about ten to twelve months of age.

When can the bottle be eliminated?

Babies vary a great deal in this matter, as they do in all feeding matters. Some will allow themselves to be fed from a cup at twelve to fifteen months of age. Others will take juice from a cup but insist upon milk from a bottle until eighteen months of age. Do not be insistent in eliminating the bottle. Some children may require a bottle until two years of age. This will do no harm.

Is sterilization of nipples and bottles necessary?

The nipples may be sterilized, but all the bottles require is washing thoroughly with soap and hot water.

How should the baby be held during feeding?

It is best to hold him in a semierect position in the curve of your arm. In this way the air bubble he swallows during feeding will rise to the top of his stomach and will come up as a "burp" more easily. In addition, the baby will not bring up any of the milk with the burp.

Is it permissible to feed the baby in a semierect position on a small pillow?

Yes.

Is it permissible to feed the baby lying down?

Yes, but he should be picked up once or twice during the feeding to bring up the air bubble.

What can be done to help the baby bring up the air bubble?

The mother puts him over her shoulder and holds him there for several minutes. Sometimes stroking his back or gently patting him will help.

How soon after feeding can the baby be put down in a lying position?

It is best to keep him upright for ten to fifteen minutes after a feeding.

At what age can the child be fed in a high chair?

When he is able to sit up comfortably for about ten to fifteen minutes. This will be somewhere between four and six months of age.

What is the significance of hiccups?

They are spasms of the diaphragm and have no special significance. They occur normally.

What should be done for hiccups?

In most cases, nothing should be done. A small drink of water may help end them more quickly.

Is it normal for infants to spit up or regurgitate some of their feedings?

Yes. "Burping" often brings up a lit-

585

tle of the formula. It may occur from changing the child's position or when he is taking a little too much food.

Is vomiting serious?

Occasional vomiting is not serious. It may be caused by the same factors that cause slight regurgitation. Repeated or persistent vomiting should lead you to consult your physician.

COLIC

What is colic?

It is a pain in the baby's abdomen due to spasm of the intestines.

What are the symptoms of colic?

Excessive crying, especially in the evening hours, and drawing up of the child's legs as if he were in pain; sometimes these symptoms are accompanied by extreme irritability.

What causes colic?

The exact cause is unknown. However, the following may be factors:
a. Underfeeding and hunger.
b. Excessive carbohydrates in the formula.
c. Too much butterfat in the formula.
d. Swallowing air and failure to burp.
e. Intolerance to cow's milk.
f. Immaturity of the baby's nervous system.
g. Improper feeding technique.
h. Fatigue.

How is colic prevented?

By finding out which of the above factors is the cause and by correct-ing it. It is often necessary to obtain the doctor's help in this matter.

What is first-aid treatment when the child is crying with severe colicky pain?

Be calm. Hold the baby erect, close to your body, and keep something warm near his abdomen. (Do not burn him with a hot water bottle.) Placing the child on his abdomen on a warm pad may also help to relieve the colic.

Should medicines for colic be given without a doctor's advice?

Never.

How long does colic last?

Some babies have colic for two to three months and then it disappears spontaneously.

Are second and third children in the family less colicky?

Not necessarily.

Is colic dangerous?

No.

BOWEL MOVEMENTS

How many bowel movements a day are normal for a newborn child?

Anywhere from one to five movements a day. Breast-fed babies may have more bowel movements than bottle-fed infants. Occasionally, the baby will have a movement with each feeding. As long as the consistency of the stool is good, the number of stools per day does not matter too much.

What is the normal consistency of stools?

They should be mushy or pasty or even somewhat firmer. They should have a fairly sweetish odor.

What is the normal color of an infant's stool?

Golden yellow. It may also be greenish or turn greenish-brown after standing for some time. This is normal.

Is constipation serious?

Ordinarily not. If the baby has one firm stool per day, nothing need be done about it as long as the infant is not uncomfortable.

Is it normal for some infants to strain at stool?

Yes. This will disappear as the child grows older, unless he is unusually constipated.

Can the mother help the child when he is straining at stool?

Yes. Flexing the legs on the abdomen frequently helps.

Should suppositories be given if the baby is constipated?

Only on the doctor's advice.

Is it ever necessary to stretch the anus when children are constipated?

Occasionally, but not often.

Are there ever a few streaks of blood in a constipated stool?

Yes. The hard stool stretches the anal opening and may cause a small scratch on the surface. This in itself is not serious. This can often be helped by a suppository or by making the stool softer.

How can the stools be made softer?

a. Increase the baby's water intake.
b. Increase the carbohydrates added to the formula.
c. Reduce constipating foods such as banana, Jello, junket, chocolate, cheese, oatmeal, apples.
d. Increase laxative foods such as cooked fruits and cooked vegetables.
e. Give prune juice or cooked prunes.

Can mineral oil ever be given to soften the stools?

Yes, but only on a doctor's prescription.

Are there any other medications that can soften the child's stool?

There are many medications on the market that will perform this function, but they must be given only on a doctor's prescription.

Is it permissible to use laxatives to soften the stool?

Usually not. The eagerness to remedy constipation may produce a diarrhea in a baby. This is a much more serious condition and a much more difficult one to control.

DIARRHEA

What is diarrhea?

Too frequent stools. In an infant this may mean ten to twelve or fifteen per day.

587

Infant Feeding and Bowel Function

Is the character and color of the stools usually changed in infant diarrhea?

Yes. The stools may show undigested material and may be greenish or greenish brown in color and may have a foul odor.

Are diarrheal stools irritating to the child?

Yes. They may cause a rash on the buttocks.

What is the significance of blood or mucus in the stools?

The appearance of blood or mucus is due to prolonged irritation of the mucous membrane lining of the intestinal tract and is an indication that the child needs medical treatment.

What are the causes of infant diarrhea?

a. Faulty technique in preparation of the formula.
b. Excessive carbohydrates in the formula.
c. Allergy to cow's milk.
d. Introduction of a new food that is irritating.
e. Excessive amounts of laxative foods.
f. Infection within the intestinal tract.
g. Infection elsewhere within the body.

What is the treatment for infant diarrhea?

a. Skip one or two feedings to give the intestinal tract a rest.
b. Give only boiled water in small amounts until feedings are resumed.
c. Start feedings with more dilute formulas, preferably with less carbohydrates and fat.
d. Give smaller amounts during the first few feedings, perhaps only one to two ounces per feeding for a day or two. Supplement the lack of formula with boiled water.
e. Add a bland, constipating food such as mashed ripe banana, raw, scraped apple, and a little pot cheese that has been thinned with boiled water.

How long does diarrhea last?

It may be a very short-lived, temporary digestive upset, or it may persist for some time and be a symptom of a more serious general condition.

Can paregoric or other medicines be used to stop diarrhea?

These medications should be given only under a doctor's direction.

Should a laxative be given to stop diarrhea?

No. This is incorrect treatment.

When can a normal diet be resumed after an attack of diarrhea?

When the child has had several hard, firm movements for a period of two to three days. At first, small amounts of the baby's normal diet should be given, and then the amounts should be increased gradually.

Can milk be resumed after diarrhea?

If the baby has been on a formula, the formula should be resumed gradually. If he has been on whole milk, use diluted boiled milk until his stools have returned to normal. Slowly return to full strength, unboiled milk if that is what the baby was taking prior to the diarrhea.

What should be done if the diarrhea is persistent and severe?

Contact your physician and get instructions from him. Stop all feedings until he calls.

Is vomiting serious when associated with diarrhea?

Yes. The baby will then lose fluids and minerals from his body tissues, which must be replaced quickly.

Do cases of diarrhea have to be treated in the hospital?

Serious cases should be; mild cases may be treated at home.

What treatment is carried out in the hospital for severe cases of diarrhea?

Oral feedings are discontinued, and the baby is given the proper amounts of nourishment and fluids through the veins.

What is the outlook for severe cases of infant diarrhea?

If treated early in their course, practically all cases recover. The serious cases and deaths from infant diarrhea that used to occur many years ago are now a thing of the past, owing to improved methods of treatment.

Were these cases of diarrhea once called "summer complaint" or "summer diarrhea"?

Yes.

For how long a period is hospitalization necessary in a case of severe infant diarrhea?

Approximately seven to ten days. The child must be hospitalized until the diarrhea and vomiting have stopped, the infection has cleared up, and the infant has returned to his normal diet schedule.

Are special formulas used for diarrheas?

Yes. In some cases, the infant is not put back on his original formula but is given a new formula containing skimmed milk or a fat-free mixture. Some physicians use a milk-free or soy-based formula.

How long are these special formulas continued after an attack of diarrhea?

For a few weeks.

Are episodes of diarrhea ever recurrent?

Occasionally. In these instances it is necessary to find the underlying cause and treat it strenuously.

What are the common causes for recurrent diarrhea?

a. An allergy.
b. An infection in the intestinal tract.
c. A form of celiac disease. (See Chapter 32, on Infant and Childhood Diseases.)
d. An abnormality within the intestinal tract.

How can one tell if an infant is allergic to cow's milk?

Usually there will be vomiting, colicky pains, loose stools, or mucus in

589

the stools. Occasionally there will be a rash, particularly on the face. There may also be failure to gain weight or actual weight loss.

Is there often a history of allergy in the family of a child who is allergic to cow's milk?

Yes. A careful history will often reveal another member of the family with a food allergy.

What is the treatment for an allergy to cow's milk?

Do not give the child cow's milk.

Is allergy to cow's milk a common condition among children?

A very small percentage of children cannot take cow's milk because they are allergic to it.

What substitutes may be used for cow's milk?

A prepared synthetic milk produced from soybean.

Is this substitute for milk satisfactory?

Yes. It contains all the elements necessary for the infant's growth and development.

Should other milk products be ex-cluded from the diet of an allergic baby?

Yes. Cheeses, butter, etc., should not be given.

Can a child allergic to cow's milk ever take milk?

Yes. Usually after the child is a year or eighteen months of age, he will lose this allergy and can then be put back on regular milk. This must be done slowly after testing the child with small amounts.

When the child is allergic to cow's milk, should vitamins and juices be given?

Yes. These are added in the usual way.

If a child is allergic to cow's milk, is it possible that he will demonstrate other allergies?

Yes. For this reason it is important to be cautious in adding any new food to the diet of such an infant.

Can allergy to milk be a serious condition in children?

There are occasional children who may go into collapse when given cow's milk. In such a case, make sure to avoid giving cow's milk again.

34 INFECTIOUS AND VIRUS DISEASES

(See also Chapter 12 on Blood and Lymph Diseases; Chapter 18 on Contagious Diseases; Chapter 50 on Parasites and Parasitic Diseases; Chapter 75 on Upper Respiratory Diseases)

What are the causes of infectious diseases, and what are examples of each?

a. Bacteria (typhoid fever, pneumonia, etc.).
b. Protozoa (amebic dysentery, malaria).
c. *Rickettsia* (typhus fever, Rocky Mountain spotted fever).
d. Virus (influenza, smallpox, measles).
e. Fungus (athlete's foot, blastomycosis).

What is the difference between bacteria and viruses?

Bacteria may be seen under the ordinary microscope; viruses are too small to be seen except under a very high-powered electron microscope. Bacteria are too large to pass through certain earthenware filters, whereas viruses are small enough to pass through these filters.

Do bacteria and viruses require living cells for their growth and multiplication?

Bacteria do not. They can be grown, and they multiply, on nonliving substances; viruses, however, cannot grow or multiply except in the presence of living tissue cells, either animal or human. New tissue culture techniques have resulted in the identification of large numbers of new

591

viruses, some of which produce syndromes now recognized as distinct diseases.

How are viral diseases spread?

By contact, by droplet infection in the air, and by intermediates (vectors) such as mosquitoes, lice, ticks, etc.

Do bacteria and viruses respond to antibiotic and chemical agents in the same manner?

No. Many bacteria are killed or inactivated by the antibiotic and chemotherapeutic drugs (penicillin, the mycin group, the sulfa group, etc.), but viruses are not so affected.

Does one attack of a virus disease protect the individual against further attack?

Not always. In many instances, as in smallpox, measles, polio, etc., this does hold true. But there are other diseases, such as the common cold, influenza, etc., that can occur many times in the same person.

How can immunity against virus diseases be obtained?

By the development and use of vaccines made from dead or weakened viruses. Poliomyelitis and influenza vaccines are examples. Measles vaccine (from both live and attenuated viruses) and vaccines for German measles and mumps are other examples.

Is there an effective vaccine for the common cold?

Not as yet. Recent work, however, seems to hold hope for the future development of such a vaccine.

TYPHOID FEVER

What is typhoid fever, and how is it transmitted?

Typhoid fever is a generalized disease caused by the typhoid bacillus. It is transmitted from infected food, milk, or water (usually contaminated by sewage). It can be spread by flies but also by direct contact with infected material.

What is a "typhoid carrier"?

This is a "healthy" person who had typhoid fever at one time, who recovered from it, but still harbors the live germs in his body. He can act as a source of widespread contamination in a community, especially if he has anything to do with the handling of food.

What are the methods of preventing the spread of typhoid fever?

Purification of water supplies and pasteurization of milk are essential measures. Typhoid carriers, when discovered, must be prevented from handling food that is to be used by other people. Typhoid fever must be recognized early, and the patient must be isolated from healthy people. All of the typhoid patient's belongings and all of his excretions must be sterilized and kept from contact with other people.

Is vaccination against typhoid fever effective?

Yes, small "booster" doses are effective in maintaining immunity even if taken only every three or four years. Typhoid vaccine should be taken under the following circumstances:

a. When traveling in a country where the water purity is doubtful and where the disease is known to exist.
b. During typhoid epidemics.
c. When there has been contact with a patient who has the disease.

How is a positive diagnosis of typhoid fever made?

There is a special blood test that becomes positive during the second week of the disease. This is called the Widal test. Also, the germ can be grown in the laboratory from the patient's blood, urine, or stool, usually during the first week of the disease.

How common is typhoid fever in the United States today?

With the establishment of pure water supplies, the proper handling of food supplies, and the proper isolation of the occasional case, this disease is now quite a rarity in the United States. Also, the advent of the newer antibiotic drugs can kill the typhoid germs readily and thereby prevent the patient from spreading the disease. Only about eight hundred cases per year have been reported in recent years.

What is the incubation period for typhoid fever?

Approximately ten to fourteen days.

How long does it take for the disease to run its course?

Usually, about four to six weeks.

Are there any serious complications of typhoid fever?

Yes. Rupture of the intestines and in-testinal hemorrhage are the two most serious complications, but they do not occur very often.

How soon can the typhoid patient be allowed out of bed?

He can sit up in bed after his temperature has been normal for one week. He may get out of bed about three or four days later.

How can one tell when the typhoid patient is cured?

When repeated stool examinations and cultures are negative for the typhoid germ. This will insure the fact that the patient is not a typhoid carrier.

What is the present-day treatment for typhoid fever?

a. Bed rest.
b. Intravenous fluids to combat the dehydration caused by diarrhea.
c. Large doses of Ampicillin or Chloromycetin, both of which are effective antibiotic medications.

VIRUS PNEUMONIA
(See Chapter 41 on Lungs)

MALARIA

What is malaria?

It is an infectious disease caused by one of four different types of parasites. It is transmitted by the bite of an infected mosquito or by the transfusion of blood from a malarial blood donor.

Infectious and Virus Diseases

Does malaria occur in the United States?

Yes. There are not too many cases, except in the southeastern states. Most cases occur in tropical countries where there are many swamplands in which the mosquitoes breed readily. It is difficult for people in the United States to comprehend that malaria is still one of the world's greatest health problems — particularly in the tropics.

How is the diagnosis of malaria made?

By the finding of a malarial parasite in the blood cells of the patient. The disease may be suspected whenever there are periodic chills and high fever in a person who has recently been in a malarial area.

Is there a vaccine to prevent malaria?

No.

How can the disease be prevented?

a. By eliminating or controlling the mosquitoes' breeding places, by the use of adequate mosquito netting and screens in an area of infected mosquitoes, and by placing protective screening around the malarial patient so that he will not be bitten by a mosquito that will then spread the disease to a healthy individual.
b. By taking a drug known as chloroquine in doses of 300mg. per week.

Is there an effective treatment for malaria?

Yes. Most cases respond well to drugs such as primaquine and chloroquine, which are now used instead of the old standby remedy, quinine. A more resistant form of malaria caused increasing difficulty among our armed forces in Viet Nam, requiring searches for new drugs and new treatment regimens.

Do malarial attacks tend to recur over a period of years if the disease has not been completely eliminated by treatment?

Yes. Formerly, patients often would have malaria on and off for many years.

YELLOW FEVER

What is yellow fever, and how is it transmitted?

It is a disease caused by a filtrable virus and transmitted by the bite of a female mosquito *(Aëdes aegypti),* which has previously fed upon the blood of a yellow fever patient.

Is yellow fever ever seen in the United States?

No. The last epidemic occurred in New Orleans in 1905. It is prevalent, however, in Western Africa and in certain parts of South America.

Why is the disease of importance today?

Because of the widespread air travel to areas in which yellow fever is prevalent. Great caution must be taken not to introduce even a single case from an infected area. It is also important that travelers from this country remember to be vaccinated against yellow fever before traveling to infected regions. The disease may masquerade as typhoid, malaria, influenza, dengue, or some form of hepatitis.

DENGUE FEVER

What is dengue fever?

It is one of the tropical fevers—also called breakbone fever—caused by a virus and transmitted by the bite of a mosquito.

Can dengue fever be prevented?

Yes, by controlling or eliminating the mosquito that transmits the disease. DDT must be sprayed over the area of the mosquitoes' breeding places.

Is there a vaccine that will prevent dengue fever?

No, but studies are in progress to produce a live attenuated vaccine against this condition.

Does dengue fever occur in the United States?

Occasional cases do occur in the southeastern states.

RELAPSING FEVER
(Recurrent Fever or Tick Fever)

What is relapsing fever, and how is it transmitted?

It is a disease characterized by bouts of fever with periods of apparent recovery that are followed by recur-

ring bouts of fever. It is caused by a spirochete germ and is transmitted by the bites of lice or ticks.

Where is relapsing fever found?

The louse-borne type is common in Europe, Africa, and India. The tick-borne type is common in the United States.

Is there a vaccine that will protect against relapsing fever?

No.

TULAREMIA
(Rabbit Fever)

What is tularemia, and how is it transmitted?

It is an acute disease caused by a bacillus and characterized by the appearance of a skin sore or ulcer, and it is accompanied by fever that resembles typhoid fever. It is a disease of wild animals, especially rabbits, and is spread among animals by the bites of bloodsucking insects. During the past ten years, the incidence of tularemia has exceeded that of tetanus.

How do humans get tularemia?

Most human cases occur in hunters, butchers who skin rabbits or other animals, and farmers and laboratory workers who handle or breed infected rabbits.

How can tularemia be prevented?

By being extremely careful with the handling of wild rabbits and rodents. Care must be exercised in removing ticks from the fur of such animals,

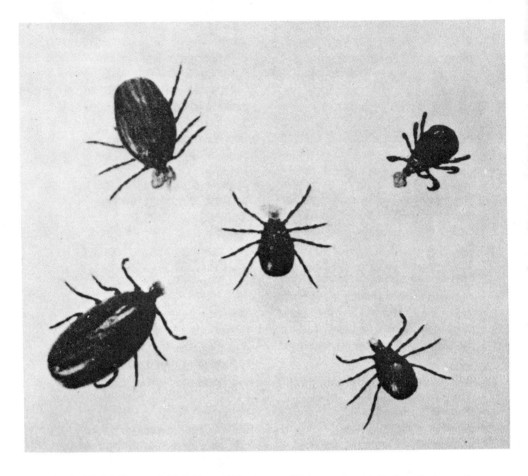

Ticks Which Transmit Tick Fever. Other types of ticks can transmit other diseases, the most serious of which is Rocky Mountain spotted fever. The large size of one tick in the accompanying photograph is caused by the fact that it is gorged with blood that has been sucked from its host. Ticks often double or triple in size after they have fed on blood for a day or two.

and proper clothing must be worn to avoid tick bites. Any wild game that is to be eaten must be very thoroughly cooked.

What is the treatment of tularemia?

Streptomycin, tetracycline, or Chloromycetin usually cure the disease within a short period of time.

THE RICKETTSIAL DISEASES

What are the rickettsial diseases, and how are they transmitted?

They are a group of infectious diseases, with fever, caused by *Rickettsia,* which are germs smaller than bacteria but larger than viruses.

They are transmitted to man by the bites of lice, fleas, or mites, or by the attachment of ticks to the skin.

Which diseases are caused by the Rickettsia?

Epidemic typhus fever, Rocky Mountain spotted fever, South American spotted fever, Q fever, scrub typhus, trench fever, and rickettsialpox. Brill's disease is a type of typhus fever seen in America and probably represents a flare-up of a former attack of epidemic typhus fever in a patient who may have had that disease when he lived in Europe, many years prior to the present attack.

How may these diseases be prevented?

By the eradication of fleas, mites, body lice, ticks, and by the control of their breeding places. In tick-infested areas, it is important to inspect the body at frequent intervals to discover any tick attachments to the skin. At night it is important to use netting to keep insects out.

Are vaccines effective against any of these diseases?

Yes, against typhus fever and Rocky Mountain spotted fever. However, tetracycline and Chloromycetin are of value in the treatment of these diseases if administered promptly. Control of Q fever in man depends upon control of the disease in animals, especially those raised for meat and milk.

Are the rickettsial diseases serious?

Yes, particularly Rocky Mountain spotted fever and certain types of typhus fever, which may lead to death in a rather high percentage of cases if not treated properly.

INFECTIOUS OR EPIDEMIC JAUNDICE
(Spirochetal Jaundice or Weil's Disease)

Is infectious jaundice the same disease as infectious hepatitis?

No. This disease is caused by a spirochete germ and is transmitted by contact with rats, either by eating or drinking food or water that has been contaminated by rat feces or urine, or occasionally by a rat bite.

Where is infectious jaundice most commonly found, and who is most apt to develop the condition?

It is most common around wharves, mines, and sewers, because rats are more apt to be found in these places. Miners, sewer workers, and wharf men are therefore more apt to contract the disease.

BRUCELLOSIS
(Undulant Fever, Malta Fever, Mediterranean Fever, Gibraltar Fever)

Is brucellosis primarily a disease of humans?

No. It affects animals, usually cattle, swine, and goats. It is caused by a germ called *Brucella.* It is transmitted to man by contact with the secretions and excretions of the above animals and by the drinking of contaminated milk.

597

Infectious and Virus Diseases

Is brucellosis contagious from man to man?

No.

Who is most apt to contract brucellosis?

It is considered an occupational disease among veterinarians, meat packers, butchers, dairy farmers, and livestock producers.

What are the symptoms of brucellosis?

Fever, chills, body aches and pains, profuse sweating, and loss of weight. The fever is usually intermittent with long periods of normal temperature. These symptoms may go on for as long as a year or more, and if brucellosis becomes chronic and is untreated, the symptoms may go on for many more years.

Is there an acute form of this disease?

Yes. This lasts only about two to three weeks and must be differentiated from typhoid fever, malaria, or tuberculosis.

How can brucellosis be prevented in man?

By pasteurization of milk. Also, people who handle meat must protect themselves by wearing rubber gloves. All skin lesions should be properly cared for in these people. Infected animals should be detected and destroyed.

What is the treatment for brucellosis?

Tetracycline has been found to be most effective in this disease.

PLAGUE
(Black Plague, Bubonic Plague)

What is plague?

It is a serious disease, which occurred in huge epidemics throughout Europe and Asia in ancient times and in the Middle Ages. It was known as the Black Death. The last great epidemic occurred in India in the early 1900s.

Is plague very common today?

No. There have not been any great epidemics since extensive programs for its extermination have been carried out.

How is the plague transmitted?

The bacteria that cause plague are found in fleas on the bodies of rats. Thus the fleas from rats get onto the bodies of humans and transmit the disease.

How does one prevent the plague?

By the extermination of rats.

What are the symptoms of plague?

Fever, severe chills, vomiting, great thirst, morning diarrhea, blood spots on the skin, and enlargement of the lymph glands.

What is pneumonic plague?

This is a form of the disease that involves the lungs. It can be transmitted from person to person by droplet infection.

Is plague a serious disease?

Yes. It formerly carried with it a tremendous mortality, but today, with streptomycin and tetracycline used together, the mortality has been reduced from over 90 percent to less than 20 percent.

LEPROSY

What causes leprosy?

It is believed to be caused by a germ called Hansen's bacillus.

Is leprosy very contagious?

No. This is a very common misconception. Leprosy is only mildly contagious, and its method of transmission is relatively unknown.

Is leprosy found in the United States?

Yes, mostly in the southern and Gulf states, but the number of cases is small.

What are the symptoms of leprosy?

There may be lumps and thickening of the skin, loss of hair, deformities of bones and joints, and loss of sensation in various areas of the body due to nerve involvement.

What is the outlook in cases of leprosy?

It depends upon the extent and type of involvement. In some cases, after a certain amount of damage has been done, there may be spontaneous disappearance of symptoms that return at a later date. Other cases go on for twenty years or more.

Is there any effective treatment for leprosy?

Yes. Several sulfone drugs have been used with favorable results. Treatment is carried on in the National Leprosarium, a special government hospital in Louisiana. With early diagnosis and well-planned treatment, the prognosis for arrest or cure of leprosy is now favorable.

INFECTIOUS MONONUCLEOSIS
(Glandular Fever)

What is infectious mononucleosis or glandular fever?

It is an infectious disease, probably caused by a virus, which often occurs in mild epidemics among children and young adults in schools, colleges, and other institutions.

How is infectious mononucleosis transmitted?

Probably by air-borne droplet infection.

After exposure, how long does it take for infectious mononucleosis to develop?

Anywhere from five days to two weeks.

What are the main symptoms of infectious mononucleosis?

Fever, headache, generalized aches and pains, and swelling of the lymph glands in the neck, armpits, and groin. The spleen becomes enlarged, and certain changes occur in the blood cells. A very prominent symptom at the onset of the disease may be a sore throat.

How can the disease be definitely established?

By certain specific blood examinations.

What is the usual course of infectious mononucleosis?

It is a self-limited disease with recovery in one to three weeks. The outlook for complete recovery is excellent except in very rare instances. A certain small number of cases may be prolonged for several months.

What are the complications of infectious mononucleosis?

There are not too many, but they may be serious. They include:
a. Throat infection.
b. Liver involvement, with jaundice and hepatitis.
c. Rupture of the spleen.
d. Involvement of the nervous system, with meningitis or encephalitis. This occurs rarely.

What is the specific blood test that clinches the diagnosis of this disease?

The heterophile agglutination test.

Is there any specific treatment for infectious mononucleosis?

No. Antibiotics have been used to prevent secondary bacterial infections, but there is no known cure for the disease itself. Bed rest is very important during the period of fever and for a few days thereafter and should be prolonged in cases in which liver involvement is suspected. Even though there is no specific treatment, it must be remembered that almost all cases get well by themselves.

Is infectious mononucleosis transmitted by kissing?

It is thought that this occurs, particularly among young adults.

If someone has the type of I.M. (infectious mononucleosis) that persists for several weeks, or even months, must he remain isolated and stay in bed?

No. If his temperature is normal, he may be permitted to return to school or work. But such a person should avoid close contact with others, as he may still be capable of transmitting the disease.

RABIES *(Hydrophobia)*

What is rabies, and how is it transmitted?

It is an acute infectious disease of animals, especially dogs and cats, caused by a virus, which affects the nervous system. The virus is present in the saliva of infected animals and is transmitted by the bite of the animal to another animal or to a human.

What is the incubation period of rabies?

Usually about two weeks, but prolonged periods up to two years following an animal bite have been recorded in rare instances.

What are the symptoms of rabies?

Fever, restlessness, and depression.

600

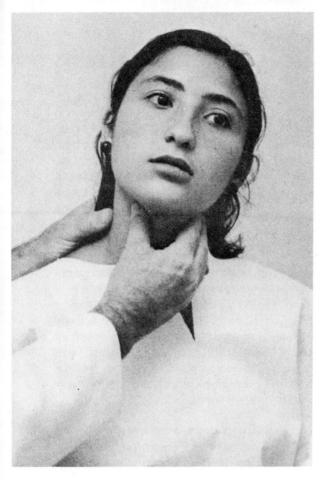

The lymph glands in the neck are almost always swollen in **acute infectious mononucleosis.**

In infectious mononucleosis the blood smear will show an increased number of monocytes. The two dark-staining large cells at the left are monocytes.

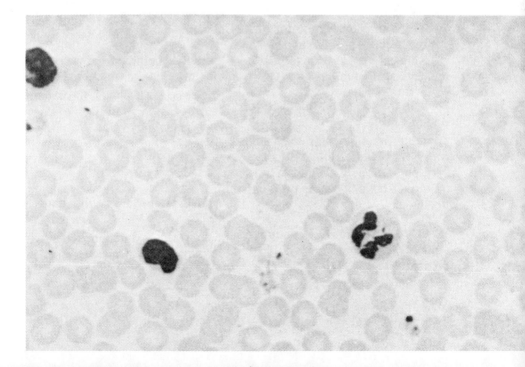

Infectious and Virus Diseases

The restlessness leads to uncontrollable excitement and convulsions. There is excessive salivation and painful spasms of the throat muscles. Death occurs in three to five days. Because of the spasms of throat muscles, there is fear of drinking or swallowing, thus the term "hydrophobia."

What should be done to a dog or other animal that bites a human being?

It should be kept under observation for about two weeks. If it does not become ill or die in this period of time, its bite may be considered harmless, and the animal can be released to its owners. If the animal becomes ill, it should not be killed but allowed to die naturally, since this will make the diagnosis easier. An autopsy should then be performed and the animal's brain examined to obtain positive proof that the animal had rabies.

Can rabies be prevented and controlled?

Yes, by the impounding and destruction of stray dogs and cats and by the mass inoculation of licensed dogs and cats against rabies.

What is the local treatment for a dog or cat bite?

Thorough washing with soap and water for a period of five to ten minutes is sufficient. Cauterization is no longer considered to be good treatment.

Is there an effective vaccine against rabies, and when should it be used?

Yes. Antirabies vaccine is very effec-

tive in preventing the disease, but it must be used cautiously as it sometimes has toxic effects. When the animal that caused the bite is known to have the disease or cannot be examined because it cannot be located, immediate vaccination against rabies should be begun. In cases in which the dog is thought to be healthy and can be observed, the animal should be watched for fourteen days. If the animal remains healthy, it is not necessary to vaccinate the human. If the dog becomes ill and dies, immunization of the bitten person should be started at once. Recent attempts to actively immunize high-risk groups such as veterinarians, mail carriers, and speleologists (cave explorers) with a new duck embryo vaccine have been very successful.

Can rabies be prevented if one waits several days after the bite before starting the vaccination?

Yes. It is safe to wait and see what happens to the animal before starting to give rabies vaccination.

If a human being once develops rabies, what is the outcome?

Rabies is fatal in almost 100 percent of cases, and there is no known treatment of any value.

TETANUS *(Lockjaw)*

What is tetanus, and what causes it?

It is an acute infectious disease causing spasm of muscles and convulsions. The spasm of the jaw muscles accounts for the name "lockjaw." The disease is caused by a bacillus that can survive in extreme heat or cold for many years because it forms inert "spores" that may become activated after they enter the body of a human.

How is tetanus transmitted?

The germ is distributed widely throughout the world, especially in soil that has been contaminated or fertilized by animal or human feces. Wounds, especially deep puncture wounds that are contaminated, form excellent sites for the development of tetanus. The germ forms a toxin, which acts upon nerves in the brain and spinal cord and leads to muscular spasms and convulsions.

What is the incubation period of tetanus?

Between five and ten days, but it may vary from two days to two months.

How is the diagnosis of tetanus made?

A history of recent injury or operation is given. The wound appears infected, and upon taking cultures of the pus, the tetanus germ is found. The symptoms must be distinguished from those of meningitis, rabies, or other conditions.

How can tetanus be prevented?

By the use of:

a. Tetanus toxoid—for active immunization of people liable to injuries, such as gardeners, farmers, soldiers, mechanics, children, athletes. Immunity with toxoid is prolonged but is best "recalled" by boosters given about every four years and also at the time of injury.

b. Tetanus antitoxin (TAT)—for passive immunization. Once an injury has occurred, this will afford protection of short duration.

What is the outlook once tetanus has developed?

It depends upon the promptness with which treatment is begun. The mortality rate is very high, especially in the very young and very old. The mortality rate varies from 30 to 100 percent. If the patient survives the first nine or ten days, his chances for full recovery are considered improved.

What is the treatment for tetanus?

a. Huge doses of antibiotics.

b. The giving of large doses of tetanus antitoxin.

ANTHRAX

What is anthrax, and how is it transmitted?

It is a highly infectious disease of animals, which is caused by the anthrax bacillus and can be transmitted to man directly or indirectly. It occurs chiefly in goats, cattle, sheep, horses, and hogs. Thus, people who have contact with these animals are prone to develop the disease.

How do humans develop anthrax?

The germs usually enter the skin through a small cut or laceration on the hands of people who habitually handle the animals mentioned above. Also, by breathing in anthrax germs, the lungs may become infected. Or if infected material from

603

the animals is swallowed, intestinal involvement may develop.

What is the treatment for anthrax?

Antiseptic dressings and antibiotics should be applied to local wounds, and antianthrax serum should be given in large doses.

What is the outlook once anthrax has developed?

Four out of five people will recover if properly treated.

Is anthrax common?

Not anymore, because people who handle animals that have anthrax sores are now fully aware of the possibility of catching the infection. Such people now take proper precautions. No potent vaccine is as yet available for human use in preventing the disease in people who handle infected animals.

ECHO VIRUS DISEASE

What is ECHO virus disease?

It is a contagious viral infection affecting the intestinal, respiratory, and nervous systems and is seen most often in young children and, occasionally, in adults. It frequently occurs in large epidemics.

What are the symptoms and course of ECHO virus disease?

Fever, headache, pain and stiffness in the neck and back, vomiting, sore throat, abdominal cramps, and diarrhea. The usual course is spontaneous with complete recovery within three to five days.

Are specific medications necessary to cure ECHO virus disease?

No. Usually aspirin for the aches and pains and drugs to relieve the vomiting and diarrhea are sufficient. Antibiotics are not indicated.

Is ECHO virus disease serious?

No, but it is sometimes erroneously diagnosed as polio or meningitis, thus alarming the family.

CHOLERA

What is cholera?

It is a disease affecting the intestinal tract and caused by a bacterium usually transmitted by water through fecal contamination.

Where does it occur?

Mostly in Asia, especially in India and Bangladesh. No cases have occurred in the Americas for about fifty years.

What are the symptoms?

Severe diarrhea with "rice-water stools," followed by extreme dehydration.

How serious is the disease?

Until recently it carried a 30 to 60 percent mortality rate.

What are the most effective methods of prevention?

a. Effective quarantine of known cases.
b. Careful hygiene and general sanitation to prevent contamination of water supplies.
c. Vaccination of all individuals

traveling to or through areas where there is danger of endemic or epidemic cholera.

What is the treatment for cholera?

a. Prompt administration of huge amounts of fluids containing salt. This is to combat the great dehydration so characteristic of cholera. If the fluids cannot be given intravenously, the patient should drink large quantities of saltwater.
b. Administration of the antibiotic tetracycline.

How effective is treatment in cholera?

Very effective if started early in the course of the disease. Mortalities have been reduced markedly.

AIDS

What is AIDS?

AIDS (Acquired Immune Deficiency Syndrome) is caused by a virus called HTLV-III/LAV that attacks and destroys T-cell lymphocytes. T-cell lymphocytes are white blood cells that protect the body against infections. When they are present in insufficient numbers, the body's ability to overcome bacterial, viral, or other harmful invaders is diminished.

How is AIDS transmitted?

AIDS is transmitted through exchange of body fluids during sexual contact or by direct contact with blood from infected persons. Most cases are found among promiscuous male homosexuals. Some cases occur from ordinary penis-vaginal heterosexual contacts, but the number is small. Other cases are found among intravenous drug users who share a needle with someone infected with the virus, or who use unsterile needles. (Now that donor blood is tested for the AIDS antibodies before being used, cases of transmission via transfusion have been virtually eliminated.)

How is the disease transmitted by male homosexuals?

Mainly through anal intercourse, since the virus is present in the semen (the fluid ejaculated during orgasm). Sex with multiple partners increases the chances of exposure to someone who has AIDS or who has been exposed to the virus. AIDS is not common in homosexuals who have only one partner.

Why is anal intercourse more likely to spread AIDS than vaginal intercourse?

It is thought that the mucous membranes of the anus and rectum are more likely to tear and permit the virus to enter the body than the vaginal mucous membranes.

Do most people exposed to the AIDS virus develop the disease?

No, the majority do not develop the disease, but they should monitor their health carefully. Some persons develop a milder form of the disease called AIDS Related Complex (ARC), which may or may not develop into AIDS.

605

Infectious and Virus Diseases

Does AIDS come about from an occasional nonsexual contact such as shaking hands or eating with someone who might have AIDS?

AIDS is not transmitted by handshakes or sneezes, or even light social kisses. It is not transmitted in swimming pools or spas, or from drinking vessels or toilet seats.

Can deep kissing transmit AIDS?

It is theoretically possible since the saliva occasionally contains the virus, but this form of transmission has not been documented.

How is AIDS transmitted through heterosexual contact?

Mainly through an infected male who is both homo and heterosexual (bisexual), or who is an intravenous drug user. Also, sexually active heterosexuals who have many contacts, especially with prostitutes, are at a higher risk of acquiring AIDS.

Do newborn children ever have AIDS?

The AIDS virus can be transmitted by an infected mother to her offspring during pregnancy, even if the mother is not ill. Such infected mothers usually have been intravenous drug users or Haitian.

Can someone be tested to see if he or she is harboring the AIDS virus?

Yes. Certain blood tests will tell. The most commonly used test, the HTLV-III/LAV antibody ELISA (enzyme linked immunosorbant assay), is an extremely sensitive test that detects antibodies in blood created by the immune system when the HTLV-III/LAV virus enters the body. Because of its extreme sensitivity, it reacts to other conditions besides the presence of HTLV-III/LAV antibody. Consequently, it is not a test for AIDS itself and probably only a small number of persons who test positive will develop AIDS.

However, they may be infectious to others.

Can someone get AIDS from being a blood donor, or from receiving a transfusion of blood, or from products obtained from blood?

No. All needles used in taking blood for a transfusion are sterile and are used only once and then thrown away. Since blood is tested to make sure it is free from possible AIDS virus contamination, transfusions and blood products are unlikely to be routes of transmission in the future.

What are the main symptoms and signs of AIDS?

Loss of appetite and weight; persistent unexplained fatigue and weakness; unexplained fever; enlarged lymph glands; infections that stubbornly resist treatment; dry, persistent cough that is not related to smoking or a cold; blue/black discolorations on or under the skin or white spots in the mouth. Eventually, infections such as pneumonia or blood poisoning overwhelm the body and the patient dies. Other patients develop malignancies, especially of the lymph glands and skin.

How long does it take to contract the symptoms and signs of AIDS?

It is thought that it usually takes any-

606

where from two to seven years after infection with the virus before signs of the disease develop.

Is AIDS curable?

Not at present. Treatment consists only of combating the infections as they arise.

Do most people with AIDS eventually die of the disease, and how quickly does AIDS kill?

Yes, at present most people die. Patients usually have the active disease for one or more years before an overwhelming infection carries them away. But there is hope for the future.

What can male homosexuals do to avoid AIDS?

Shun promiscuity; avoid intercourse if they are aware that they harbor the AIDS virus; use a condom during anal intercourse.

What can heterosexuals do to avoid AIDS?

Shun sexual contacts with promiscuous partners; use a condom to minimize exchange of body fluids; avoid sexual contacts with people who are at a high risk for AIDS, such as those who are drug addicts.

Is the number of AIDS cases likely to increase within the next few years?

Yes, for the following reasons:

1. Many hitherto unreported cases are now being reported.
2. Many people who were infected with the virus during recent years have not yet shown active symptoms of the disease.
3. Drug addiction has not diminished significantly. However, the fear of contracting AIDS may alter ihe incidence of new cases by changing the sex habits of male homosexuals. A high percentage of male homosexuals now limit their activity to just one partner.

How long do physicians think it will be before satisfactory measures will be available to combat AIDS?

Most researchers think that an effective vaccination against the AIDS virus will not come about until 1990, or later.

CHAPTER 35

INHERITED AND CONGENITAL CONDITIONS

(See also Chapter 18 on Contagious Diseases; Chapter 43 on Medications and Drugs; Chapter 57 on Pregnancy and Childbirth; Chapter 79 on X ray)

What is meant by an inherited characteristic?

It is a trait or bodily characteristic that is passed on from one generation to another. Such a trait or characteristic is determined by units within the nucleus of the germ cells called chromosomes or genes.

What is DNA?

It is the basic substance, found in the nucleus of cells, responsible for transmitting hereditary characteristics.

What is deoxyribonucleic acid?

It is the full name for DNA.

What is meant by a congenital condition?

A trait or bodily characteristic with which one is born, usually as a result of something that happens to the embryo during its development or at birth. For example, if the mother develops German measles during the early weeks of pregnancy, this is likely to affect the growing embryo and produce blindness, heart disease, and other conditions. Under such circumstances, these conditions would be regarded as congenital, since they occurred during the formation of the embryo and were *not* inherited.

Do inherited characteristics tend to follow any pattern of inheritance?

Yes. The Mendelian law governs inheritance.

What is the difference between a dominant and a recessive characteristic?

A dominant characteristic is much more likely to appear in the offspring

608

BROWN EYES

BLUE EYES

PARENTS:

One pure brown eyes
and one pure blue eyes

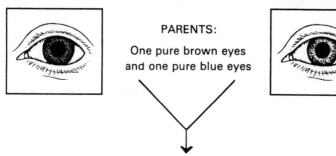

CHILDREN:

Eyes brown (dominant) with blue recessive

PARENTS:

with brown dominant and blue recessive

CHILDREN:

¼ will be pure brown	½ will be brown dominant and blue recessive	¼ will be pure blue

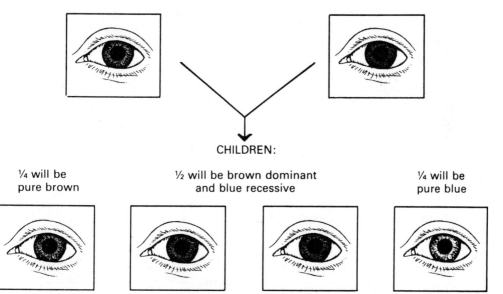

The Mendelian Law. *The illustration above is a schematic representation of the Mendelian Law as it applies to the inheritance of eye color. The same law applies to the inheritance of other physical characteristics.*

than a recessive one. For instance, with one brown-eyed and one blue-eyed parent, the chances are that more of the children will be brown-eyed, as brown eyes are the dominant characteristic. When a child has parents with black hair but is born with red hair, red hair is the recessive characteristic.

Are most inherited defects and deformities dominant or recessive characteristics?

Most of them are recessive characteristics and will appear in only a small percentage of cases.

Do inherited characteristics sometimes skip generations and appear in subsequent generations?

Yes.

If someone has an inherited deformity, is there a tendency for his children to have this deformity?

Yes, but it must be remembered that inherited defects occur in only a small percentage of offspring. However, a family with known inherited defects has a much greater chance of having children with these defects than does a family in which there are no known inherited abnormalities.

Is it safe for two people, each of whom has a family history of inherited deformities, to marry one another?

Yes, but they must carefully consider the possibility of passing on an abnormality to their children. It is wise for such a couple to seek expert advice before having children.

Is it safe to marry a blood relative?

It is safe to marry a relative, but it is wise not to have children when the relationship is close. This is apt to bring out undesirable recessive traits.

Is it safe to marry into a family in which there is known insanity?

Yes. Insanity is not inherited, although the tendency to inherit personality disorders may occur in some families. Environmental factors are usually much more important.

What are some of the common inherited traits and abnormalities?

Color blindness, skin color, eye color, hair color, harelip, clubfoot, cleft palate, twinning or other multiple birth tendencies, body build, mental deficiency, hemophilia, etc. Also, certain allergies and tendencies toward development of other diseases may be inherited.

Is cancer inherited?

No, although the tendency toward the development of tumors might be inherited.

Can paternity be determined accurately?

Yes. By means of certain blood studies, it can be determined with a good degree of accuracy.

Can events in the life of a pregnant woman alter the physical development of the unborn child?

Illness in the mother may produce a defect in the development of her embryo. Also, excessive drinking, smoking, and use of drugs can cause physical and developmental defects. Emotional upsets that affect the mother during her pregnancy will *not* influence the child.

Can x-ray radiation or exposure to radioactive substances alter the characteristics of offspring or produce abnormalities?

Excessive exposure to x rays or radioactive substances during the early weeks of pregnancy might influence and disturb the normal development of the embryo. Also, it is now thought that excessive x-ray radiation in the region of the ovaries may cause alteration of some of the cells so that an abnormality might crop up in a child or grandchild. This entire subject is now undergoing very intensive investigation.

Can the taking of certain medications and drugs during the early months of pregnancy alter the physical or mental characteristics of the offspring?

Yes. It has been found recently that there are many drugs that can injure and cause malformations in the embryo during the first few weeks or months of its life. For this reason, mothers are cautioned never to take any medicines except those that are precisely prescribed by the attending physician.

Is it possible to avoid having children who will inherit abnormalities from their parents?

This question is related to the general problem of preventive medicine in relation to hereditary disease. First, it might be well to avoid having children with a mate whose family is known to have inherited diseases. Second, relatives who marry one another should seriously consider the advisability of having children. This relationship, called consanguinity, may bring out undesirable, latent hereditary traits. Further, couples in whose families inherited diseases exist should seek genetic counseling before having children. Parents can now be tested for a sickle-cell trait and for a tendency toward passing on Tay-Sachs disease. If both parents exhibit these tendencies, it is perhaps best if they do not have children.

Are intellect and intelligence inherited?

It is difficult to assess the relative roles of heredity and environment in this connection. It is known, however, that intelligent people have a greater tendency to have intelligent children. How much of this is due to their environment we cannot now state. It is known that mental retardation is often inherited or may result from a birth injury or infection.

Should people who have one abnormal child risk having other children?

Many abnormalities are now known to be the result of conditions that occurred during pregnancy or at birth and therefore would not affect subsequent children. Of the inherited conditions, many are recessive, and

611

the chance of other children being affected is small. Expert medical advice is available and should be sought in such cases.

Should people with inherited defects marry and have children?

They may marry, but they should consider carefully whether they ought to have children, and the advice of medical experts should be obtained. Some inherited conditions are recessive and will affect only a few scattered members in a family tree. Other inherited disorders run a dominant pattern, and the chances of their appearance in the children are great. In such cases it might be wiser for a couple to adopt a child rather than have their own.

Should people who have had defects such as clubfoot or harelip, etc., exercise more than the usual care in the selection of a mate?

Yes. They ought to avoid having offspring with anyone with a similar family history of defects.

Is longevity inherited?

No, but the tendency toward longevity may be inherited. (See Chapter 5, on Aging.)

Should one exercise caution in marrying into a family in which there are several members who have had epilepsy or mental disorders?

Yes.

Are weight and height characteristics inherited?

Height is much more likely to be in-

herited than weight. Weight will depend upon one's eating habits.

Is it serious if a pregnant woman develops German measles?

Yes. If it occurs during the first few months of pregnancy, it may lead to blindness, deafness, heart disease, or mental retardation in the offspring.

Are personality traits inherited?

Heredity may play a role in the development of personality, but it is probably a small one. The most important contribution to personality development is the environment in which the child grows up.

Is there any truth to the statement that a "black sheep" is one who has inherited certain unfavorable characteristics from an ancestor?

No.

Are criminal tendencies inherited?

No.

Is there any such thing as inheriting a "weak character"?

No.

Are many diseases inherited?

No. Your physician will be able to inform you precisely as to which diseases are inherited. They are relatively few in number.

INHERITED OR CONGENITAL CONDITIONS ASSOCIATED WITH MENTAL AND PHYSICAL RETARDATION

What are some of the factors associated with inherited and con-

genital diseases that are accompanied by mental and physical retardation?

a. The inheritance of defective genes.
b. The development of chromosome abnormalities as in mongolism, Klinefelter's syndrome, and Turner's syndrome.
c. Inherited defects in metabolism.
d. Defects secondary to skull or brain malformations.
e. Conditions that affect the mother during her pregnancy, such as German measles, syphilis, or other infections.
f. Extremely poor nutrition of the mother during pregnancy.
g. The ingestion by the mother of certain harmful drugs during the early weeks and months of her pregnancy.
h. Exposure of the mother and the young embryo to excess radiation.
i. Difficulties during childbirth, especially those associated with the delay in the baby's breathing.
j. Marked jaundice of the newborn baby, as in erythroblastosis (Rh-factor disease).
k. Causes after the child has already been born, such as meningitis, encephalitis, severe head injuries, lead or other type poisonings, etc.

What are some of the more commonly encountered metabolic disorders causing mental retardation?

a. Phenylketonuria, otherwise known as PKU disease.
b. Galactosemia.
c. Maple syrup urine disease.
d. Tay-Sachs disease.
e. Wilson's disease.

What causes PKU disease?

It is caused by the absence of an enzyme that acts on one of the protein elements in the food. Improper metabolism of this element accounts for the accumulation of abnormal metabolic constituents in the brain.

Is PKU disease inherited?

Yes.

Can PKU disease be recognized early in an infant's life?

Yes. There is a blood test (Guthrie test) that can be done on the baby's blood when the baby is three to four days old. There is also a urine test that can detect PKU disease when the baby is four to six weeks old. Many states in the country now have mandatory laws requiring that the Guthrie blood test be done prior to the newborn child's leaving the hospital.

Can PKU disease be treated successfully?

Yes, if it is recognized early. It is first necessary to discover the particular protein that is not being metabolized properly. When this has been discovered, this protein is completely eliminated from the infant's diet. Under such circumstances, it is possible to avoid the ultimate brain damage that is associated with this condition.

How common is PKU disease?

It occurs approximately once in every ten to twenty thousand births.

What is galactosemia?

It is a disease characterized by a disturbance in the metabolism of the

613

Inherited and Congenital Conditions

sugar present in milk. There is no disturbance, however, in fruit or cane sugar metabolism.

Can galactosemia be detected early in an infant's life?

Yes. There is a blood test for the presence of the enzyme necessary in the metabolism of milk sugar. Also, one can test for the presence of sugar in the urine in very young babies.

Can galactosemia be prevented or treated?

Yes, by eliminating milk sugar from the child's diet. This means that the child will have to have a milk substitute instead of regular milk.

What is Tay-Sachs disease?

See Chapter 32, on Amaurotic Familial Idiocy.

What is Wilson's disease?

It is a condition in which there is a disturbance in the metabolism of copper in the body that allows it to accumulate in the brain, liver, eyes, and other organs. Eventually, the accumulation of copper will interfere with the function of these structures.

Is there any way to treat Wilson's disease?

Yes. There is a substance that can be given to the child that will aid in the removal of excess copper from the body.

A Microcephalic Child. A congenital condition, microcephaly literally means small head. Mental retardation usually accompanies this condition, as the small skull inhibits brain development.

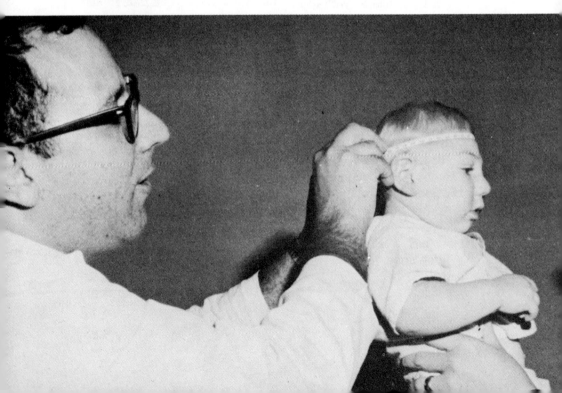

Are there any other forms of metabolic disorder that can produce mental retardation?

Yes, new conditions—most of them, fortunately, are very rare—are being discovered all the time.

GENETIC MEDICINE

What is meant by the term "genetic medicine"?

This is a new, rapidly developing science that deals with the circumstances and conditions influencing and surrounding inheritance. With the development of new high-powered microscopes, the actual chromosomes and genes can now be seen and studied microscopically.

What is a karyotype?

The chromosomal characteristics of an individual. Karyotype charts are arranged so that chromosomes are paired and placed in order, from the largest to the smallest. By studying these chromosomes under a microscope, one may detect defects.

Is it possible to determine defects in a newborn child by examining his chromosomes or genes?

It is now possible to examine a child's chromosomes by scraping a few cells from the inside of his mouth or by examining the cells in his blood. The chromosomes can be classified and sorted out, but this is not yet possible to do with the genes. A considerable number of defects have been uncovered by examination of chromosomes.

What diseases can be spotted by examination of the chromosomes?

It has already been determined that Down's syndrome, Klinefelter's syndrome, and Turner's syndrome are caused by defects in the chromosomes.

Is it possible that a day will come when one will be able to spot defects in the genes?

Yes. Recent advances in genetic medicine make it highly likely that the day is not far off when one will be able to note potentialities for health and disease through the study of the genes.

Is it possible that in the future some diseases can be eliminated as a result of genetic studies?

Yes. A day may come when we will be able to discover certain characteristics within the genes or chromosomes that might lead to the development of such diseases as diabetes, cystic fibrosis, or even cancer. Once the basic abnormality creating these tendencies is discovered, ways may be found to eliminate them.

Can birth defects sometimes be diagnosed before a child is born?

Yes, by a procedure known as *amniocentesis*. This is carried out by inserting a needle into the pregnant uterus through the abdominal wall. A small amount of the amniotic fluid surrounding the fetus is withdrawn and is examined under a high-powered microscope. It may reveal the presence of cells that contain abnormal chromosomes, thus denot-

615

Working on Karyotypes. *A geneticist analyzes a karyotype and measures the matched pairs of chromosomes in the chart.*

ing the presence of a defective fetus. Further studies of cells may reveal metabolic disorders that can cause any one of several diseases in the newborn child.

What is meant by the term "genetic engineering"?

Genetic engineering is a new science that attempts to alter and im-

prove the genes or to transplant them from one form of living matter to another.

What is hoped to be accomplished by genetic engineering?

There are genes in people that tend to cause bad traits as well as good traits. By altering "bad" genes, scientists hope to be able to do away with-some of the defects and illnesses caused by their inheritance.

Is experimentation in the altering of genes now being carried out?

Yes. Under very strict control, much progress has been made in altering genes in bacteria. Alteration of human genes is still far in the future.

What benefits might come from altering genes in bacteria?

Recent experiments have been carried out whereby genes from the human pituitary gland in the base of the skull have been implanted in bacteria, resulting in those bacteria producing the human growth hormone. Other experiments in gene transfers have resulted in bacteria producing insulin and a cancer-fighting substance known as interferon.

Are there certain dangers to genetic engineering?

Yes. New forms of bacterial or animal life may be created through genetic engineering. As a consequence, if not strictly controlled, new forms of harmful bacteria to which we have no immunity may be brought into being.

What is genetic counseling?

It is a service that physicians trained in genetic medicine should give to all people who fear that their offspring might inherit certain diseases or defects.

Can genetic counselors predict with any degree of accuracy whether a particular couple will produce a healthy or defective child?

Yes. If one looks over the list of inherited diseases discussed in this chapter, he will find many conditions whose inheritance can be predicted with considerable accuracy.

Who is most likely to have children with inherited defects?

a. Couples who have a history of an inherited defect or disease in both sides of the family. Thus, a male and female who both have diabetes will have children with a very great chance of being diabetic.

b. Certain inherited defects and diseases are known to be dominant in character. These conditions are much more likely to be inherited than defects or diseases that are recessive in character.

CHAPTER **36**

THE INTENSIVE CARE UNIT (ICU)

(See also Chapter 8 on Anesthesia;
Chapter 26 on First Aid in Emergencies;
Chapter 29 on Heart; Chapter 58 on
Preoperative and Postoperative Routines)

What is an ICU?

An ICU, or Intensive Care Unit, is an area in a hospital where specialized care is given to the desperately sick patient. In the ICU, the patient is monitored constantly and receives a great deal more attention from physicians and nurses than could possibly be given in a ward or in a private or semiprivate hospital accommodation. A well-equipped ICU has sophisticated equipment, which permits moment-to-moment monitoring of the patient's condition. In addition, it is able to render immediate treatment when critical situations demand it. Most ICUs are staffed so that a physician is always present and on duty, and there is a nurse for every three patients.

Does the ICU care for the terminally ill?

No. The ICU is a facility that ministers to those who are critically ill but are potentially curable.

What specific advantages does an ICU have over ordinary, routine hospital care?

a. The constant presence of highly trained attending physicians and nurses.

b. Equipment to assist respiration, such as respirators, suction apparatus, oxygen, etc. Also, equipment to insert a tube into the trachea or, in extreme cases, instruments to perform a tracheostomy.

c. Cardiac monitoring equipment, which records every heartbeat for

618

twenty-four hours each day. Then, if heart action appears to be failing, medications are always on hand to help support it.

d. Dialysis equipment, for use when the kidney function shows evidence of failing.

e. ICU patients have priority for any laboratory or x-ray test that may be required at any time of the day or night.

f. The patient in the ICU is supported by the presence of medical technologists to insure the proper maintenance of all therapeutic and monitoring devices.

Is it important that laboratory tests be taken frequently on patients in the ICU?

Yes. It is essential to maintain the body's chemistry at normal or near-normal levels at all times. There is a great tendency for patients in shock, and among those who have severe impairment of their heart, lung, liver, or kidney function, to get into chemical imbalance. This may mean that their body fluids are too acid, or in some cases, too alkaline. If one of these abnormalities persists, the patient may not survive.

The monitoring of one's blood volume, blood gases, and blood components, such as the number of red blood cells and the quantity of hemoglobin in those red cells, is vital, too.

Can imbalances in one's chemistry or deficiencies in one's blood be helped through treatment?

Yes. Intravenous medications can be given to improve chemical balance.

Blood transfusions can be given to replace blood loss.

Do all hospitals have an ICU?

Accredited hospitals do have an ICU. However, the number of beds in the unit, the amount of specialized equipment available, and the ratio of physicians and nurses to patients will vary according to the size of the hospital. The larger the hospital, the more beds will be set aside for an ICU.

What proportion of a hospital's beds should be designated for the ICU?

Approximately 5 percent.

Do hospitals that specialize in cancer treatment or in heart surgery usually require more ICU beds than the ordinary general hospital?

Yes.

Does the ICU accept only patients with specific illnesses?

No. Any critically ill patient is eligible for care in the ICU.

Do some hospitals have separate ICUs for individual departments?

Yes, some of the very large hospitals may have a surgical ICU separate from a medical ICU.

What are some of the newer devices in an up-to-date ICU?

a. Automatic respiratory devices to breathe for a patient who is unable to breathe on his own.

b. Electronic devices to monitor heart action.

619

The Intensive Care Unit (ICU)

c. Computerized multichannel devices to record on a visual screen various vital signs.

d. An alarm system to instantly alert the staff to any change in the patient's condition.

Are the nurses on duty in an ICU specially trained?

Yes. Most have taken courses in the recognition and treatment of critically ill patients. Their special training enables them to render treatments that the regular floor nurses do not perform.

Are patients often sent to an ICU prior to surgery?

Yes, if they are in such poor condition that the risks of surgery are too great for them to survive. Treatment in an ICU may so improve their condition that surgery may become possible.

Are patients frequently referred to the ICU after serious operations?

Yes, but only if they are in a "high-risk" category for developing life-threatening, postoperative complications. Very elderly patients, patients with advanced heart or blood vessel disease, patients with serious chronic lung ailments, patients with advanced kidney disease, etc., are candidates for admission to the ICU after major surgery. Also, patients who have encountered serious complications during an operative procedure are often sent to the ICU.

Does care in an ICU substantially increase one's chances for survival?

Definitely, yes.

When is an ICU patient transferred back to his room?

When the physicians in the ICU conclude that his vital signs are stable and that he needs no assistance to function on his own.

How long may a patient remain in the ICU?

Some patients may require care in the ICU for only a few hours; others may need several days, or even weeks, until they can function without the special supportive measures given in the ICU.

CHAPTER  # THE KIDNEYS AND URETERS

(See also Chapter 25 on Female Organs; Chapter 42 on Male Organs; Chapter 59 on Prostate Gland; Chapter 73 on Transplantation of Organs; Chapter 76 on Urinary Bladder and Urethra)

What is the location and structure of the kidneys?

The kidneys are two bean-shaped, reddish brown organs covered by a glistening, thin capsule. Each kidney measures approximately four inches in length, two inches in width, and approximately one and a half inches in thickness.

The kidneys lie on either side of the posterior portion of the abdomen, high up in the loin, behind the abdominal cavity, and beneath the diaphragm.

How do the kidneys function?

The kidneys are composed of hundreds of thousands of tiny units known as nephrons, which empty into microscopic ducts known as tubules. Each nephron is a small, independent chemical plant that forms urine as the plasma of the blood passes through. The nephrons empty the urine they produce into collecting tubules and then on into the pelvis of the kidney; thence, via a tubular structure called the ureter, into the urinary bladder.

What are the main duties of the kidneys?

Approximately one-fourth of the blood output of the heart is conveyed to the kidneys. The nephrons extract waste and toxic chemicals, excess minerals, and water from the blood, which passes through them. It is also the function of the kidney *not to extract* certain needed chemicals and substances from the blood.

Can one live a normal, healthy life with only one kidney?

Yes, provided the remaining kidney functions normally.

621

The Kidneys and Ureters

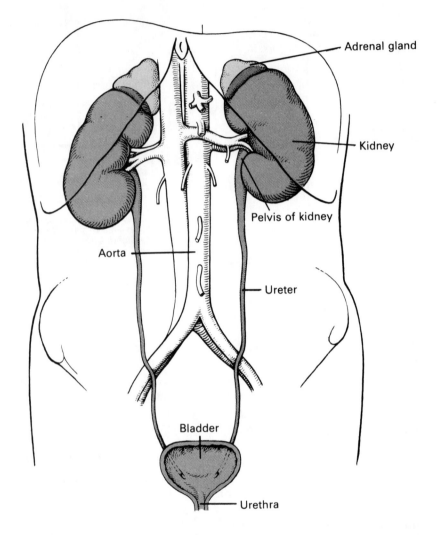

Adrenal gland

Kidney

Pelvis of kidney

Aorta

Ureter

Bladder

Urethra

What happens when kidney function is damaged?

a. There is an excessive accumulation of chemical wastes and toxins in the bloodstream.
b. Excessive loss of essential chemicals from the bloodstream into the urine occurs.
c. As a result of impaired kidney function, the tissues of the body are supplied with blood and solu-

Normal Kidneys and Ureters. *The kidneys manufacture urine, which is secreted down through the ureters and into the urinary bladder. Obstruction to the flow of urine down the ureters may cause severe damage to kidney substance and may eventually result in total loss of kidney function on the obstructed side.*

622

tions with improper chemical components. Eventually, if kidney function deteriorates beyond a certain point, such a severe chemical upset occurs that life cannot continue.

How can one tell if his kidney function is normal?

a. By analysis of the urine.
b. By chemical analysis of various constituents of the blood.
c. By x-ray examination of the kidneys and the rest of the urinary tract.
d. By special kidney function tests.

Is urine analysis always a good test for kidney diseases?

No. There are occasions when a kidney may be seriously damaged and yet the urine specimen may appear to be normal. However, by and large, urine analysis is a simple, rapid, and inexpensive initial test for screening.

Is diabetes a kidney disease?

No. Diabetes is essentially a disease of the pancreas, but the diagnosis is aided by examining the urine. (See Chapter 19, on Diabetes.)

What are the common causes of impaired kidney function?

a. Any generalized severe infection or inflammation.
b. Mechanical obstruction of the outlet of the kidneys.
c. General abnormalities of the kidneys that have existed since birth.
d. Tumors of the kidney.
e. Poisons that have been taken into the body and that damage kidney structure.

f. Interference with blood circulation to the kidneys.
g. Metabolic or hormone disease.
h. Abnormal concentrations of minerals in the bloodstream or dehydration.

Does swelling of the legs, the abdomen, and the face always indicate kidney disease?

Not necessarily. There are many other conditions that may cause this swelling.

Is it necessary to drink large quantities of water to make the kidneys function normally?

Let your thirst be your guide. This will usually provide sufficient fluid for adequate kidney function.

Are the advertised drugs that supposedly "flush the kidneys" beneficial?

No. Normal kidneys do their own flushing, and abnormal kidneys cannot be beneficially "flushed" by these drugs.

Do backaches usually indicate kidney disease?

The majority are not related to kidney disease. Certain types of backaches may be symptoms of a kidney disorder, but the diagnosis requires an examination by a physician.

What is the relationship between high blood pressure and kidney disease?

Long-standing high blood pressure over a period of years may eventually cause kidney disease due to disturbance in the circulation of the kidney.

623

The Kidneys and Ureters

Conversely, severe kidney disorders often lead to high blood pressure. It has been found within recent years that narrowing of the renal artery, the main artery to the kidney, can also cause high blood pressure.

Is it ever possible to cure high blood pressure by surgery upon the blood vessels to the kidney?

Yes. It can now be determined accurately by special x-ray techniques whether the major artery to the kidney is narrowed. If this condition is found to be present, plastic surgery upon the renal blood vessel can often be carried out successfully. If the narrowing is due to arteriosclerosis, the inner lining of the artery is reamed out, and a patch graft made of Dacron is applied. This will increase the blood supply to the kidney, in many instances eliminating the cause for the high blood pressure.

Does albumin in the urine always indicate kidney disease?

Not necessarily. However, the presence of albumin must be considered to be indicative of a kidney disorder until further testing and procedures prove otherwise.

Does frequency of urination indicate kidney disease?

Sometimes frequency of urination is caused merely by excessive drinking of fluids or by nervous tension. On the other hand, disorders such as diabetes or enlargement of the prostate may be the cause of frequency of urination. Repeated episodes of frequency of urination should lead to a thorough investigation by your phy

sician to rule out disturbance in kidney function or disease of the kidneys.

Does bedwetting indicate kidney disease or a weak bladder?

No. Most cases have their origin in emotional disturbance or may be due to excessively deep sleep.

Is salt restriction in the diet essential to a person with kidney disease?

Only in certain types of chronic kidney disease, namely, when undue amounts of fluid are already being retained by the body.

Can excessive eating of meats, eggs, or the intake of too much salt cause kidney disease?

No, but these foods are often restricted in patients who have advanced kidney disease.

Does smoking hurt the kidneys?

It can affect them indirectly by causing decreased arterial circulation, and it may increase the incidence of cancer.

Is drinking of alcoholic beverages injurious to the kidneys?

Large quantities of alcohol may damage the kidneys, as it will all other tissues. It is well for a patient suffering from serious kidney disease not to drink alcoholic beverages.

Is the taking of large amounts of spices and condiments injurious to the kidneys?

Not usually. However, it can act as a temporary irritant when there already is disease in the urinary tract.

What is the significance of blood in the urine?

This should indicate that something is wrong somewhere in the urinary tract, and the patient should seek medical advice promptly.

Does blood in the urine always indicate kidney disease?

No. The source of the blood may be the ureter, the bladder, or the urethra leading from the bladder to the outside. Occasionally, blood may appear in the urine without any underlying disease. However, such patients should consult their doctor to be sure.

Does cloudiness of the urine or pain on urination indicate kidney disease?

Not necessarily, although it may indicate that there is some disturbance within the urinary tract. Patients with such symptoms should seek medical advice promptly.

What is Bright's disease?

This is an old term, named after a famous physician, which denotes a variety of kidney diseases. In most instances, it denotes glomerulonephritis.

What is nephritis?

This is also a broad descriptive term denoting a diseased functioning of the kidneys.

GLOMERULONEPHRITIS

What is glomerulonephritis?

This is a specific disease that affects the nephrons of the kidney. It is caused by inflammation of the nephrons and may, if not checked, lead to scarring and destruction of these structures with consequent impairment of kidney function.

What forms of glomerulonephritis are there?

a. Acute glomerulonephritis.
b. Chronic glomerulonephritis.
The acute stage may last from a few days to a year or more; the chronic stage may last as long as the patient lives. There is also an intermediate stage known as subacute glomerulonephritis.

How common a disease is acute glomerulonephritis?

It is quite common, especially among children.

What causes acute glomerulonephritis?

Although the cause is not known, it usually appears shortly after a bacterial infection, most often after an infection caused by a streptoccocus germ, which is commonly the cause of sore throats, tonsillitis, and scarlet fever.

What is the usual course of acute glomerulonephritis?

It usually lasts for several weeks and then subsides spontaneously. It is estimated that in children with acute glomerulonephritis, 75 to 90 percent will get well without resultant kidney damage.

Is acute glomerulonephritis ever fatal?

Yes. In about one out of twenty

625

cases, the patient may not survive this disease.

What are the symptoms of acute glomerulonephritis?

The patient may give a history of a previous acute infection, such as a severe sore throat. Blood and albumin may appear in the urine with varying degrees of elevation of the blood pressure and tenderness over the kidney region.

At what age is acute glomerulonephritis most frequently seen?

Seventy percent of all cases occur before age twenty-one.

Is this type of nephritis hereditary?

It is not thought to be hereditary, although there is a certain tendency for the condition to occur in families.

Is there any way to prevent getting nephritis?

All acute infections, especially sore throats, tonsillitis, and scarlet fever, should be treated promptly and thoroughly by a physician.

Is there any specific treatment for acute glomerulonephritis?

No. However, with proper rest and supportive measures, the majority of people will make a good recovery.

Is there any specific treatment for chronic glomerulonephritis?

No. However, people with chronic glomerulonephritis may live normal lives for many years if they take care of themselves by observing certain dietary precautions and avoiding acute infections.

NEPHROSIS

What is nephrosis?

It is a general term relating to certain types of kidney disorder in which there is generalized water-logging and swelling of the body tissues. This swelling and water-logging may be visible in the face, abdomen, and legs. There is also a loss of large quantities of body proteins, elevation of certain of the fatty substances in the bloodstream, and a lowering of the basal metabolism of the individual. There are many different specific causes of nephrosis.

Who is most likely to get nephrosis?

Children between the ages of two and seven years.

Is nephrosis a very common disease?

It is relatively rare.

What is the treatment for nephrosis?

This depends upon the primary cause. General measures include diet and salt restrictions. Cortisone and related steroids are used in certain types of nephrosis with gratifying results.

Is it necessary to restrict salt intake in treating nephrosis?

Yes. Since retention of salt causes retention of water, it is important to restrict this substance.

Is restriction of meat, eggs, and other proteins recommended in nephrosis?

No.

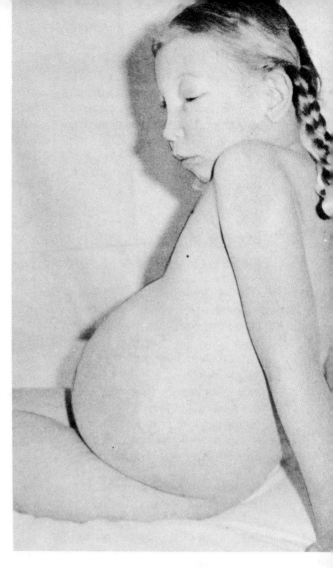

Nephrosis. This photograph shows an eight-year-old child, with an advanced case of nephrosis. Fortunately, nephrotic children can now be helped greatly by the use of some of the newer drugs, such as cortisone, etc.

What is the recovery rate from nephrosis?

In former years, about half the children with nephrosis would die. Today, with newer methods of treatment, three out of four will get well.

UREMIA

What is uremia?

This term denotes the abnormal chemical changes in the blood as well as the associated symptoms that appear in the advanced stages of kidney failure, when the kidney is unable to eliminate waste products.

Can a patient with uremia recover?

Yes, provided the cause is found and is capable of being eliminated. As an example, if it is caused by an obstruction of the ureter or the kidney outlet and this is promptly relieved, the uremia will subside, and the patient will get well. If the uremia

627

represents the terminal stage of chronic nephritis, the only cure may be through a kidney transplant. Dialysis, the use of the so-called "artificial kidney," may keep these people alive until a kidney is available for transplant.

PYELONEPHRITIS (Kidney Infections)

What is pyelonephritis?
A bacterial infection of the kidney including the outlet of the kidney.

What causes pyelonephritis?
It is caused by bacteria, which reach the kidney through the bloodstream, or by extension from other portions of the genitourinary tract, such as the bladder, the prostate, the cervix, the vagina, or the urethra.

Who is most likely to develop pyelonephritis?
Pyelonephritis is seen quite often in children as an acute infection, but is also quite common in adults. Females, especially pregnant women, are most likely to develop kidney infection, since they are more prone to develop bladder infections. Also prone are diabetics and people who are debilitated or who have certain neurological disorders.

What are the symptoms of pyelonephritis?
High temperature, possibly with intermittent chills, backache, tenderness over the kidney area, frequency of urination along with painful void-

ing and blood in the urine. Nausea, vomiting, and lack of appetite are common. Examination may reveal pus and bacteria in the urine and an elevated white blood cell count.

Are both kidneys usually affected at the same time?
No, but this can occur in some cases.

What is the treatment for kidney infections?
a. Drinking large quantities of fluids so as to flush out the pelvis and ureters of the kidneys.
b. Antibiotics to take care of the infecting organism.
c. Bed rest and a bland diet.
d. Medications for relief of pain.

What is the usual course of kidney infections?
If properly treated, almost all patients get well. It is important to discover whether there is an underlying obstruction of the ureter which might have caused the urine to dam up and become infected, and it is important to eradicate any infection elsewhere in the body that might have precipitated the kidney infection.

How long is one usually ill with these infections?
Anywhere from a few days to several weeks.

Do antibiotics always prove effective in curing pyelitis or pyelonephritis?
In almost all instances, provided the correct antibiotic drug is found for the particular bacteria causing the

628

infection, and provided that other urinary tract defects are corrected.

Is hospitalization necessary in kidney infections?

The average case can be treated well at home. However, if the temperature is very high or if the pelvis of the kidney does not drain out its infected urine, then hospitalization is advisable.

What special hospital treatments may become necessary if the case does not respond to ordinary treatment?

The urologist may be called upon to pass a catheter (a long rubber tube) into the bladder and then up into the ureter in order to drain out any infected urine blocked in the pelvis of the kidney.

Is surgery necessary for pyelitis or pyelonephritis?

Usually not. However, if an abscess forms in or around the kidney, operative drainage may be necessary. Similarly, if the kidney infection is secondary to some other kidney disease such as stones, surgery may be required.

Will frequent follow-up visits to a physician aid in preventing recurrence of kidney infection?

Yes.

Do kidney infections have a tendency to recur?

Yes, if there was a delay in the treatment of the initial attack or if treatment was inadequate. In these cases, lasting damage to the kidney occurs, which may permanently impair its function.

Is it true that people with diabetes are more prone to develop kidney infection?

Yes.

Does chronic kidney infection lead to the development of other diseases?

Yes. People with this condition often form stones, develop high blood pressure, and may eventually develop uremia.

KIDNEY STONES

What is the composition of kidney stones?

They are a combination of inorganic salts such as calcium, phosphorus, ammonium, etc., or they may be composed of organic compounds such as uric or amino acids.

What causes the formation of kidney stones?

In certain instances the exact cause is known. For instance, in gout, there is a high concentration of blood uric acid and a high concentration of uric acid in the kidney excretions, causing the precipitation of uric acid stones. Similarly, in disorders of calcium metabolism, there is a precipitation out of calcium compound stones in the urine and in the kidneys. However, in most situations, the exact mechanism is not known, but there are many theories:
a. Improper diet.

b. Chemical imbalances in the urine, cause unknown.

c. Disorders of the endocrine glands, especially the parathyroid glands in the neck.

d. Vitamin deficiencies.

e. Infections within the kidney.

f. Poor drainage in one or more parts of the urinary tract.

g. Living in areas where hard water causes stones.

Do kidney stones appear as frequently in both sexes?

No. They are somewhat more common in men.

Do kidney stones occur at any age?

Yes, but they are much more common in adults during the fourth, fifth, and sixth decades of life. Children do not get kidney stones very frequently.

What symptoms are caused by kidney stones?

In some instances the stones are quiescent and cause no symptoms. This type may be discovered accidentally. Usually, they cause pain, blood and pus cells in the urine, and, not infrequently, they impair kidney function.

Do kidney stones tend to be single or multiple?

They are more often single, but they may be multiple. When multiple stones are encountered, they may be found in both kidneys.

Is there much variation in the size of a kidney stone?

Yes. They vary in size from tiny frag-

ments like grains of sand to stones that form an outline or cast of an entire kidney (staghorn or coral stones).

Must all kidney stones be removed surgically?

No. Many of them pass spontaneously. Some are quiescent, causing no pain, infection, or interference with kidney function. The latter may be left alone. The stones that should be removed are those that appear to be too large to pass, those that cause obstruction and infection, those that cause constant pain or periodic attacks of severe pain, and those that appear to be causing progressive damage to kidney function.

Are there any *medications* that can be taken to dissolve kidney stones?

There are some dietary programs, such as low-phosphorus diet, an alkaline ash diet, or an acid diet, which may help to retard the growth of a stone or may help to prevent new stones from forming. There are also some drugs that have somewhat the same effect (Basaljel, acid salts, alkaline salts, etc.). New research gives promise that uric acid stones may be dissolved through medications.

Are there any *solutions* that can be used to dissolve stones?

There are solutions that are helpful in reducing the size of stones, and in some cases they actually dissolve them. However, these solutions must be brought into direct contact with the stone for a sufficient length of time to permit this to take place. This

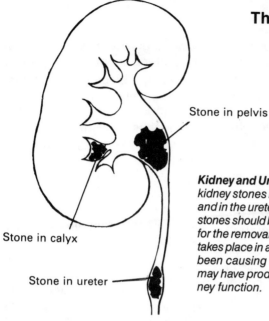

Stone in pelvis

Stone in calyx

Stone in ureter

Kidney and Ureter Stones. This diagram shows kidney stones located in the pelvis of the kidney and in the ureters leading from the kidney. Such stones should be removed surgically. Operations for the removal of stones are safe, and recovery takes place in almost all cases. If the stones have been causing obstruction for a long time, they may have produced permanent damage to kidney function.

means that if the stone is in the kidney, catheters must be put up to the kidney and left there for several days. This form of treatment is not universally applicable and cannot be used as a standard method. There have, in fact, been fatalities reported with improper use.

Do kidney stones ever recur after they are once removed or passed?

Yes. However, dietary regulation, large fluid intake, the use of certain drugs, and the elimination of infection and obstruction of the urinary tract help to prevent their re-forming. Despite all precautions, in a small percentage of cases, stones will form again.

What are stones in the ureter?

The ureter is the tubelike structure connecting the kidney with the bladder. Stones rarely form primarily in the ureter, but kidney stones often

pass down into the ureter and lodge there. When discovered there, they are known as ureteral stones.

What symptoms accompany stones in the ureter?

The principal symptom is excruciating pain of a colicky type. This may be so severe as to defy the effect of the most powerful painkiller. If the stone causes blockage of the flow of urine from the kidney, fever may result. If the urine is infected, the fever may be very high and may be accompanied by severe chills. Nausea, vomiting, and constipation are also common symptoms. Urinary discomfort, urgency, and frequency may be present. Blood in the urine is found in most cases.

What is the treatment for ureteral stones?

First, the pain must be controlled; next, if infection is present, it must be

The Kidneys and Ureters

treated by the use of the antibiotic or sulfa drugs. If pain and infection cannot be controlled adequately, drainage of the kidney must be performed. This is done by passing a catheter beyond the stone through a cystoscope. If the catheter cannot be passed beyond the stone, then the stone must be removed surgically.

Is surgery always necessary in the treatment of stones in the ureter?

No. Most stones in this location will pass spontaneously. If no infection supervenes, if the pain does not recur, and if the flow of urine is not blocked, then it is advisable to await the spontaneous passage of the stone. This may happen at any time within a period of several days or weeks.

When is surgery required for a ureter stone?

a. When the stone is obviously too large to pass.
b. If there is prolonged obstruction of urine.
c. If there are recurrent attacks of severe pain.
d. If infection persists.
e. If kidney function becomes impaired.

Can a stone ever be grasped by an instrument passed through a cystoscope?

Yes, when the stone lies near the bladder, stone-grasping instruments are sometimes successful in bringing the stone down through the ureter. If this method fails, then surgery must be instituted.

632

Is the surgical removal of a stone in the ureter a serious operation?

It is a major procedure but carries with it virtually no mortality.

How long is the usual hospitalization period after surgery for a ureter stone?

Five to seven days.

Will the patient be able to live a completely normal life after surgery for a kidney stone?

Yes.

Should a patient who once had a kidney stone be checked periodically by his physician?

Yes. He should also follow all of the precautions mentioned previously to prevent re-formation of stones.

KIDNEY TUMORS

Who is most likely to get a tumor of the kidney?

Tumors of the kidney occur at any age, in either sex. However, the majority occur after the age of forty. One special type, called Wilms's tumor, occurs in infancy and childhood.

Are all kidney tumors malignant?

No, but the malignant tumors are seen more often than the benign ones.

What is the technical name for the most common malignant kidney tumor?

The most common kidney tumor is a renal cell carcinoma.

How can one diagnose the presence of a kidney tumor?

By physical examination and by special x rays of the kidneys, such as pyelograms, arteriograms, and CAT scans.

What is an intravenous pyelogram?

It is an x-ray procedure in which a radiopaque solution is injected into the bloodstream. The solution is excreted by the kidneys, and as it is being excreted, it outlines the kidneys, which are visualized by taking an x ray.

Is an intravenous pyelogram a painful or dangerous procedure?

No. However, if the patient is markedly allergic, special precautions must be taken before this procedure is carried out.

Are pyelograms important in making a diagnosis in other kidney diseases besides tumors?

Yes. They will show the presence of many other abnormalities within the urinary tract. They are also valuable in making a diagnosis of prostate enlargement or the presence of stones in the prostate gland.

What other diagnostic tests are valuable in making a diagnosis of kidney disease?

a. Angiograms, which show the outlines of blood vessels to the kidneys. Variations from normal often indicate the presence of kidney cysts or tumors.
b. Sonograms (ultrasound) frequently demonstrate kidney tumors or cysts.
c. CAT scans (computerized axial tomography) can often outline kidney cysts or growths.

What symptoms and signs do kidney tumors produce?

a. Blood in the urine.
b. Pain in the loin over the kidney region.
c. The presence of a mass or lump in the kidney area.
d. Fever.

What is the treatment for a kidney tumor?

Prompt removal of the entire kidney and surrounding tissue and lymph glands. Preliminary x-ray therapy and postoperative x-ray treatments are also advised in certain types of kidney tumor.

Is the removal of a kidney a serious operation?

Yes, but if the opposite kidney is normal, the removal of one kidney will not adversely affect life.

Is kidney removal (nephrectomy) a dangerous operation?

No. Recovery, with an uncomplicated postoperative course, is the usual outcome.

How long is the patient in the hospital after an operation for removal of a kidney?

Eight to ten days.

CYSTS OF THE KIDNEY

What are some of the common forms of cystic disease of the kidney?

a. Solitary cysts of the kidney. This

633

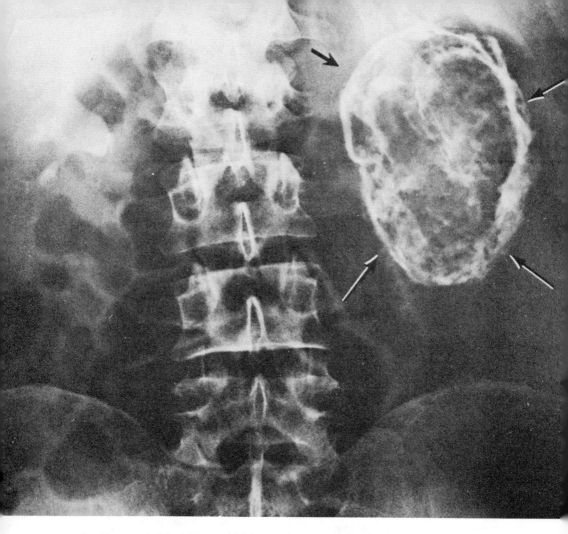

A solitary cyst of the kidney which has undergone calcification is easily seen on an x-ray.

type usually does not impair kidney function.

b. Congenital polycystic kidneys. This is a condition with which one is born and is characterized by numerous large and small cysts, usually of both kidneys. Kidney function is impaired in this type of disease as the individual grows older. This condition occurs in families.

634

What are the symptoms in polycystic kidney disease?

As the patient grows into adulthood, there may be pain in the kidney area, blood in the urine, infection, elevated blood pressure, and a large mass in the abdomen.

What are the symptoms of a solitary cyst of the kidney?

Usually there are no symptoms. Occasionally, there may be pain and blood in the urine.

What is the treatment for polycystic kidneys?

There is no effective treatment for cysts themselves. However, since the advent of the artificial kidney, these people can be kept alive until a time when a kidney is available for transplant.

What is the treatment for a solitary cyst of the kidney?

The cyst itself is removed, leaving the remainder of the kidney in place. Once in a great while, a solitary cyst can be treated by withdrawing the fluid and injecting a solution that induces the cyst to close itself off. This is not, however, the most common method of handling solitary cysts.

CONGENITAL DEFECTS OF THE KIDNEY *(Birth Abnormalities)*

Is the kidney subject to many types of congenital abnormalities?

Yes. There may be only one kidney instead of two; there may be one or two small additional kidneys; the kidneys may be in the wrong position in the body (ectopic kidneys); both kidneys may be on the same side of the body; the kidneys may be joined across the midline of the body (horseshoe kidney); the collecting portions of the kidney (pelvis) may be duplicated; the ureters may be duplicated.

An important abnormality is the presence of a narrowing or stricture at the kidney pelvis at the junction between the kidney and ureter. Such a condition may impede the normal flow of urine and eventually lead to obstruction of the kidney.

Do most congenital abnormalities of the kidneys cause symptoms?

No, with the exception of the strictures that cause the symptoms listed above.

Are these abnormal kidneys more prone to infection?

Yes.

What is the treatment for the congenital obstruction at the junction between the kidney and the ureter?

Where there is advanced obstruction

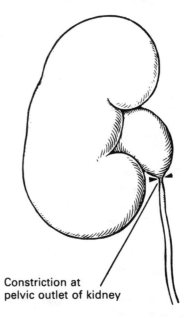

Constriction at pelvic outlet of kidney

Constriction at the Outlet of the Kidney. Such a condition often requires surgical reconstruction to relieve the obstruction to the flow of urine.

635

of the kidney or where the kidney function is impaired, surgery is indicated.

What surgery is carried out for obstruction of the kidney at its junction with the ureter?

A plastic operation is performed to widen the passageway. Formerly, simple attempts to dilate the stricture with dilating instruments were made in some cases. But this frequently resulted in infection and added damage to the kidney.

Are operations for obstruction at the kidney outlet serious?

Yes, but they are not dangerous. They may involve a long hospitalization, usually three to four weeks, and the patient may have to carry tubes that are inserted to splint and drain the area while healing takes place.

Are the results of these operations successful?

Yes, in the great majority of cases.

KIDNEY INJURIES

What are the common causes for kidney injuries?

a. Automobile accidents.
b. Athletic events such as football or boxing.
c. A fall from a height with a direct blow to the kidney area.

How can one tell if he has a kidney injury?

a. By noting pain and tenderness in the kidney region.
b. By noting blood in the urine.

What is the treatment for kidney injuries?

For the minor injuries, which make up the great majority, bed rest is the main form of treatment. If the bleeding is alarming and the x ray shows a badly damaged kidney, surgery may become necessary for removal of the organ or drainage of the blood and urine that have escaped from the injured kidney.

Can a damaged kidney ever be restored surgically?

Yes. If the damage has not been too extensive, the kidney may be sutured instead of being removed.

Is it often necessary to operate for a kidney injury?

The great majority will get well without surgery.

How can one tell whether surgery is necessary?

By noting whether the urine clears and whether there is evidence of restored kidney function. If blood continues to appear in the urine and kidney function fails to return, or if the patient's general condition deteriorates and there is swelling in the loin, surgery is indicated.

TUBERCULOSIS OF THE KIDNEYS
(See Chapter 74 on Tuberculosis)

Is tuberculosis of the kidneys often a primary disease?

No. It is usually secondary to tuberculosis of the lungs.

636

How does tuberculosis reach the kidneys?

The germs are carried to it through the bloodstream.

What are the symptoms of kidney tuberculosis?

Frequent, painful urination and bloody urine compel consideration of tuberculosis among the possible diagnoses.

How is the diagnosis of tuberculosis of the kidney made?

By finding the tuberculosis germs in the urine. It is often necessary to inoculate animals (guinea pigs) with the urine to see whether they develop tuberculosis several weeks later. There are also characteristic x-ray findings that help to make the diagnosis. When tuberculosis has involved the bladder, cystoscopic examination will reveal a characteristic appearance. Findings in the scrotum and prostate also may suggest kidney tuberculosis.

What is the treatment for tuberculosis of the kidney?

In the early stages, the disease may be arrested with the use of some of the newer antituberculosis drugs. If the disease is limited to one kidney and has already produced marked destruction, the use of drugs *and* surgical removal of the kidney may be indicated. Where both kidneys are involved, drug treatment is preferable. The drugs most often used are isoniazid, Myambutol, para-aminosalicylic acid, and streptomycin.

If tuberculosis is limited to one kidney and that kidney is removed, can a cure be obtained?

We do not speak of cures in tuberculosis, but rather of *arrest* of the disease. If the disease is limited to one kidney, its removal will arrest the disease.

"DROPPED KIDNEY" OR "FLOATING KIDNEY"

(Nephroptosis)

What is a dropped, or floating, kidney?

A kidney that has become detached from its moorings and drops to an abnormally low position in the body.

What type of person is most likely to have a floating kidney?

Thin individuals, especially women.

Is a dropped kidney more likely to be seen on the right side?

Yes.

What are the symptoms of a dropped kidney?

If any symptoms are present, they will consist of backache and abdominal pain. The kinking of the outlet of the kidney may interfere with the ready outflow of urine. This may result in a so-called "renal crisis," with attacks of severe colicky pain in the kidney area.

Is it necessary to treat a dropped kidney that causes no symptoms?

No.

637

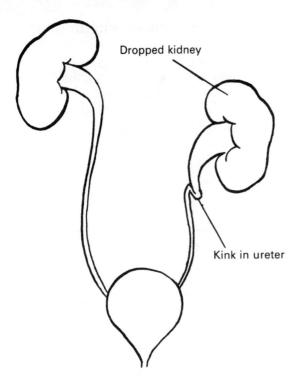

Dropped kidney

Kink in ureter

Dropped Kidney. *In certain people, a kink develops in a ureter associated with a dropped kidney, and this will cause marked pain in the loin. People who are very thin or who have lost large amounts of weight are especially subject to this condition. Symptoms often improve when the patient gains weight. In other cases, it is necessary to operate to tack down the kidney in a more normal position.*

What treatment is indicated when the dropped kidney does cause symptoms?

a. Medical management, with a special diet to increase body weight and the wearing of a support or corset to keep the kidney in its proper position.

b. A surgical procedure in which the kidney is fixed by sutures into its normal position. Such an operation is called a nephropexy, but it is seldom found necessary to perform.

TUMORS OF THE URETER

Are tumors of the ureter very common?

No. They are extremely rare.

What forms do tumors of the ureter usually take?

The great majority of them are malignant.

What are the symptoms of tumors of the ureter?

Blood in the urine, obstruction to the passage of urine into the bladder, and eventual infection.

How is the diagnosis of a tumor of the ureter made?

By x-ray studies of the urinary tract and by noting obstruction on attempted passage of a catheter up the ureter.

What is the treatment for a tumor of the ureter?

Removal of the ureter along with its

638

kidney and a portion of the bladder surrounding the entrance of the ureter.

Are operations of this type serious?

Yes, but recovery can be expected in the great majority of cases.

Can tumors of the ureter be cured by surgery?

Yes, when they are discovered at an early stage and when the operation, as outlined above, is carried out.

How long a hospital stay is necessary after operations of this type?

Eight to ten days.

URETEROCELE

What is a ureterocele?

A cystic formation at the bladder end of the ureter due to an abnormal opening of the ureter into the bladder. There is also a weakness in the wall of the ureter in its lowermost portion, probably the result of a birth deformity.

What are the symptoms of a ureterocele?

There may be no symptoms at all, and the condition may be discovered accidentally during the course of a routine investigation for some other condition in the urinary tract. Ureteroceles can, however, be the cause of a chronic infection in the bladder and kidney and can also, by blocking the outflow of urine, damage the ureters and kidneys.

What is the treatment for a ureterocele?

If it is a small one, it can be treated successfully by enlarging the opening of the ureter into the bladder. Some ureteroceles may be treated through a cystoscope by either burning off a portion of the cyst or by shaving off a portion of it. If the ureterocele is large, it may be necessary to operate and remove it through an opening made in the bladder.

Are operations for ureteroceles successful?

Yes.

Are these operations dangerous?

No.

TRANSPLANTATION OF KIDNEYS

Can kidneys be successfully transplanted from one individual to another?

Yes. The technical procedure is perfectly feasible, as outlined in the accompanying diagram. However, difficulties following transplantation of a kidney often ensue when the rejection reaction sets in, and this may occur anywhere from a few weeks to a few months after the operation has been performed.

What causes a kidney to die after it has been successfully transplanted?

A phenomenon known as the *rejection reaction* takes place. All people have antibodies whose duty it is to

639

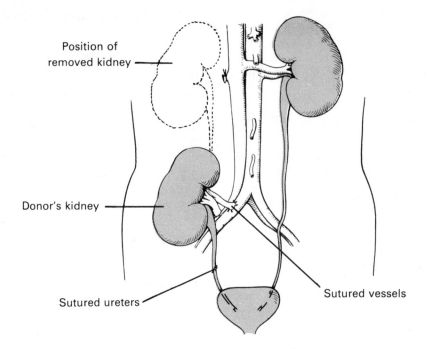

Position of removed kidney

Donor's kidney

Sutured ureters

Sutured vessels

Kidney Transplant. *The dotted outline shows where the diseased kidney was situated. The new, or donor's, kidney has been transplanted lower in the abdomen, creating a shortened ureter, which will be less likely to deteriorate.*

protect against invading foreign bodies. Tissue cells from other animals or humans are judged by the host to be a foreign body, and the normal protective mechanisms of the host are mobilized to destroy them. Thus a transplanted kidney will be attacked by the white blood cells of the host, which will cause the grafted organ to die.

When is kidney transplantation indicated?

It is performed only as a lifesaving measure in a patient who would otherwise die due to kidney failure. In this category, one would place conditions such as uremia, polycystic kidneys, chronic inflammation of the kidney due to multiple stones or overwhelming infection, or a malignant tumor of a kidney in a patient who only has one kidney.

What kidney transplants are most likely to succeed?

It has been found that permanent survival of a grafted kidney is most likely to take place when the organ is transplanted from one identical twin to another. Also, survival is more apt to occur when matching of the donor and recipient through tissue typing occurs.

Can anything be done to overcome the rejection reaction?

Yes. There are many measures that can be taken to tide the host over the period when the rejection reaction is

640

at its height. Various drugs can be given to slow down or entirely stop the host from producing the antibodies that will kill the transplant.

How successful are kidney transplants?

Kidney transplants have been carried out successfully in more than two out of three people upon whom the operation has been done. It is now possible to keep the transplanted kidney alive for many years in approximately half the patients who undergo this form of treatment.

What can be done if the transplanted kidney fails to survive?

a. The patient can be placed on the artificial kidney (dialysis) temporarily.

b. The patient can be reoperated and a new kidney from another donor can be inserted.

When a kidney transplant is carried out, is it usually placed in the normal position in the upper back?

No. It has been found that it is much better to place the kidney in the pelvic region and to attach the blood vessels of the kidney to the iliac vessels in the pelvis. In this position, there is the greatest chance of the transplant functioning satisfactorily. Also, the ureter in this position will be much shorter in length, thus enabling it to function more satisfactorily.

Are operations for kidney transplantation serious?

Yes, they are. It must be realized that these procedures are only carried out on those who would otherwise succumb to kidney failure. A kidney is never transplanted to an individual who has at least one functioning kidney.

The artificial kidney is a life-saving device for patients whose kidneys fail to function. The patient's blood circulates from him through the artificial kidney which filters out accumulated poisons. The cleansed blood is then returned to the patient's body.

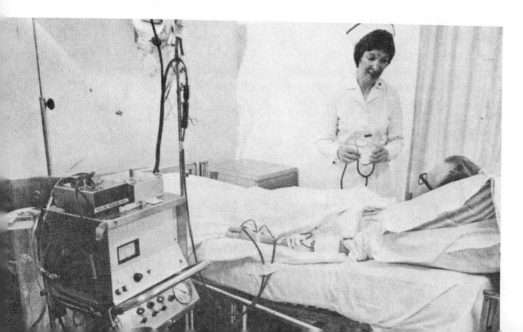

CHAPTER 38

LABORATORY (PATHOLOGY) TESTS AND PROCEDURES

(See also Chapter 12 on Blood and Lymph Diseases; Chapter 19 on Diabetes Mellitus; Chapter 31 on Immunizations and Vaccinations; Chapter 34 on Infectious and Virus Diseases)

What is a pathologist?

A physician who specializes in the study of disease and in laboratory medicine and who works closely with other physicians as a consultant in the diagnosis, prognosis, and in some aspects of the treatment of disease.

What are the usual duties of a pathologist?

To interpret laboratory tests performed upon patients, to examine human tissues that have been removed from patients, and to determine the cause of death in certain cases by making autopsy examinations. The hospital-based pathologist usually has additional duties of teaching and active participation in various hospital committees.

In addition to the above duties, is the pathologist responsible for the operation of a clinical and pathologic laboratory?

Yes.

What types of tests do these laboratories usually perform?

a. All types of tests on blood, such as blood chemistries, drug levels, hormone levels, enzyme levels, number and types of blood cells, levels of blood gases, blood cultures for bacteria, titers of antibodies, and levels of coagulation factors.

b. All types of tests on urine, such as routine urine analysis, urine chemistries, hormone levels (including pregnancy tests), drug levels, and urine culture for bacteria.

c. Stool analysis.

d. Sputum analysis.

e. Analysis of the stomach and duodenal contents (gastric analysis).

642

f. Bone marrow analysis.
g. Pus cultures.
h. Spinal fluid examinations.
i. Examination of fluid or material from various other cavities of the body, such as lung taps or abdominal taps.
j. Serologic tests to detect antigens or antibodies in serum, cells, or tissues.
k. Cytologic examinations, in which cells taken from the body are examined for malignancy.

Why is it necessary for a patient to make a special appointment before going to a laboratory for a test or series of tests?

Appointments are advisable because it is often necessary for the patient to make special preparations, such as not eating for a certain number of hours before coming to the laboratory. Many tests cannot be carried out unless special instructions are given beforehand as to how to prepare for them.

Is it usually best to have blood tests performed upon a fasting stomach?

Yes, especially for those blood tests concerned with the chemistry of the blood. In those instances, a twelve-hour period of fasting often precedes the test.

HEMATOLOGICAL BLOOD TESTS

What is a complete blood count, and how is it taken?

A complete blood count is usually obtained by passing a sample of venous blood through an automatic blood analyzer, which then prints out the number of red cells, white cells, hemoglobin content, and other blood indices calculated from this data. The test can be taken at any time and without special preparation.

What is a differential blood count, and how is it taken?

This test is done by examining a blood smear on a glass slide under a microscope for the different cells present and obtaining a percentage of the various types of white cells present. A complete blood count and differential blood count will reveal diseases like anemia, leukemia, or infection.

Is it painful when the vein is punctured for a blood test?

There is only very slight pain if a good sharp needle is used.

How does the taking of a blood count show anemia?

By counting the number of red blood cells, noting the amount of hemoglobin in the cells, and noting the characteristic appearance of the blood under the microscope.

Can a pathologist diagnose the varying types of anemia by examination of blood?

Yes. There are many types of anemia, and the treatment for each may be different.

How does a blood count indicate an acute infection?

By an increase in the white cell count

643

and an increase in the number of bands (white cells with nuclei containing no lobes).

Is the taking of a white blood count frequently important in determining the seriousness of the illness and in determining whether or not an operation is necessary, such as in the case of a possible appendicitis?

Yes. This is a most valuable test in helping to make a decision.

What is hemoglobin?

The iron-containing pigment in red blood cells that carries oxygen to the cells throughout the body.

Why is it necessary to have a blood test before tonsils are removed?

The tendency of the tissues to bleed and the blood to clot should be recorded before tonsils are removed. When these tests, known as bleeding time and clotting time, are normal, the surgeon can proceed without fear of hemorrhage due to an abnormal condition of the blood.

Can anemia be successfully treated by blood transfusions?

Blood transfusions may temporarily correct the deficiency, but they do not relieve the underlying cause of the anemia and therefore cannot produce a permanent cure. There is one exception, and that is when anemia has been caused solely by sudden hemorrhage. In this instance, blood transfusion can bring about a cure of the anemia.

Can the taking of a blood count determine whether a child has lead poisoning?

Up to a certain point, yes. In microscopic examination, the red blood cells usually show anemia and a characteristic stippled appearance. This disease was quite prevalent in the days when toys were coated with paint containing lead. The child would chew on the toys and develop lead poisoning. Even today, painters who use leaded paints in their work are subject to this disease.

What is a sedimentation rate?

This is a test performed after drawing a small amount of blood from a vein in the arm. The withdrawn blood is placed in a special glass tube containing an anticoagulant, and the blood cells are allowed to separate out from the plasma. The rate at which the blood cells drop to the bottom of the tube is called the sedimentation rate. It is a rough index of the presence or absence of inflammation somewhere in the body. The more rapid the sedimentation rate, the more likely that an inflammatory process exists.

SEROLOGIC TESTS

What is a serologic test?

Serum is tested for the presence or absence of antigens and antibodies, which indicates the presence or absence of disease.

What are antigens and antibodies?

An antigen is a substance, usually a protein, which, when introduced into

Laboratory (Pathology) Tests and Procedures

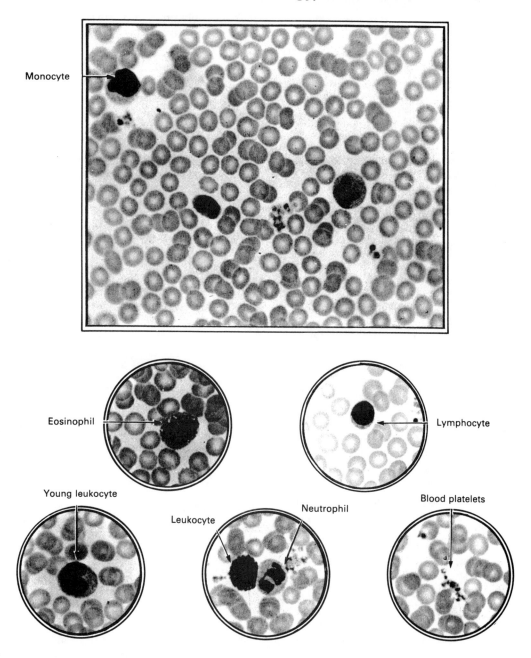

Monocyte

Eosinophil

Lymphocyte

Young leukocyte

Leukocyte

Neutrophil

Blood platelets

Blood Smear. *This photomicrograph shows what blood cells look like under the microscope. Variations in the size, shape, and number of blood cells are frequently diagnostic of specific diseases, and the pathologist also learns a great deal about all aspects of the patient's health merely by examining a sample of blood under the microscope.*

645

the body, stimulates the production of antibodies that react specifically with the antigen. Antibodies are protein substances produced by the immune system of the body and are part of the defense against attack by bacteria, viruses, parasites, and other antigens.

Are there different blood tests to determine the presence or absence of syphilis?

Yes. These serologic blood tests consist of two general groups of procedures: (1) the nontreponemal antigen tests (e.g., VDRL) and (2) the treponemal antigentest (e.g., the *Treponema pallidum* immobilization test). The second group of tests are highly specific and sensitive as compared with the first group of tests.

What is a dark-field examination?

This is a test whereby material is taken from an ulcer or other lesion suspected as being syphilitic and examined directly under a special microscope. The finding of typical spirochetes is diagnostic. The test should be performed only by individuals who have special training and experience in the technique.

Is the diagnosis of syphilis made from the blood test alone?

Never. The clinical history, physical examination, and findings are just as important as the results of the blood test.

BONE MARROW ANALYSIS

What is a bone marrow study?

A test in which a small amount of marrow is obtained from the breastbone or some other bone by placing a needle into it. It enables the physician to see how well the blood is being formed and whether it contains tissues or cells that should not normally be present.

Is a bone marrow test painful?

There is only very slight pain, since a local anesthetic is used before the needle is inserted.

Is a bone marrow study important in determining the presence or absence of blood diseases and various types of anemia?

Yes. It is an extremely valuable test and should always be done whenever there is doubt as to the exact diagnosis.

Who should perform a bone marrow test?

A physician who has specialized in the diagnosis of diseases of the blood.

BLOOD TRANSFUSIONS

When are blood transfusions most valuable?

a. When there has been an acute, sudden loss of blood due to disease or injury.
b. When an acute loss of blood is anticipated, such as when a major operation is to be performed.
c. To give the patient a temporary lift until his own bone marrow can resume the manufacture of blood, as after a prolonged or debilitating disease that has produced anemia.

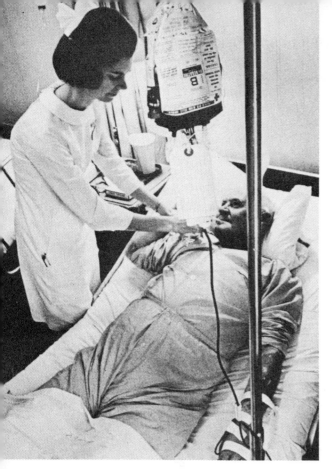

Patient Receiving a Blood Transfusion. *The bottle at the side of the bed contains blood. (Most of it has already dripped into the patient's vein.) Blood is obtained from donors and is stored in the laboratory until needed. It is essential that the blood grouping of the donor be the same as that of the recipient. Such cross-matching of bloods is carried out in the laboratory before the transfusion is given.*

Should blood transfusions be given under the direct supervision of a physician?

Yes, most emphatically. A transfusion means taking blood from a healthy individual and injecting it into a patient. This is a serious procedure and is sometimes associated with complications demanding expert knowledge.

Who should perform the blood grouping (typing) preparatory to the giving of a blood transfusion?

A well-qualified laboratory employing expert technicians should always be used to type the patient's blood.

Accidents occur if correct typing and crossmatching are not performed.

What complications can occur from giving the wrong type of blood?

Chills and fever, jaundice, or even death may ensue from giving improperly crossmatched blood.

Should people know their blood groups (types) so that if an accident should occur they can be transfused more quickly?

Yes. It is wise to know one's own blood group. The blood must always be reexamined prior to transfusion.

647

Laboratory (Pathology) Tests and Procedures

The blood to be given must always be matched with the recipient's blood before transfusion.

When given under proper supervision, are blood transfusions safe?
Yes.

What are some of the complications of blood transfusions?
a. Chilis and fever. This is a common complication.
b. Allergic reactions such as hives, asthma, etc. When this occurs, the transfusion is usually stopped.
c. Jaundice. This may occur as long as three to four months after the transfusion has been given.
d. Shock, from giving the wrong type of blood or contaminated blood. This is an extremely rare event.

Can infants and children be given transfusions?
Yes.

Are there satisfactory methods for combating reactions to transfusions?
Yes. Most reactions can be mitigated by proper medical treatment.

What is meant by an "exchange transfusion"?
This is a special type of blood transfusion usually performed on newborns who have a blood condition known as erythroblastosis. It attempts to exchange all or most of the infant's blood for new blood and thus gets rid of the blood causing the disease. This must only be performed by an expert in the field.

What is meant by an "intrauterine transfusion"?
Within recent years it has been found possible to transfuse the fetus while it is still in its mother's womb. This is done in cases where erythroblastosis (Rh factor disease) is suspected. By an ingenious procedure performed under fluoroscopic x ray, a needle is inserted through the mother's abdominal wall, through the wall of her uterus, and into the fetus. Blood is transfused directly to the fetus in this manner, thus protecting the child against the development of erythroblastosis.

How successful have intrauterine transfusions been?
When performed by an expert, the number of instances in which erythroblastosis has been prevented is quite large.

What is a blood bank?
There are special blood laboratories set up in large hospitals and institutions where blood is collected from donors and is stored. Blood may be kept for periods up to three weeks prior to use. It is an excellent idea, because the bank tries to maintain a supply of blood of all types to meet any emergency.

BLOOD CHEMISTRY

What is a blood chemistry?
It is a test performed on blood to determine the amount of the various minerals and chemicals circulating in the body.

Laboratory (Pathology) Tests and Procedures

CHEMICAL ANALYSIS OF BLOOD

	Normal	Abnormal
Urea nitrogen	12 to 15 milligrams per 100 cc.	Increased amounts may indicate kidney disease (nephritis, etc.).
Glucose-sugar	80 to 120 milligrams per 100 cc.	Increased amounts may indicate presence of diabetes mellitus.
Uric acid	4 to 8 milligrams per 100 cc.	Increased amounts may indicate presence of gout.
Nonprotein nitrogen	25 to 45 milligrams per 100 cc.	Increased amounts may indicate kidney or genitourinary disorder.
Creatinine	1 to 2.5 milligrams per 100 cc.	Increased amounts may indicate inability of kidneys to excrete urine (as in obstruction due to markedly enlarged prostate gland).
Cholesterol	130 to 240 milligrams per 100 cc.	a. Increased amounts may indicate a tendency toward premature hardening of the arteries. b. Increased amounts are also seen in some pregnant women and in disorders of the thyroid gland.
Calcium	9 to 11 milligrams per 100 cc.	Increased amounts may indicate overactivity or a tumor of parathyroid glands in neck.
Sodium	137 to 143 milli equivalents per liter.	Decreased amounts may occur from excess vomiting or loss of body fluids, thus endangering normal body processes.
Chlorides	585 to 620 milligrams per 100 cc.	Decreased quantities usually result from loss of salt from the body. Excessive loss is incompatible with normal body function.
Phosphorus	3 to 4.5 milligrams per 100 cc.	Variation in amounts may indicate functional disorder of the parathyroid glands in the neck.
Potassium	4 to 5 milli equivalents per liter.	Marked alterations occur in many disease states and may cause disturbance in heart function. Potassium quantities must be in balance with sodium quantities.
Bilirubin	0.1 to 0.25 milligrams per 100 cc.	Increased quantities may indicate jaundice, obstruction to normal flow of bile from liver, or liver disease.
Phosphatase	1.5 to 4 units per 100 cc.	Increased quantities indicate obstruction to flow of bile, or jaundice.
Icterus index	4 to 6 units.	Increased reading indicates presence of jaundice.
Total protein	6.5 to 8.2 grams per 100 cc.	Decreased amounts are seen in debilitated states, in chronic illness. *(continued)*

649

CHEMICAL ANALYSIS OF BLOOD (cont.)

	Normal	Abnormal
Serum albumin:	1.5 to 2.5 grams per 100 cc.	A reversal so that the ratio is below 1,
Globulin	2.5 to 3.0 grams per 100 cc.	indicates poor protein metabolism.
pCO$_2$	35–45 mmHg.	Increase indicates acidosis; decrease alkalosis.
pH	7.35–7.45	Increase indicates alkalosis; decrease acidosis.
pO$_2$ *(Arterial)*	95–104 mmHg.	Increase indicates alkalosis; decrease acidosis.
Amylase	80–160 Samagyi Units.	Increase indicates pancreatitis.
SGOT	<40 I.U.	Increase may indicate liver disease, myocardial infarction, etc.

What are some of the usual chemicals and minerals tested for when a blood chemistry is taken?

a. Albumin.
b. Bilirubin, total.
c. Bilirubin, direct.
d. Blood urea nitrogen.
e. Calcium.
f. Carbon dioxide content.
g. Chloride.
h. Cholesterol.
i. Creatinine.
j. Inorganic phosphorus.
k. Iron.
l. Potassium.
m. Protein, total.
n. Sodium.
o. Triglyceride.
p. Uric acid.

Are blood chemistries valuable in diagnosing the presence or absence of disease?

Yes. In certain instances, the diagno-sis cannot be made without a characteristic blood test.

Are characteristic findings in the blood chemistry helpful in determining treatment for disease?

Yes. The quantity of a certain chemical circulating in the blood is often an essential factor in deciding what form of treatment should be given.

Does life ever depend upon the amount of certain chemicals circulating in the blood?

Definitely, yes. An excessive amount of certain chemicals, or an excessive lack of certain chemicals, may throw the patient into shock, coma, and may eventually lead to death.

Can blood chemicals be artificially replaced?

Yes. One of the most common forms of treatment for serious disease is to

650

have certain of the chemicals, which may be lacking, given by mouth or by injecting them under the skin or directly into the bloodstream.

Are blood tests valuable in determination of various types of jaundice?

Yes. A distinction can usually be made between obstructive jaundice, which is due to the prevention of outflow of bile from the liver, jaundice that is due to an inflammation or disease within the liver, and jaundice due to an excessive destruction of blood.

Are blood tests valuable in detecting the quantity of cholesterol in the blood?

Yes. The presence of an increased amount of cholesterol in the blood is called hypercholesterolemia. Many investigators feel that hardening of the arteries is associated with an excessive amount of cholesterol in the body.

Are there any blood tests that give information about metabolism?

Yes. A determination of thyroid hormones and thyroid-stimulating hormones gives information about metabolism. These tests aid the physician in determining the state of underactivity or overactivity of the thyroid gland.

Are there any reliable chemical tests on blood specific for cancer?

No. However, the presence in blood of carcinoembryonic antigen, Alpha Feto protein, or the prostatic component of acid phosphatase is noted in some types of cancer. The presence of high levels of these substances in blood by themselves are not specific for the diagnosis of a particular cancer. They are useful aids in the diagnosis and the follow-up of cancer treatment.

GLUCOSE TOLERANCE TEST

What is a glucose tolerance test?

A test in which the fasting patient is given a known amount of glucose (sugar) by mouth, and the blood is tested at intervals thereafter to note the quantity of sugar in the blood. A curve is then constructed from which important information can be drawn.

What will a glucose tolerance test curve show?

a. Whether the patient is a diabetic.
b. Whether the patient has too little sugar in his blood (hyperinsulinism).
c. Characteristic changes in certain other hormonal disturbances.

Will blood tests in diabetic patients usually show an excessive amount of sugar?

Yes.

BLOOD CULTURES

Of what value are blood cultures?

In diseases in which one suspects that bacteria are circulating in the bloodstream, blood is taken to the laboratory and is cultured to see if bacteria will grow from the blood.

651

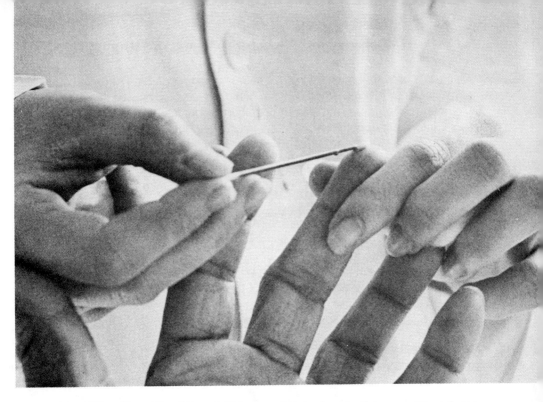

Taking Blood for a Blood Count. This procedure is almost painless, and the information to be gained from the blood count is very important. People should have a complete blood count performed whenever they have been ill for a period of several weeks or more.

What types of diseases may show positive blood cultures?

Cases of blood poisoning (septicemia).

BLOOD GASES AND ACID-BASE STATUS

What are blood gases?

When we inhale oxygen and exhale carbon dioxide, these gases are transported by blood between the tissues and the lungs. The oxygen and carbon dioxide content of blood can be determined along with the pH, base excess, and other data by passing a sample of blood through a blood-gas analyzer.

What is meant by acid-base status?

Human metabolism generates the production of acids that are first buffered and then excreted mainly via the kidneys and lungs to maintain the neutrality of body fluids. These mechanisms maintain the neutral acid-base status of the body. Disturbances of acid-base status are broadly divided into two groups: (1) acidosis (acid excess relative to base) and (2) alkalosis (base excess relative to acid). Each is subclassified depending on whether it is primarily a respiratory or metabolic disturbance and whether the condition is compensated or noncompensated.

What are the common causes of respiratory acidosis?

A respiratory acidosis occurs when carbon dioxide is poorly exchanged by the lungs due to an inadequate ability of the lungs to exhale the gas or due to an obstruction to the passage of the gas from the blood into the lungs. Some examples are: (1) chronic obstructive lung disease (chronic bronchitis and emphysema) and (2) severe restrictive lung disease (pulmonary edema and pulmonary fibrosis).

What are the common causes of respiratory alkalosis?

When an excessive amount of carbon dioxide is exhaled by the lungs,

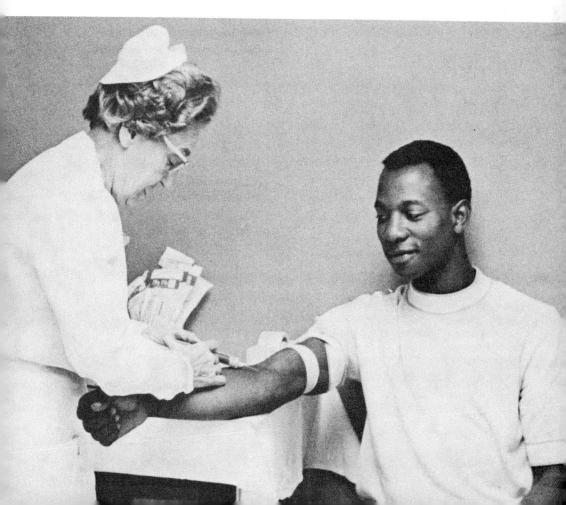

Vein Puncture. *Patient having blood removed from vein in arm. The main reason for withdrawing blood from a vein is to analyze it for chemical constituents. Many diseases can be diagnosed by noting abnormalities in the chemical components of blood. There is only slight pain when the vein is punctured.*

usually as a result of hyperventilation, alkalosis occurs. Some examples are: (1) a severe decrease in the amount of oxygen that can pass through the lungs into the blood (2) a severe decrease in the oxygen-carrying capacity of blood and (3) excitement or anxiety.

What are the common causes of metabolic acidosis?

When an excessive amount of acid is produced by the body or an excessive amount of base is lost by the body, metabolic acidosis occurs. Some examples are: (1) diarrhea (2) diabetic acidosis and (3) renal failure (accumulation of acid in body fluids).

What are the common causes of metabolic alkalosis?

When acid is lost by the body or a base is retained or ingested, then metabolic alkalosis occurs. Some examples are: (1) vomiting (loss of acid) (2) excessive ingestion of base, as in the "milk-alkali syndrome" and (3) prolonged gastric suction (loss of acid).

Are the words "alkaline" and "base" synonymous?

Yes.

URINE ANALYSIS

When is it usually best to collect one's urine for testing?

Most urines, except for certain special tests, should be collected in a clean bottle as the first specimen passed in the morning.

What are the substances usually tested for in a urine analysis?

a. Albumin.
b. Sugar.

Laboratory technicians performing chemical analysis upon a specimen of blood. It usually takes two to three days before chemial analysis of blood is completed.

c. Acidity or alkalinity.

d. Presence or absence of pus.

e. Presence or absence of blood cells, both red and white.

f. Presence or absence of bile pigment, as in cases of jaundice.

g. Presence or absence of casts (microscopic forms denoting kidney damage).

h. Presence or absence of crystals of certain chemicals.

What can be learned from the presence or absence of these substances in the urine?

Examination of urine gives valuable information concerning the state of health of the kidneys or other portions of the urinary tract. In addition, it may suggest the presence of diabetes, liver disease, etc.

Does the finding of abnormal substances in the urine always denote the presence of disease?

Not always. Sometimes these are transient findings. It is therefore important to repeat urine tests at regular intervals before making a diagnosis of disease.

Is it often wise to double-check findings on urine analysis by testing the blood?

Yes. Urine analysis is a helpful test but not always a conclusive one.

PREGNANCY TESTS

Are pregnancy tests conducted on the urine?

Yes.

How accurate are pregnancy tests?

Most laboratories report about 95 to 98 percent accuracy in their pregnancy tests.

If the examination by the physician does not seem to coincide with the pregnancy test, is it wise to repeat the test?

Yes. It is occasionally necessary to repeat the urine pregnancy test several times before coming to a definite conclusion.

How are pregnancy tests carried out?

Pregnancy tests are based on the detection of human chorionic gonadotropic hormone (HCG) in urine by using the principle of antigen-antibody reaction. The test is performed on a slide or in a test tube and requires a small quantity of urine. These tests have largely replaced tests using animals. There is also a reliable pregnancy test performed by examination of the serum in the blood.

How long does it take to get the result of a pregnancy test?

Results can be obtained in a few minutes with some methods or in a few hours using other methods. The latter are usually more reliable.

How soon after a woman thinks she is pregnant would a pregnancy test show a conclusive result?

For utmost reliability, a woman should not have the test performed before the tenth day following the day of the first missed menstrual period. In many early pregnancies, human chorionic gonadotropic levels may be so low as to yield negative results; these tests should be repeated within one to two weeks for conclusive results.

Is the pregnancy test always positive if there is a pregnancy in the Fallopian tube?

No. The pregnancy test in tubal (ectopic) pregnancy is not nearly as important as the physical examination performed by the physician.

R$_H$ TEST

What is an Rh test?

An Rh test determines the presence or absence of the Rh factor in the blood. It is done whenever a person's blood is typed.

Should all pregnant women have Rh-factor blood tests done upon them?

Definitely, yes.

Why is the Rh factor important in pregnancy?

It is particularly important in pregnancy because Rh-negative women (those who lack the Rh factor), when married to men who are Rh-positive, may carry an embryo which is Rh-positive. These women may become sensitized to the Rh factor in the unborn child. Under ordinary circumstances, this does the mother no harm, but it may affect the baby.

If a mother is Rh-negative, will her baby require a blood transfusion?

The baby will require a transfusion only if the mother has been sensitized to the Rh factor and antibodies produced by the mother affect the baby. The fact that the mother is Rh-negative does not in itself mean that her baby will require any treatment at all.

What is erythroblastosis?

This is a condition in the newborn in which blood cells are destroyed in huge quantities because of difficulties with the Rh factor.

Is erythroblastosis a dangerous condition?

Yes. If not treated promptly, it may lead to the death of the infant.

Should the fact that a woman is Rh-negative influence her to avoid having more children?

No. An Rh-negative mother can be injected with a substance known as RhoGAM within seventy-two hours after a child is born. This injection will protect her next child from developing Rh-factor disease.

Is it possible for an Rh-negative woman married to an Rh-positive man to bear an Rh-negative infant?

Yes.

Is it possible for an Rh-positive woman to bear a child who will have complications due to other blood factors?

Yes. Other factors in the blood may at times cause trouble, but these are usually of far less importance and severity than the Rh factor.

How can one predict whether an

unborn child will have trouble because of the Rh factor?

The mother's blood can be tested for anti-Rh antibodies during the course of her pregnancy. These afford a rough index of what may be expected when the baby is born.

What are antibody studies?

These are tests to determine whether the body has produced antibodies.

What is the danger of antibodies in a person sensitized to the Rh factor?

The antibodies have no effect on the person so sensitized unless they are transfused or get an injection of Rh-positive blood. In this case, a severe reaction may develop.

Can a sensitized woman who remarries bear normal children?

Yes, if the new husband is Rh-negative or of a blood group other than the one that caused the original sensitization.

Will an erythroblastotic baby be a normal baby if it survives?

If the damage to the baby incident to the disease is minimal, and this is usually the case, such a baby will almost always develop normally.

Is there any difference between an erythroblastotic baby and a blue baby?

Yes. A blue baby is one who has a congenital disease of the heart or lungs. An erythroblastotic baby is one who suffers as a result of his

mother's sensitization to the Rh factor in the blood.

Is there any way of preventing the development of erythroblastosis in babies to be born to a mother known to have been sensitized to the Rh factor?

There are no injections or drugs known at present that will prevent the disease.

Can the first child of an Rh-negative woman have erythroblastosis?

This is rare, but it can happen if she has previously been sensitized to the Rh factor by means of an injection or transfusion containing the Rh factor.

What is the treatment for erythroblastosis?

Exchange transfusion to replace the baby's Rh-positive blood with the donor's Rh-negative blood.

GASTRIC ANALYSIS

What is a gastric analysis?

A test whereby the secretions of the stomach are removed, and the constituents are analyzed.

What is looked for in a gastric analysis?

a. The presence or absence of hydrochloric acid, which should normally be secreted by the cells lining the stomach.
b. The presence or absence of lactic acid, a substance that should not normally be present in the stomach.
c. The presence or absence of

657

blood, which should not normally be present in the stomach.

d. The presence or absence of cancer cells, which, by special tests, can be noted in the gastric secretions of those who have cancer of the stomach.

In what conditions are gastric analyses most important?

a. In pernicious anemia. In this condition an absence of hydrochloric acid is found.

b. In an ulcer of the stomach or duodenum. In these conditions an excessive amount of acid is often found.

c. In tumors of the stomach. In such conditions, the presence of lactic acid or even the presence of actual cancer cells may be determined on analysis of the gastric content.

d. In tuberculosis, when it is suspected that sputum is being swallowed.

How is a gastric analysis performed?

By placing a tube into the mouth or nose and passing it down into the stomach.

Is this a very painful test?

Not at all, although it is somewhat unpleasant.

How long does a gastric analysis take to perform?

This is determined by the purpose of the test. It may take only a few minutes, or it may require three hours to complete.

Should a gastric analysis be performed on a fasting stomach?

Yes.

Where are gastric analysis tests carried out?

Usually in the office of a well-equipped laboratory. Also, the test is frequently performed upon hospitalized patients.

Is there any danger involved in having a gastric analysis test performed?

None whatever.

PAPANICOLAOU TEST

What is a Papanicolaou smear?

It is one in which cells are wiped from the surface of various organs, usually the uterine cervix or vagina, for the diagnosis of cancer. It has a high degree of reliability when performed by persons trained in cytology. These smears, generally known as Pap smears, can also be taken from cells found in the woman's spu-

Opposite page:
Gastric Analysis. *This diagram shows a rubber tube that has been inserted through the nose, down the esophagus, and into the stomach in order to perform an analysis of the stomach contents. The contents are analyzed for the presence or absence of acid, blood, and other substances. Gastric analysis, while uncomfortable, is not a painful procedure; most people undergo it without complaint.*

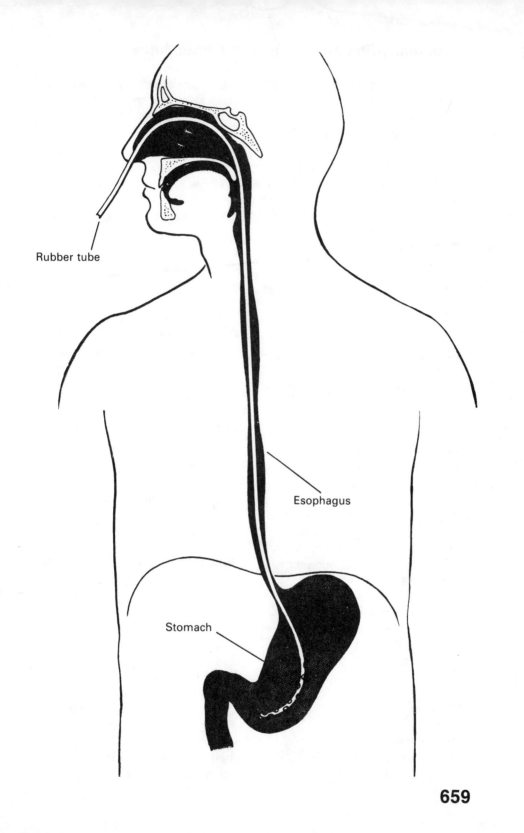

Rubber tube

Esophagus

Stomach

659

tum, urine, or discharges from the nipple.

How are Papanicolaou smears performed?

By taking a cotton swab and scraping off the superficial cells from the surface of the cervix or vagina. Cells from sputum, from urine, or from nipple discharge are also prepared by smearing them on a slide and examining them under a microscope.

Is this a painful or unpleasant test?

Not at all.

Who should take Papanicolaou smears from the cervix or the vagina?

A gynecologist, any examining physician, or a specially trained nurse.

Should all women undergo Papanicolaou tests?

Yes. It is now advised that every adult female have a "Pap" test performed at least once every year. In this way, very early curable cancers can be discovered. Some of these early cancers, known as cancer *in situ,* are 100 percent curable through surgery.

Can a woman who is virginal have a Pap test performed upon her?

Yes, as it is only necessary to insert a small applicator with a swab of cotton into the vagina.

BIOPSY

What is a biopsy?

It is the removal of tissue by a physician or surgeon, who sends it to a pathology laboratory where it is examined grossly and microscopically in order to make a diagnosis.

Where are biopsies most likely to be taken?

In hospitals or in physicians' offices.

What is meant by a needle biopsy?

This is a test whereby a needle is placed into a diseased area, and cells or contents are withdrawn and examined by the pathologist.

Is a needle biopsy as accurate as an ordinary biopsy?

Usually not, because the amount of tissue that can be obtained with the needle is so small that it makes interpretation difficult.

What is an incisional biopsy?

It means taking a scalpel and cutting into a diseased area and removing a portion. This fragment is subjected to gross and microscopic examination by the pathologist, who then makes a diagnosis.

What is meant by an excisional biopsy?

This means removing the entire diseased area, which is then submitted to gross and microscopic examination by the pathologist.

What is meant by a "frozen section"?

This means taking tissue from the patient while the patient is on the operating table and having it immediately submitted to microscopic examination by the pathologist.

Are frozen-section examinations infallible?

No. The methods by which the tissues are frozen and subjected to immediate microscopic examination are not as accurate as the usual, more time-consuming methods of preparing tissues for examination in a pathology laboratory.

What is the value of a frozen-section examination?

It will tell the surgeon whether a diseased area is malignant or not, thus indicating whether or not a more extensive operation is necessary.

When are frozen sections particularly useful?

In determining whether a mass is cancerous. The pathologist will usually be able to make a diagnosis from this examination. If the frozen-section examination reveals that the mass is not cancerous, a less extensive operation is performed. However, if a cancer is diagnosed on frozen section, then the surgeon proceeds to do a more extensive operation. This extensive operation is withheld for a few days if the pathologist informs the surgeon that there is the slightest doubt regarding the diagnosis.

Is the pathologist only asked to do frozen-section examination to determine the presence or absence of cancer?

No. There are many situations in which the surgeon is operating to remove inflammatory tissue. He can learn through a frozen-section biopsy whether his operation has extended beyond the region of inflammation.

Is the pathologist ever called into the operating room?

Sometimes. Especially when it is necessary for the pathologist to see the entire tumor and decide what tissue is needed for examination to obtain a diagnosis.

What are some of the tissues frequently submitted for frozen-section biopsy examination?

a. Skin, to determine the presence or absence of a malignancy.
b. Tissue taken from the bronchial tubes or larynx.
c. Brain tissue and tissue from the spinal cord.
d. Thyroid tissue.
e. Parathyroid tissue.
f. Lymph nodes.
g. Tissue from the tongue or gums.
h. Tissue from the lungs.
i. Liver tissue.
j. Tissue from the spleen.
k. Tissue from the pancreas.
l. Kidney tissue.
m. Adrenal gland tissue.
n. Tissue from the ovaries or testicles.
o. Tissues from the cervix or lining of the uterus.
p. Bone tissue.
q. Bone marrow tissue.
r. Tissues from the fat or muscles of the body.

SPUTUM ANALYSIS

Why is sputum analysis carried out?

a. For determining the presence or

661

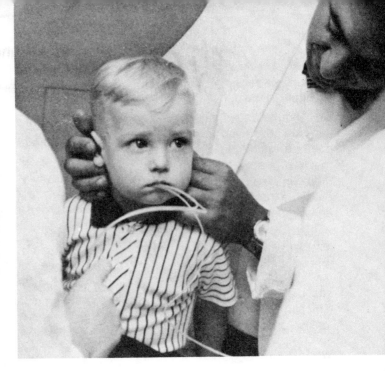

Sputum Analysis. Saliva is being removed by suction from a young child. The saliva, or sputum, will be subjected to laboratory analysis.

absence of the germ causing tuberculosis or other lung infections.

b. For analysis in certain cases of asthma.

c. For determining the presence or absence of malignant cells in possible cancer of the lung.

How is the sputum analyzed?

Concentrated smears are made, and these are examined carefully under the microscope by the pathologist. Cultures are made to isolate the offending bacteria.

STOOL ANALYSIS

For what conditions is the stool analyzed?

a. For any of the diarrheal diseases, such as dysentery, etc.

b. In cases of sprue or celiac disease.

c. In cases of anemia if the cause has not been determined through other means.

d. For any condition in which parasitic invasion is suspected.

e. For conditions in which there is bleeding into the intestinal tract.

f. For colitis or any other infection involving the large bowel.

Is it important for a fresh specimen to be analyzed?

Yes. The specimen has to be brought to the laboratory almost immediately after it has been passed; otherwise the bacteria, parasites, enzymes, etc., in the stool may be lost.

PUS CULTURES

Why are cultures made from pus?

It is very important when pus has been evacuated from the body to de-

662

termine the particular germ that has produced the infection.

How is this done by the pathology laboratory?

By growing the germs on appropriate culture media.

What is the advantage of finding out the particular germ that has caused an infection?

The treatment rendered will be dictated by the exact nature of the germ that has caused the infection. Different germs vary in their susceptibility to drugs; the appropriate drug must be used to combat a given infecting organism.

LUNG TAPS *(Thoracentesis)*

Why is a lung tap performed?

a. To remove fluid that may have accumulated in the chest cavity.
b. To determine whether a germ has caused a pleurisy, and to identify it.
c. To determine the presence or absence of any malignant cells in a case of possible cancer of the lung or in the coverings of the lung.

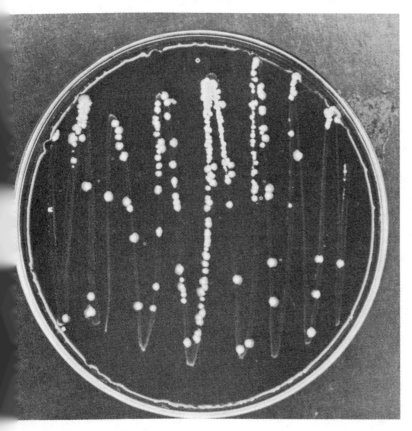

Bacterial Culture. This is a photograph of an actual laboratory culture showing living colonies of bacteria. This plate proves that the pus taken from an abscess of a patient contains active, live, growing bacteria. By noting the various characteristics of these bacteria and by placing them on a slide and examining them under a microscope, it is possible to determine exactly which bacteria is the cause of the infection.

Laboratory (Pathology) Tests and Procedures

Are lung taps painful?

There is very little pain. A local anesthetic will probably be given before the needle is inserted.

Where are the lung taps carried out?

Either in the laboratory, the doctor's office, or the hospital.

ABDOMINAL TAPS
(Paracentesis)

Why are abdominal taps carried out?

a. To remove fluid that may have accumulated in the abdominal cavity.
b. To determine the presence or absence of bacteria that may have caused a peritonitis.
c. To determine the presence or absence of malignant cells.

Is an abdominal tap painful?

The pain is not very great, as some local anesthesia will be given before the needle is inserted into the abdominal cavity.

GUINEA PIG INOCULATIONS

What are guinea pig inoculations used for?

Material is taken from a patient's body and is injected into a guinea pig in order to determine the presence or absence of tuberculosis.

How long does it take for a report to be given when a guinea pig inoculation has been carried out?

It takes approximately six weeks.

SPINAL TAPS

What is a spinal tap?

It is a procedure wherein a needle is inserted in the back and into the spinal canal, and spinal fluid is withdrawn.

Is a spinal tap painful?

No. It causes only slight discomfort, as it is common practice to inject Novocain into the sensitive structures prior to inserting the needle into the spinal canal.

Why are spinal taps carried out?

a. To determine the presence or absence of infection within the spinal fluid and brain coverings.
b. To determine the presence or absence of increased pressure within the spinal canal, which may be caused by the presence of a tumor of the spinal cord or brain.
c. To instill air or opaque substances prior to examining the spinal cord and brain by x ray for the presence or absence of tumors or other disease.